Red Hat Linux System Administration Handbook

Mark F. Komarinski
Cary Collett

D1511589

ISBN 0-13-025395-2

90000

9 780130 253958

Prentice Hall PTR
Upper Saddle River, NJ 07458
http://www.phptr.com

Editorial/Production Supervision: *Wil Mara*
Acquisitions Editor: *Mark L. Taub*
Cover Design Director: *Jerry Votta*
Cover Art: *Daniel Corley*
Manufacturing Manager: *Alexis R. Heydt*
Marketing Manager: *Kate Hargett*
Editorial Assistant: *Michael Fredette*

Prentice Hall books are widely used by corporations and government agencies for training, marketing, and resale. The publisher offers discounts on this book when ordered in bulk quantities.
For more information, contact
Corporate Sales Department,
Prentice Hall PTR
One Lake Street
Upper Saddle River, NJ 07458
Phone: 800-382-3419; FAX: 201-236-7141
E-mail (Internet): corpsales@prenhall.com

Printed in the United States of America
10   9   8   7   6   5   4   3   2   1

ISBN 0-13-025395-2

Prentice-Hall International (UK) Limited, *London*
Prentice-Hall of Australia Pty. Limited, *Sydney*
Prentice-Hall Canada Inc., *Toronto*
Prentice-Hall Hispanoamericana, S.A., *Mexico*
Prentice-Hall of India Private Limited, *New Delhi*
Prentice-Hall of Japan, Inc., *Tokyo*
Simon & Schuster Asia Pte. Ltd., *Singapore*
Editora Prentice-Hall do Brasil, Ltda., *Rio de Janeiro*

Table of Contents

Thanks and Acknowledgments . . . .*xi*

Chapter 1   *Introduction* *1*

1.1 Oh No! Not Another Linux Book! 2
1.2 Linux Theory 2
1.3 Is It Really Free? 2
1.4 Why Linux? 3
1.5 Is Linux SYSV or BSD? 4
1.6 Support 4
1.7 What You Need 4
1.8 Red Hat Recommended Settings 5

Chapter 2   *Installation* *7*

2.1 Getting Linux 8
2.2 Preparing for the Install 9
2.3 Performing the Install 12
2.4 LILO Installation 19
2.5 Linux and Other Operating Systems 20
2.6 Upgrading Red Hat Linux 21
2.7 Migrating from Other Distributions 23
2.8 Applications CD 23
2.9 Summary 33

Chapter 3 *Linux Boot and Shutdown* *35*

3.1 LILO 36
3.3 Kernel Boot 40
3.4 init 43
3.5 What's a Runlevel? 43
3.6 When Something Goes Wrong 45
3.7 The Red Hat Rescue Diskette 47
3.8 System Shutdown 47
3.9 Keeping a PC Safe from Reboots 49
3.10 Summary 51

Chapter 4 *Account Administration* *53*

4.1 Adding Users 53
4.2 Deleting or Disabling Users 56
4.3 Using Shadow Passwords .57
4.4 Using PAM 57
4.5 Linuxconf 62
4.6 Interaction with Users 76
4. 7 Summary 77

Chapter 5 *RPM* *79*

5.1 Binary RPM Installation 81
5.2 Source RPM (SRPM) 82
5.3 Other RPM Utilities 82
5.4 Summary 84

Chapter 6 *Networking with Linux* *85*

6.1 TCP/IP 86
6.2 INETD 96
6.3 Network Applications 98
6.4 AppleTalk 111
6.5 Network Information Services (NIS and NIS+) 120
6.6 Routing with Linux 126
6.7 Internet Agencies 129
6.8 Summary 132

Chapter 7 *Printing and Print Sharing* *133*

7.1 Connecting Printers to Linux 133
7.2 Serial vs. Parallel vs. Ethernet Printers 134
7.3 Configuring a Printer 135
7.4 Print Filters 136
7.5 Printers on the Network! 136
7.6 Managing Print Queues 138
7.7 Ghostscript 139
7.8 Summary 140

Chapter 8 *Samba* *141*

8.1 Setting Up an MS Windows Network 142
8.2 Installing Samba 143
8.3 Linux SMB Connections 148
8.4 SWAT (Samba Web Administration Tool) 149
8.5 Installing Linux Printers on Windows 155
8.6 Summary 157

Chapter 9 *Email* *159*

9.1 Using m4 Files 162
9.2 You Have Mail! 162
9.3 MIME 164
9.4 The .forward File 164
9.5 Mailing Lists 167
9.6 Qmail: An Alternative to Sendmail 169
9.7 Remote Email (POP and IMAP) 174
9.8 Summary 176

Chapter 10 *Setting Up FTP Services* *177*

10.1 FTP under Red Hat Linux 177
10.2 Configuring wu-ftpd 178
10.3 Anonymous FTP 180
10.4 ProFTPD 181
10.5 BeroFTPD 184
10.6 TFTP 186
10.7 FTP Clients 186
10.8 Summary 188

Chapter 11   *Applications for Linux* *189*

11.1 Office Products, Word Processors, and Editors 189
11.2 Drawing, Graphics, and Image Viewing and Manipulation . .194
11.3 Scientific Programs 196
11.4 Emulators 198
11.5 Summary 200

Chapter 12   *Linux Database Software* *201*

12.1 MySQL and mSQL 202
12.2 Other Native Linux DMBSs 210
12.3 Summary 213

Chapter 13   *Programming Languages* *215*

13.1 C 216
13.2 C++ 217
13.3 Perl 218
13.4 Python 219
13.5 Lisp, Scheme, and Guile 222
13.6 Java 223
13.7 Tcl/Tk 224
13.8 SQL 225
13.9 PHP 226
13.10 Other Languages 227
13.11 Summary 230

Chapter 14   *Web Serving* *231*

14.1 Web Server Software 232
14.2 Hardware Issues 234
14.3 Apache and ApacheSSL/Stronghold 235
14.4 Logging 245
14.5 Databases and Web Servers 245
14.6 Setting Up a Killer Web Server 245
14.7 Streaming Audio and Video 249
14.8 Summary 250

Chapter 15   *X Windowing System* *253*

15.1 X Concepts 253
15.2 Setting Up X Using Xconfigurator 254
15.3 Setting Up X Manually 255
15.4 gdm 258
15.5 Using X Window Managers 258
15.6 User Programs 272
15.7 X Resources 274
15.8 X Applications 275
15.9 Using Remote Displays 284
15.10 Major X Libraries 285
15.11 Commercial X Resources 286
15.12 Summary 287

Chapter 16   *Securing Linux* *289*

16.1 Physical Security. 290
16.2 Software Security 290
16.3 Denial of Service Attacks 294
16.4 Network Security 295
16.5 Packet Filtering with Linux 299
16.6 Summary 306

Chapter 17   *Kernel Administration* *307*

17.1 Customizing Your Kernel 307
17.2 Which Kernel? 308
17.3 Getting Ready 308
17.4 Adding Kernels to LILO 309
17.5 Modules or Compiled In? 310
17.6 Dive On In! 311
17.7 Summary 321

Chapter 18   *System and Network Monitoring* *323*

18.1 Syslog 323
18.2 Network Monitoring 326
18.3 Network Monitoring Distributions 331
18.4 Summary 332

Chapter 19   *Backing Up Your Data* *333*

19.1 tar and mt 334
19.2 cpio 337
19.3 dump and restore 338
19.4 Commercial Backup Products 339
19.5 Backup Strategies 341
19.6 RAID and Disk Mirroring 342
19.7 Summary 343

Chapter 20   *Talking to Your Peripherals* *345*

20.1 Scanners 345
20.2 Modems 347
20.3 Tape Drives 348
20.4 UPS 348
20.5 3D Cards 350
20.6 USB Support 350
20.7 Adding a New Hard Drive 350
20.8 PCMCIA Devices and Laptop Machines 353
20.9 ZIP and JAZ Drives 354
20.10 Quick Guide to Serial Ports 356
20.11 CD-ROMs and CD-R Writers 359
20.12 Summary 361

Chapter 21   *Connecting to the Internet* *363*

21.1 Overview 363
21.2 Software Versions 364
21.3 Networking 364
21.4 PPP 366
21.5 IP Masquerading 373
21.6 Summary 375

Appendix A *377*

URLs To Keep Track Of 377
URLs Referenced in This Book 378

Appendix B *383*
    Problems Using Very Large Hard Disks .383
    Linux-allocated Devices 388
    Additional /dev Directory Entries 398

Index *401*

Thanks and Acknowledgments

Mark would like to thank:

All the people who helped out on this book and gave some good suggestions based on our previous books. First and foremost is my wife, Brenda, who helped keep me writing (and somehow sane) during the past few months. My parents, Peter and Mary Kay, along with my brothers, Derrick, Scott, and Allen, and sister, Kathleen, for all their motivation and help while writing, get thanks as well. I'd also like to thank all the people who have spent time coding or even testing Linux software. The entire Linux community has worked for years to make the quality software that makes your system so easy to use.

Cary would like to thank:

My wife! Not just for not killing me while I was writing this book, but also for supporting me and lending massive amounts of help in proofreading and editing. Next, I want to thank Mark for asking me to help with this book; it's been quite an experience. I don't want to repeat it soon, but maybe in a year or so. . . . Also, I'd like to thank one of my close 'net friends, Paul Saab. Paul and I have been experimenting with bleeding-edge and/or strange freeware for years now. Without him I would likely never have begun many of the pursuits which helped me gain the knowledge I've spewed forth here. Lastly, I'd like to thank John Shipman and Jason Van Patten for being both fonts of technical knowledge and the sources of much mirth, which from time to time during this busy time I was sorely in need of.

Together we would like to thank:

Mark Taub, Audri Anna Bazlen, Wil Mara and Camie Goffi from PTR. They were very supportive and helpful while we worked on this project. Also mentions (and hellos!) to A. Rich and Nelson Chadderdon from Oceanwave Consulting (`http://www.oceanwave.com`), Daniel Corley (`http://www.wayga.net/~dcorley/`), and the gang over at Plan9 MUSH for keeping us entertained when we probably should have been writing.

Last, but certainly not least, our reviewers, Jason VanPatten and John Duprey. Their efforts and knowledge of Linux helped tune this book for you.

Once your Linux system is up and running on the Internet, you can check out the official *RedHat Linux System Administration Handbook* Web site at `http://rhlsah.wayga.net/`. Or you can email the authors at `rhlsah@wayga.net`.

Linux is a trademark of Linus Torvalds, but the software itself is free. The `wayga.net` domain is owned by Mark F. Komarinski, and he won't give it to you. He owns it. The `ratatosk.org` domain is owned by Cary Collett, and Cary won't give it to you either. All other trademarks are owned by their respective companies.

Introduction   1

What's this Linux thing?

Linux is probably one of the fastest growing operating systems around. It has about 10 million worldwide users, and that number is growing each day. For something that started as an idea by a college student in Finland in 1991, that is pretty darn good.

Linux is now used everywhere there is a need for a good, robust operating system. Companies run their businesses on Linux, but many may not know it. It is used for email servers, WWW servers, and to provide file and printer access for Microsoft and Apple machines, and even other UNIX machines.

This is a guide to give you (the reader) as much knowledge as we (the authors) have attained in our years of Linux administration. Our administrative projects have been varied, but they all have had a common base—managing users, email, the network, hardware, and making sure that we didn't mess up anything too badly while trying to make an improvement.

1.1 Oh No! Not Another Linux Book!

This is not just a Linux book. This is *the* Linux book. Anyone can write some theoretical book about the way networks should run, but how many of these authors are actually network administrators? How many are stuck in the trenches, reading the cryptic man pages to `printcap` while users are complaining about their printouts? We've been there, we are there, we will be there. We enjoy it.

The proof of this attitude exists throughout the book. While everyone else goes on about IDE drives, we personally and professionally recognize the power of the small computer systems interface (SCSI) bus and use it in our systems. It's more expensive and, at times, a pain to work with, but the benefits are enormous.

Anyone can tell you how a program like Samba is set up, but what happens in the real world where things aren't quite the same as they are in the man pages?

1.2 Linux Theory

The UNIX theory is "Do it your way," but Linux is more than a slogan for a chain of hamburgers. Linux allows you to not only choose what you want on your hamburger, but also what's in it, how the cow is grown, what spices are added to the mixture, and how long it is cooked. Linux gives you all the same abilities that commercial UNIX packages (such as Solaris or AIX) give, plus a lot more.

1.3 Is It Really Free?

Yes and no. The Gnu's Not UNIX (GNU) Public License (which is how Linux is licensed) says that you can charge for a binary distribution, but the source code must be either included or available for the cost of duplication. In these days of the Internet and CD-ROMs, the cost for duplicating is low indeed.

Note that this really covers only the Linux kernel, and the GNU utilities included with most distributions. This does not prevent a company like Red Hat from assembling all these programs, adding a few special ones (installation and administration scripts, for example), producing a CD-ROM, and charging you $80 for it. The Linux kernel and source code is there. The source code to all the other GNU utilities is either also available or pointers to the source code exist. Thus, these companies have met their end of the GNU license. Many of these also sponsor Linux-related events or offer free CD-ROMs to software contributors.

Companies such as Red Hat have a more expensive product, but they add things that may not be covered by the GNU Public License (GPL). For example, Red Hat sells a copy of their distribution for three different architectures for about $80.

1.4 Why Linux?

So why would you (or your company) want to use Linux in a personal or business setting? The answer goes past the shortsighted "anti-Microsoft" response. Microsoft makes a fair product for a new user. But so does Apple. Linux gives you things that Windows 95 can only dream about:

- Source code for the entire kernel.
- Full configurability of the operating system.
- Ability to turn features of the system on and off without rebooting.
- Full 32-bit operating system, or 64-bit for the Alpha and Sparc series processors. As new chips arrive (Pentium III and Merced), Linux will be ported to these new chips.
- Access to the 25 years of software experience that make up the UNIX world. This includes compilers, Web servers, editors, games, and Internet tools.
- A growing application base with generally rapid and responsive software development, a supportive user community, and growing commercial acceptance.

As an inexpensive Web server, Linux will beat NT hands down for performance on equivalent hardware. As a network server, a Linux machine hidden in the corner of an office can handle a small workgroup or a large office with months between reboots (usually to either upgrade the kernel or add new hardware). With the emergence of Java[1] as a truly portable language, companies can easily port their software to Linux just as fast as applications for NT or Windows 98. Many commercial applications (Netscape, WordPerfect,

---

[1] Linux was one of the first operating systems to handle Java applications in the kernel.

Applix, Motif, Oracle) are already available for Linux, with more being added.

1.5   Is Linux SYSV or BSD?

The simple answer to this is "Yes." Linux takes the best of System Five (SYSV) (like startup files) and the Berkley System Distribution (BSD) (`ps aux`, `getty`) and combines them. As a downside, some features of each are missing (like streams) and you should make yourself aware of what features of each are in Linux. If you're compiling or porting software, you will probably find better luck writing towards BSD. Check the man pages for system calls for more information on this.

1.6   Support

Contrary to popular belief, commercial support for Linux is available. While there is seldom a need for it, Red Hat has telephone and email support for their Linux distribution. With the number of users that have Linux on their machines, devices from the latest 3Dfx-based 3D cards to the Mattel Power-Glove have drivers available, and everything in between. The support is often somewhat better than from other operating systems, as the author of a particular driver is sometimes available via email and is often willing to help if your driver is not behaving properly. Some hardware drivers have released patches within 24 hours to users.

More companies are starting to add 24x7 support for Linux, including large companies such as HP.

1.7   What You Need

So what do you need to run Linux? It varies greatly, depending on what you want to do with it. If you're going to use Linux to dial up the Internet, a low-end Pentium will suffice. If you want to have a dial-in pool to give access to traveling engineers or salespeople, a 100-Mhz 486 is great. If you want a killer development system or something to write a book with, a Pentium II or K6-III will do just fine.

What? You have a spare Sparc Classic with nothing better to do? Turn it into a Linux Samba server. Let the people running Windows 98 or NT access

Network File System (NFS) partitions without having all that messy NFS software installed on their PCs. While it's doing that, it could also handle POP email for the same group of people.

You just bought that great new Alpha machine and NT is having trouble with it? Slap Linux on there and be up and running before you remember what NT stands for.

Here are the minimum suggestions for running Linux:

- 386 or better (or Sparc, Alpha, or Macintosh).

- 8 Mb of memory.

- Industry Standard Architecture (ISA), Video Electronics Standards Association (VESA), or Personal Computer Interconnect (PCI) bus.

- Graphics card, monitor, and keyboard.

Once you have these items assembled, you can use the instructions with the Linux distribution to install Linux on your system.

1.8   Red Hat Recommended Settings

Red Hat recommends the following for installation:

- 386sx or better CPU, including the Pentium family of processors.

- 120MB of hard drive space for a minimal install. 500MB is recommended for a typical install, and about 800 for a full install of all software on the Red Hat CD. You should set aside more space if it's a development system.

- 16MB of RAM.

- CD-ROM or network card.

- 3.5" floppy (in case you don't support booting from CD-ROM).

See the next chapter for information on installing Red Hat.

Installation 2

Here we try to cover a few common installation types from servers to desktop systems, as well as some of the pitfalls that are encountered when dealing with very old, very obscure, or very new hardware.

Depending on your needs, desired setup, and hardware, installing Linux can be as easy as pie or more like taking a tiger by the tail. Anyone who has installed an operating system knows this is true for almost any OS, particularly on the x86 platform.

Red Hat has gone out of their way to provide a very clean, easy, and user-friendly installation. Recent releases include autodetection of some cards, allow for a LAN or Internet install, and provide for pre-configured default installations to let you get started quickly. Red Hat also is the only company to have distributions that install on x86, Sparc, and Alpha-based systems. Once installed, the distributions are pretty much all the same.

The 6.0 release of Red Hat adds a number of new features to one of the best Linux distributions, and many of these we cover later in this book:

- The latest 2.2 kernel, which provides improved support for RAID and SMP.
- GNOME, the windowing environment and the Enlightenment Window Manager.
- KDE Window Manager.
- Better support for laptops.
- Three default configurations, "workstation" and "server", to automatically set up and install a system with a minimum of questions, plus a custom that allows for a more personalized configuration.
- The latest versions of most software.

If you have an existing Red Hat system and want to upgrade, check the section on upgrading later in this chapter. You may also want to review the sections on booting since you will need to use a boot floppy or CD-ROM.

While we are focussing here on the x86 platform, much of this information is applicable regardless of the architecture you are using.

2.1   Getting Linux

Red Hat has three versions of their distribution that are available to you.

First is the "100% official" release, as Red Hat calls it[1]. This shrink-wrapped version sells for about $80, has three CD-ROMs, a boot diskette, two manuals with installation and getting started guides, and 30 days of telephone support. This release is available in most computer stores and bookstores. Of the CD-ROMs, one is for binary installation of packages, and the other CD-ROM in the jewel case contains source code for all the applications that have source code. The third CD is not in the jewel case. That is an application CD full of trial versions of commercial applications. We cover the contents of this CD later in this chapter. If you are new to Linux, this is the version for you.

The second release is the Power Users version of Red Hat. This includes CD-ROMs with the install and source code, but no application CD, no manuals, and no telephone support. This version is available only from Red Hat

---

[1] We'll call this the official release from here on.

via their Web site and is recommended for users who are familiar with Linux. The cost for this release is about $40.

The third release is the least expensive and most widely available. Red Hat makes a free version of their distribution available on their FTP site and various mirrors. This release is free to modify, and many companies put this FTP distribution on a CD-ROM and sell it for about $2, plus shipping. Since Red Hat does not sell this, there is no manual, application CD, or telephone support. If you're very familiar with Red Hat, you can use this method. You may also choose this method if you want to perform an installation over the Internet or LAN via FTP or NFS.

We should also note some of the distributions (such as Mandrake) that are based on the free Red Hat distribution, but have changes in the distribution that may not be to everyone's tastes or needs. These distributions use the RPM package format, and in some cases, may use the source code used to compile Red Hat. For example, Mandrake uses KDE as their default window manager instead of GNOME, which is used by Red Hat. Mandrake also compiled all the applications to make use of the Pentium chip. This makes applications faster on Pentium and above chipsets, but these same applications may not be as fast for 386- or 486-based machines. Aside from this, Mandrake 6.0 claims to be 100% compatible with Red Hat 6.0, so much of what we describe here will work with Mandrake. Other distributions may differ.

2.2   Preparing for the Install

Below we give an overview of the installation process. In the next section, we cover some of the more problematic steps and give some examples.

CD-ROM

If you have a newer motherboard that supports booting from CD-ROM (as well as a CD-ROM reader, obviously!) and are installing from a CD-ROM, you are in luck. The CD-ROM supplied is bootable and thus you do not need to make boot floppies. You will need to check the documentation with your system or motherboard to determine how to boot from the CD-ROM, as many systems default to booting from the first hard drive or floppy drive.

Sun Sparcs and Alpha-based machines typically support booting from CD-ROM, and so they don't require boot floppies.

Boot Floppies

If you are not so fortunate, you will have to make at least one disk to boot from to start the installation. There are four boot floppies that you may need, depending on your setup:

1. The normal boot floppy, called `boot.img`. This is used for 90% of the installations. If you are not installing over a network, and are not using PCMCIA devices to perform the installation, this floppy will work for you.

2. The boot floppy for a network install, called `bootnet.img`. This image is needed if you are installing over a network, be it from a local FTP or NFS server, or from over the Internet from Red Hat or one of its mirrors.

3. The PCMCIA supplemental boot floppy (`pcmcia.img`). This image is needed only if you require PCMCIA services to install Red Hat. If your laptop has a built-in CD-ROM, this floppy is not required. However, if you have a CD-ROM that is accessed via a PCMCIA card, or perform a network install using a PCMCIA network card, you will require this diskette.

4. The rescue diskette (`rescue.img`). This diskette is Linux on a floppy. You can't perform an install using this floppy, but if you run into problems and need to boot Linux, you can use this floppy to get access to the rest of the system.

The files, or images, as they are more properly called, for the disks are located on the CD-ROM in the `images/` subdirectory. The images cannot simply be copied onto a floppy. They must be transferred in raw mode. If you are starting this procedure from DOS or Windows, you will need the `rawrite` program from the `dosutils` directory. If you have Linux or another UNIX-like operating system, you can use the `dd` command.

The various images can all be found in the `images/` directory of the Red Hat CD. If you are getting Red Hat from an FTP site, you will first need to locate the root of the Red Hat mirror. Of course, if you are on Red Hat's FTP site itself, this is trivial. Once there, you can find a duplicate of the CD-ROM directory tree for the latest stable version of Red Hat at `current/i386/`. If you are using the Sparc or Alpha distributions, replace `i386` with `sparc` or `alpha`, respectively.

You will need to download the `RedHat/` subdirectory if you want to make a local copy for installation.

The next few paragraphs pertain to the x86 version of Red Hat. We make notes where the procedure differs from the Sparc architecture. The Alpha platform presents a more complicated scenario. There are so many differently supported boot methods, we cannot cover them here. Check the Alpha installation addendum at `http://www.redhat.com/corp/support/manuals/RHL-6.0-Manual/alpha-inst/booklet/`. The Official release also contains a very detailed installation manual that covers this procedure.

For a local CD-ROM or hard disk-based install, you need `boot.img`; for network-based installs, you need `bootnet.img`. For a Sparc, you need either `boot32.img` for non-UltraSparc-based machines (like the Sparc 5 or Classic), or `boot64.img` if you are installing on an UltraSparc.

To write the raw image to format a 1.44MB floppy, and then write the image to it, use the following commands. These commands only work for an existing Linux setup.

```
# fdformat /dev/fd0H1440
Double-sided, 80 tracks, 18 sec/track. Total capacity 1440 kB.
Formatting ... done
Verifying ... done
# dd if=boot.img of=/dev/fd0 bs=1440k
1+0 records in
1+0 records out
```

Repeat this procedure for the other images, if necessary. Sparc users will also want to make a ramdisk image using `ramdisk.img`.

Next, you should gather all the information you can about the hardware in your system. For the most part, the Red Hat installer will automatically detect what hardware you have. Occasionally it will fail, however, and you will have to fall back on the documentation when the installer prompts you for hardware parameters. One example of this is the sound configuration, as Red Hat can recognize only Plug and Play or PCI sound cards. Other sound cards (like older Sound Blasters) will require manual configuration. Having the IRQ and I/O address information ahead of time will be very helpful.

Kickstart

If you will be installing Red Hat on a number of systems, you will want to examine Red Hat's kickstart installation. This allows you to pre-configure an installation, create a single boot floppy with it on it, and go crazy installing Red Hat. The kickstart feature is available only for local CD-ROM and NFS installs. The `doc/README.ks` file contains information on performing kick-start installs.

2.3   Performing the Install

Now you are ready to start the installation. If you have a CD-ROM and your system will boot from it, insert the CD-ROM and restart. Intel users may have to change the boot order in the BIOS for this to work. Sparc users with PROM versions of 2.0 or higher can issue a `boot cdrom` command while in the new command mode; older PROM versions use the command `b sd(0,6,0)`.

If you need to boot from floppy, insert the boot floppy and restart. Once again, you may need to change the BIOS setting for the boot order. If you are going to install via the network, boot with the floppy that has `bootnet.img` on it, otherwise, boot with the `boot.img` floppy. Sparc users issue either `boot floppy` or `b fd()`, depending on the PROM version, either 2.0 (or greater) or less, respectively. You will be prompted for other disks if they are needed.

The system will start up, and you will be presented with a screen with a few Red Hat menus. Press ENTER to let the Linux kernel start and proceed to the installation program.

First, you will be asked for a language and keyboard type. Select the language and keyboard type that matches your system.

Next, you will be presented with a choice of installation sources. If you have a CD-ROM and a CD-ROM reader, put the CD-ROM in and proceed. Otherwise, select the method you want to use. Of course, if you booted from CD-ROM, we assume you will install from it.

If you are booting with `bootnet.img`, you will be asked for networking information. The kernel will try to automatically detect your Ethernet card, and you will be asked for a method of assigning IP information. Check with your network administrator for this information. If you are the network administrator, it is best to choose `Static IP` and fill out the requested information. You will then be asked for an NFS or FTP server, along with a directory containing the base of the Red Hat install directory. This should be the directory that contains files like `RedHat`, `images`, `doc`, `misc`, and so on. Once this information is entered, Red Hat will initialize the Ethernet card and attempt to find the requested NFS or FTP site.

Once you have selected the install method and the installer has located the distribution, you are prompted for the type of installation. The choices are `server`, `workstation` and `custom`. In the first two cases, the installer partitions the disks and installs a set of packages most commonly used for the type you chose. In the second case, you partition the disk yourself and select the packages you want installed. The first two choices will overwrite existing partitions. If your machine dual boots to another OS, you will want to use the custom setup. Server and workstation installations are great for installing on fresh systems.

See below for notes on partitioning your hard drive using `fdisk`. The size of your partitions depends on the size of your hard drive and how much you want to install. A full install is about 1.1GB, and can go down to about 200MB. With that in mind, we recommend splitting up the partitions as follows:

- `/`—About 100-200MB (note that this includes `/tmp`).
- `/opt`—About 200MB, but since many post-install applications get installed here, you may want to make this larger.
- `/home`—Variable and depends on how many users you will have. If you are using NIS and have `/home` automounted from another system, you do not need to create it.
- `/usr`—Should be the largest, since that is where the majority of the software goes for installation.

Once this is complete, you will be asked what partitions hold what filesystems. This is where you assign partitions to `/` (root), `/usr`, `/opt`, `/home`, and whatever other filesystems you want to set up. Swap space is already configured, so you don't need to set that.

With this setup, swap space is initialized. You will want to format the swap space in almost all cases and make sure that it performs the check for bad sectors. The swap space is formatted and added to the system, and you get the same choice for the partitions you just created. For most cases, you will want to format all partitions except `/home`.

If you chose a custom install, you are prompted to select groups of packages such as `SNMP tools` or `SVGA Games`. You can also opt to select individual packages within a group. A full install (selecting `Install Everything`) will take up about 1.1GB of drive space. However, this will have more programs than you would ever need. A minimal install can be done in as small as 200MB.

The system will then format the partitions you selected to format, and the actual file installation will start. You'll get a screen showing the current package being installed, along with a description and two horizontal bars. The upper bar shows the percent complete of the package and the lower bar represents the percent complete of the entire installation. You will also get estimated times for the total time and size of the install, along with the time remaining for the install. You will see the actual time and size of the install as well.

When the installation is complete, you will be asked what kind of mouse you have. Red Hat can detect if you have a PS/2 mouse, but not a specific manufacturer. Select the mouse that most closely resembles yours. These days, the majority of mice are generic PS/2-style. If you have a two-button mouse, select `emulate three buttons`. If you have a three-button mouse (or a wheeled mouse), you can leave that option blank and select `OK`.

You will also be prompted to enter configuration information for your network card if you have one. Linux will try to autodetect your Ethernet card and ask the form of configuration you want. If it cannot detect your Ethernet card, you can choose it from a list of cards and chipsets that are supported. The options for IP configuration are:

- `Static IP`—Information is stored in a file on the local system.
- `BOOTP`—An older method of dynamic IP allocation. Replaced by DHCP on many NT-based networks.
- `DHCP`—Dynamic Host Configuration Protocol. It is similar to `BOOTP`, but provides more information and is also used by Windows. NT Server (and Linux, of course!) can act as DHCP servers on a LAN. We cover DHCP in more depth in the networking chapter.

If you chose a net-based install, this has already happened. In this event, you will be asked if you want to keep the existing information.

You can set the time zone in the next screen. If your hardware BIOS is set to GMT, you can set this here, and Linux will take it into account when determining the time.

Depending on the packages you installed, you can select what you want to start on bootup. For the most part, you will want to leave this as is and change it later. However, if you know that some things do not need to be started at bootup all the time (like the `httpd` for a non-server), you can prevent them from starting and taking up RAM and CPU space.

Printer setup is next, and you are allowed to set up local and remote printers that use LPD or SMB. You can set the printer type and location for use on bootup.

Next is one of the more important (from a security perspective, anyway) setups—the root password. Set a password that is hard to guess, is not written anywhere, and so on. You hopefully know the drill about passwords. After this, you can set up some authentication methods. If you are using NIS, you can set it here, along with the NIS domain. You can then either probe the network for an NIS server or manually specify one. Most of the time, you will just want to probe the network. To increase security, you can select use of shadow passwords, which prevents users from even finding out what the encrypted password is. You can also select MD5 encryption for passwords, which allows for longer passwords and better encryption.

A boot disk is a good idea, as you never know when you will get a problem booting, especially if you install Windows 98 or NT later on, which re-writes the MBR (Master Boot Record) and will erase LILO if installed in the MBR. Speaking of LILO, you install that after creating the boot diskette, and you have the choice of putting LILO either on the MBR or on the first sector of the Linux boot partition. We talk more about LILO later in this chapter and in the next chapter as well.

During the installation, Red Hat will attempt to find out what kind of video card you have. If it can be detected, the correct X server for your video card is installed. If not, you can select the video card from a list. You'll next get asked for monitor type. You'll need to select this from a list, and if your monitor is not there, you can select Generic Monitor or Generic Multi-sync. If you know the specifics of your monitor, you can select Custom. Be sure you have the technical specifications of the monitor handy when entering this information. Once this is complete, X will attempt to start up and present a screen. If you see the screen and the menu, click the Yes button. If you can't see the box or X doesn't start properly, you can go back and change your settings. Once all this works, you'll be asked if you want to boot directly into X on startup. This fires up a display manager so that you get a graphical login screen. This is really the same as booting into runlevel 5 (that's what this option sets). Runlevels are covered in the next chapter. You can find out more information about X and its configuration in the chapter on the X Windowing System.

Last, you will be prompted to remove the floppy disk and/or CD-ROM and reboot. Once the system reboots, you'll get a LILO prompt and you can start up Linux!

Using fdisk to Partition Your Disk

Unlike MacOS or MS Windows installations that typically use one partition for the whole disk, Linux installations want to have the disk divided into several partitions, sized according to their intended use. At least one of these partitions will be used exclusively for swap space. It is still possible to run

Linux with only a single native partition and use a swap file, but this is not recommended. This is because having multiple small partitions can limit damage in the event of a power failure. A small root partition reduces the chances that the root partition will get corrupted, allowing you to at least boot and try to restore the system by hand before performing a full reinstall. On the downside, a small root partition may fill quickly.

At a bare minimum, you should set up partitions to keep the system software separate from third-party software and user files plus the swap space partition.

Swap space is similar to temp space under Windows or virtual memory in MacOS: it is space on disk that can be used to supplement the physical memory (RAM) if needed. Of course, it is about two orders of magnitude slower than the main memory.

A common, but arbitrary, rule of thumb is to make the swap space somewhere between one and two times the size of the physical memory. Depending on what the system is to be used for and how much RAM it has, you may want or need to assign more swap space than this, possibly spread between multiple partitions.

Assigning partitions for use under Linux is easy for a new drive or new system. However, if Windows is already installed and you want to use that drive, you'll need to shrink the existing Windows partition. You will then have enough space on the hard drive to create Linux partitions. If you're a fan of commercial software, try using Partition Magic, which allows you (from Windows or Linux) to modify partitions on-the-fly. From Windows, you can shrink the size of a Windows partition and assign the remaining space to Linux. Also available is the free `fips` package; however, the authors have not used this package, so your experience with this program may vary. For new users, getting a new drive is recommended.

When the install program drops into `fdisk`, you will see a prompt like this:

```
Command (m for help):
```

The `m` command lists this page of helpful information:

```
Command (m for help): m
Command action
   a   toggle a bootable flag
   b   edit bsd disklabel
   c   toggle the dos compatibility flag
   d   delete a partition
   l   list known partition types
   m   print this menu
   n   add a new partition
```

```
o    create a new empty DOS partition table
p    print the partition table
q    quit without saving changes
t    change a partition's system id
u    change display/entry units
v    verify the partition table
w    write table to disk and exit
x    extra functionality (experts only)
```

If this is a completely new installation, you will want to destroy any existing partitions. Type p to list the current partition table and then use d to delete the factory-created partitions.

When creating your partitions, keep in mind the machine's intended use. For a desktop workstation, a simple partition scheme is probably fine. For a server, you will likely want to set aside partitions for /tmp (where temporary files are written), /var (where most log files are kept), and/or the mail spool, /var/spool/mail.

Another advantage of making separate partitions for an area like /var is that it isolates those files from the system area. Thus, a runaway log file can only fill the logging partitions and leave the system untouched.

There are two types of partitions: primary and extended. The disk can, at most, support four primary or extended partitions total. Extended partitions, however, are really just containers for more partitions, called logical partitions. Extended partitions are not mountable or usable as regular filesystems, but logical partitions are. SCSI disks can have up to 15 logical partitions in an extended partition and IDE disks up to 63; ironic in view of the fact that SCSI disks are available in larger sizes.

In any event, you need to make some partitions. The following is a short example using the first IDE drive:

```
# fdisk /dev/hda
```

Make a 2 GB partition:

```
Command (m for help): n
Command action
   e    extended
   p    primary partition (1-4)
p
Partition number (1-4): 1
First cylinder (1-20784): 1
Last cylinder or +size or +sizeM or +sizeK ([1]-20784): +2000M
```

Make an extended partition:

```
Command (m for help): n
Command action
   e    extended
   p    primary partition (1-4)
e
Partition number (1-4): 2
First cylinder (4336-20784): 10000
Last cylinder or +size or +sizeM or +sizeK ([10000]-20784): 20784
```

Now make a logical partition within the extended one just defined:

```
Command (m for help): n
Command action
   l    logical (5 or over)
   p    primary partition (1-4)
l
First cylinder (10000-20784): 10000
Last cylinder or +size or +sizeM or +sizeK ([10000]-20784): 12000

Command (m for help):
```

Continue this process until you've made all the partitions you need, or are out of disk space. By default, `fdisk` sets the filesystem type to `Linux Native`, which is another name for Linux's `ext2` filesystem.

You will need to change the filesystem type for any partitions you want to use as swap space.

```
Command (m for help): t
Partition number (1-5): 5
Hex code (type L to list codes): l
```

0 Empty	a OS/2 Boot Manag	65 Novell Netware	a6 OpenBSD
1 DOS 12-bit FAT	b Win95 FAT32	75 PC/IX	a7 NEXTSTEP
2 XENIX root	c Win95 FAT32 (LB	80 Old MINIX	b7 BSDI fs
3 XENIX usr	e Win95 FAT16 (LB	81 Linux/MINIX	b8 BSDI swap
4 DOS 16-bit <32M	f Win95 Extended	82 Linux swap	c7 Syrinx
5 Extended	40 Venix 80286	83 Linux native	db CP/M
6 DOS 16-bit >=32	51 Novell?	85 Linux extended	e1 DOS access
7 OS/2 HPFS	52 Microport	93 Amoeba	e3 DOS R/O
8 AIX	63 GNU HURD	94 Amoeba BBT	f2 DOS 2ndary
9 AIX bootable	64 Novell Netware	a5 BSD/386	ff BBT

```
Hex code (type L to list codes): 82
Changed system type of partition 5 to 82 (Linux swap)
```

Keep in mind that many BIOSes require the kernel and other files needed at boot to reside wholly within the first 1024 cylinders of the disk, and usually in a primary partition.

Because of this limitation, you should make sure your root partition (/), resides wholly within this range or make a separate partition named /boot near the front of the disk for your kernel and auxiliary boot files.

Once you are finished, enter w to commit your changes and exit, returning to the install.

2.4   LILO Installation

LILO stands for Linux loader. It is what is actually run by your system's BIOS at bootup, normally called a bootstrap program (since it pulls the system up by its bootstraps). It must be installed on the first IDE hard disk if IDE disks are present. If you have a SCSI-only system, it must be on a disk whose SCSI ID is 0 or 1. LILO allows you to boot your choice of operating systems at bootup, allowing you to boot Linux, DOS, Windows, and so on. LILO also allows you to pass commands to the Linux kernel on startup. We cover more of LILO in the next chapter.

Red Hat's installer gives you the choice of installing LILO in the MBR or on the first partition of the first hard drive. You may also install LILO in the root partition where Linux was installed. If you have another boot loader (like System Commander), install LILO to the root partition. This leaves the previous boot loader intact, while allowing you to boot Linux using LILO.

If you have other operating systems that LILO can boot, you will be given the opportunity to configure these as well. This includes most DOS variants, Microsoft Windows 95/98 and NT, OS/2, and SCO UNIX.

If you have a Linux/NT dual-boot system, you can also use NT's boot-loader to start LILO. This is a somewhat involved process and we summarize the steps here.

Using Linux with the NT Bootloader

You should install NT first. If you only have one disk, be sure to leave part of it free to install Linux into. Some people have reported difficulties using NT's Disk Administrator to set up the Linux partitions, so it is best to leave the Linux section of the disk unpartitioned and use Linux's fdisk to do this.

Install Linux next. The installer may report the NTFS partition as HPFS, and it may also ask you where you want to mount. Ignore these comments. After the install, if you want, you can add NTFS support to the kernel and add a mount point. When the installer asks where to install LILO, tell it the Linux boot partition. If you tell it the MBR, you will overwrite NT's bootloader. Make a boot disk for Linux as you will need this to boot to Linux until the next couple of steps are completed.

Next, you need to make a copy of the Linux boot sector for NT's bootloader to use. Issue the following command:

```
# dd if=/dev/hda2 of=/bootsect.lnx bs=512 count=1
```

Replace /dev/hda2 with the location of your LILO installation. You need to transfer this to the NT partition. You can do this by moving it to a partition that is readable by both OSes, or by copying it to a DOS (or some other Microsoft Windows) formatted disk. Regardless, bootsect.lnx needs to end up in C:\.

Now you need to edit C:\boot.ini, the NT analogue of /etc/lilo.conf. By default, this file is set to system and read-only. Remove these settings so you can edit it as follows:

```
# C:\>attrib -s -r c:\boot.ini
```

Edit C:\boot.ini and add the following line:

```
C:\BOOTSECT.LNX="Linux"
```

Reset the system and read-only attributes:

```
C:\>attrib +s +r c:\boot.ini
```

Linux should now be presented as an option the next time you reboot. Select it and you will see a message like LILO: loading zImage... and then the rest of the boot messages.

The boot sector must be transferred to NT each time a new kernel is installed. To be safe, you should probably transfer it each time to run /sbin/lilo.

For more information on LILO setup and configurations, see Chapter 3, "Linux Boot and Shutdown."

2.5　Linux and Other Operating Systems

Linux can co-exist peaceably with pretty much any other operating system. As mentioned elsewhere, LILO can boot OS/2, DOS, and even FreeBSD.

An added bonus with FreeBSD is that it and Linux can share the same swap space, as FreeBSD can use any filesystem type for swap. The only trick is to rerun mkswap on the swap partition before swapon -a in /etc/rc.d/

`rc.sysinit`. When you boot FreeBSD, it will corrupt the Linux swap signature, and not performing this step will cause Linux to not recognize the swap partition(s).

Additionally, Linux can mount FreeBSD's UFS partitions and FreeBSD can mount Linux's `ext2` partitions with a few caveats. The write support for UFS under Linux is still experimental. Files or the filesystem can become corrupted. FreeBSD cannot access (read or write) the `ext2` filesystem on an extended partition.

Other operating systems not supported by LILO can be used with Linux either with their own bootloaders or with a commercial bootloader like System Commander, which supports nearly every operating system there is for the x86 architecture.

2.6   Upgrading Red Hat Linux

Linux and Linux distributions are continually evolving. This is driven by the need for new features, bug fixes, support for new hardware, and new software integration.

Red Hat releases a new version of its distribution about every six months. Between releases they provide updates and bug fixes. You can find these on their Web site or mirror in the `updates/` subdirectory of the distribution directory for the version of Red Hat you are currently using.

Installing these intermediate upgrades is a matter of using RPM to install or upgrade the packages. Typically, you would use a command like this:

```
# rpm -U <package name>.rpm
```

If you have a number of packages you want to upgrade all at once, you can process them with:

```
# rpm -U *.rpm
```

RPM should install packages in the correct order to comply with any dependencies. You may still run into dependency problems, especially if you have some libraries in non-standard locations. You can use `--nodeps --force` to override dependency checking if you are sure the package should install and work regardless of problems RPM is reporting.

Upgrading from Previous Red Hat Releases

Upgrading to a new version is more complicated, but no more so than installation. In all likelihood, it should be easier.

It almost goes without saying that you should back up the system before starting. In particular, you should back up setup files that may get overwritten. A good practice is to make separate backups of /etc and /var.

The preliminary steps to upgrading are the same as they are for installing. You will need the same types of boot disks if you needed them before. You should also make sure you have manuals handy if you need to give parameters to the installer/upgrader during the process.

Start up the system as you would for an installation. When you are presented with the choice of Install or Upgrade from 2.0 or later, choose the latter.

The upgrade process will search for your existing Red Hat installation and update all the packages with new versions. No partitions will be formatted, and you won't get a chance to do things like create partitions or choose packages to install. The only case where additional packages are installed is where dependencies change. You'll be prompted if you need to install additional packages.

As packages get installed, some configuration files may be changed (such as the /etc/sendmail.cf file). In this case, the file on the drive is backed up to have an .rpmsave extension, making the original file /etc/sendmail.cf.rpmsave. You can find a full list of files that were modified this way by looking at /tmp/install.log after the upgrade is complete. You can then examine the changes and determine what you want to do.

To install packages after the upgrade process is complete, you can use the rpm command. Check the chapter on RPM for more information on this.

Recovering a Failed Upgrade

You should choose as reliable an upgrade method as possible. We recommend a local upgrade, if possible, from a CD-ROM or local hard disk. After that, a LAN upgrade, NFS, or local FTP is preferred. An offsite FTP-based upgrade should not be used unless absolutely necessary.

Depending on where the upgrade fails, you may be able to recover fairly easily. If the failure occurs before the actual package upgrade/installation begins, you can simply start over. If the upgrade fails during package upgrading completion, it is likely that you will have to run a full install to recover your system. But it's worth trying to run the upgrade again, just in case. If the failure occurs after package upgrade/installation is competed, e.g., during LILO setup, you can probably recover by booting from a rescue disk. Then you can finish the upgrade manually by installing LILO or other boot manager yourself.

If you purchased the Official Red Hat, you have 30 days of installation support; use it if you need it!

2.7 Migrating from Other Distributions

Unfortunately there is no magic recipe for migrating, say, a Caldera Open-Linux system to Red Hat. The only solution is to make copies or notes of your various setup files and then overwrite the system partitions/filesystems with the new Red Hat installation.

You should not need to touch your data partitions (such as /home), but you might want to back them up just to be safe. You will also need to re-create users, networking setups, and other information. It's best to consider migration as a fresh install.

2.8 Applications CD

If you purchase the Official Red Hat 6.0 CD set, a third CD (apart from the installation and source code) is provided. This CD has demos or non-commercial use licenses for applications that can turn your Linux box into a productive server. In this chapter, we'll cover some of the highlights of the applications on this CD, in the hopes that it will assist you. Remember that many of these applications are demos and may not contain full functionality. Some other applications have single-use or non-commercial licenses, meaning that the full application is installed, but only for non-commercial use. For commercial use, you'll need to purchase a license.

You can access the applications CD-ROM by mounting the CD-ROM on to /mnt/cdrom. Some installation scripts assume that the CD is mounted there. You'll need to have Red Hat installed before using these applications. Many require the X Windowing System to be installed as well.

ARDI Executor

ARDI's Executor program allows you to run Macintosh applications under X. The speed is faster than most 680x0-based machines. Much of System 6 and portions of System 7 are implemented. This application has a 30-day timeout.

Included with the Executor demo are a number of shareware games and applications to allow you to immediately test out Executor (the Risk game is great fun).

Astart LPRng

The LPRng (LPR Next Generation) is based on the BSD `lpr` application, but adds a number of features. Better accounting, security, and encryption of data going over the network make LPRng an application you might want to check out if you have a lot of network printers to manage. LPRng is free for non-commercial and educational use. Commercial licenses and support are available from Astart.

The software is installed in `/usr/local/`, and a source RPM is included on the CD-ROM as well.

EST BRU

BRU is a powerful backup program, complete with an X11 interface. It's better than using `tar` or `dump` to back up files, as you can schedule backups and select individual files for backup or restore.

Included scripts allow for incremental or full backups, which makes creating your backup strategy easier. BRU includes what it calls smart Y2K handling—a file dated 02 will be translated as 2002 instead of 1902, and files dated 98 will be considered 1998 instead of 2098.[2]

Files are installed by default in `/bru`. This is the Personal Edition of BRU, which doesn't handle things like backing up raw partitions, and is free for non-commercial use.

---

[2] This is all assuming the date for the file did not use 4-digit years to begin with, or the 32-bit second offset from 1970 to record time.

Empress Database

Empress is a well-known Linux database package, and one of the first commercial applications available for Linux. It also runs on other UNIX versions and NT as well. It includes a large number of APIs, including C, C++, ODBC, DBI, Fortran, JDBC, and Tcl/Tk. Also in the package is a powerful report writer. This 30-day demo should get you familiar with what you can do with Empress. If you're looking for a commercial application with all these features, definitely take a look at Empress.

Grey Trout NExS

The Network Extensible Spreadsheet (NExS) provides for advanced spreadsheet operations and charting. It's lightweight (taking up only about 5MB of memory) and this demo version is limited to 150 cells. The full version supports 32,767 rows by 4096 columns, allowing for very large spreadsheets. NExS can import many different formats, including CSV and TSV (comma- and tab-delimited), WK1 and WKS, and some XLS, which is used by Word 97. NExS can export to those formats, plus HTML and LateX.

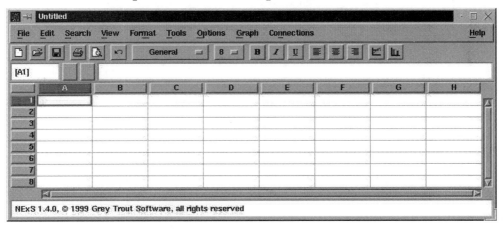

Figure 2–1 NExS spreadsheet

HKS CCVS

This credit card verification software allows an API to process credit cards online or at point of sale stations. Included are Perl, Python, and Tcl interfaces. This demo version does not actually perform any processing, but should be enough for you to write some sample programs and perform some testing.

IBM ViaVoice SDK

IBM has ported a beta version of their ViaVoice software development kit, which allows coders to write applications to take advantage of voice control. The package includes the SDK itself for C, documentation in PDF format, and some sample applications. Already programs are being written against the API (check `freshmeat.net` for applications as they get developed).

Knox Arkeia

This backup application allows for backups and restores via the network. Arkeia supports multiple client OSes, including Windows 95/98, NT, MacOS, IRIX, SunOS and Solaris, SCO, DEC Alpha, VMS, and (of course) Linux. An included GUI allows you to control the backup server from any machine. At this time, Arkeia only supports SCSI tape drives, but support will be added for other interfaces such as ATAPI.

Kuck & Associates, Inc. KCC

The KCC program is a C++ compiler with a high degree of optimization. Since it's cross-platform, you can write once, compile just about anywhere. Also included with purchase are commercial support and bug fixes, if your project requires those features. This application requires a license code, and a 30-day evaluation license can be downloaded from KAI's Web site.

Link Petra

Petra provides for remote administration of Linux machines. The RPM that Link provides doesn't modify system files at all, but you can look at the screens to see how well it works. If you'll be managing a large number of Linux systems, you can take a look at this as an alternative to `linuxconf` or other management systems.

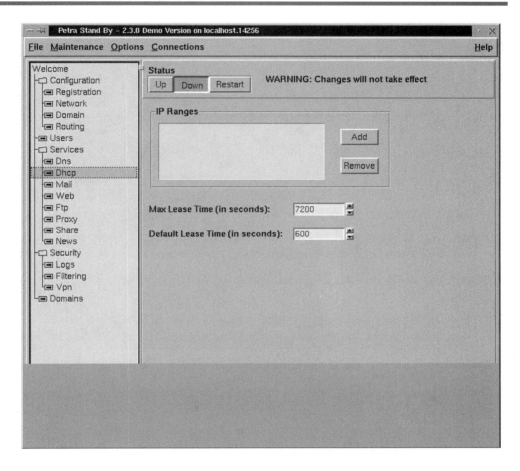

Figure 2–2 Link Petra

MayKo mxmap

The mxmap application integrates map information from NOAA or other formats and ties it into a GPS system for movement or tracking information. It supports things like zoom, routes, and access to GPS modules that are remote (connected via TCP/IP) or local.

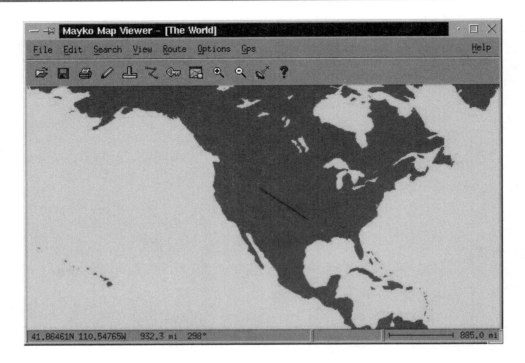

Figure 2–3   Mayko's mxmap

MetaCard

This application is a scripting tool, allowing you to create additional applications. If you have applications written for Apple's HyperCard, MetaCard will use those applications, while adding a lot of functionality. This demo includes a few sample applications such as a personal organizer. This demo is limited to 10 statements per object.

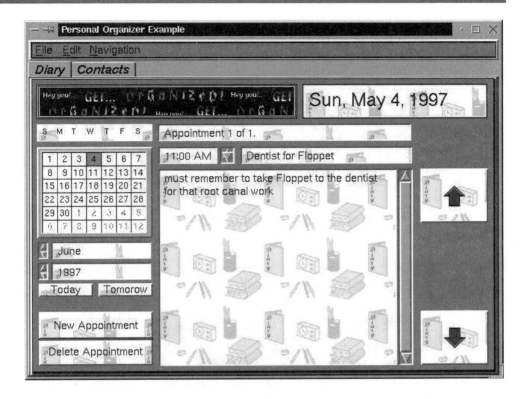

Figure 2–4 Sample Meta Cord application

MpegTV Xaudio and mtv

Ever have trouble trying to view MPEG audio or video files? You may want to try Xaudio for MPEG layers 1, 2, and the ever-popular MPEG level 3, also known as mp3. If you have MPEG-1 video files, you can view them using the MpegTV player (called mtv). Both applications are full-featured shareware applications. One advantage of the Xaudio application over other MPEG players is the Xaudio SDK, which allows you to build custom players very easily. Many dedicated MP3 players use Xaudio since the SDK doesn't require a particular interface. This makes it easy to create your interface. Included with Xaudio is a Motif MPEG player called mxaudio.

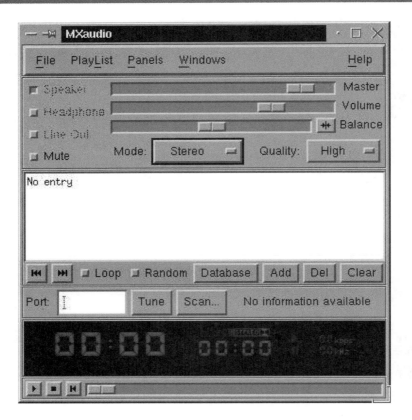

Figure 2–5   X audio

Munica NetSQL

This is a lightweight SQL server for running Web-based applications. Built into the RPM is the netsql webpak, which includes a contact manager, calendar, and newsroom. All three of these applications are available online. The license for this application is good for 180 days.

NetBeans

NetBeans allows you to develop your own Java applications, written entirely in Java. You may need to update your JVM to the latest version (available from www.blackdown.org) before you're able to use this. The version that NetBeans recommends is 1.17.

NewPlanet Code Crusader and Code Medic

Code Crusader is turning into a powerful IDE environment for C programming. The authors are taking MetroWerks Code Warrior as inspiration. Code Medic is a debugger that can interface with Code Crusader to keep an eye on the code. Included with these two applications is THX-1138, an electronic paper calculator and arrow, an email application.

Reedy Creek RPMMAIL

If you ever have problems managing the Web pages on your site (or your Webmaster has such trouble), take a look at RPMMAIL. It stands for Real-Time Page Management. Updating a Web site is done via email, and you can set who is authorized to update what pages. Email notification of pages that get updates is provided to whomever needs it, like the Webmaster.

StarDivision StarOffice

StarOffice is a competitor of the Microsoft Office suite, much like Applix and Corel's WordPerfect. However, if you want a program that can handle just about anything that Office 97 can spit out, StarOffice is it. The installation is a bit large (almost 150MB for a full install) and you have to start a single large program which can quickly gobble up your RAM. With all that said, StarOffice can read a large variety of formats, including Word, Excel, and Power-Point. It can also save files to these formats, along with exporting to other common formats.

The version of StarOffice included on the application CD is free for personal or non-commercial use. There is a code on the front of the CD holder consisting of 16 characters. This code will be needed when installing StarOffice for your use. Once installed, StarOffice will create icons for KDE or CDE so you can start up StarOffice with a single click. Under KDE, this will show up under your `Personal` menu item.

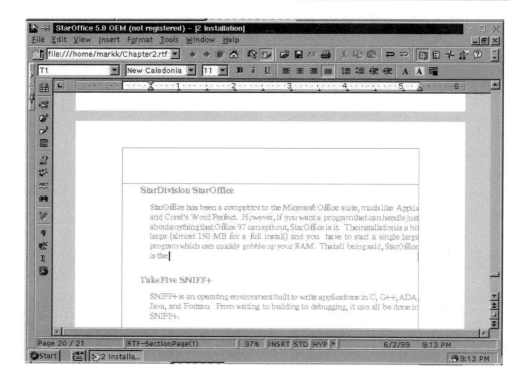

Figure 2–6   StarOffice from StarDivision

TakeFive SNIFF+

SNIFF+ is an operating environment built to write applications in C, C++, ADA, Java, and Fortran. Writing, building, and debugging can all be done in SNIFF+.

VSI - VSIfax Server

VSIfax is a fax server that can handle a number of functions. For one thing, it can handle Windows 95/98/NT clients and act as a fax server. It can also receive faxes, and, based on fax information, route a fax to the correct person. Faxes can also be sent using a Web interface.

WebTrends—Enterprise Reporting Server

WebTrends provides reports on Web usage, and it used to only run under Windows. Now there is a version for Linux that has a number of additional features, such as online reports, automatic report generation, and more.

2.9 Summary

If you have a newer system with fairly standard hardware and plan on only running Linux on it, installing Red Hat is very straightforward. Even variations such as an additional LILO-supported operating system or some not-too-esoteric hardware can be accommodated with a few adjustments.

Upgrading Red Hat is very easy and straightforward as well. Even on a slow machine, the process should only take an hour or two; on a fast machine, it could be only fifteen or twenty minutes.

When migrating from another Linux distribution, the procedure is more like installing than upgrading. There is no way to use your old system files and directories, although filesystems containing data (like /home) do not need to be touched.

Purchasers of the Official Red Hat receive 30 days of installation or upgrade support.

Linux Boot and Shutdown 3

What happens when you boot? What happens when you shut down the machine?

Booting Linux is not like starting DOS, but the concepts are somewhat similar.

The first process that Linux kicks off once the kernel has entered memory and the root (/) partition is mounted is init. The init process is always process 1. Killing this process will do the same thing as running halt or shutting down. The advantage to the Red Hat startup method is that it's the same as other commercial operating systems (OS) such as Solaris 2.

3.1   LILO

Configuring the Linux Loader

The LILO program allows you to select a boot partition for your system. If you have multiple operating systems (Linux, Windows 98, NT, etc.) all on different partitions and want to choose one to boot, LILO will let you do this.

In addition, LILO allows you to send boot parameters to the kernel before it starts up, much as the Sun architecture allows you to send boot parameters to Solaris. For example, you can specify the root drive and what devices you have installed, and pass instructions to the `init` command.

The Boot Prompt

When you start your machine up after installing Linux, you will probably have the `LILO:` prompt awaiting your command. At this point, you can choose to boot whatever operating systems were configured previously (Linux or DOS, for example). If you're starting something like DOS or Windows 95, there isn't much you need to worry about, and you can just type in DOS, Win95, or however you configured LILO when it was installed. If you forget, you can press the TAB key to see a list of what operating systems LILO knows about and will boot.

If you're starting Linux, there's a bunch of configuration parameters you can add to the end of the name you use to start Linux. For example, let's say that we configured the startup name to be `linux`.

`root=partition`—This signals Linux to use a different root partition than what is configured in the kernel. When you build Linux on one system, it assigns a default of what the current root partition is. For example, if you build a Linux kernel on an SCSI-based machine with the root partition on the first drive, first partition, Linux will assign the boot device to be `/dev/sda1`. If you were to put this kernel on a floppy drive and use it to boot an IDE-based system, it would not boot correctly since there is no SCSI system to boot off of. Adding `root=/dev/hda1`, for example, would tell the kernel to boot off of the first IDE drive, first partition. So, the same kernel can be used for multiple systems.[1]

---

[1] Assuming, of course, that all the drivers that each system needs are installed.

ro—This signals Linux to mount the root filesystem in read-only mode. No changes can be made to the filesystem when in read-only mode. The advantage is that the startup scripts can perform a filesystem check (fsck) to verify the integrity of the filesystem. If fsck succeeds, the root partition is mounted read-write and normal bootup continues. If there is a problem with fsck, the partition remains in read-only mode and the administrator will have to either do a manual fsck or reload from tape if the problem is severe. Read-only mode is used by default, so it would be rare for you to need this flag.

rw—This signals Linux to mount the root filesystem in read-write mode, as opposed to read-only mode (see above). This is dangerous, since a filesystem check of the root filesystem cannot be performed.

mem=—Some BIOSes won't recognize above 64MB of RAM in your system. Since Linux needs the BIOS to tell it how much memory is installed, systems with more than 64MB of RAM will be incorrectly reported. The mem= option tells Linux to ignore the BIOS and to determine how much memory there is. You can either use a hexadecimal address (mem=0x1000000, which is 16MB) or a number followed by k or M (16384k or 16M).
NOTE: If you lie here and tell Linux you have 128MB when you really have only 64MB, it will crash at some point. Also, due to paging and some BIOS settings, you may not have the full amount of memory accessible to your system. Check your BIOS or motherboard documentation for how much memory is used.
  Additionally, the Linux 2.2 kernel is better at recognizing more than 64MB on most motherboards. We leave this just in case you need to use it.

debug—Kernel hackers may want to use this when booting experimental kernels. Kernel messages are sent to the screen instead of being sent to disk or to the syslog facility. Most users may not need this.

init=—Specifies what program to boot as the init program. Normally, the kernel looks for /sbin/init, then /etc/init, then gives up and runs /bin/sh. This way, if the init program is corrupted, you can still get into the system.

panic=—Whenever your kernel panics, it normally waits for the administrator to come by and physically press the power or reset switch. Setting this option will allow the kernel to try to reboot x seconds after a panic. For example, a setting of panic=60 will have the kernel try to reboot 60 seconds after a panic.

vga=—LILO has the ability to change VGA video modes from the standard 80x24 to other modes, such as 80x50 or 132x44. A setting of vga=ask will provide a list of video modes and allow you to choose when it boots. Users of the 2.2 kernel can use this to select a graphical display if they're using the new Frame Buffer drivers (also known as FBcon). More documentation on Fbcon can be found in the Linux Kernel drivers under /usr/src/linux/Documentation.

If you need to configure SCSI, CD-ROM, Ethernet, and other controllers, there are a number of options to tell the kernel that you have a controller on a non-standard IRQ or I/O address, or if Linux for some reason is not probing the right IRQ or I/O address for your device. The most common is Linux not recognizing some IDE CD-ROM drives. This can be fixed by explicitly adding hdb=cdrom to the LILO boot config. This tells Linux that the second IDE device is really a CD-ROM drive. The rest of the options can be found in the LILO documentation or the BootPrompt HOWTO.

Configuring LILO

Once you have Linux started the way you want, there is a way to have LILO add your favorite options each time you boot. The /etc/lilo.conf file contains information that LILO uses each time it starts. This is where the operating systems you want to boot are configured. Here's a sample lilo.conf file:

```
# Tell LILO to install itself as the primary boot loader on /dev/hda
boot = /dev/hda
# The boot image to install; you probably shouldn't change this
install = /boot/boot.b

# The stanza for booting Linux
image = /vmlinuz              # The kernel is in /vmlinuz
  label = linux               # Give it the name "linux"
  root = /dev/hda2            #Use /dev/hda2 (first drive, second partition)
                              # as the root filesystem
  vga = ask                   # Prompt for VGA mode
 append = "hdc=cdrom"         # Tell Linux that the third IDE drive is
                              # really a CD-ROM
mem=160M                      #This BIOS does not correctly report how
                              # much memory the machine has.

#The stanza for booting MS-DOS
other = /dev/hdb1             # This is the MS-DOS partition
   label = msdos              # Give it the name "msdos"
   table = /dev/hdb           # The partition table for the second drive
```

In the above setting, the first section (the `boot` and `install` lines) configures LILO itself. The `boot` line tells LILO where to install. Since it's the first drive, LILO gets configured as the primary bootloader. If you have another bootloader such as the OS/2 bootloader or System Commander, you can configure LILO to use the Linux root partition to be a secondary bootloader. In this case, set the `boot` line to be the root partition of Linux. In the above case, that would be `/dev/hda2`. You could also take out references to other operating systems, since the primary bootloader would handle booting to other operating systems.

The section for Linux handles many of the configuration options mentioned in the previous section. The label, root partition, VGA setting, and CD-ROM are all configured. Once you choose a VGA mode that suits your needs (you'll enter a number for a video mode), you can replace the `ask` parameter with this number. One important line here is the `image` section. This line tells LILO which file to boot. Some Linux installations configure the kernel to be in the root partition (/) and some put the kernel in the `/boot` directory. You should be sure which setting you want to use when configuring LILO. A feature of the `image` line is you can boot multiple versions of the kernel all using the same Linux installation. For example, if you're developing new kernels and want to have a safe kernel around that you know boots correctly, you can create a "safe" entry in LILO. Its configuration would look something like this:

```
# Create a safe entry for Linux.  I know this kernel works.
image = /boot/vmlinuz.safe    # Boot this file.  Make sure it exists!
   label = safe               # The label for this is "safe"
   root = /dev/hda2           # Specify the root partition just in case
   vga = ask                  # Not really needed, but helpful
   append = "hdc=cdrom"       # Make sure Linux knows about the CD-ROM
```

In the event that a kernel you build doesn't work correctly and you are unable to boot it, you can just enter `safe` in the LILO prompt and boot the older kernel. Note that this will not help if there is some problem not related to the kernel, like a hardware failure or serious partition corruption.

Once the `/etc/lilo.conf` file is configured to your liking, you can run the `/sbin/lilo` command as root to install the configuration file. The next time you boot the machine, you should see the LILO boot prompt. If at some future time you need to remove LILO from your system, you can do this from DOS (and presumably Windows 98 as well) with the `fdisk /mbr` command. This tells `fdisk` to reinstall the MBR to the first partition of the first drive.

The rdev Command

The `rdev` command allows you to change parameters without using LILO. For example, you can use the `dd` command to put a Linux kernel on a diskette, then move it to another machine to boot. To change the root partition, just use the following command:

```
rdev kernel root
```

where `kernel` is the kernel file and `root` is the new root partition to use. If the kernel is on a floppy diskette (you used `dd` to put it there or `make floppy` when compiling the kernel), the command would look like this:

```
rdev /dev/fd0 /dev/hda1
```

This would configure the kernel file on `/dev/fd0` (the floppy diskette) to change its root partition to use `/dev/hda1` instead of the default. For a list of other features that `rdev` has, use the `rdev -h` command.

3.2   Kernel Boot

While the kernel is starting up, you'll see a series of messages flying across the console. Most of these messages you can catch, due to the delay while the next driver initializes. If you miss something, the `dmesg` command will list all the kernel messages since and during boot time.

Here's an example of what the boot messages look like on an AMD K6-233 machine with an Adaptec 2930 SCSI card, 3c503 Ethernet card, and an IDE hard drive. This is the standard kernel for Red Hat 6.0:

```
Linux version 2.2.5-15 (root@porky.devel.redhat.com) (gcc version egcs-
   2.91.66 19990314/Linux (egcs-1.1.2 release)) #1 Mon Apr 19 22:21:09
   EDT 1999
Detected 233867589 Hz processor.
Console: colour VGA+ 80x25
Calibrating delay loop... 466.94 BogoMIPS
Memory: 62816k/65536k available (996k kernel code, 412k reserved, 928k
   data, 60k init)
VFS: Diskquotas version dquot_6.4.0 initialized
CPU: AMD AMD-K6tm w/ multimedia extensions stepping 02
Checking 386/387 coupling... OK, FPU using exception 16 error
   reporting.
Checking 'hlt' instruction... OK.
POSIX conformance testing by UNIFIX
PCI: PCI BIOS revision 2.10 entry at 0xf0430
```

```
PCI: Using configuration type 1
PCI: Probing PCI hardware
Linux NET4.0 for Linux 2.2
Based upon Swansea University Computer Society NET3.039
NET4: Unix domain sockets 1.0 for Linux NET4.0.
NET4: Linux TCP/IP 1.0 for NET4.0
IP Protocols: ICMP, UDP, TCP, IGMP
Initializing RT netlink socket
Starting kswapd v 1.5
Detected PS/2 Mouse Port.
Serial driver version 4.27 with MANY_PORTS MULTIPORT SHARE_IRQ enabled
ttyS00 at 0x03f8 (irq = 4) is a 16550A
ttyS01 at 0x02f8 (irq = 3) is a 16550A
pty: 256 Unix98 ptys configured
apm: BIOS version 1.2 Flags 0x03 (Driver version 1.9)
Real Time Clock Driver v1.09
RAM disk driver initialized:  16 RAM disks of 4096K size
PIIX3: IDE controller on PCI bus 00 dev 39
PIIX3: not 100% native mode: will probe irqs later
    ide0: BM-DMA at 0xe800-0xe807, BIOS settings: hda:DMA, hdb:pio
hda: Maxtor 90576D4, ATA DISK drive
ide0 at 0x1f0-0x1f7,0x3f6 on irq 14
hda: Maxtor 90576D4, 5495MB w/256kB Cache, CHS=700/255/63
Floppy drive(s): fd0 is 1.44M
FDC 0 is a post-1991 82077
md driver 0.90.0 MAX_MD_DEVS=256, MAX_REAL=12
raid5: measuring checksumming speed
raid5: using high-speed MMX checksum routine
   pII_mmx   :    386.715 MB/sec
   p5_mmx    :    362.331 MB/sec
   8regs     :    344.043 MB/sec
   32regs    :    246.126 MB/sec
using fastest function: pII_mmx (386.715 MB/sec)
scsi : 0 hosts.
scsi : detected total.
md.c: sizeof(mdp_super_t) = 4096
Partition check:
 hda: hda1 hda2 < hda5 hda6 >
RAMDISK: Compressed image found at block 0
autodetecting RAID arrays
autorun ...
... autorun DONE.
VFS: Mounted root (ext2 filesystem).
(scsi0) <Adaptec AIC-7860 Ultra SCSI host adapter> found at PCI 11/0
(scsi0) Narrow Channel, SCSI ID=7, 3/255 SCBs
(scsi0) Warning - detected auto-termination
(scsi0) Please verify driver detected settings are correct.
(scsi0) If not, then please properly set the device termination
(scsi0) in the Adaptec SCSI BIOS by hitting CTRL-A when prompted
(scsi0) during machine bootup.
```

```
(scsi0) Cables present (Int-50 YES, Ext-50 NO)
(scsi0) Downloading sequencer code... 413 instructions downloaded
scsi0 : Adaptec AHA274x/284x/294x (EISA/VLB/PCI-Fast SCSI) 5.1.15/3.2.4
     <Adaptec AIC-7860 Ultra SCSI host adapter>
scsi : 1 host.
(scsi0:0:0:0) Synchronous at 5.0 Mbyte/sec, offset 15.
  Vendor: SEAGATE    Model: ST31055N         Rev: 0532
  Type:   Direct-Access                      ANSI SCSI revision: 02
Detected scsi disk sda at scsi0, channel 0, id 0, lun 0
(scsi0:0:1:0) Synchronous at 5.0 Mbyte/sec, offset 8.
  Vendor: TOSHIBA    Model: CD-ROM XM-5701TA  Rev: 0167
  Type:   CD-ROM                             ANSI SCSI revision: 02
Detected scsi CD-ROM sr0 at scsi0, channel 0, id 1, lun 0
(scsi0:0:2:0) Synchronous at 5.0 Mbyte/sec, offset 15.
  Vendor: SEAGATE    Model: ST51080N         Rev: 0913
  Type:   Direct-Access                      ANSI SCSI revision: 02
Detected scsi disk sdb at scsi0, channel 0, id 2, lun 0
(scsi0:0:6:0) Synchronous at 5.0 Mbyte/sec, offset 15.
  Vendor: QUANTUM    Model: FIREBALL_TM1280S Rev: 300X
  Type:   Direct-Access                      ANSI SCSI revision: 02
Detected scsi disk sdc at scsi0, channel 0, id 6, lun 0
Uniform CDROM driver Revision: 2.54
SCSI device sda: hdwr sector= 512 bytes. Sectors= 2069860 [1010 MB]
  [1.0 GB]
 sda: sda1
SCSI device sdb: hdwr sector= 512 bytes. Sectors= 2109840 [1030 MB]
  [1.0 GB]
 sdb: sdb1 sdb2
SCSI device sdc: hdwr sector= 512 bytes. Sectors= 2503872 [1222 MB]
  [1.2 GB]
 sdc: sdc1
autodetecting RAID arrays
autorun ...
... autorun DONE.
VFS: Mounted root (ext2 filesystem) readonly.
change_root: old root has d_count=1
Trying to unmount old root ... okay
Freeing unused kernel memory: 60k freed
Adding Swap: 120452k swap-space (priority -1)
3c503.c: Presently autoprobing (not recommended) for a single card.
3c503.c:v1.10 9/23/93  Donald Becker (becker@cesdis.gsfc.nasa.gov)
eth0: 3c503 at i/o base 0x300, node  02 60 8c dd 2b b0, using internal
  xcvr.

eth0: 3c503-PIO, 16kB RAM, using programmed I/O (REJUMPER for SHARED
  MEMORY).
Installing knfsd (copyright (C) 1996 okir@monad.swb.de).
nfsd_init: initialized fhcache, entries=256
```

There are other messages that will probably display as programs start up. For example, output of things like `fsck` will not be in a `dmesg` output. But, messages that will be added to `dmesg` include changes of CD-ROMs or floppies (`VFS disk change detected on device xx:xx`) or if modules get loaded (for PPP or the parallel port, for example).

These messages are also stored in the `/var/log/messages` file, which is the default location where `syslog` stores its messages.

3.3   init

After the boot messages you saw above, you'll see more screens of text as other programs start up. These programs are not started as part of the kernel bootup, but are started by the `init` program. The `init` program is always Process ID (PID) 1, and is started automatically by the kernel. This program then starts up the rest of the daemons and other programs.

The `/etc/inittab` file is read by `init`, which tells it what `init` level to start out on and what processes to start. This would include programs like `getty` (which is what gives you the login prompt on the console). Other scripts are run based on what runlevel you've entered.

An entry in the `/etc/inittab` file has four fields:

```
10:0:wait:/etc/rc.d/rc 0
```

Colons delimit the above fields. The first field is one unique to the file and is just an arbitrary two-letter (or -digit) sequence. The second field tells `init` what runlevel to reference this field on. In this case, it's runlevel 0. The third field is an option to `init` on what to do while the script is running. Since you don't want to cause problems by having multiple runlevel change scripts running at once, `init` will wait until the script has finished before running any other scripts. Other options include `respawn`, which will restart the process if it dies or stops (for `getty`), and `once`, meaning that the process should be run only once and never again. The fourth field lists the script or process to run. You can see how these scripts work below.

3.4   What's a Runlevel?

The runlevel of a machine determines what functionality the system should be providing. Just as Windows 98 provides a safe mode, UNIX has a single-user safe mode, plus other configurations available:

Runlevel	Functionality
0	Halt
1	Single-user mode
2	Multiuser, no NFS
3	Multiuser, with NFS
4	Unused
5	X11 console (xdm, gdm, or kdm)[a]
6	Reboot

a. In Solaris 2.x, runlevel 5 will power down the system. It won't do that in Linux.

Two of these runlevels are really for stopping or rebooting the machine. Runlevel 1 allows only root to log in, and only the root partition is mounted. This is primarily for emergency situations where one of the other partitions is corrupted. The default runlevel for Red Hat is 3, which is a typical multiuser system and starts the network filesystem daemons as well. If you're not using NFS, you can use runlevel 2 if you like. Runlevel 5 automatically starts X with a login prompt. Normally, this is the xdm process. Red Hat 6.0 uses the gdm (GNOME Display Manager), but you can change the entry in /etc/inittab to use xdm, gdm, or the KDE Display Manager, kdm.

The first script that gets run by init, no matter what runlevel you're using, is the /etc/rc.d/rc.sysinit script. This script activates swap partitions, checks the filesystem consistency on any partitions it's about to mount, and performs a few other functions we won't worry about yet. In short, the rc.sysinit script runs all the programs that would be required no matter what runlevel you'd be using.

Once the rc.sysinit script completes successfully, init goes on and calls the /etc/rc.d/rc script with an option being the number of the runlevel to enter (0-6). Here's where things get interesting.

Under the /etc/rc.d directory are six directories to look at called rc.[0-6].d. Each directory has a number of scripts that start with a "K" or an "S", a two-digit number, and a program name. The "S" is for start scripts, and they are run when init enters that runlevel. This is for starting up programs that are specific to that runlevel. The "K" is for kill scripts, and they do the reverse of the S scripts, killing any programs that are not in a runlevel. The numbers give order to the apparent chaos, as scripts with a lower number are executed first, allowing the networking software to initialize the Ethernet card before the NFS daemons try to start. In all this, the name is just a descriptive one to the user. Kill scripts are run before start scripts.

As each script starts, Red Hat 6.0 throws in a way of reporting on the success or failure of startup scripts. By default, a message will look like this:

```
Starting rwho services:                                    [  OK  ]
```

The messages you see will display OK in green. In the event of failure, you'll get FAILED in red, making it easy to spot failures. In some cases, you'll also get an error message to indicate the reason for failure. In previous versions of Red Hat, all you'd get is something like:

```
Starting rwho services: rwhod
```

You can change between the two startup modes, and you can edit the /etc/sysconfig/console file to change the entry BOOTUP=color to BOOTUP=verbose. Changing the BOOTUP to anything else will include the OK and FAILED messages, but without ANSI coloring. This file also contains information on the size of the screen, and ANSI commands to change colors.

All these scripts are links to the /etc/rc.d/init.d directory, which contains the master of all the scripts. This allows one master script to not only control starting and killing processes, but it also allows you to find all the scripts in one location.

You can change your init level on-the-fly using the telinit command.[2] The telinit command takes only one argument—the runlevel you want to go to. This has to be run as root since you don't want just anyone dropping your system into single-user mode or making it reboot. telinit will handle running all the scripts to kill or start new processes.

3.5 When Something Goes Wrong

There are only a few places in the boot sequence that will cause the kernel to not finish loading (or not load at all). These include the following:

- Can't mount the root partition—The kernel may be trying to load a partition other than the one that is really the root. Your kernel may not

---

[2]telinit is really just a link to init, so you could use init <number> instead.

have the right drivers for the hard drive loaded. This can happen with SCSI drives, where each controller has its own driver. You'll have to boot an older or emergency kernel and fix this.

- Can't automatically check the filesystem for errors using `fsck`—In this case, the system will give you a warning and drop you into single-user mode. At this point, only the root partition is mounted, and you should use `fsck` to try to fix whatever damage was done. If you can't fix the partition, you can try to remove it from the list of partitions that get mounted at boot time. If it's a necessary partition, like / or /usr, you may need to restore from backup.

- The kernel was told to start up in Runlevel 1—Check /etc/inittab to see what the default runlevel is. It should be 2 or 3. You can go to Runlevel 2 or 3 using the `telinit` or `init` commands.

- Other errors loading drivers—This usually signifies a hardware error, such as a card not being found. In general, if a non-essential card isn't working (Ethernet, sound card, serial port card, etc.), the kernel will still boot. If the card is severely damaged,[3] it can cause the entire motherboard to start to fail. Remove all non-essential cards and try rebooting again.

- Bad startup scripts—If a script in /etc/rc.d is not written correctly, it can cause the system to go into a loop and appear locked up before it gets to the point where you can log in. Note the point where the machine appears to lock up and boot into single-user mode (if possible) or boot an emergency floppy. Once you get access to the system, find the script that is causing trouble and look for any problems. You may want to keep backup startup scripts handy just in case.

To summarize, here are the things you should have ready after installing Linux:

- Emergency boot floppy—As part of the installation procedure (see Chapter 2, "Installation"), you have the option of making an emergency boot floppy.

- Root floppy with `fsck`, `mkext2fs`, `fdisk`, copies of startup scripts, and `tar` or another program to restore backups—Red Hat includes a rescue diskette on the CD-ROM that you can build in case the hard drives on

---

[3]Static electricity is one of the quickest ways to ruin a card. Be sure you're grounded before working on the inside of a machine.

your system go bad. See below for instructions on how to use the rescue diskette.

- Known good kernel on the root partition—Use the one used to install the system, if you have it available. It may not have all the drivers, but you will be able to boot.

- Screwdrivers and grounding strap—Have these handy, just in case you suspect a hardware problem.

3.6 The Red Hat Rescue Diskette

For a proper Red Hat installation, you should have four diskettes handy[4]. Two are for the install (only one disk may be needed), one for the emergency kernel that gets created after installation, and one for the rescue floppy. Using the rescue floppy and the first installation diskette (labeled boot), you can have a Linux system up and running using only the two floppy diskettes. The purpose of this is that it helps you determine where a problem is and fix it without using the hard drive, in case that's your problem. For example, if your root partition fails, you won't be able to use the emergency diskette to boot. But, if you have the boot floppy and rescue disk, you can start the system up and use fsck (which is on the rescue disk) to fix the problem.

Making the rescue diskette is as easy as making boot diskettes. Just enter:

```
dd if=rescue.img of=/dev/fd0
```

assuming that rescue.img is in the current working directory. Then, use the boot diskette to start the system. Type in rescue at the LILO prompt. You'll get prompted to insert the rescue diskette and the system will start.

3.7 System Shutdown

Shutting Linux down is somewhat easier than starting it, since all you need to do is kill off all the available processes and tell the kernel to either stop or reboot the system.

---

[4] If your CD-ROM and BIOS support booting from CD-ROM, you can skip this and just boot from the CD-ROM. You can boot rescue from the CD-ROM as well.

There are a few ways to shut the system down, depending on how and when you want it to happen. The safest way is the following:

```
sync;sync;sync;/sbin/halt
```

The three `sync` commands tell the system to sync up the internal hard drive cache and the hard drive itself. Anything that has to get written to the hard drive gets done at this time. Why three `sync` commands? There are varying reasons, but the simplest one is that by the time the last `sync` is done, the buffers have had time to clear.

There are a few other methods of telling the machine to halt, including `kill -9 1` and `telinit 0`. In typical UNIX fashion, more than one command will work. Red Hat also provides for shutdown using the `linuxconf` interface. You can read more about `linuxconf` in the next chapter.

If you choose to reboot the system, you can replace `halt` with `reboot` or `telinit 6`.

All of the above commands are for shutting down the system immediately. If you choose to have a planned shutdown and want to give users time to finish their work and log out in an orderly fashion, you'll want to use the `shutdown` command.

Shutdown Command

When `shutdown` is run, the following options are available:

- `-r`—Reboot after shutdown.
- `-h`—Halt after shutdown.
- `-c`—Cancel an already running shutdown.
- `time`—When to shut down, either +minutes or hh:mm for an absolute time. You can also use `now`, which requires a value of +0.
- `message`—Warning message to send to all users.

Once shutdown is started, only root can log in until the machine is rebooted or the shutdown is canceled.

Shutdown is a nice front-end to the `init` process, since once shutdown has determined that it's time to shut down, it sends a signal to `init` to change to Runlevel 6 or 0.

The powerd Daemon

If you have a UPS that works with Linux, then you may have the power monitor daemon (`powerd`) installed. If the power goes off and the UPS activates, it will trigger a safe shutdown in two minutes. However, if the power comes back on during those two minutes, the shutdown will cancel.

You can get a copy of `powerd` from `contrib.redhat.com`. It works with a wide variety of UPSes that have serial outputs. You can also enable network support so if you have multiple machines connected to one UPS, they can all shut down in an orderly manner.

CTRL+ALT+DELETE

Yes, the famed "three-finger salute"—CTRL+ALT+DELETE—will shut down Linux as well, in a pinch. The init process is watching for this and will shut the machine down if it receives this signal. The default setting is to run the `reboot` command immediately.

If you're in a common lab area and don't want just anyone to be able to reboot a machine on a whim, you can take a line out of `/etc/inittab` and you're all set. Unfortunately, this doesn't prevent malicious people from hitting the power switch or pressing the reset button.   The next section shows how to disable rebooting via CTRL+ALT+DELETE.

3.8 Keeping a PC Safe from Reboots

During a reboot, a Linux box has very low security. If you're trying to keep a PC safe, the standard architecture makes it very hard to do. The PC can boot an OS (DOS) that can fit on a floppy, plus contain enough programs on it to completely ruin a hard drive. A virus can infect the MBR of a hard drive, which is what Linux needs to boot, or a user can bring their own Linux boot floppy to get root access, mount the hard drive, and start editing the `/etc/passwd` file.

Additionally, the chance of users hitting the power switch or reset button is always a factor. Running any kind of program remotely on a publicly accessible system is not a good idea, as the system can go down at any time. Here are a few suggestions for keeping a publicly available Linux machine for X86 safe.

1. Protect the Basic Input/Output System (BIOS)—This is the first thing you need to do, as many of the other protections depend on this. Password-protect access to the BIOS. Most modern ones will allow this. Also, be sure that no one can open the case. Locks are available for many cases. In the event that you forget the password, you can disconnect the on-board battery or make a jumper connection on the motherboard and the BIOS will be set to its default values.

2. Prevent booting from the floppy drive—Many BIOSes allow you to specify that only the hard drive can be booted first, forcing the computer to go into Linux or another OS on bootup without checking the floppy drive. This will not only prevent booting into DOS, but may also prevent a boot sector virus or two from infecting the hard drive.

3. Use Linux only—Booting into DOS or Windows can cause trouble, especially if someone intends to harm a computer. Booting into Linux will minimize this risk, since they cannot run any DOS programs.[5]

4. Don't use LILO unless you have to—LILO can boot off another device if told to (and if you have a Linux boot disk). Putting the Linux kernel on the MBR of the first hard drive can help prevent other OSes from being loaded inadvertently.

5. If necessary, disconnect the reset and power switches—This may force you to have people nearby who can power-cycle in the event of a crash.

6. Don't give out the root password—This goes without saying, but just in case. . . it's been said.

7. Be on guard—These steps will not make your computer bulletproof, but they should help prevent major damage to Linux systems.

8. Disable CTRL+ALT+DELETE in /etc/inittab—The line you'll want to look for is probably similar to this:

```
ca::ctrlaltdel:/sbin/shutdown -t3 -r now
```

Once you have your machine secure against reboots, you can set the machine up in a lab for public use.

---

[5]If this is the case, you should also take DOSEMU off the Linux system.

3.9   Summary

In this chapter, we covered the following:

- LILO is used to start up the kernel. There are a few different ways to install it on your hard drive.
- The kernel, on bootup, displays a number of messages regarding the drivers and devices it finds.
- Back up your system often, and keep emergency diskettes handy in case of any problems.
- The `init` process is Process 1 (PID=1). Killing it will reboot your Linux machine.
- Even though the X86 architecture is not very security-conscious, there are steps you can take to secure a Linux setup.
- Killing the `init` process is the same as telling Linux to shut down.

Account Administration

4

Administering the human side of your network—the users

There is more to administration than making sure that the system itself is running properly. You must keep the users of the system running as well.

4.1   Adding Users

As you've probably discovered by now, user data and group information are stored in two files:[1] /etc/passwd and /etc/group. The /etc/passwd file stores usernames, encrypted passwords, real names, and other user information. The /etc/group file stores group information and lists the groups of which the user is a member.

There are several methods you can use to add a user. The first, and probably the most difficult, is to make an entry in the /etc/passwd file (and /etc/

---

[1]More than two if you're using shadow passwords.

group, if necessary) for the new user. The `passwd` entry looks something like this:

```
markk:0QLp0ZyXo.shE:500:500:Mark F.
  Komarinski:/home/markk:/bin/tcsh
```

As you can see, there are seven fields separated by colons. In order, these are the username, encrypted password, user ID (UID), primary group ID (GID), real name, home directory, and login shell.

To enter a new user, simply add your own line. Replace the entire encrypted field with an asterisk (`*`) or some other character. Be sure the UID is unique. Now, create the home directory for the user you entered, copy files from `/etc/skel` to the home directory, and `chown` all the files in the home directory to the new user. Once the user exists, give the user a password by using the command as root:

```
passwd markk
```

Assuming that `markk` is the UID you created, this will put a valid encrypted password in the `passwd` field, and the user can now log in. The first thing the new user should do is change their password.

If that whole procedure seems a bit complicated, there are three other methods you can use. First, Red Hat comes with a `usercfg` that will allow root to create or delete users from the system. It does all of this automatically. The downside is that it's X-based, which is not much fun for automated scripts and the like. The other option for creating users is the `/usr/sbin/adduser` command. The only option required by this program is the username you wish to create. The program will then create the user, move files around, `chown`, and so on. Both `adduser` and `usercfg` create groups and assign unique UIDs based on the last UID used above 500.

The third method is to use `linuxconf`, which we'll get to later in this chapter.

Groups

Groups and GIDs are used to collect logical groups of people together. For example, engineering would have files they'd want to share among themselves, but not necessarily with sales. Or, accounting might want to share files with each other, but not with the rest of the company. The three levels of access for Linux files are user, group, and world. User is for the individual user who owns the file. Group is the group the file and user belong to, and world is everyone else. If you belong to the `eng` group (engineers) and want anyone else in the `eng` group to read a file, make sure the file resides in the `eng` group:

```
chgrp eng README
```

Then, set appropriate permissions on the file:

```
chmod 660 README
```

This particular `chmod` command gives read and write permissions to the owner (you) and anyone else in the `eng` group. No other users have access to this file.

The `chmod` command actually uses four octal numbers (0-8) to specify permissions:

Ownership	User	Group	Others
0—no setting	0—no permissions	0—no permissions	0—no permissions
1—save text image	1—execute	1—execute	1—execute
2—set GID	2—write	2—write	2—write
4—set UID	4—read	4—read	4—read

The ownership settings are rather special in that they give some extra functionality, but they are also security holes. The "save text image" setting means that once a program has finished running, it will save only the text portion in memory to decrease the amount of time it takes the program to load later on. This can quickly eat up memory if many programs have this, but if you use some programs a lot, this may be helpful.

The "set GID" setting means that once a program runs, set the group ID of the user to be that of the file. For example, if a program is in the sales group and has its GID bit set, when you run that program, you will be in the sales group only within that program while it is running. Some email programs use "set GID" to lock files in the `/var/spool/mail` directories. The user becomes part of the "mail" group while the E-mail program is running and can write to `/var/spool/mail`.

The "setUID" setting is the same as "setGID," but works with user IDs instead. Some programs, like network snoopers, require the use of devices or functions that can be run only by root. By setting `ping` to "set UID" root, everyday users can run the `ping` program. If you set a program to "set UID," be careful. If a program creates a new shell process, it will have the UID of the owner of the file. If the owner of the file is root, this can lead to common users getting root access very quickly. All the user would have to do is start a shell, and the new shell would be running as root.

The /etc/skel Directory

This directory contains a "skeleton" user. That is, it contains files that you can use as a base for other users. It contains setup files for X, /bin/bash configuration files, and a .login. You can add to or change these files as you like, but remember that existing users will not have these changes taken into account. Only new users will see them. If you want to have common settings for all users, you can use the /etc/.login, /etc/csh.cshrc, and so on.

4.2 Deleting or Disabling Users

To disable a user account (that is, prevent the user from logging in again), replace the password in the /etc/passwd file with an asterisk (*) or some other character. Since the * isn't a valid encrypted password, there is no password that will allow you to log into that account.[2]

To delete an account, remove the entire line from the /etc/passwd file. The user will cease to exist to the system, and root cannot su to that user.

The differences? If you disable an account, the account technically still exists. That user can still receive mail,[3] has a home directory (that other people can access if the permissions are correct), and has all the rights of any other account. The user just can't log in. When an account is deleted, the system will bounce any mail that comes to that user, and all files owned by the former user will now be owned by the UID that the user had. Also, any accesses to the home directory (cd ~bob, for example) will not work.

When to Disable and When to Delete

So, when should you disable an account and when should you delete it? It depends on what information you want to keep. If you're an Internet Service Provider (ISP) and a customer cancels, you may just want to delete the

---

[2]The root user can still use su to enter that account, as su does not ask root for passwords.

[3]A deleted user can still have an entry in /etc/aliases to forward mail to another system.

account. If you're in a business and an employee quits, you'd probably want to make the account disabled for six months to give everyone else time to transfer files to other users, or to back up the account to tape.

The best criterion for this is: If the user has data in their home directory that others would want or need to access, disable the account. Once the files needed by the disabled account have been moved to other locations, delete the account. If the account has no information needed by other users, back up the home directory and any other files the user owns and delete the account.

4.3 Using Shadow Passwords

There are a few advantages to using shadow passwords instead of using `/etc/passwd`. One is that encrypted passwords are not stored in a location where just anyone can read them. The `/etc/shadow` file contains the encrypted passwords for users and is readable only by root. Thus, only processes running as root can access the passwords. Another advantage is that `/etc/shadow` stores more than just passwords. It can also store data such as the last time a user changed their password. To maintain good security, you should have users change their passwords at least once every six months or so, or immediately if there is the possibility that the password has been compromised.

The disadvantage to using shadow passwords is rather large—many Linux programs may assume you're not using them. This can cause a major headache while compiling programs. Also, many installations do not give shadow passwords by default, meaning that you'll have to put them in after installation.

Setting Up Your System for Shadow Passwords

You can easily add shadow passwords to your system, or remove them if you choose. The command to implement shadow passwords is `pwconv`. To restore a shadow password system back to using `/etc/passwd` and `/etc/group`, use the `pwunconv` command.

4.4 Using PAM

In the old days (just a few years ago), there were two big problems with the administration of user accounts:

- Managing accounts on a large number of machines.

- Ensuring security on each machine.

In the first case, it was inconvenient to synchronize /etc/passwd files on each machine, especially if you had a lot of machines to handle. NIS and NIS+ helped this situation a bit, but NIS and NIS+ had their problems. In the second case, there were a number of ways of ensuring password authentication on each machine. They ranged from your typical /etc/passwd with passwords encrypted to /etc/shadow to one-time passwords such as S/KEY. For programs such as login, rlogin, and even locking screensavers to understand the fact that a machine could have multiple ways of verifying a password, there had to be some method of verifying passwords, no matter what method you chose.

Linux is starting to get a handle on both issues. Red Hat makes it easier using the Pluggable Authentication Module (PAM). PAM creates independent modules that verify passwords and tell the appropriate program (login) that the entered password is correct. This greatly increases security (since PAM can tell passwd that a given password is too easy to guess), and also increases the ways of authenticating a user. PAM can verify passwords from a variety of sources, from NIS to an NT server to an LDAP server. PAM also handles changing passwords and can apply methods to passwords, such as timing out a password and forcing a user to change their password.

A useful starting point for information is the /usr/doc/pam*/ directory. Underneath that are three documents: *The Linux-PAM System Administrator's Guide, The Linux-PAM Module Writer's Guide*, and *The Linux-PAM Application Developer's Guide*. These three documents cover most of what PAM is as it's implemented on Red Hat. Since we're mostly concerned with system administration here, you'll probably want to print out or read *The Linux-PAM System Administrator's Guide.*

Here are some of the highlights of account administration using PAM:

PAM Configuration

The configuration files used by PAM are stored under the /etc/pam.d/ directory. Some older systems may have a pam.conf file. While the pam.conf file will be read if it exists, its use is not recommended anymore.

In the /etc/pam.d/ directory, each filename is the name of the program that will validate the service. For example, the configuration file for login is /etc/pam.d/login and the file for rlogin is /etc/pam.d/rlogin. If a service requests PAM authentication and no specific configuration file exists, PAM will check the `/etc/pam.d/other` file.

Let's take a look at the default login configuration file so it can be referenced later on:

```
auth       required     /lib/security/pam_securetty.so
auth       required     /lib/security/pam_pwdb.so   shadow nullok
auth       required     /lib/security/pam_nologin.so
account    required     /lib/security/pam_pwdb.so
password   required     /lib/security/pam_cracklib.so
password   required     /lib/security/pam_pwdb.so shadow nullok
use_authtok
session    required     /lib/securitypam_pwdb.so
```

PAM configuration files contain up to four items per line:

```
module-type control-flag  module    arguments
```

- `module-type`—The module type defines what kind of module will be defined in this entry. At this point, there are four types of modules:
  - Authentication—Used to authenticate an entered user. This is the section that checks a given password against `/etc/passwd` or `/etc/shadow`.
  - Account—This module type can restrict account access based on (for example) time of day or `login` location.
  - Session—Used to set up external services before the given service starts. Extra information can be logged to a file or to `syslog`, for example.
  - Password—Used to change the "authentication token", commonly known as the password. For a typical `/etc/passwd`, this just updates the file. For an LDAP server, this changes the password on the server. A one-time password should not use this since the password is only good once.
  As usual for configuration files, blank lines or lines that start with a # (called a hash, pound, number, or whatever) are comments and not read.
  Typical configuration files mostly contain Authentication and Password module entries.
- `control-flag`—This defines what to do on the success or failure of the module. That is, if an authentication module succeeds, will another module be checked, or will a user be given access to that service? There are four `control-flag` types:

- Required—The module must succeed for the user to be granted access. If this module fails, do not immediately report failure, but continue on to the next module if it exists. An example of this type of control flag is when a user tries to log in remotely as root. As part of the login, PAM setup checks /etc/securetty to see if where the user is logging in from is listed in /etc/securetty. If the tty is not listed there, the user will not be able to log in as root. As you can see in the sample above, the pam_securetty.so module is checked first, before the password is requested (which happens in the pam_pwdb.so). Had the securetty not been set to "required", the user trying to log in as root would have been denied login before ever entering a password. With the above configuration, the user just gets an "invalid login" error after what seems to be a normal login process (entering username and password).

- Requisite—Unlike required, if a requisite module fails, PAM immediately stops and reports failure. This is rarely used since it may give an intruder a reason as to why their authentication was denied.

- Sufficient—Unlike required, if a sufficient module succeeds, PAM immediately stops checking and reports success. This control type is used in rlogin, which checks to see if ~/.rhosts exists, and if so, allows immediate use without further checking (or asking for a password).

- Optional—Not used by default on Red Hat. Optional entries do not require success or failure to authenticate a user.

- module—The module is a full list of where each module lives. This must be a full path to a shared library. Under Red Hat, these files are stored by default under /lib/security/.

- argument—Arguments to the module are listed after the module itself. This allows you to pass items to the module to affect how it works. For example, the pam_pwdb module can look like this:

```
password    required    /lib/security/pam_pwdb.so shadow nullok
  use_authtok
```

When a password is changed, PAM knows to put the password in the shadow file. It also knows that a user can change a password that was null (but not to a password that is null, since cracklib prevents this), and to use the password given previously (that cracklib already checked and said was okay).

Increased Security with PAM

So, how do you use PAM to increase security on your system? You can easily implement many of the features that are offered by other operating systems (such as VMS or NT) that allow you to configure the kinds of passwords that are acceptable. You can also have accounts (or other services) available only at certain times or on certain days. Here's an overview of some of the modules you may want to use in your security system:

- `pam_time`—Determines what accounts have access to what services on what days. It has an external configuration file that is used by all PAM configuration files, located in `/etc/security/time.conf`. The configuration file has lines that look like this:

```
service;  tty; user; time
```

These fields represent:
- `service`—The service affected by this rule in a list (so you could `login`, but not `su`, or the other way around).
- `tty`—`tty`s where the user is attempting to access the service from. Remember that `tty` represents a local connection, `ttyp` represents a remote connection, and `ttys` represents a serial connection.
- `user`—Users affected by this rule, in a list.
- `time`—The time when this rule is in effect. Days are two-character entries (`mo` through `fr`, with `wk` being weekdays, `wd` weekend days, and `al` all days). If two items follow, the first item is unset. That is, if you enter a day string of `TuWk`, it means all days except Tuesday, or `WdAl` means all days except weekend days, which is really `wk`. Times which follow the day are listed in 24-hour format as four digits (0000-2400)
  Each of the above entries can be entered in what is called a logic list. The logic list can have three extra characters that apply: `*` to represent every possible item in the list, `|` to logically OR two items together, or & to logically AND two items together.
  For example, to prevent all logins on the `markk` account except for between the hours of 3 A.M. and 6 A.M. on Tuesday, the rule would look like this:

```
login ; * ; markk ; Tu0300-0600
```

To prevent all logins on the console except for the `markk` account, you'd do something like this:

```
login ; tty* & !ttyp* ; !markk ; !A10000-2400
```

- `pam_cracklib`—Checks a given password for "crackability," or ease of an intruder's cracking the password. The password is first compared against a dictionary (given in `/usr/lib/cracklib_dict.`) that contains a list of packed words to check against. To create a new dictionary of words to check against, use the `/usr/sbin/create-cracklib-dict` *file* command to create a new dictionary. If the password passes this check, it is then compared to the previous password for the following:
  - Is the new password a palindrome of the old one?
  - Is the change in password more than just one of changing the case of some letters?
  - How close are the old password and new one?
  - Is the password too short?
  - Is the new password a rotated version of the old one?

If all these tests pass, then `cracklib` reports success.

4.5   Linuxconf

The `linuxconf` program gives access to the configuration of your Linux system through a few methods: Web, X, Java, and text-based. Each interface is about the same, but we'll concentrate on the Web interface.

This configuration can include examining logs, creating or disabling users, network configuration, and kernel configuration. To improve configurability, non-root users can be allowed certain kinds of access to `linuxconf`. One user has access to only the logs, while another is allowed to shut down the machine, and a third has no access at all. As new modules get written, it's easy to expand what `linuxconf` can do to ease administration. Such modules include activating IP filtering or accounting to ease the construction of a firewall.

Note that using `linuxconf` over the Web does have a few security issues. It should only be used in a fairly secure environment behind a firewall or packet filter, and access should be granted only to other machines on the network. By default, Web access is turned off, so you have to explicitly activate it and set up hosts that can use it before it is allowed. However, this is the only method for non-root users to access `linuxconf`.

The `linuxconf` Web section is started via `inetd.conf`. Any connection to the `linuxconf` port (by default it's TCP 98) will start up `linuxconf` in http mode. The easiest way to get into `linuxconf` to configure the Web connection is to use the text-based interface. You can start the program with linuxconf --text as the root user. The first time you start it, you'll get some usage and navigation information, then you'll get right into it.

The Linuxconf Screen

The initial screen gives two menu items (Config and Control) and one menu button (Quit). TAB allows you to jump between the menu items and the button. The cursors allow you to move between the menu items, and the ENTER key will either select a menu item (if there is no + sign in front of it) or expand/contract submenus. Since you have more than just Config and Control available, you can press ENTER while on the Config option to see the submenus there. You'll get a list that looks like the following:

```
+Config
  +Networking
  +Users accounts
  +File systems
  +boot mode
+Control
```

With the plus signs in front of each submenu, you can see that they too have submenus (but not ad infinitum). Now let's expand the Networking menu, followed by the Misc submenu:

```
+Config
  +Networking
    +Client Tasks
    +Server Tasks
    +Misc
       Information about other hosts
       Information about other networks
       Linuxconf network access
  +Users accounts
  +File systems
  +boot mode
+Control
```

Select Linuxconf network access, which then gets you into a screen of options. First is the Enable Network Access checkbox. Since we want network access, press the SPACEBAR to select it. If the Log access box is not checked, check it now. This way, you can see who accesses linuxconf through the Web and be aware of any potential problems. Underneath all this is a list of IP address and netmask listings. A netmask is optional, but may be helpful if you want to restrict access to just a few hosts within the subnet.

Listing a class C network (192.168.1.0) or a host by itself (127.0.0.1) does not require a netmask. Any other settings should have a netmask associated with them. If you're not sure how the subnet mask works, check the networking chapter for setting up a TCP/IP network.

So, let's give access to our fake class C network and also to the local host. Use the arrow keys to put in 192.168.1.0 and 127.0.0.1 under the Network and Host fields. Then TAB to the Accept button and press ENTER. You'll go back to the original menu.

Quit linuxconf and start lynx or Netscape, pointing at http://localhost:98/. You'll get a screen similar to Figure 4-1:

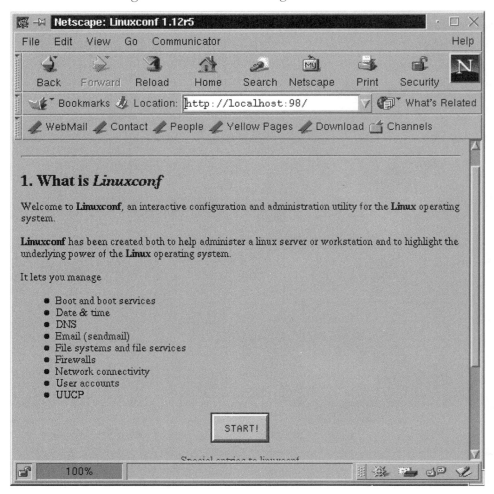

Figure 4–1   Linuxconf introduction screen

If you click on the START button at the bottom of the screen, you'll get prompted for a username and password. For now, root is the only user authorized to use linuxconf. This is the next thing we'll change, but for now, enter the root username and password.

You'll wind up with the same menu listing that you saw before, with each menu now being a hyperlink to another screen instead of actually expanding menus. Don't worry about getting lost in the menus, as the top of each page lists each set of menus you burrowed through (starting with the main page) to get where you are now. You can go back a menu level by clicking the last item on that list.

Now on to giving the "markk" (replace "markk" with your username if you like) account access to linuxconf, so you don't have to give the root username and password every time. Click Users accounts then User accounts. You'll get a list of all the local users known to linuxconf. If the markk account doesn't exist, you can click Add to create a new account. Otherwise, click the existing markk user (either way, you'll wind up in about the same screen shown in Figure 4-2).

You may notice that the root user is not in the list of users. There's a separate menu item for changing the root password. This way, you can't mess up the root settings and you'll always have something to fall back on in case of serious trouble.

In the user screen, there are a few changes from the traditional user account setup. For one thing, you may see information about expiring the password. Change this information as you see fit. By default, the password won't expire anytime soon (99999 days, or about 273 years). The minimum password change day is -1, meaning the user can change their password immediately. You can also set the account to expire after X days (if X is -1, the account won't expire) or you can set the account to expire on a specific date. If left blank and the number of days to expiration is not set, the account will never expire.

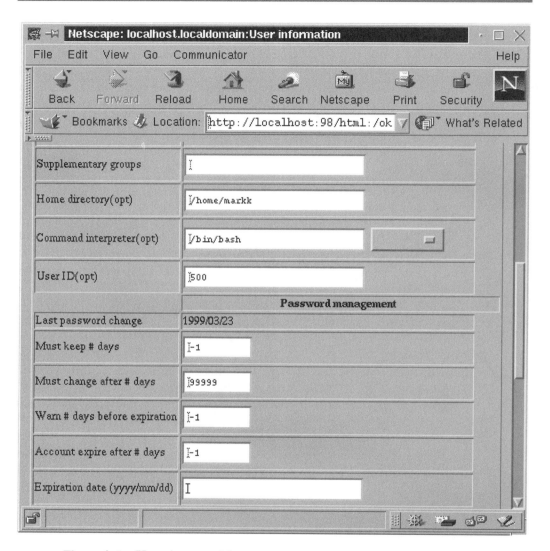

Figure 4–2   User Account Management

Next, the `linuxconf` access gives a listing of what access you want to provide to the user (see Figure 4-3). Shutdown, viewing logs, and access to PPP, POP, and UUCP management can all be denied or granted (plus access to `linuxconf` itself). Grant or deny access as you see fit. Since it's your machine and your account, you must decide if you trust yourself enough to have a certain kind of access. As you add new modules, like `Message of the Day` configuration, you may or may not get separate listings for access to those modules. Granting "superuser equivalence" gives access to pretty much everything, and may introduce security issues if you give too many users this kind of access.

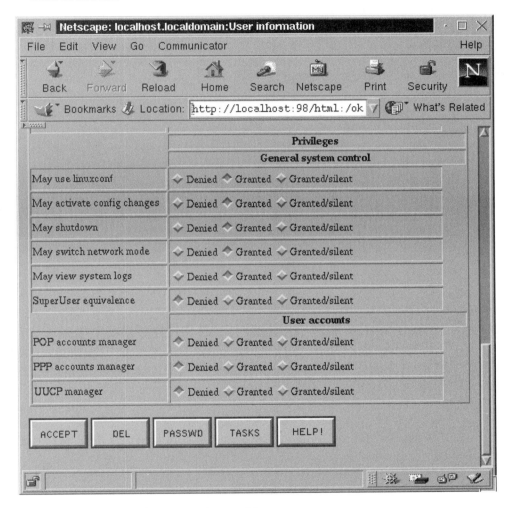

Figure 4–3 Special Account Access Management

Extra Modules

Along with the modules built into linuxconf, there are additional modules that can be added or removed to give access to other parts of the system. We've already mentioned the MOTD module, and there are modules for configuring Apache, FPTD services, DHCP, firewall administration, email, RARP, and Samba. A full list of the modules that are available can be found under /usr/lib/linuxconf/modules. They're binary files, so you won't be able to find out much more from the directory listing other than the names.

You can have root activate a module as linuxconf --setmod <module name>, where <module name> is the name of the file under the modules directory before the so. For example, if you have linuxconf version 1.12.5 and a module for setting the MOTD, the module would appear in the directory listing as motd.so.1.12.5 and the <module name> would be motd. So, you could install the MOTD module with linuxconf --setmod motd. To remove modules, use the --unsetmod switch.

The other way to activate modules is via the Web interface to linuxconf itself. Under Control and Control files and systems is the option Configure Linuxconf modules. This option allows you to enter new modules (assuming you know what they are). You'll see that treemenu is already there. After this, you can enter new modules to load (like MOTD) to add them to the system. Click Accept, then go into Control and Control panel and select Restart Linuxconf. After that, the new menus for the module become available. You may have to poke around a bit to find where the new modules were loaded.

Advanced Linuxconf—Profiles

Linuxconf also allows you to build profiles or backups of major system files. There are many purposes for this: the biggest advantage is for notebook users whose configurations may change between a home network, office network, and dial-in network. Many settings may remain the same, but network settings will be different. Linuxconf allows you to store each setting and restore it to the system on demand. Another good application of this is to store last known good settings. If you want to go tweak some network settings to see if you can get slightly better routing, you won't have to worry about the configuration. The last settings that you knew were okay (before you started tinkering) can be saved and you can then restore them on demand to get back to them.

Let's work with the two default configuration settings that come with linuxconf—Home and Office. Since the only things that really change between the two settings are networking configurations, that's all that linuxconf needs to know to backup and restore. The default is Office mode. You can see the configurations under Control, Control files and systems, and Configure system profiles. You can then examine what subsystems are backed up as part of the Office and Home configurations. So let's test it. First, archive the settings that you currently have, using Control, Control panel, and Archive Configurations. Now select Switch system profile. Switching system profiles will also archive your settings, but we'll do it twice to be on the safe side. The system profile screen shows that we're in the Office setting, and the only available profile to switch to is Home. Select that, and you'll see all the Office files backed up again. Try to restore the Home files. Since the Home files don't exist, you may see a bunch of errors. Ignore them for now.

Now you'll see that you're in the Home profile. Use linuxconf or some other tool to change your network settings. Since markk has Ethernet both at home and work, this is easy. He just changes the Ethernet settings for Home, then archives the home settings. Part of changing these settings also gives a kick to the network to make it restart with the new IP information. Once you're in the new configuration, check your network services to make sure they restarted as they should have.

Storing Profiles

Each time you change profiles, the files get backed up in RCS format. Therefore, every time you change a file, you can go back to a previous version of the same file. In the event of your messing up a bunch of files, you can use linuxconf to restore an older version of the files. It doesn't exist to do this automatically yet, but will probably arrive sometime soon. However, you should be able to use regular RCS commands to pull out older versions of files. By default, RCS files are stored in /etc/linuxconf/archive. The program that creates the RCS files is located in /usr/lib/linuxconf/lib/cfgarchive. It's a shell script, so you can see how the archives are made. You can also replace the files with a different archiving program, if you like.

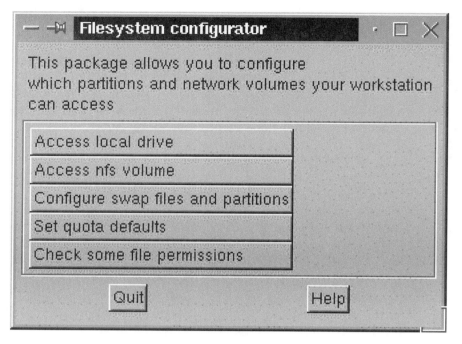

Figure 4–4   Fsconf mainscreen

fsconf

The filesystem configuration tool (`fsconf`) provides a nice front-end to the `/etc/fstab` file. The `/bin/fsconf` file is really a pointer to `/bin/linuxconf`. Since the Web interface is similar to the `/bin/fsconf` program, we'll cover this section of the program here. The `fsconf` mainscreen is shown in Figure 4-4. You can add, delete, or edit mount points for local or NFS partitions. The main screen has a total of five options, which are described in the following sections.

Access Local Drive

Clicking this option beings up a list of known mount points and options for the local drive only. NFS drives are handled in a different menu. Clicking on any of the mounts brings up a menu with options for that particular volume, including partition, filesystem type, and mount points (see Figure 4-5).

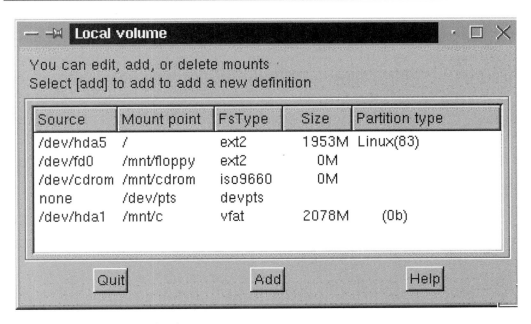

Figure 4–5 Local volume management

The `options` tab gives a view of mounting options. As you can see in Figure 4-6, we want to have the CD-ROM mounted read only, and mountable by a normal user. It's not mounted at boot time, and we don't want any applications to be able to run off the CD-ROM, nor do we want Linux to recognize any device files that exist on the CD-ROM. The final checked option indicates that no setuid programs will run. Since we don't want quota support on this volume, it's turned off. The `dump` and `fsck` levels are set to 0, indicating that we don't want this volume backed up or checked. If this were an actual hard drive, we'd set the `dump` and `fsck` levels to 1, indicating that we wanted the drive checked on bootup.

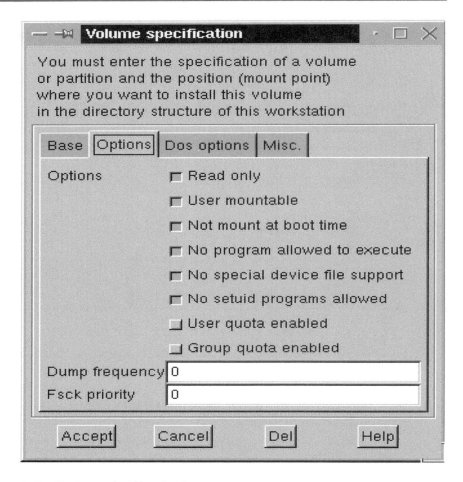

Figure 4–6   Options tab of local volume management

Because DOS (really the FAT, VFAT, and FAT32 volume types) does not recognize users or permissions, we can have Linux handle some of this for us with the DOS options tab (Figure 4-7). If you're mounting a FAT filesystem, you can have all the files appear as being owned by a specific user or group. You can also set default permissions for all files in octal format (see the section on chmod for more information on this). And lastly, you can set a default translation mode. Since Linux has only an LF (^L) as an end-of-line marker, while FAT uses CR-LF (^M^L), you have to make sure that text files get translated properly, while binary data does not get this translation applied. Linux is very good at automatically recognizing this, but if you need to set a translation mode, you can do it here. Binary indicates no translation at all, Text means translate everything, and `Auto` (the default) means to figure it out based on the filename extension. A complete list of these extensions can be found by clicking the `Help` button.

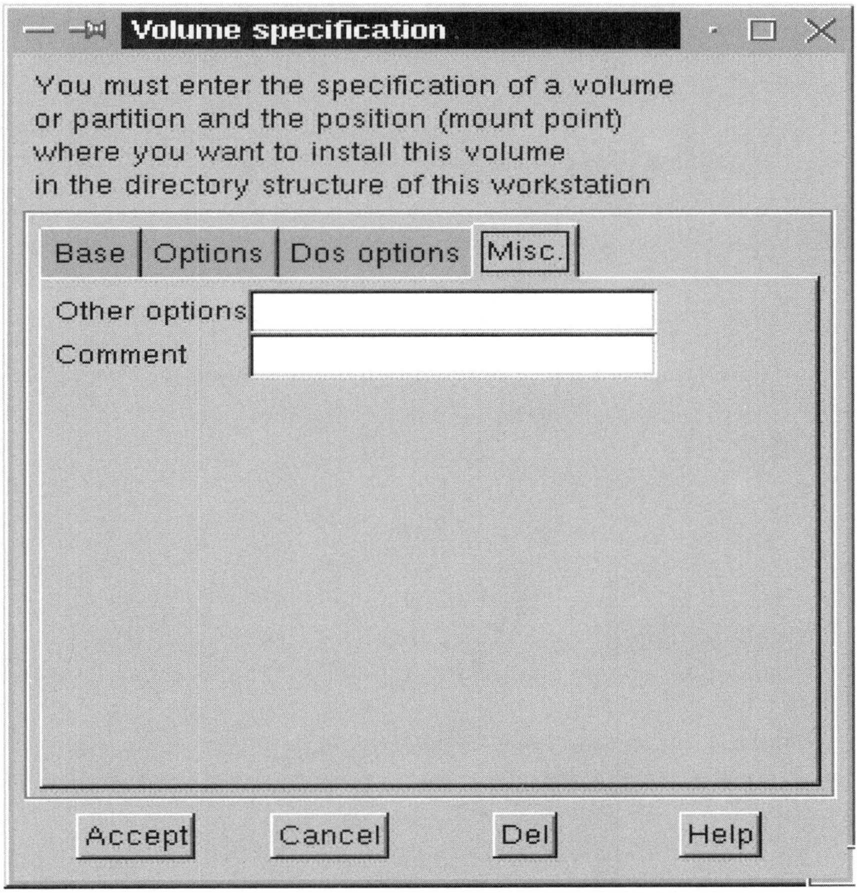

Figure 4–7 DOS options of local volume management

Under the `Misc` tab (Figure 4-8), you can use additional mount options (may not be covered elsewhere) under the `Other options` field. Comments (have no effect on the mounting of the partition) can be added in the `Comments` field.

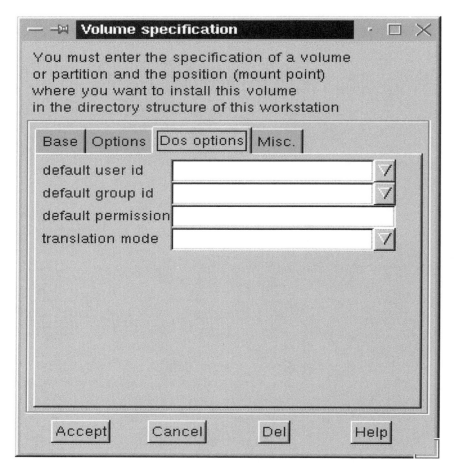

Figure 4–8   Miscellaneous options for local volume management

Access nfs Volume

The setup here is similar to local volumes, so we'll cover only the differences between mounting an NFS volume and a local volume. The main screen shows a list (if any) of known NFS mounts. Clicking on one (or clicking add) brings up the Volume specification window.

The Base tab allows you to enter the serving host and volume, plus the local mount point. The Options tab is the same as under local volumes, except there are no options for dump or fsck.

The NFS options tab has four of the most common options used in mounting NFS volumes. The Soft mount option (if checked) will return an

I/O error immediately to an application if there is a problem contacting the NFS server. With the option unchecked, called a hard mount, the request will continue indefinitely and the application may appear to hang. The `Background mount` option tells `mount` to first try mounting in the foreground, then try all other requests in the background. This allows `mount` to return without much delay, and allows Linux to fully boot even if some NFS servers are not responding. With the option unchecked, it is considered a foreground mount, and the `mount` program will either time out or wait a long time before returning. The last two options allow you to set the read and write sizes for blocks to send to and from the NFS server. The default is 1024 bytes, but you may find better performance going up to something like 8192.

Configure Swap Files or Partitions

Since swap partitions are rather easy to set up, there are not many options to configure. The `Base` tab contains the partition (or file) to use as swap, and the `Misc` tab has additional options and comments, just like local and NFS volume mounting. If you choose to use a file as a swap partition (in case you need more swap space), create a file the size of the swap partition you'll need. The easiest way to do this is to use `dd` to create a file (the `mkswap` man page uses the example `dd if=/dev/zero of=swapfile bs=1024 count=65536`, which creates a 64MB swap file), then use `mkswap` to format the space (`mkswap swapfile`). Once that is complete, you can enter the full path to `swapfile` as the partition to use and add it to the swap space.

Set Quotas

If quotas are set on a partiton, you can set up default quotas for users and groups on each partition. Quotas are set up in the following ways:

- Soft Limit—This is a limit that can be exceeded, but only for a defined amount of time. After this time, the user cannot write to the filesystem.
- Hard Limit—This limit can never be exceeded. Attempting to do so will return an error.
- Grace Period—Amount of time (in days, hours, minutes, and seconds) that a soft limit can be exceeded.

By default, soft limit and hard limit are set to -1 (none) and the grace period is 7 days. Note that these limits get applied not only to total disk space, but also to individual file size. This can be handy in preventing mailboxes from getting too big (as an example). Also note that these limits are set **per partition**.

Once the defaults are set, you can use an application like `linuxconf` to fine-tune these settings per user.

Check fs Permissions

This function does a quick check of some file permissions to make sure there are no blatant security holes. You'll either get an "OK" or a request to change some file permissions.

4.6   Interaction with Users

This section is more for the human side of interaction. The way you interact with your users determines how they will interact with you. The first thing to remember is that your users will probably not know as much about Linux as you do. They may need simple concepts or programs explained to them. Giving them a lot of low-level gibberish makes you look cool, but it probably won't answer their questions.

As an example, you could say, "Well, `sendmail` is thinking your mail host is `foo` when it should be `bar`, so I'll have to go change the `/etc/aliases` file on the NIS server to make it point to the right server." Or you could say, "The mail isn't in the right location. I'll try and move it." If you knew absolutely nothing about computers, which would make you feel better? Don't let your sadistic side get the better of you, no matter how tempting it is.

One other important thing you should do is keep your users informed. If you need to shut down the server, be sure to give everyone at least a few minutes' warning before you do it. If you have to take the server down for maintenance, do it near the end of the day and give everyone a few hours to get their work done. Just dropping people off the server may cause them to lose files and work. Also be sure that your backups work and test the backups frequently so you can be sure that you can restore them if needed.

Some administrators have the notion that the people they're assisting in their day-to-day activities are not really customers—they're just people they work with. We see it differently. Your primary job, if you're an administrator, is to make sure that the people you're helping are able to do their jobs. If they can't do their jobs, then you won't have one to do. So, it would be fair to think of the people you're helping as customers. As such, you have to be nice to them and should be ready to drop what you're doing to make sure they can keep doing their jobs.

4.7 Summary

- `/etc/password` and `/etc/group` contain all the user and group information on the system.
- File permissions are based on user, group, and everyone (world).
- PAM can increase system security.
- `Linuxconf` can assist with many routine administration functions.
- Be nice! Your users are your customers.

RPM 5

Installing new packages to your Linux system

> The Red Hat Package Manager (RPM) provides an easy way to install, remove, and verify files on your system.

Each program set (such as Apache) comes as a single file with an `.rpm` extension. After installing the `.rpm` file, all the files needed for installation are placed in the appropriate place, ready for running, including man pages, configuration files, and other documentation.

The advantages to the `.rpm` format are many:

- Dependencies—Since you may have instances where one package depends on another, RPM has dependencies to alert you if a library or other package is missing. If you do have the other files already installed and RPM doesn't know about it, such as if you compiled from source, you can tell the RPM to ignore dependency rules by using the `--nodeps` command to the `rpm` program.

- Convenient installation (typically one command to install)—A typical fresh install of a package consists of a command of the form `rpm -i` `package-1.0-1.i386.rpm`. To find out what files would be installed if you installed the entire package, you can use `rpm -qlp package-1.0-1.i386.rpm`. You'll then get a list of what files are in the package and where they will be installed. To find out the details of a particular `.rpm` file, you can use `rpm -qip package-1.0-1.i386.rpm` to get a list of the package name, description, build information, size of the installed package, and other information. This can be handy if you have a large number of `.rpm` files and don't know what they're for.

- Convenient upgrading and removal—Upgrading the version of an existing package just uses the `-U` option instead of the `-i` switch to the `rpm` command. Since you can install two packages of the same kind using `-i`, it's advisable to use the upgrade switch when in doubt. Use the `-e` switch to remove packages. If there are dependencies that would break if you removed a package, you will get an error message from the RPM. You can get around this by using the `--nodeps` option. This isn't really advisable since some system programs may be affected. For example, `glint` (see below) uses Tcl/TK. Removing Tcl/TK from your system would generate an error saying that `glint` depends on Tcl/TK.

- Easy to see what is installed on your system—The `-q` switch allows you to query the RPM database. You can query a specific package to see if it's installed (such as `rpm -q apache`) or get a list of the files that are part of a package and where they're located (using the `-ql` switch, such as `rpm -ql apache`). If you don't know the name of the package you're looking for, you can use the `-qa` switch to list all installed packages and `grep` for the package you're looking for. For example, Netscape is installed as `netscape-communicator`, `netscape-common`, and `netscape-navigator`. Using `rpm -q netscape`, you won't find the package, but `-qa` will. In addition, if you want to find out what RPM package "owns" a particular file, you can use the `-qf` switch followed by the file. If that file is listed in RPM's database, it will report which RPM package owns that file.

- Easy system verification—If you suspect there are problems with your system and want to verify that packages are installed properly, you can use the `-V` option to `rpm` to verify packages. RPM stores file sizes, modes, MD5 sums, and other information. This option will let you quickly see if a file has been erased or modified since you installed it. If you find a problem, you can use the `-U` switch to reinstall the package to its original form. You can verify all packages on your system with the command `rpm -Va`. If the verification passes, you won't see any output. If a particular test fails, you'll get a list of eight characters, followed by a "c" if it's a configuration file, followed by the name of the file. These eight characters can be:

5 - MD5 checksum failed.

S - File size.

L - Symbolic link.

T - File modification time.

D - Device file.

U - User (file owner).

G - Group (group owner).

M - File mode.

If you modified a configuration file, such as for Apache, you can expect to see at least one or more of the above failures. If you see this on a file like /bin/su or /bin/login, it may indicate a breakin attempt.

- Graphical interface available—It provides a graphical way to see what packages are installed, install new packages, verify package files, and list files in a package. If you have the install CD, you can install files directly from the CD. This provides a user-friendly way to install packages. There are other programs to install RPM files as well, such as kpackage for the KDE Window Manager.

5.1 Binary RPM Installation

RPM files typically have the following filename syntax:

```
package-1.0-1.i386.rpm
```

This syntax tells you the following four things:

package—The name of the package, usually the same name as the RPM package name.

1.0—Version number of the package. This usually refers to the version of the original source, not the RPM version.

1—Release number of the package. This refers to the RPM build, so if package-1.0 was made into an RPM file again (either because of a configuration error or other change), the next version would be called package-1.0-2.i386.rpm.

i386—Architecture for the build. You'll typically see i386, sparc, or alpha. You might see i586 or i686, which refer to packages built with a

Pentium or Pentium-Pro-specific compiler. If you're not sure and there's a choice, go for the `i386` version.

5.2 Source RPM (SRPM)

Source RPMs contain the source code for an application that either must be compiled on each individual system, or allow you to modify source code or pre-compile options before installing the software. One example of this is a program that depends on a particular library release. Another example is compiling a package to be Pentium-specific, using `pgcc` to compile the package instead of `gcc` or `egcs`. After SRPM installation, you can compile the package into a binary RPM, then install the binary RPM just like a pre-compiled package. Many SRPM files contain the original source code as a `.tar.gz` file, along with patches for it to compile as an SRPM, or to add extra functionality.

To build a SRPM into a binary, do the following:

1. Install the source RPM file (`rpm -Uvh file-2.1.src.rpm`).

2. Go to the SPECS directory (`cd /usr/src/redhat/SPECS`).

3. Create a binary RPM from the source spec (`rpm -bb -clean file-2.1.spec`).

4. Install the binary RPM (`cd /usr/src/redhat/RPMS/i386 ; rpm -UVH file-2.1.rpm`).

5. Uninstall the source RPM (`cd /usr/src/redhat/SPECS ; rpm -rmsource file-2.1.spec`).

6. Remove the source RPM (`rm file-2.1.src.rpm`).

5.3 Other RPM Utilities

In this section, we'll cover some of the utilities that make using RPM fairly painless.

RPMFIND

In case you ever wanted to find an RPM file, but didn't know where to look, there's the `rpmfind` program. A list of known RPM files are kept at rpm-

`find.net`, and in most cases, copies of the RPMs are there as well. The client application, called `rpmfind`, can search for an application name (a search for `mkisofs`, for example), can search for updates to an RPM, and also gives the option to download dependent packages. Unfortunately, `rpmfind` is not included with Red Hat, as it's not part of the distribution. You can get an RPM of the application at `www.rpmfind.net`.

RPM2CPIO

The `rpm2cpio` program converts a given RPM file to a file format that can be used with the `cpio` program. This is mostly useful for those who are using distributions not based on Red Hat, but it can also be helpful if you're running Red Hat. If you feel you may have conflicts between two RPMs, or want to install only a few files from a given RPM, you can convert the RPM to a `cpio` file. The syntax of `rpm2cpio` is `rpm2cpio file.rpm file.cpio`. The resulting `cpio` program can be extracted using `cpio -e file`, where `-e` represents "extract". After extracting the `cpio` file, you can move, install, or whatever. The only problem with this is that files installed in this manner won't be tracked by RPM. Additionally, you won't be able to use regular `rpm` commands on the installed files.

Kpackage

The `kpackage` file runs under the KDE Window Manager. It provides for management of `.rpm`, `.DEB` (debian), and `cpio` files. Packages can be installed, uninstalled, verified, and so on. The `kpackage` program is not included as part of the KDE installation on the Red Hat CD-ROM, but can be found at the KDE Web site `http://www.kde.org/`.

GnoRPM

The `GnoRPM` program is included as part of the Red Hat installation and runs under the GNOME windowing system. If you're familiar with the older `glint` application that was with previous Red Hat installs, this program is its replacement. If you're not familiar with `glint`, here's how `GnoRPM` works.

RPMs are arranged based on their use, meaning that the PostgreSQL RPMs would be located under `Applications/Databases`. Depending on what RPMs you have installed, this may be different on your system. Each icon on the left side represents a section (such as `Applications` or `Directo-`

ries) and the right side lists the contents of the section. In our example of PostgreSQL, the left side would initially contain Applications, while the right side has Directories. Double-clicking Directories moves it to the left side and puts PostgreSQL on the right side. You can then verify, query, or delete the RPM. Verifying makes sure that all files listed in the RPM have the correct permission and ownership, and that all the files exist. Querying lists the files used by the RPM so you know where they're located. Deleting the RPM removes it from the system.

Clicking on a package makes it selected, and clicking on it again unselects it. This allows you to perform the same operation on multiple RPMs (like query or delete).

You can also install RPMs. By default, new RPMs are looked for at /mnt/ cdrom/RedHat/RPMS. The /mnt/cdrom directory is the location where the CD-ROM is mounted, given the command mount /dev/cdrom. Assuming the Red Hat installation CD was in the drive, the list of RPMs used to install Red Hat would be located in /mnt/cdrom/RedHat/RPMS. In install mode, the screen will change to show what packages are not installed. You can then select packages to install. Clicking the install button would then install the RPMs on your system and remove them from the install screen.

5.4   Summary

- RPM provides a useful way of managing system files.
- Source RPM files allow you to compile programs from source with the management of RPM.
- Numerous utilities exist to assist with .rpm file installation and management.

Networking with Linux

6

Let your Linux box connect to other machines using PPP and Ethernet

One of the biggest benefits of Linux and UNIX is the built-in TCP/IP networking. This networking gives you E-mail, remote connections, and World Wide Web (WWW) access.

To connect your machine to a network, you'll need either an Ethernet card or a modem and a PPP provider.[1] Once this is done, you'll have to reconfigure the Linux kernel to take advantage of the networking hardware. There are more networking options available in Linux than just those for the Ethernet card and Point to Point Protocol (PPP), but these are the two most common methods. For example, you could use PLIP (Parallel Line IP), ATM, Frame Relay, or AX.25.

---

[1]This can be your Internet Service Provider (ISP), employer, or university.

6.1 TCP/IP

The Transmission Control Protocol / Internet Protocol (TCP/IP) is the way that UNIX machines talk to each other. This is also the primary way of connecting to and using the Internet.[2] The entire TCP/IP world (as it's defined right now, anyway) is based on a 32-bit number. This allows for about four billion hosts[3] to all be on the Internet and talking to each other. For us humans to figure this out, these 32-bit numbers are referenced by four 8-bit bytes, also known as an IP address; for example, 192.33.4.10. For the further sanity of the human race, these IP addresses can also be referenced as names (ns.psi.net) to make it easier for us to use. Note that these two addresses are not the same. Linux prefers using numbers, and we humans prefer using names. The middle ground comes in the form of the DNS (Domain Name Service), which allows for mapping IP addresses to domain names, and vice versa.

DNS works with a root nameserver, which can be located in various parts of the world. When a user has their Web browser point to www.wayga.net, the machine asks the local DNS server to map that name to an IP address. The local DNS server first looks at the root nameservers. These root nameservers know that the nameserver for the wayga.net domain is 208.197.103.125. The DNS server then connects to 208.197.103.125 and requests the IP address for www.wayga.net. The DNS server at 208.197.103.125 responds by saying that www.wayga.net's IP address is 208.197.103.125. The local DNS server stores that IP address in its cache in case it's needed again and then provides that IP address to the user application. The user application completes the connection and up pops the Web page.

DNS servers really do more than this. They also provide for the first pass at mail routing, aliases for machine names, reverse DNS, and even give basic system and location information.

At an application or system level, TCP/IP has over 65,000 ports available for connecting. This allows for FTP, telnet, E-mail, WWW, DNS, and hundreds of other functions to happen all at the same time. When a Web

---

[2]Coincidence or conspiracy? You decide.

[3]There are a few hundred thousand IP addresses that aren't used because they're broadcast or reserved numbers. Don't worry if you think that we're running out of IP addresses too quickly. IPv6 has 128-bit IP addresses (that's a 39-digit number for those of you without calculators).

browser connects to a server, Linux opens one of those unused ports and makes a connection to the server. The server monitors one specific port (port 80 for WWW), sees a connection request, opens an unused port on its side, and then tells the client what port is available for connection. Other important TCP/IP ports include port 25 (E-mail), port 23 (telnet), and ports 20 and 21 (FTP). A list of the known ports and their uses is kept in the /etc/services file. Note that for security reasons, ports lower than 1024 can be opened by root only. This is why the main Web server has to run as root, but its clients can run as other users.

TCP/IP has two main connection methods that you'll probably run into: UDP (User Datagram Protocol) and TCP (Telnet Control Protocol). UDP is a connectionless protocol. The packets are usually small, and interaction between the client and server really consists of a number of openings and closings of network connections. UDP is a bit faster and less resource-intensive than TCP, but does not guarantee transmission of a packet. NFS is a protocol that uses UDP. TCP is a connection-based protocol. The client talks to the server, the port is opened, and the connection begins. When the connection closes, it should be because both programs have finished their need for the network. TCP guarantees packet delivery, and most protocols (Telnet, HTTP, SMTP, etc.) use TCP, but the connections may be longer in time than UDP connections.

Ethernet

Ethernet was developed in the 1970s as a broadcast-style network. In the commonly used coax network, Ethernet cable was run in one long cable and each end was terminated with a 50-ohm resistor. Each machine that was on the Ethernet network hooked into this cable using a tap.

For machines to identify themselves, each Ethernet adapter has a unique address (Media Access Connector, or MAC address) assigned to it by the Ethernet adapter manufacturer. When an Ethernet adapter wants to talk to another Ethernet adapter, it sends a message containing its own MAC address, as well as the receiving MAC address, down the entire Ethernet cable. If the receiving MAC address is on that run, it gets the message. Collisions occur when two Ethernet adapters try to transmit at the same time. If this happens, both adapters stop transmission, wait a random amount of time, and retransmit. Having too many collisions indicates a network that has very heavy traffic and is running inefficiently. A link that has a high number of collisions should be broken up into two or more separate Ethernet runs.

Each Ethernet packet has to and from Ethernet addresses along with IP to and from addresses, followed by the data, and finally some error checking data to verify that a packet arrives complete. A typical Ethernet packet can be no larger than 1514 bytes. IPv4 takes up 40 bytes, and the Ethernet framing takes up another 18 bytes, leaving a maximum of 1456 bytes of data.

Even though all the other Ethernet adapters on a cable see a message, they do not answer or respond. The only message that all Ethernet adapters should receive is an Ethernet broadcast. Network monitors take advantage of this feature of Ethernet to give an overall view of a particular Ethernet run.

For a packet (say an IP packet) to get across a network to another Ethernet run, a router is used. The router doesn't look at the Ethernet header, but instead looks at the protocol being used. If the router knows that a particular packet needs to be forwarded to another network, it forwards the packet.

What allows Linux (and TCP/IP) to make connections between an Ethernet address and an IP address is the Address Resolution Protocol (or ARP) cache. When the Linux machine starts talking on an Ethernet network, it starts asking (via ARP) what the MAC addresses for other machines on the subnet are. Here's how it works:

Linux first sends an Ethernet broadcast asking for a mapping from an IP address to a MAC address. The receiving end with that IP address responds with an ARP reply, giving the IP address and its MAC address. Linux stores that MAC address in an ARP cache for future use. The cache times out every now and then, and this may happen several times a day. Don't worry, though—there are plenty of 10 Mbps for everyone on the network. If a packet has to go through a router to get somewhere else, Linux addresses the Ethernet packet to the router (or gateway), and the router then picks it up and forwards it to another network.

In the reverse situation, the BOOTP protocol involves a Reverse ARP (RARP) that announces its MAC address, asking which IP address to use. For diskless machines, or even Windows machines using Dynamic Host Configuration Protocol (DHCP), this is the way that these machines can get themselves configured. A machine that has RARP or DHCP running responds with the IP address and other information (the gateway and nameserver, for example).

Even though the Ethernet protocol is a standard, there are three main ways of actually implementing the physical layer. Thicknet is a 15-pin connection with very heavy gauge wire that is no longer in use. The best thing you can do with a thicknet connection is attach a transceiver on it to convert it to another physical layer.[4] Thinnet, or coax, runs one long wire, which has all the Ethernet adapters adding taps or T-connectors along the wire to connect. Coax is very inexpensive to implement, but a wiring problem anywhere along the cable can cause failure of the entire network. Coax also requires termination on both ends to keep the Ethernet signals from reflecting and causing network problems. With the large number of wires and connectors that can be on an Ethernet run, your chances of failure for a large-scale installation increase. The last, and preferable, setup is RJ-45, also known as 10-BaseT. 10-BaseT costs more, since you have to buy a hub, and is harder to implement, since a cable has to go from the hub to each individual machine, but only the failure of a hub would cause more than one person to have network trouble at the same time. If a wire from the hub were to become disconnected, no other users would be affected.[5] The RJ-45 connection also has the capability of running at 100 Mbps instead of the regular 10 Mbps, and most new cabling installations use Category 5 (Cat 5) cabling, which is required for 100 Mbps. Category 3 (Cat 3) is suitable for 10 Mbps.

Connecting to an Ethernet Network

To get hooked into an Ethernet network, get yourself an Ethernet card. Most should work, but you may want to check out the Ethernet HOWTO for a list of cards. For the most part, if it's from a major provider like 3Com, there is probably support for that card. Install the card in your machine and reboot. If the kernel recognizes your card, you're set for now. If not, recompile the kernel and be sure to add support for your particular Ethernet card. The first Ethernet card is usually designated `eth0`.

To add networking for this Ethernet card, you have to first initialize and set up the IP interface, then you have to set up routing for the interface you just set up. No, the two are not the same. The IP interface merely gives the kernel an IP address to work with. It still needs to know when a packet wants to go out and what interface it should use. Otherwise, you're likely to use the loopback interface and your packets will get nowhere fast.

The `/sbin/ifconfig` program will register the Ethernet card with the TCP/IP services. The typical syntax is:

```
/sbin/ifconfig eth0 netmask <addr> broadcast <addr> <IP address>
```

[4]We lied a bit. Thicknet provides for electrical isolation in areas where you might have a ground loop domain problem; for example, going between different floors in a multi-story building. Some 10-BaseT hubs have this capability as well.

[5]Unless, of course, you are the disconnected user.

The netmask and broadcast addresses are given, followed by the IP address for the interface. The interface is automatically brought up if you give it a new IP address, so you don't need to explicitly tell the interface to start.

Now that you have that, you can get the routing set up:

```
route add default gw <address>
```

This sets up a route to your gateway (firewall, router, etc). This is set up to be the default route, so any packets that Linux cannot determine how to route will be sent to this address for further processing.

The Red Hat network configuration is an excellent tool for setting up your network devices. Get your IP address, nameserver information, gateway, and netmask from your network administrator. If you're the network administrator, look further in this chapter for instructions on finding this information. Under the `Names` section, verify the hostname, domain, and IP address for your nameservers. The `Hosts` section lists what IP addresses and hostnames you have in your `/etc/hosts` file. This should contain at least your IP address and hostname. If you have other hosts you want to list here, go ahead and add them.

The `Interfaces` section lists which interfaces are available to you. The `lo0` interface is the loopback interface and is used to route TCP/IP packets to itself. Think of it as a virtual Ethernet interface. Changing it will cause problems with most other programs, including X.

You can next add the Ethernet interface and give the IP address and netmask. Don't turn on `Configure Interface with BOOTP`, but you can turn on `Activate Interface at boot time`. BOOTP is a protocol intended to dynamically assign IP addresses at boot time. The interface should be configured at boot time, so that once the machine starts, you can use the Ethernet network.

DHCP

DHCP stands for Dynamic Host Configuration Protocol. The purpose of DHCP is similar to BOOTP in that a client requests an IP address and gets one assigned to it. The similarities end there. DHCP provides much more configurability than BOOTP, including:

- Dynamic host setup—You don't need to know what every machine's MAC address is to configure it for DHCP. If DHCP receives a request for an IP and it's configured with a pool of dynamic IP addresses, it will give those IPs out. This allows you to quickly get a client on a network.

- Hostname, routing, log host, nameserver, and WINS information—All this can be sent to a client. WINS is really only good for Windows-based machines, but it can be a big help in configuring them on a network.

- Works with Windows and Linux—Linux can be configured as a DHCP client or server, and Windows machines try to find DHCP information by default.

- On-the-fly configuration—DHCP "leases" expire after a set time, and if you change a machine's configuration during that time, it will use the new configuration (even on MS Windows) without a reboot.

Aside from these features, why would you want to use DHCP on your network? The biggest advantage of DHCP is configurability. One central location stores networking information for an entire subnet. For setups where network settings are changed frequently (such as changing ISPs or changing a router IP address), all configuration is done in one location, as opposed to going to each client machine and changing the settings manually. As new machines are added to a network, they can be quickly put on the network using a dynamic IP address, then later changed to use a static IP address. This can make configuring a machine easy. For the convenience of visitors, anyone with a laptop and Ethernet card can pick up their email from the home office without tying up a phone line.

DHCP Configuration

Server Configuration
When installing DHCP on a network, the first question you should ask is: Do I want dynamic IPs or static IP addressing? That is, should hosts on the network get the same IP address every time they boot, or should you have a pool of addresses that you could use and assign as hosts request them? To us (you may do whatever you like), static IPs are the way to go in general. They allow you to use your existing DNS configuration and not have to worry about setting up a dynamic DNS server. It is advisable to leave 5 or 10 addresses available as dynamically allocated so that you can get a machine on the network temporarily.

There are two programs to give you access to DHCP services: the server software (dhcpd) and client software (dhcpcd). Note that you should have only one DHCP server on a network, and since the DHCP server also provides BOOTP services, you can turn off your existing BOOTP servers and

use dhcpd instead. These packages exist on the Red Hat CD as dhcpd and
dhcpcd. Also note that in some instances, dhcpd will be configured to automatically start on boot, so you should only install dhcpd on one machine per
subnet.

The configuration file that dhcpd uses is /etc/dhcpd.conf. This file contains MAC addresses, IP information, and router/WINS/nameserver information. Two other files that get created when dhcpd is running are /etc/
dhcpd.leases and /etc/dhcpd.pid. The .pid file contains the PID of the
running dhcpd to make stopping or restarting dhcpd easier. The leases file is
used if you have dynamic IP addresses being used in a network. It contains
information about who is being leased IP addresses, and how long the leases
last. In the event of a reboot or restart of dhcpd, the dhcpd.leases file should
not be deleted as it is re-read on the startup of dhcpd to know what dynamic
IP addresses have already been assigned.

Here's a sample configuration file for dhcpd, along with some running
commentary:

```
# What's the DNS name of this server?
server-identifier wayga.auroratech.com;
#Also identify the DNS domain that clients will be under
option domain-name "auroratech.com";
#What DNS servers should clients look at? (put at least 2)
option domain-name-servers auratek.auroratech.com, row.auroratech.com;
# Define a Class C network (192.168.1.0->192.168.1.255)
subnet 192.168.1.0 netmask 255.255.255.0 {
#Set the network mask (again)
  option subnet-mask 255.255.255.0;
  option domain-name "auroratech.com";
  option domain-name-servers auratek.auroratech.com, row.aurorat-
  ech.com;
#Define how long a lease for an IP address should be.
  default-lease-time 600;
#Max lease time, in case that's what the
# client requests.
  max-lease-time 7200;
#Specify the default router.
  option routers 192.168.1.142;
#The below IP range will be dynamically
# allocated to clients whose MAC address
# doesn't match any of the following hosts.
  range 192.168.1.46 192.168.1.50;
}
#A printer (called ipc)
host lpipc {
#MAC address for lpipc
    hardware Ethernet 0:60:b0:0f:c0:a9;
```

```
#It's FQDN (so that DNS knows what its IP is
# We could have used a plain IP address here, but why?
   fixed-address lpipc.auroratech.com;
}
#PC host
host camille {
  hardware Ethernet 0:0:bc:0f:12:d6;
  fixed-address camille.auroratech.com;
}
# PC host using a different default router.
host cyrus {
  hardware Ethernet 0:10:4b:a2:e2:4b;
  fixed-address cyrus.auroratech.com;
  option routers 192.168.1.95;
}
```

Client Configuration

The client side is easy to set up. Using the network configuration (netcfg), set the IP configuration to be DHCP and activate the Ethernet card. The dhcpcd program will automatically start, request an IP configuration from the DHCP server, and re-create any needed files such as /etc/resolv.conf for DNS information. Linuxconf (see Chapter 3) can also be configured to start up an Ethernet interface with DHCP.

You can also choose to edit files manually if you do not have X running. Look at /etc/sysconfig/network-scripts, and edit the file for your Ethernet card (usually ipcfg-eth0). Clear out any IP settings you don't want to keep, and set PROTOCOL to read DHCP.

Windows machines can merely be set for DHCP configuration via the Network Control Panel. Other UNIX machines (such as Solaris) may come with DHCP client software already installed, or you can download and compile the ISC DHCP distribution available at http://www.isc.org/.

If you choose to use all dynamic IP addresses on your network, you can use a program like lanlord (http://linux.uhw.com/software/lanlord/) to view what IP addresses have been assigned.

PPP

The Point-to-Point Protocol (PPP) is the way to connect to the Internet or a TCP/IP network via a dial-up line. As the name implies, PPP is designed to work between two machines and two machines only. This makes it ideal for dial-up applications, or even connecting remote locations via a leased line. Many 56-Kb links use PPP to carry IP traffic over the line.

PPP depends on one machine running `pppd server` on one end of the phone line, and a `pppd client` running on the machine dialing up (yours). Unlike Ethernet, you have to configure the software differently, depending on whether you're the client or the server.

PPP doesn't quite have the overhead of Ethernet since no MAC addresses are used. Also, some compression is added to the IP frames to boost the amount of data that can be sent in a packet.

Like Ethernet, PPP can carry more than just IP traffic. It can route IPX, AppleTalk, or DECNET along with IP over a PPP link. Linux does not really take advantage of this functionality, but not many people need it. Since SMB packets can be encapsulated inside TCP/IP packets, you can use Samba or NT shares over a dial-up line from Linux.

PPP Client

Setting up a PPP client requires a modem, phone line, a PPP server at some other phone number, and PPP support compiled into the kernel. Check the `dmesg` command to see if PPP support has been compiled into it. You can also check the `/lib/modules/` directory for `ppp.o` and see if it was compiled as a module. If support is not compiled into it, recompile the kernel and reboot using the new kernel.

The quick way of verifying that a PPP connection works is by doing something similar to the following:

```
pppd connect 'chat -v "+" ATDTphone CONNECT "" ogin: login word: pass-
    word' \
/dev/cua1 38400 debug crtscts modem defaultroute
```

The phone, login, and password are assigned to you by whomever is providing the PPP account. Also, change `/dev/cua1` to be the location of your modem. Remember that `/dev/cua1` under Linux is the same as COM2: under DOS and Windows. The `chat` command is used to dial the modem and provide the login and password information. Once `chat` returns success (that is, once it makes a successful connection), PPP takes over the line and starts a connection. The server and client negotiate settings like Maximum Transmit Units (MTU), compression, and a few other settings. This will take a few seconds, but once it's done, you should be able to use the `/sbin/ifcon-fig` command to examine the network connections. If you see a `ppp0` listed, you're ready to go.

To use DNS, be sure to enter a valid DNS server that you can reach in the `/etc/resolv.conf` file. Add it as in the following:

```
domain wayga.net
nameserver 192.33.4.10
```

This sets the domain and default nameserver. If you know of other nameservers, you can enter them here.

All this configuration can be filled out in scripts using the Red Hat Network Configuration Manager. You merely have to enter the phone number, line speed, modem, login, and password. All the rest of the scripts are done for you.

PPP Server

To get the PPP server software running (which, coincidentally, is the same software as the PPP client), you must have IP forwarding and PPP turned on. This allows Linux to act as an ARP proxy and answer ARP requests for an Ethernet address. If you're using a multiport serial card, you should have the drivers for that in the kernel as well.

Once this is completed, assign a bank of IP addresses that are not in use and will not be in use. These will be the addresses used for incoming connections, and there should at least be as many available as you have phone lines. You don't want to run out of IP addresses, do you?

Once this is done, create new accounts for each user that will be connecting via PPP. Many places use the name of the user with a P prepended to it. For example, if your normal dial-in name were `mark`, then your PPP dialup would be `Pmark` to signify a PPP connection. Have the user information in `/etc/passwd` look something like this:

```
Pmark:#56njvc893h:500:500:PPP user:/home/mark:/usr/local/bin/pppd
```

In the home directory of that user, create a `.ppprc`[6] file and add the following:

```
 -detach
modem
crtscts
lock
192.55.123.100:192.55.123.111
proxyarp
```

---

[6]You could presumably have the home directory for `Pmark` and `mark` in the same location, but be sure to have the `.ppprc` file unwritable by anyone but root.

This gives PPP some initial settings to work with. The -detach says to not detach from the console. The modem says to monitor the CD (Carrier Detect) line and to terminate if CD drops. The lock will lock the device, preventing anyone else from using that serial port. The two IP addresses are the address of the server (waiting for the call) followed by a colon and the IP address to assign to the client when it dials in. The proxyarp allows the server to put the PPP client in its ARP cache and respond to packets that are supposed to go to the client.

Once this has been completed, set up getty to monitor the serial ports, and dial in to make sure that the static IP addresses work. The pppstats command can give a running total of packets in and out for the line.

If you choose to use dynamic IP addresses instead of static IPs to save on IP addresses, create a /etc/ppp/options.ttyXX file for each tty file that is attached to a modem. Replace the XX with the name of the serial port, for example, /etc/ppp/options.ttyS0 for /dev/ttyS0. The content of the options.ttyXX file is the same as the .ppprc file listed above.

6.2 INETD

The inetd meta daemon is used to start programs automatically when a request comes in on a specific TCP/IP port. What happens is that inetd monitors all the ports that are in its configuration file, and when a request comes in, it starts the application and returns to watching ports. There are two files that inetd needs to work: /etc/services and /etc/inetd.conf.

/etc/services

The /etc/services file contains information about a TCP/IP port number, and a name for the specified port which is later used in the /etc/inetd.conf file. It's not often that you'll need to add entries to this, but some programs may have you do it. Here's a portion of an /etc/services file:

```
chargen         19/tcp ttytst source
chargen 19/udp ttytst source
ftp-data 20/tcp
ftp  21/tcp
telnet 23/tcp
smtp 25/tcp       mail
time 37/tcp       timserver
time 37/udp       timserver
rlp  39/udp         resource # resource location
```

```
name 42/udp        nameserver
whois 43/tcp       nicname # usually to sri-nic
domain 53/tcp
domain 53/udp
mtp  57/tcp                      # deprecated
bootps 67/udp           # bootp server
bootpc 68/udp           # bootp client
tftp 69/udp
gopher 70/tcp                   # gopher server
```

The first entry in the line is the service name. This is followed by the port number and the protocol (usually TCP or UDP), which are then followed by any aliases. As you can see above, the port where email comes in is called the smtp port and it is located on port 25. Its alias is mail, so you could run a command like:

```
[markk@wayga ~]$ telnet localhost smtp
Trying 127.0.0.1...
Connected to localhost.
Escape character is '^]'.
220 wayga.ratatosk.org ESMTP Sendmail 8.8.5/8.8.5; Mon, 1 Sep 1997
  18:54:30 -040
```

and the telnet command would connect you to TCP/IP port 25 (where sendmail is currently running).

/etc/inetd.conf

The /etc/inetd.conf file takes the port information in the /etc/services file and tells inetd what ports to monitor. Here's a portion of a sample inetd.conf file:

```
# These are standard services.
#
ftp stream  tcp nowait root /usr/sbin/tcpdin.ftpd -l -a
telnet stream  tcp nowait root /usr/sbin/tcpd in.telnetd
gopher stream  tcp nowait root /usr/sbin/tcpd gn

# do not uncomment smtp unless you *really* know what you are
# doing.
# smtp is handled by the sendmail daemon now, not smtpd.  It does # NOT
# run from here, it is started at boot time from /etc/rc.d/rc#.d.
#smtp stream  tcp nowait root /usr/bin/smtpd smtpd
#nntp stream  tcp nowait root /usr/sbin/tcpd in.nntpd
```

The entries in this file are as follows:

- Entry from `/etc/services` for what port to monitor.
- `stream` or `dgram` (`tcp` is `stream`, `udp` is `dgram`).
- Protocol (`tcp` or `udp`).
- Options (`wait` or `nowait`). `wait` says to wait until the program has finished or returned before returning to watching the port. The `nowait` option says to not wait and return to monitoring the port. If `nowait` is selected, only one instance of a program will run at a time.
- User to run as—this is usually `root`.
- Path of the program.
- Name of the program, and any options you'll want to add.

In the example from `/etc/services`, we made a connection to the mail port, but the `inetd.conf` example shows that `smtp` is not being monitored. What happened? For some high-throughput programs (`httpd` and `sendmail` are prime examples), you don't want to have a program constantly restarting since it takes a lot of time for a program to start initially. But, for a program that is already running to fork or spawn off a new process, the overhead is much less. Thus, it's better for programs like these to be constantly running and taking care of the connections themselves.

Programs like `telnetd` or `ftpd` don't need a lot of startup time, so `inetd` can handle starting up new copies as it needs them.

6.3   Network Applications

Now that the network is set up, what are you going to do with it? Most of the standard topics (Web, FTP, email) have already been covered, but the rest of this chapter will cover applications that work across the network for the benefit of everyone. DNS (the nameserver) and NFS (the network file server) are two such applications.

DNS

The nameserver is the program that matches an IP address (`208.197.103.125`) to a hostname (`wayga.net`). It also provides for matching in the opposite direction as well, informing you that the machine that has the address `208.197.103.125` is called `wayga.net`. Since one of the jobs of a nameserver is to look up and cache DNS requests from client machines, it can be used at one end of a slow link (between two offices perhaps) and reduce the amount of DNS traffic across the link. It also has provisions for forwarding E-mail addressed from one host to another and can provide backups for particular hosts in case one Web server is busy while another is idle.

In any instance where you're connecting to a TCP/IP network, you'll want to use DNS[7] for hostname resolution. The setup of this is easily done by putting a few lines in your `/etc/resolv.conf` file:

```
domain wayga.net
nameserver 192.33.4.10
```

Modify `wayga.net` to be your domain name and change the IP address to be the nameserver provided to you by your ISP. This IP address is an actual nameserver, and if you don't know your local nameserver, this IP address should work in a pinch to get you up and running. You can also put multiple nameserver entries in here, and it will search in order until it makes a connection to a DNS server.[8]

If you plan on running `named` (the DNS server software) locally, you should change the IP address to read `127.0.0.1`. Be sure to have a few other IP addresses in there in case `named` goes down.

Should You Be a DNS Server?

You should use the DNS server only in the following cases:

1. You own a domain and want to control the DNS.

2. You run a large network over a slow link.

3. You have no connection to the Internet.

For item 1, many ISPs will offer to handle your DNS serving for you, but if you're in an environment where machines change frequently, it may be easier to do it yourself than wait for the ISP to update their tables. For item 2, `named` can act as a cache to store frequently used hosts, and this will reduce some of the traffic. In item 3 . . . well . . . if there's no other DNS host on your network, someone should do it, and it may as well be you. If you don't match any of these three, you probably don't need a DNS server running.

---

[7]Yes, even if you're using NIS.

[8]Note that the search stops after the response from the first DNS server. If the first DNS server replies `host not found`, the search stops there.

If you expect to be the primary or secondary DNS server to the outside world (i.e., the Internet), you'll have to make sure the DNS host is registered with the InterNIC or another top-level domain organization. See the chapter on interacting with Internet agencies for information on getting this set up.

Once you're ready to start serving DNS, you'll have to set things up on your machine to do DNS serving.

named.boot

The `named.boot` file contains configuration information to give to `named` once it starts. It really tells `named` three things:

1. What directory the configuration files are stored in.

2. What primary DNS services it provides.

3. What reverse DNS services it provides.

There are a few other functions that `named` does, but they are a bit outside the scope of this chapter. A sample configuration file looks like this:

```
directory        /var/named
;
cache            .                            named.ca
;
primary          wayga.net                    named.wayga
primary          a-muse.org                   named.a-muse
primary          0.0.127.in-addr.arpa         named.local
```

In this case, `named.boot` is doing all three things. The `directory` statement tells `named` that any references to files are going to be in the `/var/named` directory. Next, it says that the `cache` file is going to be for all domains and is kept in the `named.ca` file. The three primary statements say DNS information for hosts is provided in the `wayga.net` and `a-muse.org` domains, and the information about those hosts is stored in `named.wayga` and `named.a-muse`, respectively. The third `primary` statement indicates that any reverse DNS requests on the `127.0.0` network (also known as the loopback device) are to be done looking at the `named.local` file.

named.ca

The `named.ca` file contains information about the root nameservers. If the local `named` program does not have the hostname information locally, it then starts looking for it in the root nameservers. Here's a section out of the `wayga.net named.ca` file:

```
.                        3600000 IN    NS      A.ROOT-SERVERS.NET.
A.ROOT-SERVERS.NET.      3600000       A       198.41.0.4
;
; formerly NS1.ISI.EDU
;
.    3600000 NS    B.ROOT-SERVERS.NET.
B.ROOT-SERVERS.NET.      3600000       A       128.9.0.107
;
; formerly C.PSI.NET
;
.                        3600000       NS      C.ROOT-SERVERS.NET.
C.ROOT-SERVERS.NET.      3600000       A       192.33.4.12
;
; formerly TERP.UMD.EDU
;
.                        3600000       NS      D.ROOT-SERVERS.NET.
D.ROOT-SERVERS.NET.      3600000       A       128.8.10.90
;
; formerly NS.NASA.GOV
;
```

DNS Database Records

Now let's look at the `named.wayga` file. This file has an example of many of the features you'll want in your files:

```
@               IN      SOA     wayga.net. enry.wayga.net. (
                1
                3600
                600
                3600000
                10800 )
                IN      NS      208.197.103.125
                IN      NS      208.197.103.21
wayga.net.      IN      A       208.197.103.125
galileo         IN      A       208.197.103.21
localhost       IN      A       127.0.0.1
wayga.net.      IN      MX      0 wayga.net.
                IN      MX      10 galileo
www             IN      CNAME   wayga.net.
mail            IN      CNAME   wayga.net.
ftp             IN      CNAME   wayga.net.
plan9           IN      CNAME   wayga.net.
```

The SOA indicates the Start Of Authority line. This line tells named which domain this file is working on. The SOA line is constant up to the point after the SOA. It then has the following information:

- Machine name acting as the DNS server.
- Contact name (replace the @ in the email address with a period).
- Open parenthesis.
- Serial number, which should be incremented every time you change the file—Since this is the first revision of the file, it has a serial number of 1.
- Refresh time in seconds, or how often to recheck the SOA record—The 3600 says to refresh once an hour.
- Retry time, or when a secondary server should retry contacting the primary server if something goes wrong.
- Expire time, or when the secondary server should flush its cache if it can't contact the primary server.
- Minimum time to live—This defines how long other servers should keep the records in their cache before flushing it out. If it's too short, named spends too much time requesting addresses it should already know, and if it's too long, the wiring IP information may be reported if a host changes ISPs or even IP addresses.
- Close parenthesis.
- NS (to indicate the nameserver).
- Name of the nameserver host (the local host).

Once the SOA is complete, you can begin adding hosts. This entry has four sections to it:

1. Name of the domain or hostname—If the name does not end in a period (.), the domain name (in our case, wayga.net) is appended. If the address ends in a period (.), it is assumed it is the Fully Qualified Domain Name (FQDN).

2. IN—This separates the hostname from the rest of the record.

3. Type of record—The record type can be any of the following:
   - A—Directly maps a hostname to an IP address. All other records must point to an A record.
   - MX—Mail exchanger, which lists what hosts will accept E-mail for that host or domain. Before the record contents, you can indicate a num-

ber for preference. In the case of `wayga.net`, the mail host is itself, but if `wayga.net` is busy or unavailable, `galileo` will accept the E-mail instead.

- CNAME—Also known as an alias, as you can see. `Ftp.wayga.net`, `www.wayga.net`, and `mail.wayga.net` are all pointers to `wayga.net`. Any DSN requests for these hosts will receive the IP address for `wayga.net`.
- HINFO—May contain host information. This is not used very much, as it can give potential crackers information about your machine.

4. Record contents—In the case of an A record, it's an IP address. For other records, it can be a hostname or system information.

Reverse DNS

If your machine is doing reverse DNS, the SOA is the same, but the records themselves are slightly different. First, as you can tell with `named.boot, the` IP address is reversed. Instead of the `127.0.0` network, it becomes `0.0.127.in-addr.arpa`. Reverse the network you're using and use that as the domain in `/etc/named.boot`. Since the network for `wayga.net` is `208.197.103`, the domain becomes `103.197.208.in-addr.arpa`.

The records for `wayga.net` and `galileo.wayga.net` would look like this if we were doing reverse DNS:

```
21    IN    PTR   galileo.wayga.net.
125   IN    PTR   wayga.net.
```

As you can see, the hostnames need a period (.) at the end, since reverse DNS can span physical IP addresses.[9] The record type is also different—PTR. The IP address needs only the portion of the network not already in the domain listed above.

Once this is complete, you can start `named` and verify your configuration with `nslookup`.

Configuring the Berkeley Internet Name Daemon 8.1 (BIND)

If you've decided to be a DNS server, be it a primary, secondary, or a mix of the two, you need to get (possibly compile) and configure BIND. It's very

---

[9] As it is, `wayga.net` is part of someone else's IP network. That's why we don't do reverse DNS. If someone did a reverse DNS lookup on us, it would report a different domain.

likely that `named` was installed when Linux was installed; if not, you can retrieve it from the official distribution sites at `ftp://ftp.isc.org/isc/bind/` or any Linux distribution site.

As of version 8.1, the configuration filename and format have changed. Since the new version of BIND is or will be shipped with newer versions of every Linux distribution, we will go over the configuration of it.

The basic 8.1-style configuration file is named `named.conf` and lives in `/etc`. It has four types of statements: one controlling access, one describing the logging, one describing the more general options, and one or more describing the zone(s) it is a server for. Comments in the file can be delineated using C or C++ style comment syntax.

BIND comes with extensive documentation, but we will try to give the most important details of it here.

The `options` statement describes what IPs to listen for and what port to use. Firewalls can complicate things and will likely require that you use a privileged port. 53 is the default port and can be specified in this statement. Lastly, the working directory for `named` specified here, `/var/named`, is fairly widely used. The zone files and any other files specified in various statements will live here in the absence of any pathing information. There are many other options which can be controlled from here; most of them have reasonable defaults (see the documentation for details).

The `logging` statement simply controls the verbosity of the logging and where log messages are sent. Each category has various channels to which output is sent, and each channel can be customized with a `channel` statement. Logging can be controlled to fairly fine detail (consult the documentation for the gory details).

Controlling what clients your server will answer queries from is done via the `acl` statement. If you have a lot of mobile users, you may need to be pretty loose with access to the name service.

Finally, the guts of the configuration file are the `zone` statements. They describe what zones the server serves, either as a master or a slave (we ignore the stub type; read about it in the documentation). A master is just that, the master authority for information in that domain (zone). A slave is a secondary disseminator of zone information, but it gets all the zone data from the zone master; no changes can be made at the slave. There is one special type used when specifying the root nameservers. It is called a hint because the `named.ca` really just supplies a list of servers, some of which will have the current list of root nameservers.

For a slave zone, you must specify at least one master from which BIND can transfer the zone records. More than one can be specified. Only one will be the real master; the others will be other slaves, which will presumably have up-to-date zone records.

Below is a basic /etc/named.conf that will be used for some examples. Currently it will answer queries from any client.

```
options {
  directory "/var/named";
  /*
   * If there is a firewall between you and nameservers you want
   * to talk to, you might need to uncomment the query-source
   * directive below.  Previous versions of BIND always asked
   * questions using port 53, but BIND 8.1 uses an unprivileged
   * port by default.
   */
  // query-source address * port 53;
  listen-on { 127.0.0.1; 208.197.103.21; };
};


logging {
  category default {default_syslog; default_debug;};
  /* Uncomment to send debugging information to my own set of files */
  /*
  channel this_security_channel {
    file "named_security.log";
    severity info;
  };
  category security { my_security_channel; default_syslog;
  default_debug; };
  */
};

zone "." {
  type hint;
  file "named.ca";
};

zone "0.0.127.IN-ADDR.ARPA" {
  type master;
  file "named.local";
};

zone "103.197.208.in-addr.arpa" {
  type slave;
  file "named.208.197.103";
  masters {
    208.197.103.2;
  };
};
```

```
zone "ratatosk.org" {
  type master;
  file "named.ratatosk";
};

zone "wayga.net" {
  type slave;
  file "named.wayga";
  masters {
    208.197.103.125;
  };
};
```

The first thing you are probably interested in is restricting the use of your nameserver.

There are five ACLs that `named` defines for you:

`any`	Allows all hosts
`none`	Denies all hosts
`localhost`	Allows the IP addresses of all interfaces on the system
`localnets`	Allows any host on a network for which the system has an interface

Defining your own is simple; the syntax is `acl name { address list }`. `name` is an alphanumeric string and `address list` is a list of IPs, IP prefixes, or the name of another ACL. It is possible to negate elements with an exclamation point (!).

For instance, to exclude machines on your LAN, you could define this ACL:

```
acl notlocal { ! localnets; };
```

It is important to keep in mind that the matches are checked against the list from left to right; as soon as a match is found, the rest of the line is ignored.Consider these two ACL entries:

```
acl first { 10.10.10/24 ; ! 10.10.10.128; };
acl second { ! 10.10.10.128 ; 10.10.10/24; };
```

Only `second` will work the way it was intended: deny the IP `10.10.10.128` name service. Since the IP prefix is tested first and matches `10.10.10.128`, the denied IP is never tested. Thus, the host you want to deny will be able to use your DNS server.

Using Your ACLs

Now that you have an idea of how to define ACLs, we'll show you how to use them.

You may want to restrict what hosts can get (transfer) your zone record to only your trusted DNS slaves, one of which we have specified in an `acl` statement as follows:

```
acl trusted_slaves {localnets; 205.157.230.253; };

zone "ratatosk.org" {
  type master;
  file "named.ratatosk";
  allow-transfer {trusted_slaves; 208.197.103.125; };
};
```

Other Important Options

```
listen-on [port]
```

This option specifies what IP address and/or port to listen to. The default port is 53. You can specify IP prefixes as well.

```
listen-on port 7777 { 208.197.103.200; };
```

If no `listen-on` is specified, the server will listen on port 53 on all interfaces.

```
include
```

This statement is used to include other files that contain valid configuration information, such as:

```
include "/etc/my_acls";
```

We've tried to cover the options you will most likely use. However, there are several potentially useful statements we haven't covered. You should spend some time looking at the documentation, which also includes some features that will be implemented in future releases.

nslookup

The `nslookup` program interacts with the nameserver to give IP information about a host or domain. This program will also allow you to examine things like `A`, `MX`, or `CNAME` records. When run with an option of a hostname, `nslookup` will contact the local DNS host and return information on that host as follows:

```
[markk@wayga named]$ nslookup wayga.net
Server:  wayga.net
Address:  208.197.103.125

Name:    wayga.net
Address:  208.197.103.125

[markk@wayga named]$
```

When run without any options, it puts you in an interactive mode, allowing you to enter hosts, set the kinds of queries, list hosts within a domain, and so on.

Entering a hostname from interactive mode will look up the host and return the results. The `set type=X` command will tell `nslookup` to report on only certain types of records (`MX`, `PTR`, `A`, `CNAME`, `HINFO`). Setting a type of `ANY` will search for all records.

```
[markk@wayga named]$ nslookup
Default Server:  wayga.net
Address:  208.197.103.125

> set type=ANY
> wayga.net
Server:  wayga.net
Address:  208.197.103.125

wayga.net          nameserver = 208.197.103.125.wayga.net
wayga.net          nameserver = 208.197.103.21.wayga.net
wayga.net          preference = 10, mail exchanger = galileo.wayga.net
wayga.net          preference = 0, mail exchanger = wayga.net
wayga.net
        origin = wayga.net
        mail addr = enry.wayga.net
        serial = 1
        refresh = 3600 (1 hour)
        retry  = 600 (10 mins)
        expire = 3600000 (41 days 16 hours)
        minimum ttl = 10800 (3 hours)
wayga.net          internet address = 208.197.103.125
```

```
wayga.net          nameserver = 208.197.103.125.wayga.net
wayga.net          nameserver = 208.197.103.21.wayga.net
galileo.wayga.net        internet address = 208.197.103.21
wayga.net        internet address = 208.197.103.125
>
```

As you can see, this is a bit more information than you got earlier. The `server` command will allow you to request information from another server. This is good for debugging, since you can now ask a remote server for information about the domain you just set up and make sure the information is correct. The last command that is rather important is the `ls DOMAIN` command, which will list all the hosts under `DOMAIN`.. Using this on the domain you have just set up will verify that all hosts are being listed.

NFS

The Network File System (NFS) allows a server to export a directory or an entire filesystem to other systems. This feature provides for not only getting the most out of hard drives, but it can also allow a user's home directory to exist anywhere on the network, just as if it were local.

Setting up NFS for use is easy, as most Linux installations start up the necessary software at boot time. All that's left is to configure the NFS servers.

If NFS isn't started on bootup, all you need to do is fire up `rpc.mountd` and `rpc.nfsd` on startup. This is a script in the `/etc/rc.d/rc3.d` directory. The one other item that needs to exist is the `/etc/exports` file. The `/etc/exports` file lists what directories can be exported to other machines.

The `/etc/exports` file has a setup of the following:

```
directory              options
```

where `directory` is the directory to be exported, and `options` are any additional options to work on that export. The options are many and can provide different options per host. Any options not enclosed in a host are assumed to be for any hosts. Options can be the following:

- `insecure`—Allows non-authenticated access.
- `ro`—Mounts read only (good for use with `insecure`).
- `rw`—Mounts read write.
- `root_squash`—Prevents the root user from having any special access to the NFS drive by mapping UID 0 (root) to UID 65524.[10] This option is off by default.

- `no_root_squash`—Allows the root user to manipulate the partition as if it were local. This is turned on by default.

- `all_squash`—Same as `root_squash`, but does it for all UIDs.

- `no_all_squash`—No UIDs are squashed (default).

Options can be prefaced with a hostname to apply them to only that host.

```
/pub wayga(rw)
```

The `wayga` machine can mount the directory in read write mode for all users (the default). The `ro` option means read only.

```
/pub/foo wayga(noaccess)
```

The `foo` subdirectory is not accessible to `wayga`. The only thing that `wayga` will see is permissions for the `foo` directory, and an `ls` of it will return only "." and "...".

Remember that unless you have a firewall or packet filter up, all NFS access will be TCP/IP-wide, unless you specify a host or group of hosts that can access that particular NFS directory.

From the NFS client, assume root power, and let's mount the `/pub` directory from above:

```
mount -t nfs wooba:/pub /mnt/pub
```

There are only a few changes in the `mount` command from mounting a hard drive or CD-ROM. The filesystem type is `nfs`, and the device name is replaced with a host:directory combo.

To have directories mount automatically on startup, you can enter them into the `/etc/fstab` file, or use the Red Hat `fstool` to add the mounts. Remember to replace the device file with the host:directory combo, and use the filesystem type of `nfs`. Once the network is started and NFS service has started, the NFS directories will mount.

One problem with NFS is that if the NFS server goes down, or the network connection between the client and server is broken, the client can effectively stop while trying to do file access. This can even include the situation where an NFS directory is in your `$PATH`. Running a command that searches through the path will cause your machine to appear to hang. There isn't a cure for it at this point. Just be sure that the server doesn't crash. Other

---

[10]Also known as the nobody user.

network filesystems are in the works that will prevent some of these problems, but they don't quite work yet. The other important point is to make sure your networking is working correctly.

One additional program you may want to look at if you have a large amount of NFS drives is the `amd` program. This program is an automount daemon, and it automatically mounts and unmounts drives as needed. It's a bit outside the scope of this chapter, but you can download the program and give it a try if you have a lot of partitions to mount.

6.4 AppleTalk

To round out the list of Linux-supported networking/file sharing protocols, we turn to AppleTalk. Using Linux as an Apple fileserver has several advantages, including:

- No limit on simultaneous users. Apple's AppleTalk, however, sets a limit of 10 concurrent users. To go beyond this limit, you must upgrade to Appleshare, which isn't free.
- It is extremely versatile. The Linux server can also, as discussed earlier, serve disks (possibly the same disks) via NFS, SMB (Server Message Block, aka Samba, used by the various Windows OSes), and IPX (Novell Netware).
- You can take advantage of the superior remote access features of Linux, which none of the popular non-Unix-based OSes can rival.
- Because Linux is truly multitasking and has less overhead than MacOS, performance will generally be better. Mac OS X, with its Unix kernel, will likely narrow this performance gap.

There are a couple of minor disadvantages. First, to provide the full functionality of the MacOS filesystem, AppleTalk and the daemons that manage the file sharing need to write some "hidden" (i.e., starting with a leading ".."; MacOS will not see them) files that tend to junk up the filesystem somewhat. It does this to implement the full functionality of the MacOS filesystem.

Second, the MacOS filesystem (HFS) supports a very loose file naming convention. Linux supports this after a fashion. Considering how restrictive traditional UNIX file naming conventions are, it supports it very well. However, some characters must escape or be encoded somehow and thus filenames may look different when viewing them from the Linux side of things.

In addition to making disk volumes available via AppleTalk, netatalk can also make local printers available to your Macs or print to a network Apple-Talk printer, which in turn could be made available to non-AppleTalk machines on your local area network (LAN).

Installing netatalk

If you are installing from RPM, which is recommended, installation simply involves downloading the latest netatalk+asun distribution from `ftp://con-trib.redhat.com` or a mirror. Then install/upgrade by running `rpm -U <rpm file>`.

Configuring netatalk

In AppleTalk, there are two levels of access: guest and registered user. Being a guest user is basically like being the nobody user in UNIX: You have highly limited access to the server and typically can write only to areas that are world-writable. Often the guest account will also have printing privileges.

Under netatalk, users authenticate themselves using the user and password information in `/etc/passwd`, that is, they must have an account on the machine. If you don't want these users to have shell access, you can give them the shell `/bin/false`. This is analogous to what is done when setting up FTP-only accounts. If you would like to let your users change their passwords by logging in with `ssh`, `telnet`, or something similar, you can give them the shell `/bin/passwd`. If you choose to do this, be sure to add `/bin/passwd` to the `/etc/shells` file so that it is a valid shell.

In the configuration files for netatalk, you define which directories are available at the two levels of access, including the home directory of registered users, if wanted. For each instance of the AppleTalk daemon, you can specify a set of directories for guests and registered users to access.

Netatalk uses five configuration files. The RPM version also uses a sort of "meta" configuration file that serves to collect much of the configuration data in one place.

AppleVolumes.default and AppleVolumes.system

The `AppleVolumes.default` file lists directories to be shared. An entry of a tilde (~) will share the connected user's home directory. An optional second entry on the line will be used for the name of the volume. Otherwise, the name defaults to the last element of the path. Note that if you edit this in `vi`, a line with only ~ on it will appear no differently than other unused lines in the `vi` screen.

```
#
# Sample AppleVolumes.default
#
~    # the user's home dir, will be named whatever the login name is
/home/ftp/pub  "Public FTP Area"  # Share the public ftp area with an
                                   # appropriate name.
 /usr/local/Archives    # Share  the  archive  area,  will  be  named
 'Archives'
```

`AppleVolumes.system` controls the mapping of file extensions to types that MacOS understands. You shouldn't have to do anything to this file except add new file extensions to it.

afpd.conf

The `afpd.conf` file holds configuration information for the AppleTalk file protocol daemon. With the RPM version and a small network, you will likely leave this file empty, making any minor configuration changes in `/etc/atalk/config`.

To set up virtual servers (in the sense that there is only one physical machine), this file is the way to go. Each entry starts with a server name and is followed by various options.

```
#
# Sample afpd.conf
#
-                                       # A server going by the hostname
foobar -address 10.1.1.34               # Server named 'foobar' bound to a
                                        # particular IP
```

atalkd.conf

`atalkd.conf` controls the interfaces to which netatalk binds, and any network numbers or zones you want to assign to them. In its simplest, empty form, `atalkd.conf` lets `atalkd` bind to every interface it finds. If it can't find all the interfaces you want it to bind to, you will have to specify them here. The simplest entry is just the interface to bind to. Additionally, zone names, network, node, and AppleTalk phase can be specified.

The phase is either 1 or 2, the latter being the default. The important difference is support for multiple zones in phase 2.

If there is more than one interface, it will automatically route between them. If there are other routers on the network, they can give configuration information to the Linux/netatalk router.

If you have more than one network, AppleTalk will break them into zones. In this case, you will want to use `atalkd.conf` to tell your server what zone to present itself as being in. You can also configure `atalkd` to listen to multiple interfaces and route AppleTalk packets among them.

Minimal `atalkd.conf` for use with multiple AppleTalk zones looks like the following:

```
eth0 -zone "Production"
```

The zone is basically a free-form string, although it must be 31 characters or less in length.

Unless you are on a very large network, you can also let `atalkd` set up its AppleTalk address. If this is not the case, you will have to assign one (or get one, if you are not in charge of the assignment of these addresses). Addresses are specified by network and node, like this:

```
-addr 45.10
```

In this example, the `45` is the network, while `10` is the node on that network.

The `-net` option is used to specify which address range is covered in this zone. This option lets you set the address range, which is automatically detected at server startup. If you have no zones, this number is irrelevant. The first number corresponds to the first network address of coverage in this range, and the optional last number corresponds to the last address covered in the address range. The address range should include netatalk's address number set with the `-addr net.node` option.

For example:

```
-net 106-110
```

The `-zone` option sets the name of the zone that `atalkd` should represent when talking on the network. This option, as discussed before, is merely a means of classification. It will be authoritatively broadcast if the `-seed` option is used and there are routers on the network whose zones don't conflict with that given after the `-zone` option.

papd.conf

The AppleTalk printer daemon reads its configuration information from papd.conf. If the conf file is empty, it will make all entries in /etc/printcap available. If you only want to make a subset of your print queues defined in / etc/printcap, you can specify them in papd.conf.

```
#

# Sample papd.conf
#
# We make two print queues available: the default 'lp' and 'lpcolor'
# a color laser printer
#
# For the first printer we also provide the location of the printer
# device driver file and the operator name for spooling.
#
B&W Laser Printer:\
  :pr=lp:pd=/usr/share/lib/ppd/HPLJ_4M.PPD:op=nobody:

Color LP:\
  :pr=lpcolor:
```

Printing to AppleTalk Printers

If you're a sole Linux user on an AppleTalk network, your first priority—and perhaps the reason you're installing netatalk in the first place—might likely be to enable printing to a network Apple printer.

Start netatalk if it's not already running. Next, probe the AppleTalk network to determine the name of the printer.

Running the nbplkup program with no arguments will list all object types in the default zone. This will typically give you a few screens of information, even on a small network:

```
# /usr/local/atalk/bin/nbplkup
    HP Color LaserJet 5M:SNMP Agent 150.128:8
    HP Color LaserJet 5M:HP Color LaserJet 5 150.128:158
    HP Color LaserJet 5M:LaserWriter 150.128:157
    HP Color LaserJet 5M:HP Zoner Responder 150.128:155
        CIC-2 BobM 4M+:SNMP Agent 150.151:8
        CIC-2 BobM 4M+:LaserWriter 150.151:157
        CIC-2 BobM 4M+:LaserJet 4 Plus 150.151:158
        CIC-2 BobM 4M+:HP Zoner Responder 150.151:152
    Judith's Laserjet 4mv:SNMP Agent 150.130:8
    Judith's Laserjet 4mv:LaserWriter 150.130:157
    Judith's Laserjet 4mv:LaserJet 4V 150.130:158
```

```
      Judith's Laserjet 4mv:HP Zoner Responder 150.130:152
XRX_DC230ST_08003E30CC89:LaserWriter 150.225:128
   ...
```

To show only LaserWriters:

```
# /usr/local/atalk/bin/nbplkup :LaserWriter
  XRX_DC230ST_08003E30CC89:LaserWriter          150.225:128
     Judith's Laserjet 4mv:LaserWriter          150.130:157
           CIC-2 BobM 4M+:LaserWriter           150.151:157
```

Let's set up the first printer returned as the default. To be thorough, we will also check the status of the printer:

```
# /usr/local/atalk/bin/papstatus -p XRX_DC230ST_08003E30CC89
spooler: ready
#
```

It appears to be okay. Next, let's test the printer by sending a file to it with pap:

```
# /usr/local/atalk/bin/pap -p XRX_DC230ST_08003E30CC89:LaserWriter
  links.ps
Trying 150.225:128 ...
spooler: ready
Connected to XRX_DC230ST_08003E30CC89:LaserWriter@*.
Connection closed.
#
```

To use the printer via the Linux lpr command, an entry in /etc/printcap for the printer must be made. (See the chapter on printing for an explanation of the details of printcap entries.) The important items to note are the AppleTalk name of the printer in the first line and the last two lines, which tell the printer daemon which input and output filters to use; in this case, the filters that come with the netatalk distribution.

```
lp|LaserWriter 1|XRX_DC230ST_08003E30CC89:\
        :sd=/usr/spool/laserwriter1:\
        :lp=/dev/null:\
        :pl#63:pw#85:\
        :mx#0:\
        :sh:sf:\
        :lf=/var/log/lpd-errs:\
        :if=/usr/lib/atalk/filters/ifpap:\
        :of=/usr/lib/atalk/filters/ofpap:
```

The spool directory, status file, and lock file need to be set up next:

```
# mkdir /var/spool/tlaserwriter1
# chown root.lp laserwriter1
# chmod 775 laserwriter1
# touch laserwriter1/lock
# chown root.root laserwriter1/lock
# chmod 004 laserwriter1/lock
# touch laserwriter1/status
# chown root.root laserwriter1/status
# chmod 664 laserwriter1/status
```

Now, start (or restart if it is already running) the printer daemon. Do this by running `/etc/rc.d/init.d/lpd (re)start`.

The 'config' Metafile

This file is only present if you installed from RPM. It contains definitions for a number of variables used by the startup script installed at `/etc/rc.d/init.d/atalk`.

One of the variables you are likely to want to change is the maximum number of simultaneous connections, `AFPD_MAX_CLIENTS`. The default is 5, which, unless you have a very small network, will likely be too small. Other options you might want to change include enabling the guest account, setting its username, and choosing which daemons to run. If you do not need to share your print queues, set `PAPD_RUN` to `No`. Similarly, if you do not want to share any filesystems, set `AFPD_RUN` to `No`.

Note that some of the options in `config` are not actually supported yet and therefore shouldn't be turned on.

Hardware Considerations

There are a few hardware caveats related to Ethernet cards. Netatalk doesn't function on cards based on DEC's Tulip chip, though it appears that activating the interface in promiscuous mode has been reported to fix this problem. Also, the driver for your card must support multicasting; check the Ethernet HOWTO to determine if your card's driver does.

Aside from these functional considerations, the best hardware investment is a good, fast disk. Spend the extra money to buy a faster disk and/or faster disk controller.

Installing from Source

The latest netatalk-1.4b2+asun distribution can always be found at `ftp://ftp.u.washington.edu/public/asun/`. When you install from source, the installation is rooted at `/usr/local/atalk` by default. There, a nominal set of directories (`bin`, `etc`, `include`, `lib`, and `man`) is created for the netatalk binaries, `config` files, and so forth.

There are only a few differences between source-based installation and RPM-based installation. The `config` directory is `/usr/local/atalk/etc`. It contains the following configuration files: `AppleVolumes.default`, `AppleVolumes.system`, `atalk.conf`, `afpd.conf`, and `papd.conf`. There is no `config` file, so you will have to edit the startup script yourself to change or add options.

Second, the startup script is named `rc.atalk`. It is installed in `/usr/local/atalk/etc/`. You will need to add a line to `/etc/rc.d/rc.local` to call it upon bootup.

Lastly, as is the case for many network services, you will need to make a few entries in `/etc/services` as well (RPM does this for you), including:

```
rtmp         1/ddp    # Routing Table Maintenance Protocol
nbp          2/ddp    # Name Binding Protocol
echo         4/ddp    # AppleTalk Echo Protocol
zip          6/ddp    # Zone Information Protocol
```

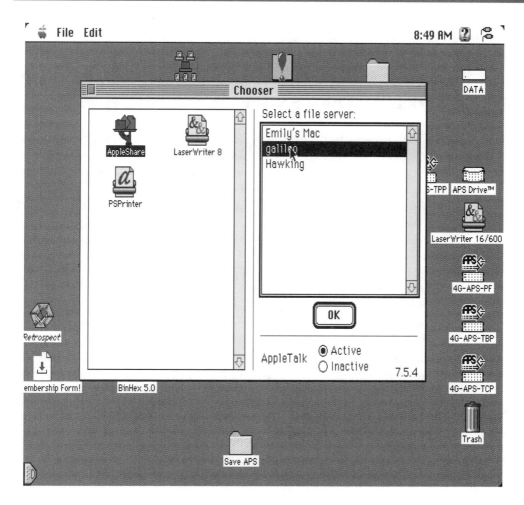

Figure 6–1   Galileo is a netatalk server.

Starting Netatalk

Once you have `config` files set up, invoke the `rc.atalk` script:

```
# /usr/local/atalk/etc/rc.atalk
```

This will take a minute or two as netatalk scopes out the network, registers itself, and so forth.

Now, go to one of your Mac clients and start the chooser. Select the new AppleTalk server, as shown in Figure 6-1, select the volumes to attach to, and watch them show up on your desktop!

6.5   Network Information Services (NIS and NIS+)

The Network Information Services (NIS) is a set of programs for managing users and various network services from one master server. Recently, an enhanced version of NIS, NIS+ has been introduced. NIS+ is more secure, works better in large networks, but is more difficult to set up.

NIS began life as Yellow Pages. Yellow Pages, however, is a registered trademark of British Telecom, so the name was changed. The original name's legacy is still around since most of the programs associated with NIS begin with "yp".

NIS stores its information in a set of directories and GDBM (GNU Database Management) files rooted in /var/yp. NIS refers to these files as "maps". The maps are then made available to other machines in the NIS domain (not the same thing as a DNS domain!) via RPC (Remote Procedure Calls). NIS also allows for secondary slave servers. Slave servers get their maps from the master and answer requests if the master is slow, much the same way secondary DNS servers work. Each subnet should have one (and only one) NIS server on it. Since clients can request NIS information through an IP broadcast, there should be one NIS slave server per subnet. Each of these slaves points to the master NIS server.

The NIS maps are built from the various setup files found mostly in /etc: passwd, group, hosts, services, aliases, and so on. It is not necessary to use every map. Often only the password and group maps are used, since most of the other files change infrequently.

One of the biggest problems with NIS is the security hole opened by broadcasting NIS requests. Anyone could set up a server that would have a chance of answering the requests. Recent versions of ypbind allow the specification of the domain server either by IP number or name.

NIS Client Setup

It is most likely that your first encounter with NIS will be as a client. Setting up your Linux machine to be an NIS client is fairly straightforward.

Red Hat makes the process of working in an NIS network easy with two scripts included with the system: /etc/rc.d/init.d/ypbind and /etc/

`rc.d/init.d/autofs`. The second script is only needed if you have auto-mount maps in your NIS server. You can also set NIS client configuration during the installation process. See the installation chapter for more information on this.

You should make sure that the time service is enabled in `/etc/inetd.conf`. If it is not, uncomment it and restart `inetd`.

You will need to set the NIS domain that you're in. Edit (or create) the `/etc/defaultdomain` file to have one line—that of the NIS domain you're in. Remember that NIS domains and DNS domains are not the same (did we mention this yet?). Newer versions of Red Hat (like the 6.0 release) use the `/etc/yp.conf` file to edit the NIS domain or a server to bind to.

By default, `ypbind` will send an IP broadcast through the network to find an NIS server. If the NIS server is on another network, or you want to prevent spoofing on the network, you can manually specify an NIS server to use. Edit the `/etc/yp.conf` file and add the hostname for the server. Make sure the host listed here is listed in `/etc/hosts`:

```
ypserver nisserver.host.com
```

In the examples below, we've assumed `/etc/passwd` is fairly minimal, containing entries for the superuser, various daemons, and so forth, but no mortal user entries.

To append the whole NIS password map to the local `/etc/passwd` file, add this line:

```
+::::::
```

You can customize access by adding additional lines starting with + or -. For example, deny the user `cary` access, but allow all others (at least to the extent they have on any other NIS client) like this:

```
+::::::
-cary
```

The "`+::::::`" entry is not mandatory. Additionally, you can control access by groups, using "@." This entry:

```
+cary::::::
+rachel::::::
+@plan9::::::
-paul
-enry
```

allows access for `cary`, `rachel`, and the group `plan9`. The users `paul` and `enry` (who are presumably in the aforementioned group) are denied.

It is also possible to override sections of information in the `passwd` map entry or to add users that don't exist in the NIS at all. For example, to give `paul` the shell `/bin/tcsh`, change `rachel`'s home directory (and allow access to only them), and add a user `surya`, use entries like this:

```
+:::::::
+paul::::::/bin/tcsh
+rachel:::::/local/home/rachel:
+:*:::::/bin/false
surya:IUg6jkhgT:506:100::/home/surya:/bin/bash
```

Next, make sure that the portmapper is starting. If you're using NFS, then the portmapper is already started. If not, use `/etc/rc.d/init.d/portmap start` to get it started. Finally, you can start with ypbind: `/etc/rc.d/init.d/ypbind start`. This will read the `/etc/defaultdomain` file, start the `ypbind` program, and connect you to the NIS server.

The nsswitch.conf File

The `/etc/nsswitch.conf` file determines the lookup order for all NIS information (unlike `/etc/host.conf`, which is only for host lookups). The example below is self-explanatory:

```
#
# /etc/nsswitch.conf
#
# An example Name Service Switch config file. This file should be
# sorted with the most-used services at the beginning.
#
# The entry '[NOTFOUND=return]' means that the search for an
# entry should stop if the search in the previous entry turned
# up nothing. Note that if the search failed due to some other reason
# (like no NIS server responding) then the search continues with the
# next entry.
#
# Legal entries are:
#
#           nisplus            Use NIS+ (NIS version 3)
#           nis                Use NIS (NIS version 2), also called YP
#           dns                Use DNS (Domain Name Service)
#           files              Use the local files
#           db                 Use the /var/db databases
#           [NOTFOUND=return]  Stop searching if not found so far
#
```

```
passwd:        compat
group:         compat
shadow:        compat
passwd_compat: nis
group_compat: nis
shadow_compat: nis
hosts:         nis files dns
services:      nis [NOTFOUND=return] files
networks:      nis [NOTFOUND=return] files
protocols:     nis [NOTFOUND=return] files
rpc:           nis [NOTFOUND=return] files
ethers:        nis [NOTFOUND=return] files
netmasks:      nis [NOTFOUND=return] files
netgroup:      nis
bootparams:    nis [NOTFOUND=return] files
publickey:     nis [NOTFOUND=return] files
automount:     files
aliases:       nis [NOTFOUND=return] files
```

Automounter Client Startup

The automounter will (as the name implies) automatically mount partitions over NFS based on an NIS map. The two typical maps used are `auto.home` and `auto.vol`, which mount off of `/home` and `/vol`, respectively. If you have these maps in your NIS domain, you can start the Linux `autofs` automounter using the following command:

```
/etc/rc.d/init.d/autofs start
```

It should be noted that the automounter under Linux performs some of the same functions as `vold` under Solaris. CD-ROMs, floppy disks, local volumes, and NFS filesystems can be automatically mounted when the user changes to a certain directory. By default, Red Hat 6.0 includes `/misc/cd` and `/misc/kernel`, which `mount` `/dev/cdrom` onto `/misc/cd` and `ftp.kernel.org` via NFS onto `/misc/kernel`. We mention the automounter with NIS, since that is the most frequently used reason for using it.

NIS+

NIS+ is Sun's successor to NIS. It has better security and handles a large number of clients. Historically, support for NIS+ under Linux was poor and limited to the client side only. Fortunately, recent Red Hat versions are based on `glibc`, which supports NIS+ more fully, though still not completely.

Despite this support, NIS+ is still much more difficult to use, particularly on the server end. We recommend that you only use Linux as an NIS+ client if you have to (if you are on a large network or are concerned about security) and not use Linux as an NIS+ server at all.

If you need to set up an NIS+ client, you will need to make a few changes to your system. First, you will need `glibc` 2.1 (for 32-bit systems, e.g., Intel machines) or `glibc` 2.1.1 (for 64-bit systems, e.g., Alpha machines). If you are running Red Hat 6.0, you have `glibc` 2.1.1 already. If not, you will need to upgrade `glibc` and recompile `gcc/g++` against the new `glibc`. Both source and binary releases of `glibc` can be found at `ftp://ftp.gnu.org/gnu/glibc`.

Second, you need the NIS+ client programs. These programs can be found at `ftp://ftp.kernel.org/pub/linux/utils/net/NIS+`. You will need two files: `nis-tools-1.4.tar.gz` and `pam_keylogin-1.1.tar.gz`. Unpack and compile them.

Assuming your NIS+ server is set up to answer requests for your client (see your Solaris documentation for how to do this), you will need to set the NIS+ domain name as you would for NIS and then run `nisinit` as follows:

```
# nisinit -c -H <NIS+ server>
```

Edit `/etc/nsswitch.conf`, making sure the only service after `publickey` is `nisplus` (`publickey: nisplus`). Next, start `keylogin`. You should add `keylogin` to the `rc` boot up sequence so that it is the daemon started immediately after portmap:

```
# keylogin -r
```

Edit the `/etc/pam.d/login` file to match this:

```
#
# /etc/pam.d/login for use with NIS+
#
auth        required      /lib/security/pam_securetty.so
auth        required      /lib/security/pam_keylogin.so
auth        required      /lib/security/pam_unix_auth.so
auth        required      /lib/security/pam_nologin.so
account     required      /lib/security/pam_unix_acct.so
password    required      /lib/security/pam_unix_passwd.so
session     required      /lib/security/pam_unix_session.so
```

Lastly, edit `nisswitch.conf`. Basically, you will want to replace `nis` with `nisplus`.

Setting Up an NIS Master Server

Make sure that you have the ypserv package installed. If you need to install it, it can be found on the Red Hat CD, FTP site, or one of their mirrors.

Next, edit /var/yp/Makefile to add or remove the maps you will be serving. The line starting with all: contains the list of maps.

Now edit /var/yp/securenets and /etc/ypserv.conf. The first defines the IPs from which the server will answer requests. It is fairly simple and well-commented.

```
#
# Sample /var/yp/securenets
#
#
# Allow localhost access. This is necessary!
#
host 127.0.0.1
#
# Allow access from machines on the local network
#
255.255.255.0 10.10.10.0
#
# Access from two class C networks 209.1.2.0 and 209.1.3.0
#
255.255.254.0 209.1.2.0
```

The /etc/ypserv.conf file lets you further customize the server's behavior at the host or network level on a per map basis. There are two types of entries: options and access rules. Options have the simple format of <option>: yes|no, i.e., the option is either on or off. Access rules have the format host : map : security : passwd_mangle. Access rules are read until a match is found for the host and map being requested, then the rule is applied.

An option that is commonly turned on is dns. The following line would tell the NIS master to consult DNS if it finds a host in its host maps.

```
dns: on
```

The following lines simulate shadow passwords for a particular network for privileged ports (those numbered under 1024) and deny access to the maps to other hosts:

```
10.10.10.0/255.255.255.0    : passwd.byname    : port    : yes
10.10.10.0/255.255.255.0    : passwd.byuid     : port    : yes
*                           : passwd.byname    : port    : yes
```

```
    *                                  : passwd.byuid    : port      : yes
```

Next, start the portmapper:

```
# /etc/rc.d/init.d/portmap start
```

and then `ypserv`:

```
# /etc/rc.d/init.d/ypserv start
```

You can verify that things are running with the following:

```
# rpcinfo -u localhost ypserv
program 100004 version 1 ready and waiting
```

Now run `ypinit` to generate the maps in `/var/yp` from the files in `/etc`:

```
# ypinit -m
```

If you are setting up a slave server, run:

```
# ypinit -s master
```

and you're ready to get the clients connected!

6.6   Routing with Linux

To start routing with Linux, you first have to have two Ethernet ports. This doesn't mean two Ethernet cards, but you do need something like an Ethernet port and a PPP connection, or something similar. Routing allows you to connect two Ethernet networks with the Linux machine in the center. Unlike a switch, which connects two physical runs and segregates the two networks on an Ethernet layer, a router segregates at the IP layer. Each side of the router has its own subnet. This is good for things like PPP dialin servers, or to create links to remote offices, to create a safe network that holds the WWW, FTP, and email servers. In the case of Linux, a router can also act as a packet filter and to provide IP masquerade services.

Let's say that you're connecting two physical networks located in the same building (say the first and second floors). You have two Ethernet cables in your hand, hopefully of the 10-BaseT variety. Now what?

Get two Ethernet cards in your system, and use `kerneld` to load in the modules. You can verify the modules are loaded by using the `dmesg` command. The two Ethernet cards do not have to be the same type, but it helps if they're different, since this allows you to explicitly know which card is which. The example below has a 3Com 3c503 and a Digital 21140-based card.

The /etc/conf.modules looks like this:

```
alias eth0 tulip
alias eth1 3c503
alias char-major-14 off
alias sound off

options eth1 xcvr=1
```

Because of the above setup, we know that eth0 (the first Ethernet port) is going to be the tulip (which is the name for the Digital/Intel chip). The second Ethernet port is the 3C503 card. The last line that starts with options tells kerneld to pass xcvr=1 when loading the 3C503 module. This allows us to use the AUI port instead of the coax port on the card.

You may want to either change /etc/conf.modules and restart kerneld, or load the modules by hand the first few times to make sure you don't have any problems. If you're using kerneld to load modules, they won't get loaded until you actually use them. You can use the Red Hat netcfg program to start up both Ethernet cards on their respective networks.

Routing Using Red Hat netcfg

The netcfg program does many of the routing setups that would normally have to be done by hand automatically and on startup. These files get stored in /etc/sysconfig and are compatible with linuxconf's routing scheme.

Routing by Hand

These commands, entered by hand, will allow you to route between two networks:

```
/sbin/ifconfig eth0 192.168.1.10
/sbin/route add -net 192.168.1.0
/sbin/ifconfig eth1 192.168.2.10
/sbin/route add -net 192.168.2.0
/sbin/route add default gateway 192.168.1.15
```

If you use these in a file like rc.local, it will work, but it is not compatible with the way that linuxconf or netcfg stores its routing information. Make sure you're not conflicting with these other methods.

Here the machine is on two networks, 192.168.1.0 and 192.168.2.0, both class C with netmasks of 255.255.255.0 and broadcasts located at the .255 IP address. Since the netmasks and broadcasts are standard for class C, we don't have to tell ifconfig about them. As soon as ifconfig gets the message to start up, it activates the module (if necessary) and configures the device. The route tells the networking section to pass packets for each kind of network to the specified Ethernet card. The final route designates a default location for packets that don't match any other route to go. In this case, it goes onto the 192.168.1.0 network to the machine with an IP address of 192.168.1.15. If this machine were acting as a company-wide router, this address would point to the router box installed by the ISP. Since Linux now knows how to route packets between the 1.0 and 2.0 networks, any packets that get directed to it to go to a network will automatically be sent there. So, 192.168.1.10 and 192.168.2.10 now become gateways for anyone on those respective networks.

This example only shows how to use static routing. There are other methods of routing, such as RIP (which is handled by routed), and OSPF (handled by gated). Since the networks we administer are not that large, and many configuration issues are only in a few locations, we prefer to use static routes so we know exactly what our networks look like. For some networks, you may need the above programs.

If you replace eth0 with ppp0, you now have a routing PPP dialin. The Linux machine is dialed into another machine, and is able to route data between the local Ethernet network and the remote PPP link. As previously mentioned, this method works for any two (or more) IP connections.

Security Issues

By default, all packets are allowed to pass between connected networks. If you want to implement some sort of security to prevent violation attempts, you'll need to get familiar with the built-in packet filtering tools ipfwadm and ipchains. The older 2.0 and 2.1 kernels used the ipfwadm command to implement packet monitoring, filtering, and accounting. The newer 2.2 and 2.3 kernels use ipchains, which implements all the functionality of ipfwadm plus some. See the next chapter for information on how to boost security between networks.

6.7   Internet Agencies

InterNIC

In the early 1990s, domains were free for the taking. If you filled out your template and sent in the form, you got yourself a domain name. Everyone thought this would go on forever, but alas...

In the mid 1990s, the National Science Foundation (NSF) started cutting off funding to the Internet and allowed commercial organizations to begin using the Internet to sell and advertise. The response was an explosive growth in the number of domains being added. This got into the hundreds of thousands per year. To impose some order on this and make up for some of the missing NSF funding, the InterNIC (`http://www.internic.net`) was created to provide for a top-level DNS domain and to register new organizations within the United States. The downside to this was a new Internet fee: $70 for the first two years, then $35 each year after. After paying this fee, you are entitled to have your domain registered in the InterNIC database and your domain can be recognized by the rest of the Internet. This doesn't mean that the InterNIC will give you anything else, like DNS services or an Internet link. You will just have your domain name registered and a pointer to a DNS server. You're still responsible for getting Internet service and a DNS server.

The InterNIC only handles U.S. domains: `.edu`, `.net`, `.org`, `.com`, `.gov`, and `.int`. Other domains, such as `.us` or other country-based domains, are not registered with the InterNIC, and you'll have to find out who handles your regional DNS service to get registered with them. Many of these have a fee, but some (like `.us`) are free or have a smaller fee than the InterNIC. To register in the `.us` domain, go to `http://www.isi.edu`. The `.us` domain doesn't give the kind of general quality that, for example, `.com` would give. For example, instead of `wayga.net`, you'd probably get something like `wayga.billerica.ma.us`. but I could still build a domain under that such as `ftp.wayga. billerica.ma.us`. In some ways, this is preferable to just a `.com` domain since it allows you to specify the location of a site (`ibm.armonk.ny.us`) directly. Foreign companies have slightly different subdivisions and may subdivide by location, type of organization (commercial, educational, etc.), or a combination of these. To find out the contacts for a particular country's top-level domain, check out `http://www.isi.edu/div7/iana/domain-names.html`.

One other thing to remember about country codes is that they may not be what you think they are. For example, .ch is Switzerland, not China, and .ca is Canada, not California.

Registering a Domain

You'll need to have a domain name first. Take one that isn't already taken (obviously), and make sure the domain you take isn't a registered trademark of someone else. Sure, you could take mcdonalds.com, but their lawyers get paid more than yours, and there's more of them. The InterNIC does not take sides in these kinds of disputes, so don't think that just because you got a domain that you own it for all time.

There are a few choices when registering a domain. The .edu is for educational institutions (mostly colleges and universities—elementary and secondary schools usually get a state-based domain). The .com is for commercial organizations that don't necessarily provide Internet access or aren't necessarily based on the Web. The .org domain is for organizations, either formal or a group of people getting together (apache.org or linux.org, for example). The .net domain is for groups that resell Internet access or provide access to other groups. And the .gov and .mil are for the government and military, respectively. This leaves you with three probable choices: .com, .net, or .org. Pick the one appropriate for your organization.

Next, you'll need up to three people. One is the technical contact, one is the administrative contact, and the third is the billing contact. The technical contact is the person who typically registers the domain and is the Manager of Information Services (MIS). The administrative contact is probably your boss. The billing contact is the one who gets the bills. They can all be the same person if you wish. These names and addresses will be compiled into the database as well, giving a handle that you can use later at the InterNIC instead of reentering your address, phone number, name, and so on.

The last important items are the primary and secondary DNS servers. Since the InterNIC doesn't provide you with DNS service, you must enter the two hosts that will be able to provide IP addresses for your domain. Two are required so that one can act as a backup, in case the primary is down or busy.

The InterNIC also asks for information such as, "What does your organization do?" Fill in all the information requested and wait. In a few days, you'll get email saying the domain was added. If you're changing a domain, the administrative, technical, and billing contacts will receive requests from the InterNIC to verify the new information. This prevents one contact from changing information without the knowledge of the other two, and it prevents a cracker from changing domain information (for example, if `microsoft.com` were to point instead to `linux.org`). This is more a denial-of-service attack and was common until the InterNIC requested verification.

whois

The whois database is a hook directly into the InterNIC hosts and allows you to see domain information and get information on the people who run the domains.

The whois database not only lets you see information about a domain, but also about people. For example, since I own the `wayga.net` domain, I have an entry in the whois database (`MK146`). Looking up this information would give my name and E-mail address. Back in the early days, this was a great way to find someone's E-mail address. But since there are millions of people on the Internet now, the only people in the whois database are domain administrators.

Using whois is easy. Just type something like:

```
whois wayga.net
```

The original version of whois looked at an inappropriate whois database (`nic.ddn.mil`, which is for military use only). The Linux version of whois should point at the right server name, but if it doesn't, you'll have to replace whois with:

```
whois -h rs.internic.net wayga.net
```

After the `whois` command, you can list names or domains and get results from the InterNIC database on who owns a particular name or get contact information for the administrators of that domain. This is especially helpful if you're trying to track a cracker in your system and know what domain they're coming from. You can then contact the administrators of the domain and alert them.

CERT

The CERT Coordination Center was founded in 1988 to coordinate security problems on the Internet. It was founded after the great Internet Worm of the late 1980s and is located at Carnegie-Mellon University in Pittsburgh, Pennsylvania. If you don't know anything about the Internet Worm, either read *The Cuckoo's Egg* by Cliff Stoll or *Cyberpunk: Outlaws and Hackers on the Computer Frontier* by Katie Hafner and John Markoff. Both are excellent books and show some real-life examples of crackers and those who track them down. Anyway, CERT's purpose is to keep administrators aware of potential security holes in the OS or the software the OS runs. These security alerts often list the type of security hole, how it can be exploited, what versions are affected, and (if available) locations of patches or ways to prevent anyone   from   taking   advantage   of   those   holes.   The `comp.os.linux.announce` group has posts every now and then from CERT related to Linux and programs it runs. Strangely enough, some of the security holes they have are not with Linux itself, but with the way a particular program was compiled, making the hole not a Linux problem at all, but a fault of whoever compiled that program.

If you have an intrusion that you need investigated, you can send an intrusion report to CERT and maybe they can help you track down the person responsible. Their Web site is `http://www.cert.org/`. It is probably best to give their site a visit before your site gets broken into so you can stay up-to-date with their advisories.

CIAC—http://ciac.llnl.gov/

The Computer Incident Advisory Capability (CIAC) is run by the U.S. Department of Energy as something similar to CERT, but it primarily provides services for the U.S. Department of Energy (DOE) and its contractors. However, it does have a number of bulletins and advisory notes that may not be at CERT. It is also worthwhile to take a look at their site to keep up-to-date with security issues.

6.8   Summary

- TCP/IP is the main protocol used by Linux.

- Ethernet and PPP are the most common ways of using TCP/IP.

- DNS provides name translation.

- NFS allows you to share information across a network.

- Netatalk allows you to communicate over AppleTalk.

- NIS allows you to distribute login information.

Printing and Print Sharing

7

Getting the most out of a single printer
across multiple machines

Print sharing allows you to set up a single printer so that everyone on the network has access to it.

Print setup and sharing under Linux give you a number of choices. You can print to a local printer, or just have Linux point to a remote printer on an AppleTalk, TCP/IP, or SMB network. You can also share your locally-connected printer with others using any of those protocols.

7.1 Connecting Printers to Linux

To use a printer under Linux, it must first be configured. By default, Red Hat configures the parallel port as a module. See the chapter on kernel configuration for more information on loading and configuring modules. Once you have the `lp` module active (you can tell by seeing something like `lp1` at `0x0378, (polling)` by using the `dmesg` command), you should be ready to print. Assuming your printer can handle plain ASCII (most do), you can send a text file to the printer by using something similar to:

```
cat /etc/motd > /dev/lp1
```

This should print a copy of your `motd` file to the printer. If you get an error, you may want to see if `dmesg` specified something other than `lp1` (for example, `lp0` or `lp2`) and try again. Once this is set up, you can get on with configuring the printer.

7.2   Serial vs. Parallel vs. Ethernet Printers

Using parallel ports is the obvious choice for driving a printer since there are no baud rates or `stty` settings to worry about and the speed is much greater (parallel ports run at about 150 Kbps as opposed to 38.4 Kb for a serial printer). But, there are limitations to the parallel port. The greatest of these is the distance. A parallel port can run only about 20 feet or so before the signal degrades too much and causes errors. A serial printer can run 50 feet at 38.4K, and much longer if you choose to use an electrical interface like EIA-530 (aka RS-422). Also, a serial cable can technically run through an RJ-45 (8-pin) wire, or three wires if you feel lucky. This is a big advantage over the 25 pins that the parallel port needs. Many low-end printers these days have only the parallel port connection, but most of the higher-end printers for workgroups or print servers have serial connections as well, or they are options available after the purchase.

And then there are the Ethernet connections you can have to a printer (see the remote printer section below). This is a great idea for some printers, since Ethernet runs through most buildings anyway. In a computer lab situation, where Ethernet is running through the room, and the server is in another room, this is an excellent idea. As long as the Ethernet printer supports the LPD protocol, and most do, you can print directly to the printer via Linux. For ease of configuration, many network printers can be configured via DHCP so that you don't need to install extra drivers to get access to them. See the networking chapter for more information on configuring DHCP for your network.

7.3   Configuring a Printer

Linux uses the BSD style of printing. That is, there is a /etc/printcap file that has to be modified, and the commands are lpr, lpq, lpc, lprm, and so on. One advantage of the BSD method over SYSV is that it makes adding printers and modifying printer setups very easy. Here's a copy of the printcap for an HP LaserJet 4L connected to the parallel port on Red Hat:

```
lp:\
        :sd=/var/spool/lpd/lp:\
        :mx#0:\
        :lp=/dev/lp1:\
        :if=/var/spool/lpd/lp/filter:\
        :sh:
```

This printcap entry is really all one line. You can tell because in the Linux world, a line that ends in \ is automatically added to the next line. Each printcap entry is one line, but that line can be extremely long. The first line (the lp:) defines the name of the printer. You can add alias names for the printer by adding |<alias> to the name definition. Once the name is given, the options can be put in any order. Here are what the above options mean.

- sd—Spool directory. This is where the files that have to be sent to the printer are stored. This is usually /var/spool/lpd/<printername>.

- mx—You can set a maximum file size that can be sent to the printer. The #0 means that there is no maximum file size. The default maximum is 1000 blocks, which equates to just under 1Mb.

- lp—The device name for output. The /dev/lp1 specifies a parallel printer, but you can also use a serial device if you wish.

- if—Input filter. Any file going to the printer gets piped to this command before being put in the queue. This is where the Red Hat Print Manager comes in and does its work, and where other magic filters get installed as well.

- sh—Suppresses printing of burst pages. Burst pages list the user, the name of the file being printed, and the job number, along with other information. Think of this as a fax cover page. In a small network, you don't need burst pages, but if you have about five or more people using the printer, it's a good idea to have it.

The `printcap` man page has a list of all the options, what they're used for, and the default settings. If you're using a serial printer, you will want to add the following settings:

- `br`—Baud rate to use. Any valid baud rate will work.
- `ms`—`Stty` settings to give to the serial port after opening and before sending data. This is usually to set up things like hardware flow control.

A sample line addition of an 8-bit connection using hardware flow and running at a rate of 38.4 Kbps is:

```
br#38400:ms=opost,cs8,-parenb,-cstopb, crtscts\
```

7.4   Print Filters

Print filters are programs that convert from multiple file types to one that your printer can understand. In most cases, this will be either PostScript (really easy to do) or PCL (harder, but not by much). The reason PostScript is so easy to use with printers is because most of the higher-end printers were connected to UNIX machines, and therefore the programs were written to output in PostScript. Now that PCL is being used more often in the lower-end printers, and since Linux is everywhere, you'll probably need some kind of converter. This is where print filters come in.

Red Hat comes with a collection of filters that can correctly change just about any file format into something that your specific printer can understand. The filters take longer to convert a PostScript file to PCL, but the output is similar, and you don' t have to spend hundreds to get a PostScript cartridge for your printer (if one is even available). Fortunately, you won't have to worry much about the filters being installed. All you need to do is configure the printer via the Red Hat `printtool` and you're all set.

Now, let's hook that printer into a network.

7.5   Printers on the Network!

When the `printcap` is set up, you'll need to restart the printer daemon (`lpd`), which should already be running and will be once Linux starts. To inform Linux of the changes on the `/etc/printcap` file, you can send a HUP signal (1 for Linux) to the `lpd` process. This will cause it to reread the `/etc/print-`

cap file and restart. From the Red Hat printtool, you can select restart lpd and this will perform the same function.

Access from Other LPD (UNIX) Systems

Once lpd is running, enter the names of the hosts that you want to have access to your printers in the /etc/hosts.lpd (for printer access only) or /etc/hosts.equiv[1] file. Once this has been done, your printer is available for access from other UNIX machines immediately. Set the rm option to the remote host and have the rp option name the remote printer. The only other option that needs to be set is sp (local spool directory). For added security, the rs option, if set on the print server side, will accept only print jobs from users on the remote machine that have accounts on the server machine. That is, a user account of the same name must exist on both machines before the print job will be accepted. The Linux lpd monitors TCP/IP port 515(tcp) for activity from print clients.

If you want to talk to a printer that exists on the network and is compatible with the LPD protocol (such as HP's JetDirect, available for many of their office printers), you can use the printtool to point directly to the printer. Just enter the IP address and type of printer it is, and printtool will do the rest.

Access via SMB (Windows Networking)

The very best way to get a Linux printer seen on a Windows network is to run Samba. We'll get into Samba in the next chapter, but we'll focus on setting up print services here. The important thing to know is that Samba should be configured to use the /etc/printcap file and BSD-style printing. That is about the entire configuration Linux needs to serve a printer to a Windows 98 or Windows NT machine.[2] Users will be able to use the standard Windows print management tools (print queues), see the entire printer queue, and even remove their job if they choose. Be sure to install a print driver under Windows for the kind of printer you have installed, as the print filter on Linux should just pass the data along to the printer.

---

[1]Using hosts.equiv could be a security hole, especially if you're in a network of Linux or UNIX machines.

[2]You could also serve another Linux (or UNIX) machine running Samba as well. That would just be silly, but still in "the UNIX way."

To print from Linux to a Windows machine, the procedure is a bit different. Red Hat allows you (via the `printtool`) to add a printer that is connected via Server Message Block (SMB), and the `printtool` takes care of the rest. The Windows machine picks up the print job and sends it off to the printer.

Windows NT can also handle the LPD protocol, so you may want to use it instead.

7.6 Managing Print Queues

Now that the printer is connected and working, people are going to try sending print data to it. At this point, it's time to put on the "print master" hat and get to work.

Print queues are FIFO (First In First Out), so the first one in line gets to have access to the printer. If one job gets stuck, or the printer runs out of paper, the queue will begin to fill and you'll be hounded by users desperately trying to find their printouts. Not to worry.

The commands you'll want to know about are `lpc`, `lprm`, and `lpq`. The `lpq` command shows what's in the queue and gives the current status of the printer, as best as `lpd` can figure that information out. Some printers will be able to tell `lpd` that they are out of paper or that the connection is down, and these errors will show up in the `lpq` listing.

The `lprm` command will remove jobs from the queue. Only root and the person who submitted the print job can remove a job from the queue. If an accidental print job is 3Mb in size and is currently tying up the queue, it may be best to remove the job. As root, you can remove all the jobs owned by a particular user with the command `lprm user`.

The `lpc` command is the "lp control." It can activate and deactivate queues and printers, rearrange jobs in the queue, and get a status of any printer listed in `/etc/printcap` (to paraphrase the man page).

`lpc` can be run interactively, or you can put the commands directly on the `lpc` command line. Here's a list of some of the more important `lpc` commands:

- `disable { all|printer }`—Disables the named printer. New jobs cannot be added, but printing will continue.

- `down { all|printer }`—Disables the named printer completely. No new jobs can be added, and printing stops.

- `enable { all|printer }`—New jobs can be added to the queue (reverse of disable).

- `restart { all|printer }`—Tries to restart a print daemon. Sometimes the `lpd` process will die or get stuck, and this will try to restart a new daemon.

- `status { all|printer }`—Gets a status of the printers and lists whether or not queues are up and whether or not printing is enabled.

- `topq printer [job..] [user..]`—Prints the jobs listed at the top of the queue.

The `lpc` man page has more on the commands available, but these will get you started with queue administration.

In the worst case scenario, where the `lpc` commands do not work, you can use the `/etc/rc.d/init.d/lpd.init stop` command to stop the `lpd` program altogether. The `/etc/rc.d/init.d/lpd.init start` command will start `lpd` up.

For more information or help on how the print services work, check out the Printing HOWTO and the Printing Usage HOWTO.

7.7 Ghostscript

Ghostscript is used by Red Hat's printing system to convert postscript into other forms that can be handled by printers. Since many desktop laser and inkjet printers can't talk Postscript; you need something that can speak both the language of Postscript, and the PCL or other printer language used by your printer.

Postscript has long been a default output method in Linux. It easily handles text and graphics, has fonts defined, and it's easy to create postscript files from just about any program. Its downsides include the fact that Postscript usually creates large files. There's also the previously listed fact that not all printers talk Postscript. Again, this is where ghostscript comes in. It has a number of defined output devices. This allows ghostscript to import Postscript and output just about anything, including an X window. While ghostscript can directly output to an X window, the ghostview program handles this a little easier, allowing you to read files from a menu instead of the command line.

For the most part, you won't have to worry about how ghostscript works since the printtool will convert from whatever format you send to whatever the printer can handle.

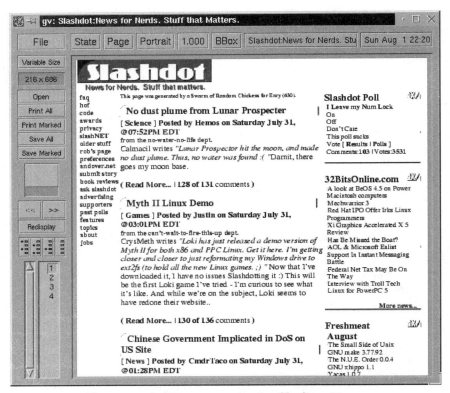

Figure 7–1   Ghostview displaying a postscript file from Netscape

7.8   Summary

- Serial, parallel, and Ethernet printers all have their relative advantages, depending on what your printing needs are.
- Linux uses the `/etc/printcap` file for controlling how the `lpd` program talks to the printer.
- Linux can talk to printers across a network, and Samba allows Windows machines to network with a Linux printer.
- The `lpr`, `lprm`, and `lpc` programs are used to manage printers and print queues.

Samba 8

How to let your Linux machine serve files and printers to Windows machines

SMB (Server Message Block) is the primary file and print sharing protocol for MS-Windows-based machines. Linux can provide services to and receive services from SMB-based machines.

The other printing and print sharing option is called Samba, developed mainly by some nice folks in Australia. TCP/IP and SMB work quite nicely together. In fact, they work so well together one could piggyback a packet of SMB data onto a TCP/IP packet.[1] This relationship is one that Samba uses to get Windows machines to talk to Linux. The latest version of Samba can be found at `http://www.samba.org/`.

Let's quickly go through a small network.

---

[1]Which itself is piggybacked on Ethernet, FDDI, ATM, PPP, or what-have-you.

8.1   Setting Up an MS Windows Network

This is actually easy, if you have Windows 98 or Windows NT. So from here on in, we'll just say "Windows" to relate to all versions of the OS, and you'll have to do some reading to match what we tell you to your particular version of Windows.

What You'll Need

First, get the Ethernet cards and drivers loaded. Also, install your backbone. The best available networking scheme for the money is 10-BaseT, as there are fewer problems that can cause the entire network to go down. But it's more expensive; you have to buy hubs, patch cables, patch panels, run one cable to each machine, and so on. But it is certainly worth the money.

If you want a cheaper Ethernet, or you have a very small network, you can get the very affordable 10-Base2. This is also known as "thinnet." All you have to be concerned about in a 10-Base2 network is that both ends are terminated with a 50-ohm resistor. Thinnet has the disadvantage that if one section of cable goes bad, the entire network goes down.

Check the chapter on networking for more on networking concepts and how to set up a TCP/IP network.

You'll also need to make sure that each Windows user has an account on the Linux server. If you want, make the shell something like /bin/false. If you want users to be able to change their passwords, set the shell to be /bin/passwd. Also, be sure to add /bin/true or /bin/passwd to the /etc/shells file. If you have an existing NT server that has passwords for user accounts, you can have Samba authenticate passwords against the NT server.

Once you have your network and Linux box set up, get the software working. Windows will allow you to use the Windows networking option to create a simple network. Be sure to use the same workgroup name across all the machines.

What's a Workgroup?

A workgroup is a logical collection of users within the same subnet. A subnet breaks users up physically, as you need a router or bridge to get from one subnet to another. A workgroup is a more logical breakdown. For example, you can have accounting, manufacturing, and sales all on the same subnet, but all in different workgroups.

Once the software has been set up, you should be able to browse the network and see all the other machines, at least those on the same subnet as you.[2] If you can't, get the software to this point. If something's wrong, you'll usually get a somewhat cryptic explanation of the problem and how to fix it.

In a workgroup, there is typically no central server. Usernames and passwords are authenticated as needed against a server.

What's a Domain?

A Windows NT domain has a central password server that authenticates users when they log into their Windows machines. Instead of checking a local password from the Windows login screen, the password gets sent to the PDC (Primary Domain Controller), which grants access to services on all the servers within that domain.

If you have a PDC on the network and choose to have Samba authenticate users off that, you can set up your network as a domain. Otherwise, choose a workgroup.

Install TCP/IP Stack

Windows 98 and Windows NT both come with a TCP/IP stack already in the installation. When Windows asks for a username and password, be sure to give the username that would work against whatever system you're authenticating.

We'll assume you know how to set up a TCP/IP network. If not, check the networking chapter for information on how to do this. Once you have the TCP/IP stack loaded on all the Windows machines, try having them ping each other, or ping the Linux box. The Linux box should also be able to ping the Windows machines.

8.2 Installing Samba

Now that the Windows machines are set up, let's go to the Linux machine. Samba is installed if you selected `DOS/Windows Connectivity` on the Red

---

[2]You won't be able to see outside your subnet unless your bridge forwards non-TCP/IP packets. A router usually won't forward SMB packets, since it deals with TCP/IP only. But since Samba piggybacks on TCP/IP, you can still connect to machines in other subnets.

Hat installation screen, and is available from the Red Hat distribution as Samba. If you don't have it, you can install an updated RPM from `con-trib.redhat.com` or `www.samba.org`.

You can examine a sample configuration file, `/etc/smb.conf`, and tune it for your network. Here's a sample copy of an `smb.conf` file:

```
[global]
  printing = bsd
  printcap name = /etc/printcap
  # The above lists the printing method.  Linux has BSD printing, so we
  use
  #  BSD printing and /etc/printcap.
  load printers = yes
  guest account = nobody
  # If a user can connect with no authentication, the above is the user-
  name
  #  that is connected.
  log file = /var/log/samba-log.%m
  admin users=markk
  # users that have full access to all files
  read prediction = yes
  dead time = 15
  workgroup=WORKGROUP
  mangled map=(*.html,*.htm)
  lock directory = /var/lock/samba
  share modes = yes
  os level = 33
  domain master = yes

[homes]
   comment = Home Directories
   browseable = no
   read only = no
   create mode = 0750
   read size = 8192
   max xmit = 8192
   # the two above try to write and read in 8kB blocks.

[printers]
   comment = All Printers
   browseable = no
   # This entry expands into each printer available, we don't want this
   #  actual entry seen in a browse list.
   printable = yes
   public = yes
   # We want anyone to be able to print, even without authentication.
   writable = no
   # Can't really store files on a printer, eh?
   create mode = 0700
```

```
[pcsoft]
    comment = PC Software
    # Comment as it shows up in a browse list
    path = /vol/repository
    # Linux directory for sharing
    public = no
    # Can users connect with no authentication?  No.
    writable = yes
    printable = no
    create mode = 0666
    # The above sets what the file permissions are on the Linux side.
    #  It's set to owner, group, and world read and write.

[accounting]
  path = /home/bob/shared
  valid users = fred bob
  # Only fred and bob can access this share.
  public = no
  only guest = no
  browseable = no
  writable = yes
  create mask = 0777
```

Much like the Windows system.ini, files are broken up into sections starting with a word in brackets; the smb.conf file does the same. [global], [printers], and [homes] are the only three reserved section headers. All others are assumed to be share names to be provided to SMB clients.

The [global] section sets options for the entire program. For example, the mangled map option says that all files that get to Samba that end in .htm should instead be written to the Linux server as .html. This makes writing files in Windows and sending them to a Web server easier.

Other options of note include the following.

- log file—When smbd fires up, this is where it will write its log file. In the above case, the name of the log file is samba-log, plus the name of the machine.

- dead time—After <dead time> minutes are up with no activity, the smb connection goes away. This is good not only to save resources on the Linux server, but it also allows Samba to recover when a Windows machine crashes. A good choice would be around 15 minutes or so.

- admin users—These users are as good as root. In fact, they have root privileges to all the shares (this should only be you or the person who is administering Samba).

- `workgroup`—The workgroup to be a part of. This should be the same name that you set earlier in Windows.

The [`homes`] section will put in the browse network section of the Windows home directory for the user. The user can then click or mount that directory and it's their home directory on Linux.

Once Samba is installed on the network, you can test it by starting `smbd` and `nmbd`. If you installed from an `.RPM` file, you can start Samba services as `/etc/rc.d/init.d/smb start`. The `nmbd` process acts as a name server for Samba, much like `named` handles DNS. Once started, you can go to an SMB client and perform a network browse. You should see your Linux machine in the list of machines (see Figure 8–1).

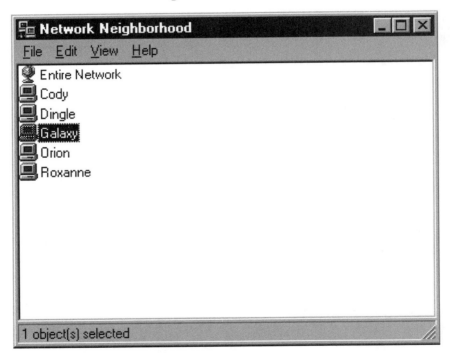

Figure 8–1   Galaxy is a Samba server.

If not, you can check through the logs located in `/var/log`. Each `smb` and `nmb` process has its own log files (`samba-log.nmb` and `samba-log.smb`). In addition, each client machine that connects to `smb` has a log file named `samba-log.`*machinename*,where *machinename* is the Netbios name of the machine.

Password Authentication

Even if you see the Linux machine listed in the browse list, you still need to connect to a share. First, there are public connections that do not require a valid login. These kinds of connections are easy to make, but are very short on security, since there is no authentication. However, it is a good start for making sure you can mount shares. If you choose to do this, set the `public=yes` option in the configuration for the share.

Let's assume you have this working (since it's not that hard to do). Let's go into connecting to a share. To do this, you have to understand how SMB transfers passwords.

There are three methods of authenticating a user to access a share. First is *user*, where a username and password are authenticated against `/etc/passwd`. This method of connection requires that the username under Linux and the SMB client match. When a user logs into Window 98, the username and password given at the login screen are sent to Samba.

The second method is to forward authentication requests to another server. This is insecure, but allows Linux to handle encrypted passwords, such as those from NT 4 running Service Pack 3 and above. This is called *server* authentication, and you have to trust the machine to which you're forwarding requests.

The third method of authentication is called *share* and does not require that the usernames under Linux and the SMB client match. When a connection is made to a share, many SMB clients (like Windows 98 or NT) ask for a password each time the share is connected.

SMB allows for both encrypted and unencrypted passwords. The good news is that encrypted passwords increase security. The bad news is that passwords are encrypted with a one-way hash. Passwords in `/etc/passwd` and the Samba password file (`smbpasswd`) don't mix all that easily. NT 4 Service Pack 3 and above send encrypted passwords by default, and the only way to change this is to go into the Registry and change it. In our opinion, there are two ways to handle this. If you have an existing NT PDC (Primary Domain Controller), set the Linux box to forward passwords to the PDC. You can do this by setting the *password server* to point to the PDC and `security=user` (both these settings are under [Global]). The other option (if you don't have a PDC) is to set up the Linux box to handle encrypted passwords. Read the `/usr/doc/samba*/ENCRYPTION.txt` file to go over what you need to do to handle encrypted passwords.

8.3   Linux SMB Connections

So now that you have the Windows machines talking to the Linux box via Samba, how do you get access to SMB shares from Linux? Easy: by using the client side of Samba and other SMB utilities for Linux.

smbfs

Linux has a Virtual File System (VFS) that provides a generic interface for mounting filesystems. One advantage of this is that it provides for mounting an SMB share like NFS or local mounting. However, instead of using `mount`, we use the `smbmount` program, which is part of the `smbfs` RPM, to mount SMB shares. The `umount` program can be used to unmount mounted shares.

Operation of `smbmount` is a bit more complicated than `mount`, but you'll get used to it after a while:

```
smbmount service mount-point [options]
```

where `service` is the Netbios name of the SMB share you want, replacing a \ character with /. A sample service is `//nebula/users` or `//auratek/market`. The `mount-point` is the local mount point in the Linux file hierarchy.

Since you have to use `smbmount` as root, and you probably don't have a root user on your NT server, you'll need to make use of the options. The two we run into most are `-U` for what user to authenticate as, and `-c` to list a Netbios name for your client machine, otherwise the FQDN is sent. Since `markk.wayga.net` isn't quite a valid Netbios name, adding `-c wayga` tells the server the client's name is just `wayga`. If the Netbios name for the client can be resolved to a hostname, you'll get asked for a password for the given username. If you want to skip this step, add `-P passwd`, replacing `passwd` with your password on the SMB server.

There are two big drawbacks to using `smbmount`. Since SMB doesn't transmit UID or GID information per file, you won't get any of that information in directory listings. And, due to the nature of NFS and SMB, you won't be able to mount an SMB share and then export it via NFS. Keep these in mind, and you'll be set.

smbclient

The `smbclient` program is part of the Samba distribution and provides an FTP-style interface to an SMB server. This is really written for use by operating systems other than Linux, or for quickly downloading a file. Since Linux already has `smbfs`, this program can be used in areas where multiple people may have access to a single machine. Operation of `smbclient` is a bit different from `smbmount`:

```
smbclient service options
```

where *service* is the Netbios name of the SMB server and its share name. Unlike `smbmount`, `service` is listed as `\\nebula\users` or `\\auratek\market`. Since the `\` is an escape character under many shells, you may need to escape it and make something like `\\\\nebula\\users` or `\\nebula\users`. Check out how your shell handles this character.

Options include `-L`, which lists shares available on a machine. The `-M` option sends text messages (remember `winchat`?). `-U user` specifies a user to connect as. If you include a percent sign (%) followed by a password, it will authenticate the user with the password, and you won't get prompted for a password.

Once connected, the commands are mostly the same as FTP. Commands like `get`, `put`, `ls`, `cd`, and `del` (even `prom`) all work the same as in FTP. Here's a description of some of the lesser known commands:

- `mget` and `mput` – Gets or puts multiple files at once.
- `prom` – Toggles prompt mode when using `mget` or `mput`.
- `lcd` – Changes directory on the client side.
- `!` or `!command` – Starts a shell or runs the given command.

8.4   SWAT (Samba Web Administration Tool)

Also part of the Samba suite is the SWAT online utility (Figure 8-2). A remote administrator with a Web browser can administer Samba configuration remotely, adding and removing shares, getting online help for configuration, and other information about the status of `smb` and `nmb`.

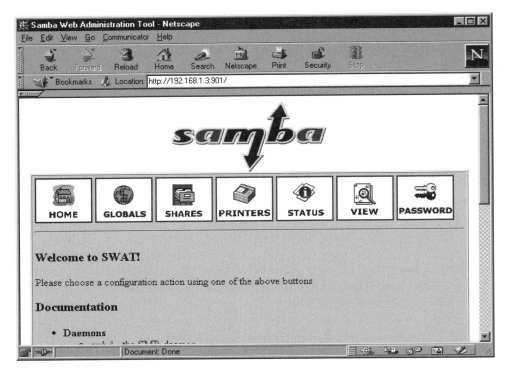

Figure 8–2   SWAT

In order to use SWAT on a machine, you must first activate it. SWAT is started from the Internet meta-daemon (`inetd`) and is disabled by default under Red Hat 6.0. You must first uncomment the line starting with `swat`, which is the last line in the `/etc/inetd.conf` file. You must tell `inetd` to reload its database, and you can do this with `/etc/rc.d/init.d/inet restart`. You can then connect to the machine at port 901, giving a URL of `http://localhost:901/` to connect. You must give the root user and password (this causes obvious security issues), but upon verification, you get access to the contents of `/etc/smb.conf`. Note that if you start making major changes to the `smb.conf` file by hand, SWAT may overwrite some of them or get confused. Be sure to back up your existing configuration before continuing.

As you can see on the screen, you are able to configure the `Global`, `Printer`, and `Share` options. `Home` returns you to the previous screen, and `Status` shows the existing status of `smb`, `nmb`, and connections from remote locations. The `View` button shows the raw `smb.conf` after being rewritten by SWAT, and the `Password` section allows you to change passwords for users remotely. Note that it defaults to changing the root password, so use this option with care.

Globals

These options provide a base that affects all shares, including workgroup configuration, logging, tuning, browsing, and WINS configuration (Figure 8-3).

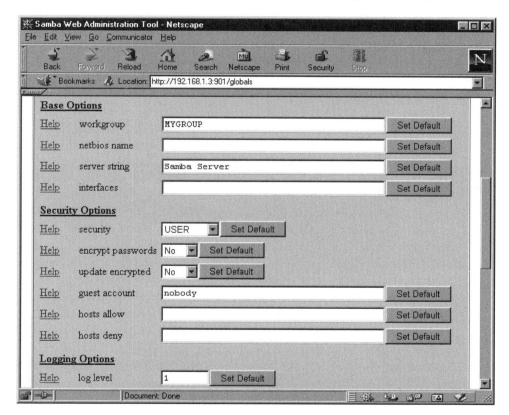

Figure 8–3 Global Options in SWAT

Most of the options have already been explained, but we'll go over them again...just in case. The workgroup is the SMB workgroup to join. Set this to the same as your clients, so everyone can browse your Samba server easily.

Base Options

The `netbios name` should be used if you want to have a shorter name that appears as the Netbios name. You probably won't need to set this, but it can be done if your Netbios name gets set to be your FQDN (see the section on `smb-mount` for more on this). The `server string` sets the comment as it appears in a browse list. By default, it sets to `Samba server`, but you can change this to suit your needs. The `interfaces` field is used if your Samba server acts as a router or has multiple Ethernet interfaces on it. You can specify an IP network address and netmask as either 192.168.1.0/24, known as a bitlength since we're masking the first 24 out of 32 bits, or 192.168.1.0/255.255.255.0, known as a bitmask. Put a space between the two entries here.

Security Options

Here you list the kind of security you want to have. The first security option we described under "Password Authentication" above. If you have chosen to use encrypted passwords on your machine (after reading `/usr/doc/samba-2.0.3/docs/textdocs/ENCRYPTION.txt`), set `encrypt passwords` to `Yes`. The `update encrypted` setting is used to assist in building an encrypted password database. As users log in, their password is encrypted using the SMB hash, and then it is stored. Once all accounts have been encrypted in this format, you can turn the `update encrypted` off. The `guest account` is the account to be used when no authentication is provided. Some shares have no passwords required to access them. Even in these cases, some valid Linux user must access the file on the Samba side. In this case, that user is "guest".

The `hosts deny` sets up a list of hosts (space-separated) to be denied access to the server. They can be either IP addresses or FQDNs, meaning an entry could have `192.168.1` or `markk.wayga.net` in it. In the first case, you would block off the entire 192.168.1.0 network, and in the second, you would block off access to a single machine. The `hosts allow` sets up hosts to be allowed access to the server. In the event of a conflict between a deny entry and an allow entry, the allow entry wins out. Going back to the example, the `hosts allow` could have `192.168.1.5`. You would then block the entire 192.168.1.0 network, except for 192.168.1.5, which could access the server.

Logging Options

As the log level increases, more data is captured to the log file. Setting a `log level` value of 0 indicates that no logging is to be done. The logs are kept per machine, and are by default stored in `/var/log/samba`. If you have a host called "`saturn`" that uses Samba, the log file for Samba's interaction with `saturn` is kept in `/var/log/samba/log.saturn`. To keep log files from getting too large, there is a default limit of 50KB per log file. If the log file gets bigger than that, it gets backed up as an `.old` file and a new log file is created. A log file of 0 means that there is no upper limit on log file size.

Tuning and Printing

Here you can enter OS-specific tuning options, mostly related to the TCP/IP stack. You will probably not need to change from the default of `TCP_NODELAY`, which is said to be one of the biggest boosts in performance for sending data to a Windows client. You can check `/usr/doc/samba-2.0.3/docs/textdocs/Speed.txt` for more information on tuning Samba for high-performance environments.

The `printcap name` contains the location of the `printcap` file. There should be no need to change it from the default of `/etc/printcap`.

Browse and WINS Options

These two sections are somewhat related, so we'll cover them both here. When an SMB network is set up on a local network, each of the machines in that network sees the others and has an election to see who will handle browse requests from clients. That is, when you start up the `Network Neighborhood`, where do you get the information? In an NT-only environment, this would be your PDC. In a Samba-only environment, this would be `nmb` (the Netbios name daemon). In a mixed environment, it depends on the settings you have in these sections.

The `os level` is a number that is really a bias in the election on the local network, and can be between 0 and 255. To give you a number to pick from, Windows 95 and 98 clients have an `os level` of `2`, and an NT server has a level of `32`. Anything higher than this will win a local election, except against other Samba servers.

If the `preferred master` is set, Samba will force an election on startup, and give itself a slight advantage in the election process. If `local master` is set, then Samba will participate in elections, with the `os level` specified earlier. The `domain master` option selects whether or not Samba will try to allocate a special Netbios name to collect workgroup information across subnets. If you have a PDC, you should set this to No, as the PDC will automatically try to allocate this special name.

WINS is the Windows Internet Name Service. It is essentially a Netbios-to-DNS conversion, so it helps if all the machines on your network have the same Netbios name as DNS. The nmb program can act as a WINS server for your local subnet. However, there can be only one WINS server per subnet. More than one will cause some problems on your network.

Shares

The shares section provides configuration of the Samba shares (Figure 8-4). The default share available for configuration is the special Homes section. Entering a new share next to Create Share and clicking the Create Share button can create new shares. Once created, a share can be selected from the Choose Share list. Clicking Delete Share will remove the share.

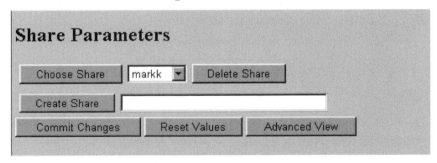

Figure 8–4   Choosing, creating and deleting shares

Once you have a share selected, you can start to change the configuration from the defaults to what you want (Figure 8-5). The defaults are: directory is /tmp, no comment to appear in the share listing, read-only access, and guest (non-authenticated user) is denied access to the share. In addition, the share is available (authenticated users can access it) and the share will show up in browse lists.

You'll want to change these settings based on what you want your share to do. Let's say your Linux machine is a CD-ROM server to other users on the network, and the CD-ROM is mounted on /mnt/cdrom. Change the Comment to read CD-ROM service and change directory to /mnt/cdrom. Guest access depends on how secure your network is and how secure you want the data on the CD-ROM to be. If you care who accesses this share, leave the guest user as No; if it doesn't matter, set the option to Yes. Since the CD-ROM is read only to begin with, leave the read only option as is. The hosts allow and hosts deny entries are tab-, colon-, or space-separated lists of hosts to allow or deny to this share, respectively. In the case of a conflict between an allow and deny entry, the allow entry will win out. This is the same option as in the `Global` section, but it only applies to this share. As for the last two options, `browsable` means that the share shows up in browse lists of the machine. With this turned off, a user would have to manually specify the share to connect either using the `net use` command from Windows or `smbmount` on UNIX. The last option, `available`, indicates if a share is to be activated by Samba. If `no`, then the share is not available at all. If `yes`, the share is available to users to whom we allow access. Since we want other users to use this share, we set this to Yes.

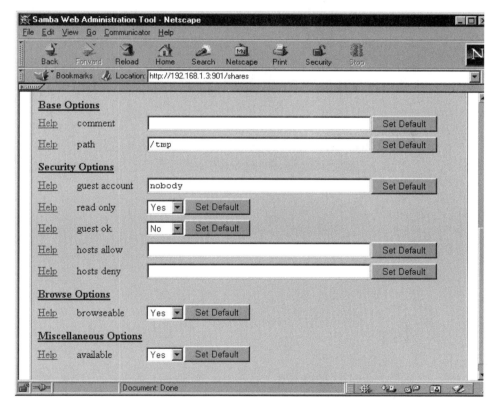

Figure 8–5 Share options

8.5 Installing Linux Printers on Windows

Samba knows enough (via the `printing = bsd` and `printcap name = /etc/printcap lines`) to load in all the printers available in `/etc/printcap` and make them available to SMB clients. The Linux side does not require any changes, but you may want to make sure that the `/etc/printcap` file is set successfully and you can print. Since it uses LPD, Samba will also deal with any remote printers as well. Any printer you can get to from Linux will be available from Samba (see Figure 8–6).

The Windows side may be a bit more complicated. More sophisticated print drivers that demand to talk directly to the printer may cause you some problems. Our advice is to get a printer that supports either PCL or Post-Script. This way, you can at least send data to the printer. Be aware that more printers coming out these days may be using the "Windows Printing System," which will work only with Windows. If you have a printer that accepts PCL or PostScript, you can install generic drivers in Windows to print to the Samba printers. We have had some success with using an Apple LaserWriter as a PostScript printer, and an HP LaserJet 4 as a PCL printer.[3]

We go more into using an SMB server as a print server in the previous chapter on printing.

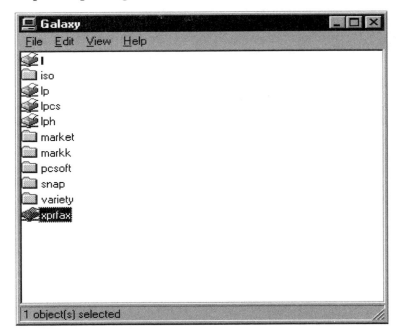

Figure 8–6   Printers available from Samba

---

[3]Your experience may vary. Try other print drivers under Windows and see how well they work.

Once the printers and shares are configured, you can let your users loose. Be sure to keep an eye on the log files to monitor any problems if they show up.

8.6   Summary

- Samba is an easy way to share drive space and printers with Windows 98 and NT machines.

- SWAT allows you to easily administer your Samba configuration.

Email 9

Sendmail, mailing lists, email clients, and POP/IMAP (remote connections)

This chapter shows you how to set up sendmail, set up simple mailing lists for customers, clients, or groups of people, review some of the email clients available, and set up remote connections using the POP (Post Office Protocol) and IMAP (Internet Message Access Protocol) mail standards.

Email (electronic mail) was one of the first methods for communicating over what is now the Internet. Email allowed short messages to route across various machines. In the early days (1987), you often had to manually specify all the machines (or hops) an email message would have to route through to get to the end host. With TCP/IP as the communication method, things are a bit smarter in that you don't need to know how to get to the end host—as long as some machine along the way knows how to route the email for you. The technical name for the email that you get on the Internet is known as Simple Mail Transfer Protocol (SMTP). There are a few other protocols that work with SMTP, such as POP and IMAP, but we'll get to those later. You can find more information about SMTP in RFC 821.

The primary program that is the Mail Transport Agent (or MTA) is send-mail. There are others available, but sendmail is pretty much the standard for most Linux installations. You may have seen that really thick book with a bat on it that gets you into the nitty-gritty of sendmail. It gets really nitty-gritty.[1]

The upshot of all this is that you don't always need sendmail to set up a simple email server. The one thing you should know about sendmail is this: Always be sure you have the latest version. Each version of sendmail, while patching various bugs, seems to have a security problem with it. Sometimes it seems like you need to upgrade your sendmail software more often than the Linux kernel.

Enough of that. Let's get to the typical sendmail options you'll see on start-up. Most Linux installations have sendmail kick in on bootup. Red Hat (being SYSV-ish) has an /etc/rc.d/init.d/sendmail.init script that runs on star-tup. An installation could start the actual command like this:

```
echo -n "Starting sendmail: "
daemon sendmail -bd -q1h
echo
touch /var/lock/subsys/sendmail
```

As you can see, the sendmail program starts with the -bd and -q1h options. The -bd signifies that sendmail should start up as a daemon and run in the background, waiting for connections, much the same way that a Web server is always running, waiting for a connection. The -q1h means that sendmail should go through its queue at least once an hour and try to send any data in its queue.

There are a number of reasons why an email message would be held in a queue. For example:

- You have a dialup-only connection to the Internet, and you send a note while you're not connected.

- The remote host is not dialed in (same thing in reverse).

- The remote host is down for upgrades or it crashed.

- There is no connection to the remote host (the network is down).

In any of these cases, you'll want to make sure that your email gets through. Leaving the email in sendmail's queue allows you to do this. A machine directly connected to the Internet or on a LAN can change this to

---

[1]If you have anything to do with setting up sendmail, get this book.

ten minutes (-q10m), since you're more likely to be connected to the Internet all the time. In case you're interested in what's currently in the queue, the mailq command will list what sendmail has. The mailq program will also list the reason why an email message is stuck in the queue. If there is a lot of email in the queue, you may have a network or configuration problem.

You can verify that sendmail is running by connecting to TCP port 25.

```
[markk@wayga ~ ]# telnet localhost 25
Trying 127.0.0.1...
Connected to localhost.
Escape character is '^]'.
220 wayga.net ESMTP Sendmail 8.7.6/8.7.3; Fri, 18 Apr 1997 00:26:18 -
  0400
```

As you can see, the connection works, and there is a bit of information about the host we connected to: status number, hostname, type of SMTP (Extended SMTP), the Sendmail program (instead of qmail or the like) version 8.7.6, and the current time and date that the computer thinks it is.

The configuration options for sendmail are typically located in /etc/send-mail.cf. Examine the file if you like, but don't change anything unless you know what you're doing! Small changes can render your email system useless. As always, back up files that you want to edit, just in case.

A few options you may want to note:

- OA—Can set another file that contains aliases. We'll get into this with majordomo.

- Mlocal—Specifies what program will act as the Mail Delivery Agent (MDA). This can be something like /bin/mail or /usr/bin/procmail (we'll get to this later, too!).

- DS—Contains a pointer to a "smart" relay host. If you have a very slow connection to the Internet or don't have DNS set up, you can specify another machine to accept all your email and deliver it for you. For dial-up links, you only have to send the email once, and a machine that is permanently connected to the Internet can hold it in its queue.

- Cw—This option works if you have one Internet host that has multiple names (for example, wayga.net and ratatosk.org). This entry will allow you to specify which hosts you will receive email as.

9.1   Using m4 Files

One option that many versions of sendmail has is the option to have your
`sendmail.cf` file automatically generated. This will allow you to keep a small
file that has most of the options you wish to use. When upgrading sendmail,
you need to recompile only `sendmail.cf` to have the latest updates to that
file. The m4 macro language is excellent for doing this, and sources for various types of `sendmail.cf` files are included.

If you decide to use the m4 files, be sure to download the source code for
sendmail, as the Red Hat distribution does not include m4 files by default.
The m4 processor is installed by default, however, and is located in `/usr/bin`.

9.2   You Have Mail!

Once email has arrived at your system, there are a few things that happen to
it before you actually get alerted to new email. First, sendmail checks to see
if you have a `.forward` file in your home directory. If so, then sendmail will
forward the email to whatever address is specified in the `.forward` file. If
you're using `procmail` and you have a `.procmailrc` file, sendmail will run
`procmail` and follow the rules in it. After that, sendmail appends the email to
a file called `/var/spool/mail/<USER>`, where `<USER>` is the username. This
file does not need to be created when making a new user; sendmail will take
care of that the first time the user gets an email message.

Creating mail aliases allows incoming mail to get routed to a different user
or program, even if there is no user account with that name on the system.
This will have a larger impact once we get to managing mailing lists. For now,
you may want to examine the `/etc/aliases` file to see what aliases are currently defined. This is a method of having a mail alias that really sends the
mail to someone else, or a group of people. For example, a common `/etc/`
`aliases` file may contain the following:

```
MAILER-DAEMON:  postmaster
postmaster: root

# General redirections for pseudo accounts.
bin:        root
daemon:     root
games:      root
nobody:     root
uucp:       root
```

```
# Well-known aliases.
manager:    root
operator:   root

# Person who should get root's mail
root:       mark
mfk:        mark
bren:       brenda
bdk:        brenda
```

You can see that there are a number of aliases listed, most of them pointing to `root`. In some cases (`bin` and `nobody`), the accounts exist, but no one should ever log into those accounts. In this case, any email that gets sent to `bin` or `daemon` merely gets forwarded to `root`. Also, note that `postmaster` is set to `root`; in most situations, the person who administers the mail also administers the rest of the system. The MAILER-DAEMON is mostly for mail errors. These errors get sent to `root` as well.

Later on, you see a few user aliases. These aliases are set up so that anyone sending email to `mfk@wayga.net` will go automatically into the `mark` account. There is no `mfk` account, but people can send email to that address. The same is true of anyone sending email to `bren@wayga.net` or `bdk@wayga.net`. A small business could have email aliases of `mark.komarinski`, `mfk`, `m.komarinski`, `markk`, `mark.k`, and any other unique permutation of a name in case outside customers forget an email address. It is something that's often overlooked, but it is very important to keep in touch with customers.

Once the mail is delivered to the correct account, a process called `comsat` runs; `comsat` is what actually tells the shell that you have new mail. Once the shell gets that information, it may notify you of it. The `biff`[2] program tells you if you'll receive notification, and it also lets you turn it on or off. The `y` option to `biff` will turn mail prompting on, and `n` will turn it off. There are also X versions of `biff` to give you graphical notification that email has arrived.

Now that you've received an email message, how are you going to read it? This is the job of the MUA, or Mail User Agent. This is the only area the end-user is going to interact with directly. There are dozens of programs available from the low-feature (mail) to the high-feature, full-screen (elm, pine, mutt) to the graphical (Netscape).

What is used for mail reading is pretty much up to the user. For example, many people prefer pine over elm. If you plan on having many users, it's best

---

[2]Why name the command `biff`? Turns out that's the name of the author's dog. Under UNIX, if you write it, you name it.

to install a few MUAs aside from `/bin/mail`. Red Hat's installation provides a number of different MUAs to suit everyones' needs. Each MUA has advantages.

9.3 MIME

When SMTP was first designed, it would handle only 7-bit (plain ASCII) data. Hence the "Simple" in the protocol name. With things like JPEG images, sound files, application data, and compressed files to be sent through email, there had to be some way of sending binary (8-bit) data through a 7-bit stream. The first method of handling this was via the `uuencode` program. This program would turn two bytes of 8-bit data into three bytes of 7-bit data. The file size was two-thirds larger, but it would now squeeze through the 7-bit path that SMTP provided. Another problem in addition to the file size was that the remote side had to decode the data (`uudecode`). This turned into a tedious procedure, the sender encoding the data and manually including it in a mail file and the receiver trying to strip out all the mail headers, text, and signatures to get to the `uuencode` file and then decode it.

In the early 1990s, the Multipurpose Internet Mail Extension (MIME) was developed to do this, and it is used today on the Web for determining file types. MIME encoded each data type such that any MIME-capable mail reader would understand what kind of data was in the message. Once a file type was detected, each individual user could have a file (`.mailcap`) that would list what file types you knew about, and what application to run once you found that file type. For example, if a JPEG image were sent, the receiving side might start up the `xv` program and display the image in an X window. Another user might have it set up so the image was converted into PostScript and sent directly to the printer.[3] Most mailers today have the ability to handle MIME mail, and there should be little to no interaction that you as an administrator have to worry about.

9.4 The .forward File

When mail comes in, the `.forward` file is checked. If it exists, the email is sent to the address listed in the file. This is helpful if you have multiple

---

[3]This is a good example of "the UNIX way"—there's more than one way to do anything.

accounts on the Internet and want all the email to come to one location. An example of `.forward` shows another feature of the file—instead of an email address, you can have a command. The `vacation` program, which isn't available in Red Hat (but is on the CD-ROM), allows you to put a program in the `.forward` file. Each time email comes in, the program is run. The `vacation` program stores the email and then sends a custom message back to the email sender, notifying them that you're on vacation (or out of town, out of the office, out of your mind, etc.). The sender then knows that the email got through.

Procmail

If `procmail` is installed as the Mail Delivery Agent (MDA) on your system (check the `Mlocal` entry in your `sendmail.cf` to find out), you can immediately use it to filter all your incoming mail. If not, you can put a reference to `procmail` in your `.forward` to run each time new mail arrives. Procmail is used to process mail as it comes in. This can include putting all email from the "Plan9 MUSH Advisory Committee" in one mailbox separate from everything else, or filtering all that annoying email you get from `billg@microsoft.com` by sending it to `/dev/null`.[4]

If `procmail` is set up to be the default local mail handler, setting `procmail` up for use is easy. Create a `.procmailrc` file and start adding rules for `procmail` to filter. If `procmail` is not your local mail handler, you have three options:

1. Make `procmail` the local mail handler (the man page has the suggested changes you can make to the `/etc/sendmail.cf file`). If you're using m4 configuration files, add `FEATURE(local_procmail)` to your file.

2. Run `procmail` periodically, or use `cron` to filter out an existing mailbox. This still allows you to use `.forward` (in the event of a vacation and the like), but the mail is not always sorted and you will have to wait.

3. Put a reference to `procmail` in your `.forward` file. Note that this won't let you forward all that easily. In the `.forward` file, put a line in that looks like the following:

---

[4]Anything sent to `/dev/null` is immediately discarded. This is called the "bit bucket." Thanks to the fact that Linux is a 32-bit OS, its bit bucket is one of the fastest around.

```
"|IFS=' '&&exec /usr/local/bin/procmail -f-||exit 75
  #YOUR_USERNAME"
```

As you can guess, option 1 is the best, as it requires the least amount of effort on everyone's part.[5] Here's a copy of a sample .procmailrc file:

```
PATH=/bin:/usr/bin:/usr/bin
MAILDIR=$HOME/Mail        #you'd better make sure it exists
DEFAULT=$MAILDIR/mbox     #completely optional
LOGFILE=$MAILDIR/from     #recommended

:0:
* ^From.*mark
from_me

:0
* ^Subject:.*Flame
/dev/null
```

There are three sections to matching a line and performing some action on it, also called a recipe. A recipe starts with a line that has at least :0. After the :0, you can include some flags (for example, H will scan only the headers). Pattern matching is done for any lines that start with an asterisk (*). The rest of the line is sent to egrep[6] literally. If all of the lines match (the lines are ANDed together), then the appropriate action is taken. If not, it moves on to the next recipe.

There can be only one action line, and this is the one that does not start with an * or :. An action starting with ! will forward the program to the specified user. An action starting with | will start a shell and pipe the email to that program for processing. Anything else will be assumed to be a filename to append (or create if it doesn't already exist).

These two examples show that all mail that has a From line and ends in mark (which will be any email sent by me) will be put in the ~/Mail/from_me mailbox. The second example shows that all email that starts with the word "Subject" and ends in "Flame" will be sent to /dev/null (the bit bucket).

The thing to know if you just want to delete mail out-of-hand is that you have to be absolutely sure that your logic is correct. For example, if you delete all mail that has the word "Flame" in it, then you could potentially lose

---

[5]Except the system administrator, who has to install the software and make sure that sendmail isn't busted. Oh wait. That's you. Scratch that.

[6]egrep = extended grep, and the syntax is not exactly the same as with plain grep.

messages with a subject such as "Flame broiled burgers free until 10 AM." OK, so it's a poor example. You may want to store mail you want to delete for a while and then examine it just to be sure you don't lose anything important.

9.5 Mailing Lists

Mailing lists allow larger groups of people to communicate via email. In many cases, it is preferable to using USENET since mailing lists do not need approval from anyone other than the administrator to be created.

Anyone with a machine connected to the Internet can create a mailing list on any subject. Getting members to subscribe to it is a different issue, however.

Mailing lists can control who subscribes. The mailing list administrator can make it so anyone can subscribe, or he/she can make it so that the administrator is the only one who can add new members to the mailing list. The administrator can also remove offending members if a problem arises.

Mailing lists can control content. This isn't as bad as it sounds, since it is the alternative to the anarchy that is USENET. The administrator can set the list up to be open and provide a healthy discussion area (such as for developers working on a piece of software). Alternatively, the list can be set up such that the administrator has to approve each piece of email that gets sent to the list, like moderated USENET groups. Moderated lists are good for news releases, humor lists, or any other list where the amount of discussion is low.

Majordomo

The best mailing list program in use has to be majordomo. Majordomo provides all the features listed above, plus adds a few other features, such as sending out regular digests, or archiving for future use. We'll get back to these later on.

The first thing that needs to be set up is majordomo itself, if it's not already installed. The source for it is located on the CD-ROM. You need to have Perl 5 installed on the system (as well as GCC, of course) to use it. First, create a majordomo user. Given the eight-character limitations of Linux's usernames, the username will have to be shortened to `majordom`. Thanks to `/etc/aliases`, no one ever has to know this. You should also create a home directory for the `majordom` user. This can be `/home/majordom` if you like, or `/usr/local/majordom` if you prefer, or anywhere you have space.

Su to majordom,[7] copy the `majordom1.94.1.tar.gz` file to the home directory, and uncompress/untar the file. Make any kinds of modifications to the `majordomo.cf` file; then just use the `make` command to create it. Once installed (which should be in the majordomo home directory), you need to make only one change to the `/etc/sendmail.cf` file. You should already have one OA (or O alias file) entry listed. Underneath that, put in the following:[8]

```
OA/home/majordomo/majordomo.aliases
```

This sets up an additional file to handle aliases. It also makes it easier for the majordomo administrator to add new mailing lists, and that person does not need root access to modify the lists.

Now, on to creating the lists themselves. Let's create a (fictional) list called `gastro`. It will be an open list for sharing recipes, so anyone can join, and anyone can post a note to the group.

In the `~majordom/majordomo.aliases` file (we'll call it the alias file from now on, in case you chose to use `/etc/aliases` instead), add the following:

```
gastro:                     "|/home/majordom/wrapper resend -l gastro
   gastro-list"
gastro-list:                :include:/home/majordom/lists/gastro
owner-gastro:               mark
gastro-owner:               mark
gastro-request:             "|/home/majordom/wrapper
   majordomo -l gastro"
gastro-approval:            mark
```

This sets up the basics. The list itself will be `gastro@host`, the owner will be `mark`, and any requests to join the list will be sent to `majordomo` as well. Normally, users would send email to `majordomo@host` to subscribe, but different mailing list software works in different ways.

Once the aliases are set up, you can initialize the lists using:

```
echo "config gastro gastro.admin" | mail majordomo
```

and the lists will have some default configurations put in. If you choose to change the defaults (and you should!), edit the `~majordom/lists/gastro.config` file. This has all the configuration settings for the particular list.

---

[7]You set up a password for the `majordom` user, right??

[8]Note that this is a bit of a security risk, as root should really be the only person who can create new aliases. If you want, leave this statement out and use `/etc/aliases` instead of the `majordomo.aliases` file.

Now that your mailing list is set up, you should be able to email to the list by just sending mail to `gastro@host`, and the email will be sent to all the subscribers of the `gastro` list. There are a number of extra features that majordomo has, and you should check out the Web site for more information and to get the latest updates.

9.6 Qmail: An Alternative to Sendmail

One of the better known replacements for sendmail is called qmail. There are two reasons for its popularity: ease of use and security. This doesn't mean that qmail is best for everyone, since there are a number of changes that your system has to go through to use qmail. It's also not perfect in a large installation (yet) because of some of the ways that sendmail and qmail differ. The configuration for qmail is much simpler than sendmail, but it doesn't offer the "Swiss army knife" of Mail Transport Agents (MTAs) that many expect to see.

Here's a few of the ways in which qmail and sendmail differ in methodology:

- *Mail file location*—Sendmail prefers to use `/usr/spool/mail/user` as a location for incoming mail. Qmail prefers to use `~user/Mailbox` as a location for storing mail files. This is for two reasons. First, putting the mail in the user's home directory provides for better quota checking and prevents overfilling a central location. Second, there are fewer security problems since there isn't a central location to store files.

- *Permissions*—Sendmail runs almost always as root, or with root privileges, to write files and so forth. Qmail runs as root only when necessary and otherwise runs as a qmail user, which has no special permissions.

- *Mailing list integration*—Sendmail has external programs to create and it administers mailing lists (majordomo and listproc). Qmail supports a method where individual users can have their own mailing lists and administer them themselves with no extra accounts or permissions.

- *Size*—Sendmail is a monolithic MTA, where everything is done in the program itself. Qmail has a number of smaller programs to handle each aspect of mail receipt, delivery, sending, and so forth.

Installing Qmail

You can download qmail in either RPM format or source code (also called a tarball, due to the fact it's in tar format). Both files can be found at `http://`

www.qmail.org/. If you download in RPM format, be sure to remove the sendmail RPM from your system to avoid conflicts. The RPM is in source format, but handles many of the functions of building and installing qmail, and adding the users and setting up initialization scripts for use with Red Hat.

After you get the qmail-1.03.tar.gz file, untar and uncompress the file. This will create a qmail-1.03 directory with the source code in it. Review the INSTALL file so you know what the full install procedure is. This procedure allows you to build and install qmail without affecting the sendmail you probably already have installed until you're satisfied that qmail is working correctly. Qmail resides in the /var/qmail directory, so you'll need to create that directory and remember that so you can monitor that directory. Next, you'll need to create users for qmail to use. Since security is a big component of qmail, these new users will need to be created to separate qmail from the root user and regular users.

Now for the simple part. Enter make to build qmail. The compile should take a few minutes to complete, and you'll be ready for the installation and testing. The biggest problem you may run across is the fact that your home directory and .qmail files cannot be group- or world-writable. This will show up in the logs as something like:

```
Feb  8 16:50:00 wayga qmail: 886974600.032889 delivery 10:
  deferral: Uh-oh:_.qmail_file_is_writable._(#4.7.0)/
```

In this event, just find the .qmail file it's referring to and change the permissions. You'll also want to check for other copies of the sendmail program floating around the filesystem (like in /usr/sbin/, for example), and change those to use qmail. Also while testing, remember that mail is no longer being delivered to /usr/spool/mail/user, but to ~user/Mailbox.

Once the testing and configuration are done (the INSTALL file is pretty thorough on this), you can then tell your users about the changes and start using qmail.

A few notes you should know of if you're considering changing MTAs:

- If you're upgrading or changing software to something you're not used to, always use a staging machine. There are instructions in the FAQ file on how to upgrade slowly from sendmail to qmail with a minimum of fuss and trouble. This upgrade path allows you to use both qmail and sendmail until you get the bugs worked out and move to qmail completely.

- You may not want to put qmail on a connection that goes down frequently. One of the features of qmail is that it continually tries to deliver mail. If the Internet link goes down often, you could be in a situation where qmail is trying to deliver lots of mail at the same time. If you have a dialup link, it might be worth it to check out the serialmail program, which is designed to send out email on demand (i.e., when the link is up).

- In addition to the `/usr/spool/mail` directory changing, the `.forward` file is ignored in favor of the `.qmail` file. The `.qmail` file has a number of features that can't be put in `.forward`, but programs that operate on `.forward` won't work anymore.

Once qmail is configured and working properly, you'll need to make sure that you can deliver mail to each user (check their mail file and the `syslog` output in `/var/log` to make sure mail is being delivered properly).

There are a few things that you will notice once qmail is installed. For the benefit of your users, you should warn them ahead of time.

- As previously mentioned, mail now gets stored in `~user/Mailbox` instead of `/usr/spool/mail/user`. You'll need to make sure that the `MAIL` environment variable is changed (see `/etc/profile`). There are two problems with the `/usr/spool/mail` approach to delivering mail. First, it's a security risk. Second, the way sendmail does local mail delivery is prone to losing mail if the mail directory is mounted via NFS or if the server goes down while writing email. The "Mailbox" format in qmail makes sure the email is written to the disk before it reports success back to the main qmail program. If there is a locking problem or the machine goes down while a message is being delivered, it will get delivered when the machine restarts or the lock goes away.

- Qmail does not look in the `.forward` file anymore for forwarding email to other users. The replacement file, `.qmail`, handles this. The nice thing about this is it allows you as a user to create your own simple mailing lists. For example, if you wanted to create a simple mailing list related to this book, you could create a `.qmail-linux` file in your home directory. That file then would get a list of the people you wanted to be on the list. Once this was done, any email sent to your address would get sent to the entire list. You could even have a `.qmail-default` to catch all `enry-*` email that came in. Note that this isn't a very full-featured mailing list system as it doesn't handle automatic subscribes or unsubscribes. This is where ezmlm comes in (see next section).

- Qmail also does not use `/etc/aliases` at all. There is a global way of setting up email aliases, which is a bit easier to use. The alias user is used by qmail to handle addresses that don't exist. For example, you could have `~alias/.qmail-markk` contain the line:

```
enry@wayga.net
```

to forward email that comes in for `markk@wayga.net` to `enry@wayga.net`. A common use of this is setting up postmaster, abuse, or root aliases.

• The `root` user does not receive email. Due to the number of security problems this could cause, it was determined that `root` should be aliased to someone else (like the actual administrator of the machine). This makes cracking a root account much harder.

Ezmlm

The ezmlm package allows for easy mailing list setup. It has all the functionality commonly needed in mailing list applications: automatic subscribe/unsubscribe, moderated lists, and digest creation (handled by `ezmlm-idx`). Unlike many other mailing list applications, ezmlm is command-based—there should be no need for the mailing list administrator to edit files. Another feature of ezmlm (and qmail) is that mailing list creation and administration do not require access to the root account.

By default, many of the ezmlm programs get installed in `/usr/local/bin/ezmlm`. The install instructions are in the INSTALL file (located in the `ezmlm-0.53` directory) and are straightforward. Once installed and tested, users can create their own mailing lists with the following commands:

```
ezmlm-make ~/list ~/.qmail-list user-list host
```

This creates the mailing list. The mailing list itself is contained in `~/list`. This mailing list is not moderated in that anyone can subscribe and unsubscribe. If you want a private mailing list where only the moderator can add and remove members, you can add the `-P` option. Once the mailing list is created, you can just remove `~/list/public` to create a moderated list or create the file to create a public list:

```
ezmlm-sub ~/list email
```

This subscribes `email` to `list`. The new member is subscribed to the list.

```
ezmlm-unsub ~/list email
```

This unsubscribes `email` from `list`.

```
ezmlm-list ~/list
```

This lists the members of `list`.

Once a list is created, the `user-list-subscribe` and `user-list-unsub-scribe` email addresses are created for users to subscribe and unsubscribe. If the mailing list is moderated, these mail addresses will not work and the moderator will have to manually add new members. An extension to ezmlm, `ezmlm-idx`, provides for more moderation and archiving.

Ezmlm Files

Once a mailing list is created, you'll find the following files in the directory:

`Archive/`	Contains an archive of the mailing list. Messages are numbered from 1 on. If the `archived` file exists, no messages will be archived.
`Archived`	If this file exists, ezmlm will archive messages.
`Headeradd`	Contains a list of headers that will be added to email sent by ezmlm.
`Headerremove`	Has a list of headers that will be removed from email that gets sent out by ezmlm.
`Key`	This file has some random binary data to prevent forging subscription requests.
`Num`	Contains the number of messages sent so far.
`Public`	If this exists, users can subscribe and unsubscribe without the help of a moderator. If it doesn't exist, only the moderator can add or remove users.
`Text`	Directory containing files that ezmlm will send back as administrative messages. You can change these files if you want.

9.7   Remote Email (POP and IMAP)

POP (Post Office Protocol) and IMAP (Internet Message Access Protocol) are two of the standards for receiving email from a remote machine. The best example of remote email use is in an office situation where there is a Linux server and Windows (or Mac, or other UNIX) clients also running on the network. The clients can receive their email in a number of ways (Eudora, Netscape, PC-Pine, etc.) and still have one central mail server.

Each protocol has strengths, weaknesses, and assorted Mail User Agents (MUAs) that support them. Both are available in a Red Hat install setup ready to run. Authentication of email is done by the same PAM scheme that is used to log in. One of the advantages of using POP or IMAP is that little user setup is required. You can typically install and run client software without any trouble.

POP

POP (Post Office Protocol, defined in RFCs 937 and 1225) was one of the first methods for retrieving and sending email to/from a remote machine. The protocol is rather simple. You can get, list, and delete mail. That's about it. The good thing about it, though, is that you can pick up your email at the office from home. The downside to POP is that the email on the server is often deleted once it gets sent to you.[9] So, while you can get your email from work to home, you then have to send the email back from home to work, or else you won't have any email at work. Netscape, Outlook, and most PC-based Internet email programs handle POP.

The POP server (`popper`) is included in a typical Red Hat distribution as part of the `imap-4.5` RPM. To use it, configure the client software so that the server matches the Linux box. The username and password are the same as in `/etc/passwd`. Remember that any email downloaded gets stored on the local machine, so make sure that user drives are backed up regularly. One option to look at is the `Don't delete from server` option, which might be named differently on some clients. This option leaves the email on the server after delivery. If you have two locations where you want to read your email from (work and home, for example), you can leave this option off on the

---

[9]To be fair, this is a problem with the applications that use it, not the protocol itself. POP can be set up to leave email on the server, which can fill the server up very quickly.

office email system, and turn it on at home. This way, all your email gets downloaded at work, and you can only get new email from home. IMAP is a much better solution to this problem.

IMAP

IMAP (RFC 2060) was created to handle some of the deficiencies of POP. IMAP is designed to be a client/server setup, where the server keeps the mail until the client requests that it be deleted. In POP, all the email is downloaded at once, which is a bit of a problem for large messages over slow links. IMAP allows for downloading only the body of a message when it is required, allowing you to quickly download header information and then read only the messages you want to read. Email can be stored in different files (often called folders) to allow you to organize your email easier. These folders remain on the server side and can be accessed by the client software at any time.

Another big feature of IMAP is disconnected mode, sometimes called offline mode. If the client supports it, you can have the client download one or more folders to your local machine, usually by selecting an option called `go offline`, `download folders`, or `offline mode`. You can then read, modify, delete, reply, and so on without being connected to a network. When you return to your network, you can return to online mode and synchronize the client and server. A list of clients and their support for IMAP can be found at the official IMAP home page, `http://www.imap.org`. Both Netscape Communicator and MS Outlook support IMAP and offline mode.

The IMAP server is included with Red Hat in the imap-4.5 RPM, and is configured to get files from `/var/spool/mail`. To configure it for use with qmail, you'll need to recompile the server. Client setup is about the same as for POP; set the server name and the username/password. One option that you may want to look at is the `server directory` option. This option tells the client what directory on the server contains the mail folders (not the `mbox` or new mail – that's hard-coded on the server). By default, this is the user's home directory, and if a user does not store other files in that directory, you're okay. However, if you share user home directories via Samba or NFS, you'll want to change the server directory to something like `~user/Mail`. The downside to this is that you have to set it each time you configure someone for IMAP. The benefit is that your users won't confuse their email with their regular files.

By default, `mbox` (mail that was read in and not put in another mail folder) is stored in `~user/mbox`, which is actually the same file used by the UNIX `mail` program. New mail is checked for in `/var/spool/mail`. If you need to change this, you'll have to recompile the software. The easy way to do this is to get the `.src.rpm` file from the Red Hat FTP site or source CD-ROM and compile it. You can find out more about installing and compiling source RPM files in the RPM chapter.

9.8   Summary

- Sendmail is the default way of sending email.
- You might benefit from using qmail.
- MIME allows you to email binary data from one person to another.
- POP and IMAP allow you to get your email from remote locations.

Setting Up FTP Services

10

Virtual, anonymous, and more

The File Transfer Protocol (FTP) is one of the most frequently used services available on the Internet. Setting up an anonymous FTP server is fairly straightforward. Other services, like virtual FTP hosts and FTP-only accounts, are a little more tricky.

10.1 FTP under Red Hat Linux

Along with telnet-like applications, FTP is one of the most basic TCP/IP services. Red Hat Linux comes with a clone of the standard FTP UNIX command-line FTP client, as well as the more full-featured `ncftp`. The default FTP daemon under Red Hat is `wu-ftpd`.

We will cover the setup and configuration of `wu-ftpd` for anonymous and user access, as well as the setup of virtual FTP servers. Next we'll talk about setting up these services with two other FTP daemons: ProFTPD and Bero-

FTPD. Then we will cover some of the basics of using FTP and `ncftp`.
Lastly, `tftp` (trivial FTP) will be covered briefly.

10.2 Configuring wu-ftpd

The `/etc/ftpaccess` file is the main configuration file for `wu-ftpd`. Three of
the directives warrant special attention: `class`, `autogroup`, and `guestgroup`.
The `class` directive defines classes of users, while `autogroup` combines
classes into groups. The `guestgroup` directive tells `wu-ftpd` to treat users
from the list of groups given like anonymous FTP users, but rooted within
their home directories. This means that the `bin`, `lib`, and `etc` directories
must be set up in the user's home directory as they are under `/home/ftp`.

An example `/etc/ftpaccess` file is:

```
#
# /etc/ftpaccess
#
# The class directive takes three or more arguments. The first is the
# name of the class, then the typelist (one or more of real, anonymous
# or guest separated by commas ONLY), then the list of patterns for
# matching against incoming hostnames
#
# Note that if no class matches the host, access will be denied.
#
# Define two classes. One for any users in hosts in the .edu and .us
# TLDs named 'all', a second for real users from hosts in the
# ratatosk.org domain, and a third for anonymous users from
# ratatosk.org.
#
class   all        real,guest,anonymous  *.edu *.us
class   ratatosk real                    *.ratatosk.org
class   ratatosk-anon anonymous *.ratatosk.org
#
# Lock users from the group 'ftponly' to their home directories
#
guestgroup ftponly
#
# Define the email address that will be substituted for the
# %E magic cookie. See the man page for ftpaccess(5) for information
# on the use of magic cookies
#
email @ratatosk.org
#
# Set the number of login failures (5 is the default). After 3
# login failures the connection will be closed
#
```

```
loginfailures 3
#
# Define the files to be automatically displayed and when
# logging in and changing directories
#
message /welcome.msg  login
message .message      cwd=*
#
# Notify the user of the last modified date of a file named README
# upon login, a file starting with
# README upon changing directories and a file named README.NOW
# upon changing to the /pub/incoming directory
#
readme  README  login
readme  README* cwd=*
readme  REAMDE.NOW cwd=/pub/incoming
#
# log commands of guests (as defined by guestgroup) and log
# inbound transfers of real users and outbound transfers of
# everyone
#
log commands guest
log transfers real inbound
log transfers all outbound
#
# Control which classes have access to some commands/services.
# usertypes or classes can be specified. Wildcards can be used
# for class names.
#
compress        yes             all
tar             yes             ratatosk*
chmod           no              guest,anonymous
delete          no              guest,anonymous
overwrite       no              guest,anonymous
rename          no              guest,anonymous
#
# The shutdown message. See the man page for ftpaccess(5)
# for the format of this file
#
shutdown /message_shutdown
#
# Define an IP-based virtual host.(wu-ftpd doesn't support IP-less
# virtual hosts. Set up the root, the login banner and the log file
#
virtual 10.10.10.45 root /home/ftp_vhost1
virtual 10.10.10.45 banner /etc/banners/vhost1.banner
virtual 10.10.10.45 log /var/log/ftplogs/vhost1.log
#
# deny connections from goober.edu, displaying a file containing
# a message to them.
```

```
#
deny *.goober.edu /.deny.message
#
# don't let files named passwd, group or core be retrieved
#
noretrieve passwd group core
```

As you can see, wu-ftpd is highly configurable! Support for virtual hosts is limited, though. Only the root, banner, and log files are configurable. The rest of the directives in the ftpaccess file are applied to all FTP connections.

There are a few other files you need to know about. For the most part, they control access on a per-user basis. The /etc/ftpusers file lists users, one per line, who should be denied access. To give only FTP access to a user, specify /bin/false as the user's shell. This will effectively deny shell logins, but allow FTP access. Note that /bin/false must be in /etc/shells or the user will be denied any sort of access.

10.3 Anonymous FTP

If anonymous FTP was selected when Red Hat was installed, then some of your work is already done. The anonymous FTP client account is set up as well as the directory framework under /home/ftp. If anonftp isn't installed, grab the anonftp RPM package off the distribution CD or a Red Hat FTP mirror and install it. Similarly, if wu-ftpd is absent, obtain and install its .rpm.

Setting Up Anonymous FTP

In the instructions below, /home/ftp is the home of the anonymous FTP user as specified in the /etc/passwd file.

The FTP daemon, ftpd, recognizes the anonymous user and adjusts some aspects of the account. The root directory for access is set to /home/ftp. This means that access is limited to the directories and files in /home/ftp at best. Permissions can, of course, restrict access further. Because the filesystem root is changed, several directories and files need to be set up to allow the necessary minimum level of functionality. The anonftp RPM does this.

The directory structure should be set up as follows:

- /home/ftp—should be owned and only writable by root.
- /home/ftp/bin—should also be owned and only writable by root. /home/ftp/bin should be owned by root and contain the follow pro-

grams: `compress`, `cpio`, `gzip`, `ls`, `sh`, `tar`, and `zcat` (as a link to `gzip`). They should all have the mode `---x--x--x`; `chmod 111 ~ftp/bin/*` if this is not the case.

- `/home/ftp/lib`—should contain `ld-linux.so.2`, `libc.so.6`, `libnsl.so.1`, and `libnss_files.so.1`.

The `etc` subdirectory should have mode 111 also, and should contain the files `group`, `passwd`, and `ld.so.cache`.

If you want listings to translate user and group IDs into names, you will likely need to add additional entries to `/home/ftp/etc/passwd` and `/home/ftp/etc/group`. Both should have mode 755 and contain `passwd` and `group` files that associate IDs with names. The encrypted password field is not used and should contain an asterisk (*). The only fields that need to be present are username, UID, and GID.

The upload and download directories can be created under `/home/ftp/pub`. For anonymous users to upload to a directory, it should be owned by FTP (and writable by the owner!). This will allow others to upload and read from the directory. You can, of course, change ownership and permissions to allow the level of access you desire.

The user `ftp` should have an entry in `/etc/passwd` similar to this:

```
ftp:*:14:50:FTP User:/home/ftp:
```

FTP is a service controlled by `inetd` and, as such, requires an entry in `/etc/services`. Once again, this should be set up already, but if it is not, add an entry like this:

```
ftp `  21/tcp
```

A corresponding entry in `/etc/inetd.conf` needs to exist as well. The `wu-ftpd` RPM sets this up. It should look something like:

```
ftp    stream  tcp    nowait  root  /usr/sbin/tcpd  in.ftpd -l -a
```

10.4 ProFTPD

A relatively new FTP daemon is the Professional FTP daemon (ProFTPD). While `wu-ftpd` aims for performance, ProFTPD aims for security and configurability. ProFTPD's configuration file uses a syntax similar to Apache (which also aims to be highly configurable).

Some of the features it boasts are single-file configuration, per-directory
configuration using `.ftpaccess` files, the ability to be run as a standalone program without the need of the `inetd` meta daemon, and anonymous FTP,
without the need for a private system directory tree. Some specific security
features include running as a non-privileged user (in standalone mode) and
no support for running external programs (like `tar` and `gzip`.)

The source code for ProFTPD can be found at its home page, `http://`
`www.proftpd.org`, and usually a recent binary RPM version can be found at a
`ftp://contrib.redhat.com mirror`.

There are few differences between the source and binary distributions. If
you install from source, the configuration file, `proftpd.conf`, is installed in `/`
`usr/local/etc` and the server binary (`proftpd`) in `/usr/local/sbin`. The
RPM installs `proftd.conf` in `/etc` and the binary in `/usr/sbin`.

As mentioned above, ProFTPD aims to be highly configurable and uses
configuration syntax similar to Apache. Below is a sample configuration file.
It doesn't adequately cover all the various options, but it tries to give examples of the more useful ones. For a complete explanation of all the configuration directives, consult the ProFTPD home page.

```
#
# A sample proftpd.conf.
#
# A few basic directives:
#

ServerName                      "ProFTPD at ftp.ratatosk.org"
ServerType                      standalone
#
# Send connections which don't match any virtual hosts to the
# default server (instead of giving the 'no server available'
# message.)
#
DefaultServer                   on
#
# Port 21 is the standard FTP port.
#
Port                            21
#
# Set a ridiculously high idle timeout (# of seconds without
  activity
# the server waits before closing the connection.)
#
TimeoutIdle 1800
#
# Turn off name DNS look ups. This prevents stalls on DNS lookups
# and generally helps performance.
```

```
#
UseReverseDNS no
#
# Normally, ProFTPD binds to the specified port(s) on all address
# on a machine. This directive tells it only to bind to specific
# addresses, as specified in <VirtualHost> containers or with
# the 'Bind' directive.
#
SocketBindTight on
#
# Bind to a address
#
Bind 10.10.10.2
#
# Umask 022 is a good standard umask to prevent new dirs and files
# from being group and world writable.
#
Umask                       022

#
# Set the maximum number of child instances, which is also
# the maximum number of simultaneous connections. Note that
# this option is ignored. If you want to limit the number of
# instances when running under under inetd, you will have to
# run and inet daemon that supports this.
#
MaxInstances                30
#
# The user and group that the server runs as.
#
User                        nobody
Group                       nobody
#
# The Directory container groups options for an entire directory
# tree.
#
<Directory /*>
  #
  # Default to files being overwriteable, unless denied by Unix
  # permissions.
  #
  AllowOverwrite            on
</Directory>
#
# An anonymous configuration rooted at the home directory
# of the user 'ftp'
#
<Anonymous ~ftp>
  User                      ftp
  Group                     ftp
```

```
#
# Don't require the shell to be listed in /etc/shells before
# allowing a connection.
#
RequireValidShell            off
#
# Make "anonymous" an alias for "ftp"
#
UserAlias                    anonymous ftp
#
# Limit the of simultaneous anonymous logins
#
MaxClients                   10
#
# Set the file containing the welcome message and the file
# containing the message to be displayed up changing directories
#
DisplayLogin                 welcome.msg
DisplayFirstChdir            .message
#
# You can nest Directory containers. Here we deny uploads
# in general...
#
<Directory *>
  <Limit WRITE>
    DenyAll
  </Limit>
</Directory>
#
# ...but allow them in incoming while denying directory listings
#
<Directory incoming>
  <Limit WRITE>
    AllowAll
  </Limit>
  <Limit READ>
    DenyAll
  </Limit>
</Directory>
</Anonymous>
```

10.5 BeroFTPD

BeroFTPD is another new FTP daemon. It is based on `wu-ftpd` and uses the same configuration files. The main enhancement made over `wu-ftpd` is more full-featured virtual server support. Additional enhancements include support for email notification, better on-the-fly compression, additional logging options, an `include` directive for use inside `ftpaccess`, a built-in `ls` command, and support for Kerberos5 for secure logins.

A recent version of BeroFTPD in binary RPM format can usually be found in the Red Hat `contrib` area. The source code is available from `ftp:/` `/bero.x5.net/pub/`. As of this writing, the current version is 1.3.4.

Virtual FTP Servers

As mentioned, BeroFTPD has enhanced support for virtual FTP servers, including support for IP-less virtual hosts. In addition to `wu-ftpd` virtual host support (private banners and messages), BeroFTPD supports individual configuration files, `ftpusers`, `ftpgroups`, `ftphosts`, and `ftpconversions` for each virtual FTP server.

To make full use of virtual host support under BeroFTPD, you need to add a couple of lines to the `ftpaccess` file and create an `ftpservers` file. Two directives must be added to `ftpaccess`:

```
root      /ftp
logfile   /var/log/xferlog
```

These specify the default `root` and `logfile` locations of the virtual hosts, as well as the `root` and `logfile` for connections to the "real" server.

`ftpaccess` should contain a line for each virtual host that defines the directory where the configuration files for that host reside. These can also be defined on a per-domain basis.

```
cheese.ratatsk.org    /etc/ftpd/config/cheese.ratatosk.org
foobar.com            /etc/ftpd/config/foobar.com
10.10.10.76           /etc/ftpd/config/hey.you.com
```

Within these directories, you can create configuration files to customize the server just as you would a standalone server. Note that the virtual host's file completely overwrites directives from the master `ftpaccess` file and nothing is inherited from the master configuration files except for the default `root` and `logfile` locations from `ftpaccess`.

Another useful feature is limiting throughput for particular files. The syntax of this directive is: `throughput <root-dir> <subdir-glob> <file-glob-list><bytes-per-second><bytes-per-second-multiply><remote-glob-list>`. For example:

```
throughput /home/ftp * README,help.* oo - *
throughput /home/ftp/pub/dogs *cat* * 2000 0.8 *.nm.us
```

The first line tells the server not to restrict (the oo means no throughput restriction) the download throughput of files named README and those starting with help. under the /home/ftp directory tree. The second entry restricts the throughput of any files in subdirectories with cat in their name under /home/ftp/pub/dogs to 2000 bytes/second. In addition, subsequent downloads by the same client will be at a throughput of 20% less than the previous download. So, the second download will be at 1600 bytes/second, the third at 1280 bytes/second, and so on.

There are, of course, many other directives that are not covered here. You should consult the man pages for ftpaccess and other related files.

BeroFTPD has the benefit of being closely related to wu-ftpd: Users of wu-ftpd will find migrating to it fairly simple and its performance comparable. On the other hand, it is not as configurable as ProFTPD, which, while not having the best performance, has the added advantage of a single, centralized configuration file for everything.

10.6   TFTP

Trivial tftp is a very simplistic FTP service. It has no user validation and no ability to change directories or to list the contents of directories. It can get or put files in binary or ASCII mode. That's it. The only restrictions on the reading or writing of files are that they must exist and be "publicly" readable or writable, respectively. "Publicly" in this case means read/write privileges for the user the server is running as. Therefore, it is a good idea to run the server with the lowest privileged user necessary. The server takes one argument, which is a directory to set as the tftp root. If one isn't specified, the default of /tftpboot is used.

Some remote devices may require a tftp host for part of their booting process, but, in general, tftp is used fairly rarely. By default it runs as root, but is disabled in inetd.conf. If you need to offer this service, uncomment it and change the user it runs as.

10.7   FTP Clients

FTP clients range from the fairly limited featured, stock ftp to full-screen, feature-rich NcFTP to Web browsers with limited features to full-featured graphical clients such as gFTP and XFTP.

Today, probably the most common way to access anonymous FTP sites is with a Web browser. These are typically the only clients that support anonymous FTP well. It is possible to access sites with a username and password with URLs of the form `ftp://username:password@host.name/`. You should leave `password` empty, however, to avoid displaying it in clear text. Your browser should then provide a pop-up for you to enter it in.

There are also a number of other FTP clients, ranging from the simple command line like the `ftp` program to full-screen clients like NcFTP to graphical clients like XFTP.

ftp

The `ftp` program is a command-line-based program. It is not particularly friendly, but should always be available on any Linux (or UNIX system).

NcFTP

NcFTP is a full-screen (still ASCII) FTP client. It sports a number of features, including:

- A list of shortcuts for FTP hosts, including storage for usernames and passwords (if so desired) for each host.

- Automatic connection as anonymous (sends `anonymous` as the username and a string you supply as the password defaults to `username@host`; the anonymous FTP password is stored in the `.ncftp/prefs` file of your home directory).

- The screen is split into a command typing area and an output area.

- File and directory name completion using the TAB key.

- Viewing of remote files with a pager like `less` or `more`.

- Support for wildcard expressions when putting or getting files, without having to use separate `mput` or `mget` commands.

- Support for FTP: URLs, for example, `ftp://www.snerdwump.org/pub/wump-1.2.4.tgz`.

- Batch operation.

gFTP

If Gnome is installed, you can also use gFTP, which is a graphical FTP client that makes full use of the Gnome environment. It allows for drag-and-drop if you are running a window manager that is Gnome-compliant, such as WindowMaker or Enlightenment.

gFTP's features include multithreading for multiple simultaneous downloads, proxy support, passive and active transfer modes, immunity to buffer overflows from malicious FTP servers, directory listing caching, bookmarking, and editing of local and remote files.

XFTP

XFTP is an X/Motif-based FTP client. It supports things such as selecting groups of files for upload or download. It can also move files between other computers (i.e., neither of them needs to be running XFTP, though they both need to be running some form of `ftpd`).

Local and remote files can be viewed with a built-in pop view or with a user-specified viewer such as `emacs`, `less`, or `more`. Additionally, you can specify a program to use for various graphic formats.

Finally, the interface allows for a large amount of user configuration.

10.8 Summary

FTP is an incredibly useful service—one of the few that has not been eclipsed by the Web. (Things like Gopher, Archie, and WAIS are all but dead now, replaced by Web equivalents.)

Most of you will, at worst, have to set up an anonymous FTP server and possibly make sure your users can access their accounts via FTP. This can be trivial if your machine was set up to handle FTP initially, as most Linux boxes are. You may have to create a few files and directories, however.

The trickier things to set up are FTP-only accounts and virtual FTP clients. Hopefully, we've provided enough information to get you started

- By default, anonymous FTP is rooted at `/home/ftp`.
- Not all FTP clients are created equal; a graphical interface isn't a guarantee of ease of use.

Applications for Linux

11

Linux can be more than just a server—there are a growing number of desktop applications for it as well

This chapter is a survey of the more popular applications for Linux. These applications run the gamut from integrated office suites to symbolic math programs to emulators for running software from other operating systems.

11.1 Office Products, Word Processors, and Editors

In this category fall the multitude of office suites, standalone word processors, spreadsheets, editors, and publishing tools.

Applixware

Made by Applix, Inc. (`http://www.applix.com/`), Applixware is probably the most complete and tightly integrated office suite available for Linux. It is still not as slick as similar products from Corel, Claris, or Microsoft, but it is making strides toward that goal.

Applixware is invoked by typing `applix` at a shell prompt. This brings up the main window (Figure 11–1), from which you can start Words (a full-featured word processor), Graphics (a drawing tool), Spreadsheets (a spreadsheet program), Presents (a presentation editor), Mail (a mailer that supports local or POP mail), and Builder (a tool for creating macros and custom Applixware applications).

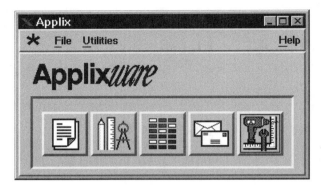

Figure 11–1   Applixware main window

Applix Words

As mentioned above, Applixware is very tightly integrated. Documents can be shared between applications and inserted into documents made by different applications (see Figure 11–2).

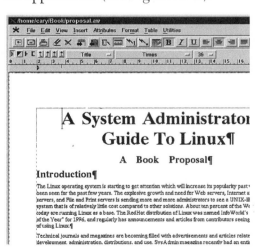

Figure 11–2   A document opened in Applix Words

WordPerfect

Corel's WordPerfect 8 has been ported to Linux and is free for non-commercial use (`http://linux.corel.com`). WordPerfect is probably the most feature-rich word processor available for Linux.

The downside of using WordPerfect is that the rest of Corel's office products have not been ported with it, so it does not have a nice, well-integrated office suite to interact with.

Figure 11-3 shows the 30-day evaluation version of WordPerfect 7.

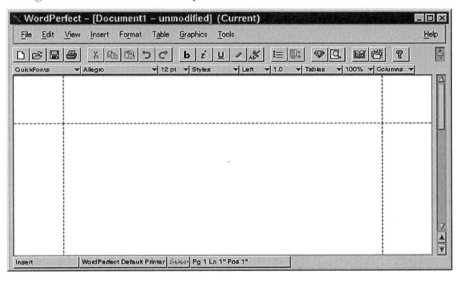

Figure 11–3　WordPerfect for Linux

Plan

Plan is a freeware schedule manager. It requires Motif or LessTif (see below) to compile. It allows for sharing appointment information between users and various methods of notification (see Figure 11–4).

Figure 11–4   The Plan application

TeX/LaTex

TeX is the original UNIX typesetting program. It is not a word processor and has no editing environment. TeX files can be created with any text editor. They are subsequently processed by TeX to create a formatted document. Some word processors (such as LyX) write their files as TeX, so you can get a WYSIWYG screen with the power of TeX.

Because TeX source is plain text and because TeX is free and has been ported to virtually every platform, documents created with it are completely portable.

When a TeX or related file is processed, the output is sent to a DVI (device independent) file. DVI is a flexible format that can be viewed with a simple, lightweight viewer or translated into other formats, for example, PostScript, for printing.

Over the years, a number of extensions and utilities for TeX have been developed:

- LaTeX—By far the most common TeX extension. LaTeX is actually a set of macros to allow a higher level of interaction with TeX, which makes it easier to use. It provides specific modes for articles, books, and letters.

- BibTex—A bibliography and citation system. It will also allow you to build bibliographies for a particular document from a larger, possibly shared, bibliography.

- SliTex—Specially designed for making overhead slides or large-print documents for presentations.

- MakeIndex—A utility for creating an index for a TeX or LaTeX document. It supports up to three levels of indexing.

- HyperTeX—An extension for TeX that lets you create hyperlinked documents. The source then passes on the hyperlinking information to the `.dvi` file, which can subsequently be translated into Acrobat format. (Acrobat is essentially an overlay for encoded, compressed PostScript that supports hyperlinking.)

- LaTeX2HTML—A utility for translating LaTeX source files into HTML files. It will create a hyperlinked table of contents, translate mathematical formulae into embedded GIFs, and properly handle references and footnotes.

TeX is supported by the Comprehensive TeX Archive Network (CTAN). CTAN can be accessed at `http://www.tex.ac.uk/`, where you can find information on LaTeX and other TeX extensions.

Xemacs

Xemacs (see Figure 11–5) is an enhanced version of GNU `emacs` for X. Xemacs is an incredibly full-featured editor. It has editing modes for dozens of file types, including HTML, C, Perl, Python, C++, `Makefile`, TeX, LaTeX, and FORTRAN, just to name a few.

Additionally, Xemacs supports speech synthesis and voice control. This, combined with its USENET News read, Web browser, and mail reader, make it an obvious choice for sight-impaired users.

Xemacs supports editing of multiple buffers in multiple frames. Frames can also be split into sub-windows, either vertically or horizontally.

Xemacs can also be run in a screen mode. In this situation, you will lose some functionality, mainly that relating to frames and pull-down menus.

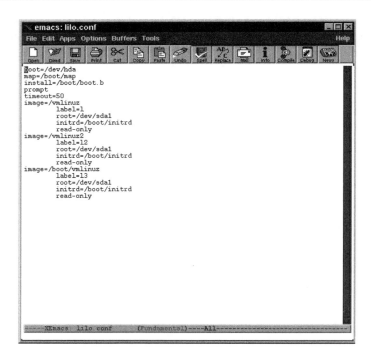

Figure 11–5   The Xemacs editor

11.2 Drawing, Graphics, and Image Viewing and Manipulation

Xv

Xv is a shareware image viewer and translator. It supports GIF87, JPEG, TIFF (compressed and uncompressed), PostScript, PPM, PGM, PBM, Sun Rasterfile, TARGA, FITS, IRIS RGB, and PM (whew!). It can read, write, edit colors and gamma corrections, process a number of algorithms (oil painting, edge detection, blurring, and sharpening), and crop.

GIMP

The GNU Image Manipulation Program (`http://www.gimp.org/`), or GIMP, is an image composition, authoring, and photo retouching tool. It is the closest thing to packages like Adobe Photoshop available for Linux.

It is very extensible and relies on an active user community to write plug-ins to extend its functionality. Plug-ins include image processing algorithms, scanner hooks (so you can scan an image directly into GIMP), and file formats. There are extensive tutorials on writing your own plug-ins, and the program is very easy to use.

Xfig

Xfig is a freeware drawing tool for X (see Figure 11-6). It supports the drawing of interpolated lines, various polygons, grouping of objects, scaling, copying, and embedding text using many PostScript fonts. It ships with most distributions of Linux.

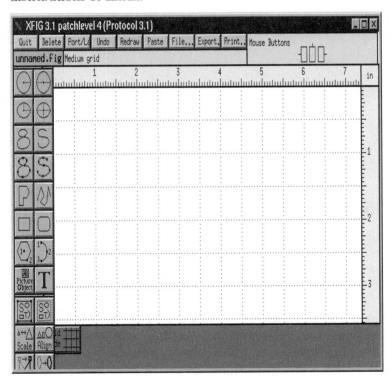

Figure 11–6 The Xfig drawing tool for X

Xpaint

Xpaint is similar to Xfig, but more oriented toward painting rather than drawing (see Figure 11-7). It is free as well and ships with most Linux distributions.

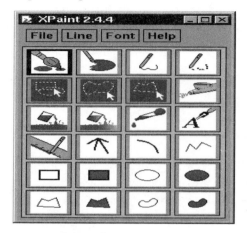

Figure 11–7   The Xpaint program for X

Mapedit

Mapedit is an image map editing program from Boutell.Com, Inc. It can create client-side and server-side image maps. It supports GIF, JPEG, and PNG image formats. It is very easy to use; even Windows users tend to find it easier to use than similar tools for Windows 98. More information can be found at http://www.boutell.com/mapedit/.

11.3 Scientific Programs

Maple

Maple is a program for performing symbolic (as opposed to numeric) mathematical operations. The latest version has not yet been released for Linux.

Maple is a very powerful computation package. It also supports 2D and 3D plotting and animations. It has a scripting language for creating procedures and macros. The procedures can be exported to C or FORTRAN.

Figures 11-8 and 11-9 are a couple of screen shots from the demo version of Maple V Release 3.

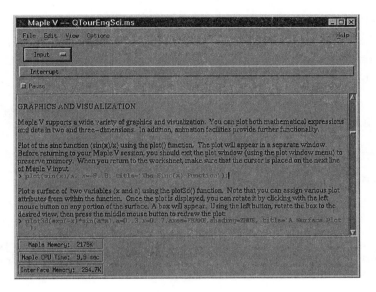

Figure 11–8 An example screen from the Maple application

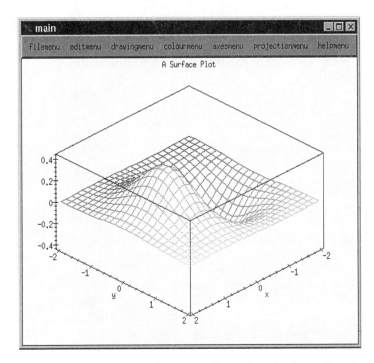

Figure 11–9 An example screen from the Maple application

Mathematica

Developed by Wolfram Research (http://www.wolfram.com/), Mathematica is another symbolic manipulation package. One of the best features of Mathematica is that its kernel can be run on a separate machine from the front-end. This allows the front-end to operate independently on a client machine with other desktop applications while the kernel executes on a server machine with lots of RAM and a nice big CPU.

There is no demo or evaluation version of Mathematica available.

11.4 Emulators

Executor

ARDI (http://www.ardi.com/) makes a Macintosh emulator for Linux and a number of other platforms as seen in Figure 11-10. A free demo is available on the application CD included with the Official Red Hat 6.0. The list of completely and mostly usable software is quite long.

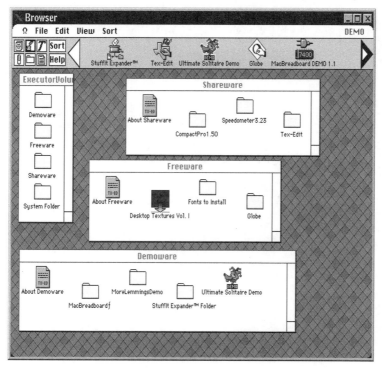

Figure 11–10   ARDI Macintosh Emulator window

Wabi

Wabi is a commercial MS Windows 3.1 emulator developed by Sun Micro-systems. It has been ported to Linux by Caldera. It provides for cutting and pasting between applications, remote display, application sharing between users, Winsock networking, OLE (Object Linking and Embedding), DDE (Dynamic Data Exchange), access to serial and parallel ports, and many other features.

Wabi has a few limitations. It requires 8-bit color, so if you are running X with 24-bit color, your server will need to support 8-bit pseudo-color. IPX/SPX connectivity is not available, nor are virtual device drivers. See `http://www.caldera.com/doc/wabi/wabi.html` for more information.

Dosemu

Dosemu is a freeware DOS emulator. It can run on the console or under X in its own window. The best place to get information on Dosemu is the HOWTO, which can be found at any Linux mirror site.

Acrobat

Adobe (`http://www.adobe.com/`) makes Acrobat Reader for Linux. It is available for free and, as far as we know, this is the only Adobe product for Linux right now.

LessTif

LessTif is a freeware clone of Motif. It is still in beta, but a large number of Motif-based programs compile with it already. Additionally, precompiled programs that use the shared version of the library will run with it.

Some of the programs that can be run and/or compiled with Xmotif are:

- Xemacs.
- Plan.
- Netscape Mozilla.
- Xmcd (Motif-based CD player).

LessTif's home page is `http://www.lesstif.org/`; the source code, a list of compatible applications, the FAQ, and much more can be found there.

11.5 Summary

As Linux's popularity has grown, so has commercial support for it, which in turn helps feed Linux's popularity. As we said at the beginning of this chapter, this is only a sampling of the applications available for Linux.

One of the areas that Linux is weakest in is graphics- and illustration-related applications. There are no applications that are on the level of Quark Xpress, Adobe Photoshop, PageMaker, or Illustrator. Many of these applications exist for other versions of UNIX, so it should not be too difficult to port them to Linux (or other free Unices).

Linux Database Software **12**

A cornucopia of database management systems!

Linux has benefited in the realm of DBMSs by being a UNIX-like OS. A number of software vendors have ported their database servers to Linux. Better yet, a few have even been developed under Linux. In the last year or so, major commercial database makers have also made versions of their systems for Linux.

This chapter actually started as a section, but it got so big and DBMSs are becoming such an important aspect of computing, we made it a chapter. We first talk about two very popular, lightweight servers in detail. Then we have a less detailed listing of other native database servers. Finally, a description of a couple of databases with partial Linux support round out the chapter.

This is not an attempt to enumerate every database server for Linux. It is a list of databases we've used and/or found interesting. For a more complete listing of commercial databases, see the Linux Commercial HOWTO.

Lastly, let's go over a few acronyms and terms for those of you who are not very familiar with the world of databases:

- SQL—Structured Query Language, a language for performing queries on relational databases.
- DBMS—Database Management System.
- Key—A column or set of columns that organizes a table. Often, but not always, keys will be unique, that is, a particular combination of values of the columns that make up the key must be unique (for a one-column key, this means each value in the column must be unique).
- Schema—An interrelated set of tables and/or databases. Also a description of how a set of tables are joined via keys.
- RDBMS—Relational DBMS.
- ODBMS—Object Oriented DBMS.

12.1 MySQL and mSQL

These two servers are often mentioned together as they developed somewhat in parallel and MySQL was initially based off of mSQL. Both are used for similar tasks as well.

mSQL

mSQL stands for mini-SQL, a shareware database server (free for non-commercial use). It supports, as its name suggests, a subset of the normal SQL specification. Additionally, it has some extensions to SQL. Before we go any further, it is probably best to list what mSQL can't do so you can decide if it's worth your while to use it for your particular application.

- There is no grants database or "logging in" to the database. Access is granted to users listed in /etc/passwd to read and/or write on a per-database basis.
- Databases can be accessed locally via a UNIX domain socket or remotely via a TCP/IP socket. If you grant TCP/IP access to a database, you do so for all usernames, even though the username on the remote host is not necessarily the same person as on the local system. There is no method for finer grained remote versus local access control.

- It does not support the BLOB data type and is thus not really suitable for storing large blocks of data.

- It has no ALTER command. This means that, for example, once a table is created, columns cannot be added, removed, or changed. While you may think that careful planning can minimize the inconvenience of this, don't. Invariably, some outside force, be it a new product, new marketing strategy, or simple oversight will force you to alter your carefully planned database schema.

- It is single-threaded, meaning it can only process one query at a time. As long as the load is not too heavy and the queries not too complex, this shouldn't really be a problem. What exactly too heavy and too complex mean will depend on your system and may require some experimentation on your part.

Despite these shortcomings, mSQL is still a useful database server. For small datasets with a simple schema and low likelihood of simultaneous accesses, it is well-suited. There are several other reasons you might want to use mSQL:

- It is lightweight, consuming only a small amount of system resources when simply running (as opposed to monsters like Oracle and Sybase, which require many megabytes of RAM simply to start up).

- It is free for non-commercial use and the shareware fee for commercial use is only $200.

- It has a large install base and widespread support on the 'net.

- As a side effect of its popularity, most of the more popular languages have support for mSQL: C (the API is for C), Python, Java, Perl, Tcl, PHP.

- It has two enhanced LIKE operators: RLIKE, which allows use of the regular expression library, and CLIKE, which is case-insensitive. Since there is a separate RLIKE that implements regex, LIKE and CLIKE do not need to and thus are faster than most other SQL operators, which typically implement at least a subset of regex's functionality.

Lite and W3-msql

These two additional packages are a part of the standard mSQL distribution.

Lite is a scripting language designed for use with mSQL. Its syntax is similar to Perl. Its variables are dynamically typed, arrays are dynamically sized, and variable names start with a $. Its chief advantage over other languages is its tight integration with mSQL.

W3-msql is a Web interface to Lite that is embedded in HTML and server-side parsed. Also included is W3-auth, an access control package for W3-msql. It supports users and groups and gives somewhat finer access control than the non-Web access control file. In some ways, W3-msql is very similar to PHP, though it lacks support for other databases and is simply not as full-featured. See the Web serving chapter for more information on PHP.

Some Other Notes

mSQL's author claims that it will manage up to 4GB of data, but suggests that other system limitations will make such a large database impractical under mSQL. It's not entirely clear how this number is arrived at, if it comes from a real-life example, or to how many rows it corresponds.

Linux 1.3 or higher is required. Earlier versions do not have full `mmap` support, which mSQL 2 requires. Additionally, you should have the kernel sources installed to ensure that you have all the necessary libraries and header files.

For an example of how to install mSQL, see the Web serving chapter.

MySQL

An increasingly popular free database server, MySQL started off as an enhanced version of mSQL 1. It attempted to add a more complete set of the ANSI SQL specification, plus some enhancements. Today it implements nearly all of ANSI SQL and a bevy of additional features.

Like mSQL it implements a `regex` `LIKE` separate from `LIKE` to enhance performance. It is also fairly lightweight, though not light as mSQL.

Some things that MySQL supports that mSQL doesn't include are:

- Expanded SQL, including things like an `ALTER` `TABLE` clause (allowing for columns to be added or dropped from a table after it is created) and embeddable functions that operate on all datatypes.
- More datatypes—especially BLOBs, binary large objects. It also supports varying sizes of existing datatypes, e.g., tiny, small, medium, and large integer types.
- Usernames and passwords independent of `/etc/passwd`. This is nice for CGI use. Rather than having to allow the user `nobody` read and pos-

sibly write access to the database, you can require a valid MySQL user-name/password combination that you could ask for on a form. The level of access a user has can be controlled on the operational (selecting, deleting, updating, preloading, and shutting down the server), database, and host levels.

• Optimized queries, including optimizations for joins (all joins are done in one pass).

• It is multithreaded and able to handle multiple requests concurrently. This mean that subsequent queries will not have to wait on a large, time-consuming query that was presented to the server first.

• It has much looser licensing requirements. Basically, unless you are going to sell MySQL, you don't need to purchase a license for it.

• It is currently serving larger databases (as many as 50 million rows) than mSQL. This isn't to say that mSQL couldn't handle so large a database, it is just an empirical observation.

Some disadvantage of MySQL include:

• Not as lightweight as mSQL.

• More complex access control system, which is probably the most difficult aspect of MySQL to master.

In the past year or two, MySQL's popularity has exploded. It has replaced mSQL in many places. Virtually every common programming language has a module or wrapper that implements the C API. Support on Internet mailing lists and on the Web is excellent.

In general, if you are frustrated with mSQL's limitations or licensing, you should definitely look into MySQL. If your favorite language doesn't have an interface and you know a little C, it is probably worth your while to port mSQL modules to MySQL.

Installing MySQL

MySQL is free in almost every circumstance, the one exception being that if you wish to sell it, you have to purchase a license. Getting a legal copy of it for your use is thus simply a matter of FTPing the distribution. The source code is available, or if you choose, you can get a Linux binary distribution. Binaries also exist for Solaris and SunOS, as well as a growing number of other OSes.

MySQL's home page is `http://www.tcx.se/`; there are also numerous mirrors: in the U.S. (`http://www.buoy.com/mysql`), Australia (`http://mysql.bluep.com/`), and many others, all listed on the home page. Also on the home page are pointers to FTP for MySQL, the documentation home page, mailing list, and contributed software.

Compiling and Installing MySQL

If you choose to compile MySQL yourself, you will need a multithreading library. If you have Red Hat 5.02 or later, the threading is built into the C library. Otherwise, you will need the `LinuxThreads` library. You will also need a C++ compiler, presumably g++ under and libg++. Note that libg++ is distributed separately from GCC/g++/gobj-c, just as GNU `libc` is. Lastly, you will need recent versions of GCC, at least 2.7.2; GNU `make`, at least 3.75; and libc 5.4.12 or glibc 2.0.2.

GNU `autoconf` is used, so the common sequence of configure, make, and make install works. Useful options for the MySQL configure are:

`--prefix==/path/to/mysql/install/base`	Where to install MySQL
`--localstatedir==/path/to/mysql/datafiles`	Where to keep the datafiles.
`--without-server`	Only compile client libraries and binaries.
`--enable-shared`	Build libmysqlclient as a shared library.

Other configure options can be listed with the `--help` option. You may also want to run an optional make check before installing.

We're not going to go into a lot of detail about how to deal with a troublesome compile, since you can always fall back to a binary distribution. One thing to note is that unpacking the binary distribution and installing from the compiled source distribution will place things in slightly different directories. The binary distribution creates a directory named `mysql-<version>` and subdirectories for libraries, header files, and program files. Installing from the source makes `mysql` subdirectories in `/usr/local/lib` and `/usr/local/include`. This is important to keep in mind if you compile MySQL-dependent programs or modules.

Beyond making sure that you have the right versions of the tools needed to compile, there is little to check. If you run into trouble, `mysql` mailing list is probably the best place to ask for help. Information about it can be found in the FAQ at the MySQL home page or any of its mirrors.

Once you have MySQL compiled, you can run the optional make check and then proceed to running the make install. This will install MySQL in subdirectories of your install base as follows: binaries in `bin/`, libraries in `lib/ mysql`, header files in `include/mysql`, and the data area will be in `var/`.

Installing from a Binary Distribution

Unpack the tarball where you want the `mysql` directory to be created. It will create a directory named `mysql-<version info>-<platform info>`; you can then create a link using `ln` or just rename it to `mysql`. The MySQL binaries will now be in `/usr/local/mysql/bin`, libraries in `/usr/local/ mysql/lib`, header files in `/usr/local/mysql/include`, and `/usr/local/ mysql/data` will be the home of the data files and subdirectories.

Setting up the Grants Database and Other Data Files

The next step in our installation is to set up the grants database. Unless you've done some fiddling after the installation, you should just be able to run it and let it do its thing. What it does is set up tables for access control for users. These users do not need to be system users, that is, they do not need `/etc/ passwd` entries.

The name of the grants database is simply `mysql`. It has three tables: `db`, `host`, and `user`. The `db` table lists access for the combination of user, database, and host from which the user is connecting. host controls access for the pairing of host and database. Finally, `user` combines host, user, and password.

To initialize the `mysql` database, you need to run `mysql_install_db`. If you used a binary distribution, run the following command in the directory created when you unpacked the archive type:

```
scripts/mysql_install_db
```

If you compiled from source, run the above command in the top level of the source tree. This will set up root as a "superuser" when connecting locally, lock out remote users, and force other local users to be granted access on a per-database level in the `db` table. It will also set up db to allow any access to the test database, or any database starting with `test_` to any user. It will start the MySQL daemon, `mysqld`, for the first time as well.

Since the grants database is probably the most complex aspect of using MySQL, we'll give a few examples here. There are a few things to remember when manipulating the access tables:

- Passwords are stored encrypted.
- The tables are sorted, putting wildcard and " " entries last. The first match is then used. Host table is sorted first, then user, and last, for the db table, database.
- The host table is only consulted if the host field in the user table is " ". Then the privileges that are listed by the user table are logically **AND**ed with those in the host table.
- The results of the previous step are **OR**ed (once again in the logical sense) with the user table.
- If there is no matching entry in db, the matching entry from host is **AND**ed with the matching user entry.

To start manipulating the mysql database, as root, enter:

```
mysql mysql
```

If you installed from a binary distribution, you will likely have to specify the path to the mysql binary.

The following set of entries will lock out all local users that don't otherwise have an entry for a particular database in db:

```
INSERT INTO user VALUES
    ('localhost','','','N','N','N','N','N','N','N','N','N','N');
INSERT INTO user VALUES
    ('myhost','','','N','N','N','N','N','N','N','N','N','N');

INSERT INTO host VALUES ('localhost','%','Y','Y','Y','Y','Y','Y');
INSERT INTO host VALUES ('myhost','%','Y','Y','Y','Y','Y','Y');
```

In the above and following examples, myhost stands for the name of the computer where mysqld is running.

Now, to grant the user cary full access to the database notebooks, we would add this row to the db table:

```
INSERT INTO db VALUES
    ('%','notebooks','cary','Y','Y','Y','Y','Y','Y');
```

If we wanted to give all other users access to the data in notebooks, but not let them modify the table:

```
INSERT INTO db VALUES ('%','notebooks','','Y','N','N','N','N','N');
```

To give the user mark full access with the password osprey from any host:

```
INSERT INTO user VALUES ('%','mark',pass-
    word('osprey'),'Y','Y','Y','Y','Y','Y','Y','Y','Y','Y');
```

To test your access control, you can use mysqlaccess. The syntax is very straightforward: mysqlaccess [host] [user] [database]. There are a number of options that control the amount of and format of the output as well; the --help option lists them.

In general, it is easiest to give a user no access at all in the user table; simply set up their username and password. Then, do all the access control in the db table. Of course, superusers have to be given full privileges in user. Also, if you want to give a user shutdown or reload privileges, you can only do this in the user table as well.

Now, you may be a little worried about slinging your MySQL usernames and passwords over your LAN. You need not be worried, or at least not as worried as you would normally be since MySQL encrypts its network traffic to at least make it difficult to sniff out users and passwords. (Of course, no decryptable encryption scheme is 100% foolproof. Cracking encryption is a matter of patience, cleverness, and lots of CPU power.)

You're now ready to start populating your database! Just a couple of last notes. When storing data in binary large objects (BLOBs) or variable-length text (VARCHARs), MySQL doesn't allocate space in the table on disk until there is data there. This can substantially reduce the amount of disk space used by your data compared to servers, where space for the entire VAR-CHAR or BLOB (or TEXT in mSQL) is allocated when the row is created, regardless of how much is actually stored in it.

Contributed Software for MySQL

An Apache authorization module, which is useful if you have a large number of users and lookups in the password flat file are becoming slow.

- Another Apache module for storing your logs in a MySQL database.
- A module for running radius authentication through MySQL.
- Cryllic language extensions (MySQL already supports German and Swedish on top of English).
- A C++ interface.

- An NSAPI (Netscape API) authentication extension, which is useful in the same situations that the Apache authentication module is.

- A number of applications are written using MySQL. Using PHP or Perl's DBI, you can quickly write your own Web-based applications. Applications written to use other database systems can be easily rewritten to use MySQL in many cases.

xmysql: A GUI Interface to MySQL

An X-based interface to the MySQL client, xmysql, exists and is available from the MySQL home page. It requires the `Xforms` library for compilation. `Xforms` can be found at `http://bragg.phys.uwm.edu/xforms`. The interface allows the user to choose tables and columns by pointing and clicking, doing a good part of the query building on its own. Of course, it's likely that the user will have to enter some information in the `where` clause.

Xmysqladmin

This is an admin for MySQL. It supports the adding/dropping of databases and tables, full access and manipulation of the grants database, browsing and killing of threads, stopping and starting the server, and repair and optimization of tables.

12.2 Other Native Linux DMBSs

Freeware

PostgreSQL

Postgres (`http://www.postgresql.org/`) has been around the UNIX world for quite some time. It is not purely relational and has some objected-oriented features in its core. It's usually referred to as object-relational. In any event, in its most recent incarnation, it supports nearly all of ANSI SQL plus some extensions, including embeddable functions. PostgreSQL is considered by many to be an alternative to MySQL since it has much of the same support for SQL and includes API code for most major languages, including support for ODBC and Perl's DBI.

PostgreSQL is included with the Red Hat CD-ROM, and documentation can be found in `/usr/doc/`.

Commercial

Solid

Solid Technologies sells its DBMS for nearly every UNIX platform, including Linux for the x86 and Alpha architectures. Support for Solid is available for Python, Perl, PHP, and of course, C.

This SQL server is aimed at higher-end applications and larger businesses. A free evaluation copy is available. Client software for non-Linux UNIX systems is available too.

Solid supports a number of things you'd expect of a high-end database server:

- Online backups—i.e., the server remains running and a "snapshot" is saved.

- Crash and power failure recovery to the last checkpoint.

- Fine-grained access control (at a similar level to MySQL's).

- ODBC support.

- Automatic crash recovery.

- Symmetric mulitprocessing (SMP) support.

Solid's manuals are available online in HTML. It is designed to require a minimal amount of administration. It is easy to set up and more or less runs itself. System requirements are minimal: a couple of megabytes of disk space and a megabyte of free RAM.

Pricing for Solid's Linux product is considerably less than for other systems; as of this writing, Solid Technologies is offering the desktop version (single user, only UNIX socket connections) free for Linux.

Information on Solid can be found at `http://www.solidtech.com/`.

Empress

Empress is one of the first commercial databases for Linux. It is a relational database, like Sybase and Oracle. Empress supports these features (among others):

- Multimedia support.
- Check-pointing and rollback.
- BLOBs (binary large objects).
- Shared libraries and a C API.
- Interfaces for Tcl/Tk, Perl, and FORTRAN (!).
- A GUI builder for quickly creating graphical interfaces to Empress applications.
- Two-phase commit.
- A CGI pass-through for processing Empress HTML SQL (EHSQL), ESQL, is embedded into a document and then parsed by the CGI and passed on to the client browser.

Personal Empress for Linux is available also. More information on Empress can be found at `http://www.empress.com/`.

Texpress

KE Software (`http://www.kesoftware.com/`) is a Canadian company that makes an object-oriented (as opposed to relational) database and numerous support applications and modules. It supports relational, free text, and multimedia datatypes.

Texpress also supports massive datasets and OO features, including inheritance and extensibility. You can define methods on objects in the database. Methods can be defined for data displaying, validation, assignment, and branch expression. This effectively lets you write stored procedures and then associate them with a particular object or class of objects.

Texpress' design actually favors more complicated queries, processing them equally as fast if not faster than simpler ones. It also supports massive datasets with ease. As database applications become more and more common and complicated, these are important features to consider.

Texpress' object-oriented design typically means that data can be stored and represented in a more natural fashion and less structured data is handled better than a relational database server.

Essentia

Essentia (`http://www.inter-soft.com/`) is another database that incorporates some nontraditional technology. It employs what its developer, Intersoft, calls RISE, the Reduced Instruction Set Engine. The communication interface is kept small and well-defined. It supports both relational and object-oriented models of data management.

Essentia also sports these features:

- Journaling and consistency checking.
- Database versions—allows you to go back and examine previous states of databases.
- Incremental backups.
- Mirroring.
- Shadowing—data to be modified is copied to a shadow and not committed to disk until a checkpoint is cleared.
- Locking at the row, table, and schema levels.

Sybase

After making their client libraries available for free for Linux, Sybase has at last released a Linux version. It is available for free, without support.

Oracle

Oracle has recently ported version 8 of their software to Linux.

Informix

Of the four big DBMS makers, Informix was the first to release a server for Linux. This has helped its acceptance in the Linux world relative to its competitors.

IBM

IBM as well has released a Linux version of DB2, its relational database manager.

12.3 Summary

Linux has a fairly large and rich set of databases available for use. These range from the very lightweight mSQL to the freeware MySQL to larger commercial database servers like Empress, Solid, and Texpress to Oracle running in SCO emulation.

All of these servers have different strengths and weaknesses. If you find that one of the smaller free or shareware database servers is not fulfilling your needs, nearly every commercial server listed here offers free or low-cost personal editions and/or a trial version of their larger packages. Take a few weeks to *really* evaluate these before shelling out what could be a substantial amount of money.

Programming $\mathbf{13}$
Languages

So many languages, so little time

Aside from everything else that Linux does, it provides for some extraordinary programming languages to make repetitive tasks, or ones that don't seem easy to fix, very easy to accomplish.

Numerous programming languages are available for Linux. There are literally scores, or maybe hundreds, depending on how you choose to split a few hairs. A large portion of these, and nearly all of the more popular ones, have at least one implementation under Linux. To attempt to give even a brief summary of all of them would be a small book in itself. We have tried to cover the most important ones, those that we (or others we know) use and ones which are especially interesting. You may, of course, use any language that suits your needs, and not all languages are appropriate for all situations.

In this chapter, we take a break from the format in the other chapters. Two of the sections are written explicitly from a singular viewpoint: Perl and Python. Each of us has our own reasons for using the languages we use for a particular task. Mark still doesn't understand why object-oriented programming (OOP) is so cool and downloads endless extensions to Perl, whereas Cary recognizes the usefulness of Python and does nearly all his programming with it, including large amounts of Common Gateway Interface (CGI) work.

13.1 C

```
http://www.fsf.org/software/gcc/gcc.html
http://www.accu.org/
```

We are not extensive C programmers. We know enough to hack C up a little and write small programs, but C is such an important language in a UNIX-like system, it is rightly placed first in our list. The kernel and most of the everyday commands and tools you use are written in C. If you don't know C now, in the course of compiling and installing software, you will at least become a little familiar with it.

GCC is the "native" C compiler for Linux. It supports everything a good compiler should: optimization, debugging, ANSI C support, and POSIX compliance. More than a lot of compilers are shipped with or are available for some commercial OSes. SunOS 4 in particular had a very lame compiler, but it was enough to compile the first stage of GCC to bootstrap your way up to a full GCC compiler, which is all we ever used it for.

C is the most popular compiled language for high-performance, general programming. Because it is compiled, it is typically faster than an interpreted language like Perl or Python[1]. C is also a fairly low-level language. This typically leads to longer development times for software. On the other hand, because it is a low-level language, it is possible to tune code to achieve higher performance than high-level languages.

Because C compilers exist for virtually every OS and platform, it is usually possible to port a C program to other platforms. Architecture or OS-specific libraries obviously complicate this process (GUI libraries especially), but frequently analogs exist on the target platform.

When it comes right down to it, C is the foundation for all the other languages discussed here in that their compilers and/or interpreters are or were (some of the compiled languages can compile their own compilers) written at least partially in C. While nearly all of them offer high-level methods or func-

---

[1] These are also known as high-level languages.

tions for accomplishing various tasks, a proficient enough C programmer can write a program to do it just as fast, if not faster.

The reason people use higher-level (often interpreted) languages is that the development time for applications is much shorter. For the smaller tasks often addressed by high-level languages, the performance trade-off is more than acceptable. It is also very easy to write a program and then test it out. Since the programs written in Perl or Python are small, there are few requirements for building makefiles or waiting for code to compile. You can write and test in seconds. This is not to say that larger applications can't be written in an interpreted language. Grail is a Web browser written in Python (using its Tcl/Tk interface and the tkinter module), which has acceptable performance. Additionally, HotJava is a browser written in Java, which is a byte-compiled language; it too has decent performance. While neither is as feature-packed as Netscape, both have support for HTML 3.2 plus frames, among other things.

13.2 C++

http://www.accu.org/

C++ is an object-oriented, compiled language whose roots lie in C (as its name suggests). It is not as popular as C, mainly because both it and OOP are younger than C. C++ and C mix very well together: It is easy to link object files from either language and thus mix the two languages within an application. VRweb, a VRML scene viewer, and MySQL, a freeware database server, are two applications that do this. Since windowing systems are thought of as object-oriented, many libraries and programming for X are done solely in C++ (like the Qt library, the basis behind KDE).

GNU's g++ is the C++ compiler shipped with Red Hat. To dispel a common misconception, knowledge of C is not necessary to learn C++. While it is certainly useful to know C before learning C++, it's no more a necessity than knowing Basic before learning FORTRAN. They're two separate languages.

For applications where an OO language is better suited or desired, and the performance of a compiled language is necessary, C++ is the most popular choice. It is more and more frequently used in GUIs, databases, and other applications where classes and inheritance occur naturally and an OO approach is a more efficient way of coding.

13.3 Perl[2]

```
http://www.perl.com/
```

To begin, my primary job isn't to be a CGI programmer. There is CGI work involved, but I have a lot of little things that I work on. I need a general-purpose language where I can write fast, test fast, and get on to the next project. Since we have multiple servers, I want my code to be as portable as possible, allowing me to run on Solaris or Linux (even NT) with only minor changes.

One of the first projects I worked on involved Remedy, our call tracking software. One feature I wanted to add was the ability to have E-mail that comes in or out to be automatically added to a customer's call. This involves a few steps:

1. Make sure the Subject: line for a call has a four-digit number. This would be the call number.

2. Extract that four-digit number.

3. Take the body of the message and the sender and add them to the call.

The first two items are actually easy, since Perl was designed as a more powerful version of awk, the pattern-matching program. Searching the Internet produced a group of people who gave a Perl interface to Remedy. This interface allowed me to log in to the Remedy server, modify the database to add the new entry, and then log out. The total size of the program was under 100 lines of code, and most of it was re-used from a sample program that came with the interface.

Another project was to monitor our phone system and make a listing every day of the number of incoming calls and the average length of each call. Someone else wrote a program to get the information and dump it in a file. All I had to do was open the file, read through until I hit a certain day's records, and then add up the times. Since Perl is made for string manipulation, I can pull out the hours, minutes, and seconds of a call, convert them all to seconds, and then build a total number of seconds of incoming calls for the day. I can then divide that by the number of calls, divide again to get hours, minutes, and seconds, and dump that into another file. If you add a cron process to do this every night right after midnight, there's the program.

---

[2] Written by Mark.

Last, I have the CGI work. Most of the work on our Web site is on our internal network (some call it an intranet). This allows us to have a common repository for information—how the phones work, what drive letters are which NFS mount, even schedules listing when people will be out of the office. This last one requires the CGI work. I have a SQL database program called PostgreSQL, which (you got it!) has a Perl interface. Perl also has a CGI interface, so I can build my form and CGI script all into one compact (under 200 lines) file. In one instance, a user can enter their name, what day they'll be out, and why they'll be out. This information then gets entered into the database. In another form, a person can enter data and query the database.

Why Perl over other languages? I've known Perl for a few years and have gotten used to how quickly you can write a program and get it working. Plus you don't have to worry about all the memory, pointers, `include` files, and compiler problems that exist in C. I wouldn't want to write anything big in it, but my projects typically don't require large programs. They're mostly small programs, and probably smaller in terms of line count than a comparable C program. Why not Python or another language? I don't need the OOP that Python provides[3]. Other scripting languages (such as `sh` or `csh`) have all the functionality built into Perl already, but Perl has the form of a real language and is something I'm much more used to, coming from my Pascal and M days.

There are a host of applications I've started using, from MRTG (`http://www.mrtg.com/`) to Mozilla's Bugzilla bug-tracking program (`http://www.mozilla.com/`). These are all written in Perl and that make use of Perl's ability to have an almost unlimited number of plug-ins. From databases to Web programming to bug tracking, Perl does the job for me.

13.4 Python[4]

`http://www.python.org`

Now, unlike Mark, at least half of my job is CGI programming and ironically, I don't use Perl. I say ironically because anyone who has looked into doing CGI programming has undoubtedly noticed that most of it is done in Perl. In fact, it can be difficult to find a book that concentrates on writing CGI in any other language, but they are rumored to exist.

---

[3]Perl 5 is OOP-based, and many modules take advantage of this style of programming.

[4]Written by Cary.

I used to be a huge Perl fan, but I didn't know any better then. I was actually just happy to be writing CGI. I discovered Python on my own near the end of my tenure in graduate school and wanted to learn it, but never really had the time or didn't think I did. Finally, about six months and two jobs later, I decided to finally learn another language. I really wasn't happy with Perl. I looked into Tcl and then Python again and decided to give the latter a whirl. I wrote my first "real" Python program, a CGI script, about a year ago and haven't looked back since.

Python is an object-oriented scripting language written by Guido van Rossum. It is dynamically typed, supports multiple inheritance, user-defined types, high-level dynamic types, and classes. As alluded to above, it is often compared to Perl, as the two are frequently used for similar tasks. It is younger than Perl, and as a result, its usage is less widespread. Despite this, Python has a large number of contributed modules for tasks, ranging from HTML generation to database interfacing to complex numerical calculations.

In general, you can use Python for any task where you could use any other scripting language. Python has a very clear syntax and is more extensible than other interpreted languages, with the possible exception of Tcl. It has also been shown to scale better than the average interpreted language. As an example of this, a Web browser has been written in Python using the `Tkinter` GUI interface. While not as high performance as compiled browsers, it is certainly tolerable. It is at least as fast as the HotJava browser, which is the most similar browser, being interpreted byte codes while Python is interpreted text.

Since it was designed as an object-oriented language from the ground up, the OO orientation is a very clean one, unlike the somewhat ad hoc OO of Perl 5. Also, development of Python on other platforms has taken place more or less concurrently, so Python is extremely portable.

Why do I like Python so much? Several reasons. First, the syntax is remarkably clear; my Python programs are much easier to read than in any other language I've used (FORTRAN, C, Basic, LISP, Bourne, and C shell). Second, program development is at least as fast as it was under Perl, usually faster. Third, I have discovered that I much prefer the OO approach to programming; inasmuch as any programming language can be said to work as my chaotic mind thinks, OOP comes closer than the "old-fashioned way," plus Python is consistently OO. Lastly, longer programs are much easier to develop and maintain.

Large CGI programs are uncommon, but certainly not unheard of. Most of the CGI I do is either a few dozen lines of code (for simple applications like reading data from a database or mailing form variables) or a couple hundred lines for more complicated stuff like inserting or updating a database or building GIFs with `libgd`. Now about that occasional big CGI application...

For example, I have a CGI script that processes new and renewing subscribers to the Web sites at my place of employment. It started off as a collection of small Perl scripts which checked, minimally formatted, and mailed the form variables to a Mac, where they were processed by Leads!, a front-end to 4D (a Mac DB I'd never heard of until I started the job). Needless to say, this was not the most robust way to populate our customer database. At the time, we had one subscription site and about a half-dozen types of subscriptions.

Since I started my current job, the number of subscription sites has tripled and the number of oddball marketing deals that are made has gone from zero to a half dozen or more, depending on whether I'm counting or someone from marketing is doing it; there has been an almost geometric rise in the number of different subscriptions. What started as a collection of hacked, canned Perl scripts is now a monolithic CGI of over 1,200 lines. It verifies and cross-checks as many as 40 variables; determines whether renewing members are adding sites, users, or both; inserts and/or updates as many as six tables in our membership database (at the moment, split over two DBMSs, though not for long); and prints out a nice membership certificate suitable for framing. Despite the ad hoc manner in which the group and later single script developed the code, it is still easy to read and understand—something that can rarely be said of a 1000+ line C shell or Perl script.

As much as I like Python, there are a few things about Perl that I miss. Chief among these is the `regex` implementation in Perl. It is wonderful. Fortunately, the next version of Python will have expanded `regex` capabilities that should rival Perl's. Another is the lack of string interpolation. Since Python doesn't use a `$` or other symbol to distinguish variable names, this is difficult or impossible to do. I'm finding I don't miss the latter too terribly much these days, but I'm eagerly awaiting enhancements to Python's pattern-matching abilities.

There has been a fair bit of interest in making a compiler for Python, but this is not so straightforward, as Python is not a statically typed language (i.e., there are no variable declarations, a variable need not be of a constant size, and worse, a given variable name could represent a different type in various parts of a program, depending on what is assigned to it, though this is not particularly good programming style).

Python and GUIs

Several windowing toolkits exist for Python's various UNIX implementations. The most popular is `tkinter`, which provides an OO interface to Tcl/Tk. `Tkinter` provides the broadest cross-platform support, since it has been ported to Windows 95/NT and MacOS. There is also an extension for using the Athena and/or Motif (or LessTif if you have that instead) widget sets. With version 8 of Tcl/Tk promising a more native look and feel, `Tkinter` will likely become the GUI tool of choice for most implementations of Python.

Python on Other Platforms

Thirty-two-bit ports of Python exist for Windows 95/NT (Pythonwin) and MacOS (for both PowerPC and Motorola 68K-based Macs). WPY is a 16-bit Python for Windows 3.1 and OS/2. Additionally, a separate port exists for DOS. All of these ports, except DOS (for obvious reasons), have support for their OS's native windowing classes.

13.5 Lisp, Scheme, and Guile

```
http://www.cs.cmu.edu/Groups/AI/html/cltl/cltl2.html (Common Lisp)
http://www-swiss.ai.mit.edu/scheme-home.html (Scheme)
```

Lisp is a venerable language; its origins lie in the earliest days of artificial intelligence (AI) research in the mid-1950s. Machines like the IBM 704 and PDP-1 (yes, one not eleven) are associated with it. As computer technology progressed, Lisp was implemented on more and more architectures; no two implementations were completely interoperable so Lisp and its dialects became splintered. In the early to mid-1980s the Common Lisp specification was hammered out and an ANSI standard adopted.

Today, Common Lisp sports functions with variable numbers of arguments, a large library of utility functions (it is four decades old!), and an OOP facility. As you might guess, since it was developed for AI, Lisp also has a very sophisticated condition-handling system.

Scheme

Scheme is a much simpler dialect of Lisp. It has its own separate specification, about 50 pages in length, which lays out a conceptually elegant language. Interestingly, the Scheme specification is shorter than the index of *Common Lisp: The Language*.

Guile

Guile is an implementation of Scheme in an easily embeddable library. It aims to provide a cross-platform, machine-independent architecture for executing Scheme code. For Linux users, it is particularly important as it has been embedded in Gnome and as such is the preferred scripting language for Gnome. More information can be found at `http://www.red-bean.com/guile`.

13.6 Java

`http://www.blackdown.org/`

Sun's Java has weathered some growing pains over the last couple of years. While in many ways Java failed to live up to hyped-up expectations, it delivered on some promises and its user base continues to grow. Its architecture-neutral design (including its GUI tool, the AWT) delivers great portability. Like C++, it is an object-oriented language. Its popularity has given birth to large numbers of contributed extensions (classes) and a great deal of support on the 'net.

Java is different than the other languages here in that it is meant to be completely platform-neutral. Java code is compiled into platform-independent byte-code files that can then be run on a virtual machine (VM). Once a VM has been implemented on a machine, it will (in theory) run any "pure" Java program or applet. Sun has a program for certifying applications and Java implementations as "100% Pure Java." Part of the source licensing agreement from Sun requires that each JDK implementation pass all of Sun's compatibility tests before release. As more ports from Blackdown become available and pass the tests, they'll be posted to the Web site.

Java support can be compiled into the Linux kernel, allowing programs to be executed directly from the command line. Applets can be invoked this way as well, as long as Java binary support has been compiled directly into the kernel and not as a loadable module by setting the execute bit on the HTML file that references the applet class.

The feature that originally won Java much of its popularity is that the VM could be implemented in a Web browser and applets could run in the client

VM provided by a Web server. At first the applets were mainly "gee whiz" things such as simple animations or moving text, clocks, and simple games like tic tac toe. However, because of the enormous amount of contributed code and additional tools and specifications, such as Java DBC (Database Connectivity), "real" applets (and applications) became much more easily realized.

Information on Java for Linux, including where to download the latest developer's kit, can be found at the URL listed above. You can also get a list of what ports are available and what tests passed.

In addition to the port of Sun's JDK, there are a number of open source Java compilers and interpreters. Gcj is an extension to `egcs` that aims to compile Java source and class files to native binaries. It is still under development, but work is progressing very rapidly. For more information, check `http://sourceware.cygnus.com/java/gcj.html`.

Kaffe is a clean room implementation of a Java VM and class libraries. It too is still in the beta stage. It implements most of the JDK 1.1 specification and parts of JDK 1.2. Kaffe comes with Red Hat. For more information, go to `http://www.kaffe.org/`.

Another clean JVM is Japhar, which is published under the LGPL. More information on this developing software is available at `http://www.japhar.org/`.

Guavac is a GPL compiler for Java. It comes with Red Hat as well. Unfortunately, its home page seems to have disappeared as of this writing.

BISS-AWT is a free replacement for the Java AWT. Rather than attempt to provide an OS-specific look and feel, it aims for its own consistent look and feel across all platforms. More information is at `http://www.biss-net.com/biss-awt.html`.

APIs for interfacing Java to virtually everything imaginable exist. A search through your favorite application's contributed software list will likely turn up a Java API.

13.7 Tcl/Tk

`http://www.scriptics.com/`

The Tool command language and Tk toolkit are the inventions of John Osterhout. Tcl is both a scripting language and a C library. Tk is not a separate language, but an extension to Tcl for interfacing to X; it is also available as a C library. Tcl and Tk have been ported to MacOS and Windows, making them good choices for cross-platform application development. However, interfaces for them exist for other languages as well, most notably the `Tkinter` module for Python.

Tcl by itself is actually not a particularly good scripting language. What it is designed for is "gluing" together other languages and programs. It is arguably the most extensible language listed here, with the possible exception of Python. By using Tcl and Tk together, you can quickly develop your own graphical interfaces to text-based programs (as an example).

The latest major release, version 8, enhances the level of native look and feel for Tk across X, MacOS, and Windows. This should make it very popular for building cross-platform GUIs. Those familiar with Tcl and Tk may recall that the last full releases of them were 7.6 and 4.2, respectively, and then may wonder what happened to versions 5, 6, and 7 of Tk. The version numbers of both were synchronized and Scriptics plans to release subsequent versions concurrently.

Because of Tcl's popularity, it has interfaces to several databases (MySQL, mSQL, and Sybase) and even a Netscape plug-in. Additionally, Tcl is, as of 7.6, year 2000-compliant. Scriptics has various applications for Tcl/Tk programming, including a commercial-grade Tk GUI builder, an on-the-fly compiler, and maintenance of the current, native look-and-feel ports to MacOS and Windows.

Tcl's extensibility has allowed for several extensions to both it and Tk. Extended Tcl (Tclx) provides additional functionality with the idea of creating a more standalone scripting language. ObjTcl is just what you might guess it is—a Tcl extension that allows for the use of OOP techniques. Tix is a set of extensions for Tk written in Tk. TkPerl is an interface to Tk for Perl 5.

One of the most useful Tcl extensions is Expect. It is a tool for interacting with other command-line-driven programs that require user interaction. Thus it is possible to automate any number of tasks which might otherwise require a much more complicated solution for automation.

13.8 SQL

The Structured Query Language (SQL) is the language used to talk to relational databases. In reality, it is a set of standards to which DBMS vendors add their own extensions. Because implementations of SQL differ so much, we didn't include a link for SQL; instead, we suggest you consult the documentation for your particular DBMS. We include a list of DBMS applications in our chapter on applications and in the chapter on the Red Hat application CD-ROM.

In general, SQL's syntax is fairly simple and English-like. Some implementation features function like embedded query statements, full regular expressions, or nearly full-blown programming languages. Others may support very little beyond being able to select, delete, insert, and update.

Here are a few simple examples of common SQL commands:

```
select * from table;
```

Gets all entries from all records in `table`.

```
select name,address from customer_list;
```

Gets only name and address from all records in `customer_list`.

```
select name,address from customer_list where cust_id=1;
```

Gets `name` and `address` from `customer_list`, where the `cust_id` field is equal to 1.

```
insert into table values (1, TRUE, "abcdef");
```

Creates a new record in `table` with the values 1 (integer), TRUE (Boolean), and "`abcdef`" (text).

SQL also defines things like Access Control Lists (ACLs), rollbacks (to undo changes to the database in the event of a problem), and in some cases, embedded applications. How each of these features operate, if the DBMS has that capability, is described in the documentation.

13.9 PHP

```
http://www.php.org/
```

Finally, a language we both agree on. While PHP isn't a true language for programming, it makes writing CGI scripts a lot easier. PHP has hooks into most databases we've listed, is embedded in HTML, and is easily added to the Apache Web server. Web-based mail readers, inventory tracking systems, order forms, and other sorts of programs have been written using PHP.

Since PHP is really for Web servers, we describe it in more detail in the Web server chapter. If you have to do a lot of CGI scripting and HTML programming at the same time, PHP is worth looking at.

13.10 Other Languages

There are literally scores of programming languages, certainly more than we have space to cover in any detail here. The languages already described are among the most popular on Linux and many other platforms, but many other languages bear mentioning as well.

Many readers have surely noticed we left out some old standbys.

Oldies but Goodies

FORTRAN

http://www.fortran.com/fortran/

FORTRAN is a venerable language designed mainly for numerical calculation. Its most common incarnation on Linux is in the form of g77, a FORTRAN 77 compiler. The g77 program can also be called f77, and is actually a call to GCC with a few extra options. The latest specification is FORTRAN 90, which is not as common as FORTRAN 77. Few compilers for FORTRAN 90 exist, and no free ones exist for Linux.

Basic

http://www.fys.ruu.nl/~bergmann/basic.html

This language is not as old as FORTRAN, but still popular for its simplicity; Microsoft's Visual Basic and VBScript have played a large part in keeping it popular despite its shortcomings. It has had and continues to have many different incarnations, both interpreted and compiled. Only recently has a Basic compiler become available for Linux. This may be a good programming language to start with if someone has never coded before. It also teaches the "it's not a bug, it's a feature" method of bug control after writing 10 GOTO 10.

Pascal

http://www.pascal-central.com/

Pascal is a language that has always been popular among computer scientists, both to teach good programming techniques and as a general-purpose programming language. Free compilers exist for Linux, and Red Hat includes a p2c program that converts Pascal to C, just in case you have all those high school programming assignments left.

COBOL

```
http://www.cobol.org/
```

Despite the fact that nearly everyone we know laughs at it, more lines of COBOL code have been written than any other language. Its usage is almost completely confined to financial-related applications, but there are an awful lot of banks, finance companies, and people interested in everyone else's money. It is not a language well suited for general programming tasks, but a free compiler exists and is shipped with some Linux distributions.

Of More Recent Vintage

Most of the languages we discuss next are somewhat newer than the previous ones. Also, few of them are included in any Linux distribution. Regardless, these are useful and powerful tools that you may wish to consider using in place of the more common languages.

Smalltalk

```
http://st-www.cs.uiuc.edu/
```

It is one of the fastest growing languages on the planet. Its usage is estimated to be growing at around 60 percent a year. It is a very high-level general programming language, which typically translates into short development time. Its syntax is easier to read, and the language itself is also easy to learn.

Smalltalk is about as purely object-oriented as it gets. Everything is an object, leading to very consistent methods of handling things. Smalltalk advocates the claim that it was "designed with the human being in mind."

Icon

```
http://www.cs.arizona.edu/icon/www/index.html
```

Icon is another high-level language, very high-level in fact. Its roots are in SNOBOL, though in its current incarnation, there is little resemblance. Beyond having very powerful and extensive string and data structure processing features, it does not specifically address a particular problem set. Its syntax is similar to C, but with a much higher level of semantics.

It is well suited to systems programming, though as a high-level compiled language, it is certainly useful and is used for shorter but computationally intensive tasks. Similar to Smalltalk, it was designed with the programmer in mind. This may not be as friendly as the Smalltalk slogan, but the point is clear: Icon's high-level design allows for rapid application development.

As an aside, the name Icon is not an acronym and it was chosen for the language before the term's usage to refer to window manager "icons."

Rexx

`http://www.rexxla.org/`

According to its creator, Rexx is "a procedural language that allows programs and algorithms to be written in a clear and structured way." Rexx's syntax is not particularly unique or unusual. It was designed to be a generic macro language to be used with another application. When its parser encounters a function that it doesn't recognize, it asks the application to handle it. This way, if Rexx is used as the macro language for multiple applications, users need to learn only one macro language and the functions for each application, which presumably will be known from normal use of the application.

Eiffel

`http://www.eiffel-forum.org/`

Eiffel is an OO, compiled language, designed for rapid development of clean, reusable software. There is a strong emphasis on mechanisms and techniques to promote reliability and low bug rates.

Eiffel is an open system and several commercial implementations exist. A GPL'd implementation exists as well. SmallEiffel is still in beta development, but is very usable. More information on it can be found at `http://smalle-iffel.loria.fr/`.

Sather

`http://www.icsi.berkeley.edu/~sather/`

Sather's roots are in Eiffel. Early beta versions of it were nearly subsets of Eiffel 2.0; however, a major release later, both languages have gone their own ways. Sather was and is developed at the University of California, Berkeley, and as you might expect of a language developed at an educational institution, it is freeware.

Sather has garbage collection, multiple inheritance, is strongly typed, and its code can be compiled into C code. Its public license is very liberal to encourage users to contribute to its library.

13.11 Summary

We have literally just skimmed the surface of the scores (at least) of programming languages that are "officially" available and can be compiled for, or easily ported to, Linux. Certainly, we've tried to cover the most popular languages and those that come with most Linux distributions. More likely than not, one or more of these languages will meet your needs as a programmer. If not, a search on your favorite Web search engine will turn up collections of links to programming languages for you to try out.

Web Serving **14**

Various Web servers and extensions for Linux

How to install and configure Apache-derived Web servers under Linux, as well as popular modules, extensions, and key configuration directives are explained, and some examples of their use are given.

With the phenomenal rise in popularity of the World Wide Web (WWW), everyone wants a Web page, be it a small, personal home page where you can pull out your soapbox or a large corporate Web site where a company can distribute information (everything from press releases to hardware driver updates to troubleshooting guides), market themselves, or sell their products online. Linux has proven itself to be a robust, high-performance Web server on everything from a 386 to a DEC Alpha. Still, as with almost any application, there are hardware and software issues to be considered.

A Note on Other Information Services

The Web's popularity has forced many other information services into the background or, in some cases, into obsolescence. Notables include Gopher, WAIS, and Archie. Consequently, we make no effort to cover them in this book and refer the curious to either the Web or any of a number of texts covering Internet information services.

14.1 Web Server Software

There are a number of Web servers (HTTP daemons) available for Linux as both commercial and/or free- or shareware. Additionally, there is the choice of using a secure server versus a non-secure server. The difference between the two is the use of SSL (Secure Sockets Layer, a protocol for encrypting/ decrypting data sent via a network socket). Secure servers use it, insecure ones don't. Typically, non-SSL servers are free- or shareware, while those employing SSL are commercially developed and cost several hundred dollars.

In addition, a Web server can be forking or non-forking. Traditionally, HTTP daemons fork off child processes to handle incoming requests. Each child can typically handle a hundred or so requests, but it handles them serially; this means that heavily loaded Web servers may need to have a large number of child processes, each of which takes up additional RAM and CPU. In a server with a large `httpd` binary (especially a secure server), this can cause problems. The alternative is to have a server that multiplexes incoming connections internally. Typically, this approach has yielded severs with impressive performance.

RAM has been and looks to remain inexpensive, and CPU performance has been increasing by leaps and bounds, so one may be inclined to question whether a multithreaded server is worth the effort. However, it has certainly been one of the main aims of Linux to get as much out of a computer's hardware as possible, which obviously means writing efficient software. This said, there are no non-forking servers that equal the extensibility of the best of the forking servers. It seems likely, though, that soon the extensibility of servers like Apache and the multiplexing of servers like Boa will be combined.

Encryption, the Web, and Uncle Sam

Until recently, there were no Web browsers that supported encryption stronger than 40 bits, mainly due to U.S. export restrictions (based on the rather silly idea that no one outside the U.S. could make stronger encryption). With these restrictions gradually loosening and strong (128-bit) encryption now available on Web servers sold inside and outside the U.S., browsers are appearing which support stronger encryption. Within the U.S., it is possible to get enhanced versions of Netscape's browser, which use 128-bit encryption. For more information on encryption and security, see the chapter on security.

Below is a sampling of secure and unsecure `httpd` servers.

Non-SSL Servers

- Apache (`http://www.apache.org`)—Currently the most popular Web server, hands down. Loaded with features, it is also fast, free, and extensible.

- Boa (`http://www.boa.org/`)—A very new, very fast Web server, freely available with source code. Unlike Apache, it does not fork off child processes to handle additional clients; it multiplexes all connections internally.

- The W3C `httpd` (formerly known as the CERN `httpd`; `http://www.w3.org/pub/WWW/Daemon/`)—The first Web server, ever. No longer in production, it is included for the sake of completeness.

- NCSA (`http://hoohoo.ncsa.uiuc.edu/`)—The successor to CERN and later the basis for Apache, which has largely supplanted it.

- Roxen (`http://www.roxen.com/`)—A commercial Web and FTP server. It also uses an extension to HTML called RXML (developed by Roxen) that allows pages to be modified at download time. It is available for free, or you can purchase it, along with commercial support. Source code is available as well. Additionally, an SSL version is in progress and beta versions of it are freely available.

- WN (`http://hopf.math.nwu.edu/`)—Another freeware Web server. Not as extensible as Apache, but it has some nice features for modifying pages as they are served. (Also available paired with a Gopher server under the name GN. See `http://hopf.math.nwu.edu:70/` for more information.)

- Zeus (`http://www.zeus.co.uk`)—Another non-forking server (like Boa). It is commercial and somewhat pricey, but then you get commercial support. Source code is unavailable.

SSL Servers

- Stronghold (`http://www.c2.net`)—As its alternate name suggests, this is Apache with SSL built in. It is unlike most commercial software in that it comes with source code, and thus, none of Apache's extensibility is lost. Unlike Apache, Stronghold is not the most popular commercial Web server in its class; it is the second most popular secure server.

- Apache-**SSL** (`http://www.algroup.co.uk/Apache-SSL/`)—This is freeware Apache with SSL support. Since the SSL libraries that it uses were illegally exported from the U.S., its use within the U.S. is illegal. It is essentially the same as Stronghold as far as the actual code is concerned. Both it and Stronghold support 128-bit encryption and have done so for some time.

- Roxen (`http://www.roxen.com/`)—Roxen also comes in an SSL flavor.

- Zeus (`http://www.zeus.co.uk`)—Similar to Roxen, Zeus also comes in a secure version.

14.2 Hardware Issues

One of the primary considerations if you are using a forking server or lots of interpreted CGI is memory. Each server child obviously takes up at least as much memory as the size of the executable. Each CGI script requires the loading of its respective interpreter. Dynamic linking of the executables can alleviate the problem to some extent. There are four subsystems that you need to consider beyond the choice of a good personal computer interconnect (PCI) motherboard: memory, CPU, hard disk, and network. The PCI bus has a throughput of 133 Mb/s, which is several times faster than even an ultra SCSI 3 adapter, and is thus well-equipped to handle fast peripherals.

However, there is simply no substitute for more RAM—not swap space (your hard disk is pitifully slow compared to on-board memory), not CPU (if you are swapping to disk, your disk is what's slowing you down), and not a faster network card. RAM is cheap; buy a lot of it.

After RAM, the next most important subsystem is either disk or CPU, depending on the peculiarities of your site. If you make extensive use of CGI, SSI, or database transactions, you will probably want to put a little more CPU in your system. A note here: Don't bother with MMX CPUs. There's really no gain to be had in this situation; just get a faster CPU for the same price, or put the money into RAM or the hard disk.

In a situation where you are simply serving large numbers of static pages, a good, fast disk is probably a good investment. Spend some money to go from a fast or ultra SCSI 2 to ultra SCSI 3. We're assuming here that you have the good sense not to use IDE (or even EIDE) drives in a server.

If you need higher network throughput and are saturating your T1 (i.e., you have no LAN congestion issues), you may want to look into having your server cohosted at an ISP that has T3 access to the Internet backbone, and consider moving from 10 Mb/s Ethernet to 100 Mb/s (fast) Ethernet. A properly configured Linux Web (and/or FTP) server can saturate a fast Ethernet card and thus multiple T3s.

14.3 Apache and ApacheSSL/Stronghold

Because of its popularity, rich feature set, extensibility, and power, we will concentrate on Apache, although much of the information here will apply to any Web server.

As mentioned above, Apache is freely available with source code. Apache also provides an API. These two features allow for a great deal of customization and extensibility. Additionally, Apache is HTTP 1.1-compliant. This latest revision of HTTP introduces many performance enhancements to the protocol.

Getting Started

Since Apache is freely available, a number of Linux distributions are shipped with it, Red Hat included.

1. Where is the document root for the server? In other words, where is the directory that contains the root of the directory tree that is served when someone hits your server? It is the directory from which files are served if no path information, aside from a filename, is given (for example, `http:/ /www.ratatosk.org/davinci.html` versus `http://www.ratatosk. org/artists/surreal/dali.html`). This is typically something like `/ home/httpd/html` or `/home/httpd/htdocs` (so the second URL above would retrieve `/home/httpd/html/artists/surreal/dali.html`).

2. Where are the configuration files? Typically, `/etc/httpd/conf, / home/httpd/conf/, /usr/local/etc/httpd/conf`, or something similar is the directory used for these files.

3. Is the server running? Depending on how the server was configured when Linux was installed, the HTTP daemon may start automatically at boot time. You can use the `ps` command to check if `httpd` is running as follows: `ps -waux | grep httpd`. If it is not, you need to invoke it as root and tell it where to find the directory containing the configuration files. For example, if your configuration directory is `/etc/httpd/conf`, you would type something like `httpd -d /etc/httpd`. If the directory containing your `httpd` binary is not in your path, you will need to use the absolute path to invoke it. Typically, `httpd` lives in one of the `sbin` directories such as `/usr/local/sbin`, `/usr/sbin`, or on rare occasions, `/sbin`.

Aside from the various modules that can be used to extend Apache at compile time, there are many items that can be specified at run-time in the `.conf` files, `httpd.conf` and `srm.conf`. These two files control parameters, such as aliases for directories, aliases for icons, images, CGI scripts/programs, virtual host directives, the document root directory, the file to be served from a directory if no other file is specified in the URL, and various access control and authentication directives.

<Directory> and .htaccess

These two tools are used to modify access of all types for directory trees. `<Directory>` directives typically reside in the `srm.conf` or `httpd.conf` file. They can also occur in the `<Virtualhost>` directive (more on this later.) The `.htaccess` file resides somewhere in a directory tree of HTML documents. In both instances, directives placed in the directories are recursively effective for all the files and subdirectories in those directories. For example, to enforce basic authorization for a directory and all its contents, you could put the following in a `.htaccess` file in that directory (say `/home/web`):

```
AuthType Basic
AuthUserFile /home/cary/etc/passwd
AuthGroupFile /dev/null
AuthName Realm of the Kazoos
<LIMIT GET POST PUT>
require valid-user
</LIMIT>
```

or in a `<Directory>` directive:

```
<Directory /home/web>
```

```
AuthType Basic
AuthUserFile /home/cary/etc/passwd
AuthGroupFile /dev/null
AuthName Realm of the Kazoos
<LIMIT GET POST PUT>
require valid-user
</LIMIT>
</Directory>
```

The `<LIMIT>` directive tells the server what HTTP methods require a valid user, in this case, `GET`, `POST`, and `PUT` (`PUT` is used for file uploading).

CGI and SSI

The Common Gateway Interface (CGI) and Server Side Includes (SSI) are the two most common ways to execute external programs. CGI is designed to both receive and send information from and to the server. SSI is more one-way; mainly it sends information. SSI can do more than simply call external programs. It can also include files, echo some simple system information such as the local time, and even execute CGI.

Perl is the preemptive language for CGI programming. This is something of a double-edged sword. On the one hand, large collections of "canned" scripts for various common CGI tasks exist. It also has very powerful features for processing strings, including a large set of regular expression atoms and operators. Since CGI frequently involves large amounts of text processing, this helps to fuel Perl's popularity. On the other hand, Perl is not the easiest language to learn, nor is its syntax particularly easy to read (there are obfuscated Perl contests!).

After Perl, there are several languages that are popular for use in CGI programs: Python, Tcl, C, and Java. Additionally, there are languages that can be embedded in HTML and parsed later by a CGI program; PHP (discussed later) falls into this category. The PHP parser can also be embedded into Apache and servers based on it.

The number of books published on CGI is considerable and they cover the topic much more thoroughly than is suitable for us to do here. One criticism of most of the literature available is that it tends to focus nearly entirely on Perl, ignoring, for the most part, C, Python, and other languages. C, in particular, is very useful since, as a compiled language, CGI written in it is faster and lighter weight. Of course, development times in C are much longer.

At this point in time, all of the languages mentioned have more or less equivalent extensions/modules/libraries for dealing with the peculiarities of CGI and interfacing with everything from TCP/IP sockets to the operating system to a database. As such, the choice of a language for CGI is largely up to you. All of the above are shipped with most Linux distributions and are available for free from their respective authors.

Web Pages for Your Users

In a situation where you have multiple users on your machine, be it at an ISP or at a publisher, some of them will likely be interested in setting up a home page for themselves. This is not something that will typically consume a large amount of resources on your server, unless you have a large number of home pages or have very popular users. Additionally, serving static HTML poses no security concerns beyond those of running the server itself. All that aside, there will almost certainly be users who will want to use CGI, SSI, or some other server-parsed content that will add a dynamic element to their Web pages. Now, you have a security issue.

The various solutions range from simply allowing users full access to tools like SSI and CGI (in a situation where you trust all your users) to some sort of limited SSI/CGI to completely forbidding the use of them. You can also allow or disallow the use of them on a user-by-user basis.

In a small business, or possibly on a corporate LAN, you may likely choose the former route, while at an ISP, where you know few of the users personally, you will likely choose one of the latter two routes.

Fortunately, Apache makes controlling access to these and other tools fairly easy via the .htaccess file and <Directory> directive.

Restricting the Use of CGI and SSI

The <Directory> directive is your friend. It is the way you specify what can and can't be done in which directories. Couple this with Linux user and group permissions, and you can exercise very fine control over who can do what in which areas of your Web space.

In general, unless the server is already so insecure it doesn't matter, or you can trust your users to not inadvertently or purposefully write CGI that compromises your server in some way, you will not want CGI to be executable from arbitrary directories. Of course, if the server is accessible only to you and possibly a few others, you can leave things fairly open and not worry about it.

Additionally, you will likely want to prohibit browsers from roaming through the filesystem, be it a particular user's or the root filesystem. In other words, if a URL points to a directory that does not contain an index file, the server will return a `404` (`File not Found`) error instead of displaying the directory's listing.

To make the entire filesystem off-limits to the server, a directive like this would be placed in the `access.conf`:

```
<Directory />
 AllowOverride None
 Order deny,allow
 Deny from all
 Options None
</Directory>
```

"Wait a second! I want to serve Web pages!" Ahh... then you need to tell Apache what directories it can serve pages from. A statement like this:

```
<Directory /home/*/public_html>
 Order allow,deny
 Allow from all
 AllowOverrides IncludesNOEXEC
</Directory>
```

lets you serve pages from your users' `public_html` (this is the default directory from which files are served when a request that ends in `~username` is received) directories and lets them use SSI that doesn't execute external programs or CGI scripts, and:

```
<Directory /home/httpd/htdocs>
Order deny,allow
Allow from all
AlowOverrides All
</Directory>
```

lets you serve pages from what is commonly the document root for the server and allows all of the restrictions to be overridden. Now you can set up CGI directories in this tree. You can do this with additional `<Directory>` directives or in an `.htaccess` file. If you choose the latter route, be sure to make the `.htaccess` file not writable by the user, unless they can be trusted not to abuse the privilege. However, if you plan to have all CGI pass by you, or perhaps someone else, you may want to set up one directory that is writable by root or `httpd` only. In any event, to turn on CGI in a directory, assuming it can be overridden, using `.htaccess`, you need the following:

```
Options ExecCGI
```

There are many other options you can turn on and off, including the symbolic links, indexing, and multiviews. For details on them, look at the Apache documentation.

Other Useful Modules and Directives

Whole books have been written on Apache, and since this is only one chapter, we're only going to touch on the more interesting and useful features. We aren't going to talk about most of the directives that appear in the configuration files since it's fairly easy to understand their syntax from the usage, and they are explained fairly well in the Apache documentation.

We've already met some of them: `.htaccess`, `<Directory>`, `Options`, `AllowOverride`, `Allow`, and `Deny`, and we've given a few examples of their use. Now we'll discuss the other most common and useful directives.

- `User` and `Group`—These set the UID and GID under which the server will run.

- `ServerRoot`—This is the root of the server's directory tree. It is typically the directory where the log file, `.conf` file, and document root subdirectories are. The locations of these can be overridden on the command line or in the configuration files.

- `DocumentRoot`—This is the base of the document tree.

- `UserDir`—This is the subdirectory within a user's home directory, which is the root of that user's Web space.

- `ServerType`—This specifies the type of server (obviously), either standalone or proxy. Unless you are setting up a proxy server, this should be standalone.

- `Port`—This is the TCP/IP port at which the server will listen. Port 80 is the standard; for an HTTP request to be heard on another port, it will have to be specified in the URL like so: `http://www.wombat.net:81/`. The server must be run as root to use ports 1023 and lower.

- `Listen`—If you want the server to listen at an additional port, use this. It takes two arguments: the alias and path to the directory. The path can either be relative to the `ServerRoot` or an absolute path.

- `ScriptAlias`—Often, for security reasons, you will want to have the directories from which CGI programs can be executed outside of the directory tree. Or, you may simply want to provide a shortcut for referencing a directory containing CGI programs.

- `Alias`—Similar to `ScriptAlias`, but only non-CGI files can be served from the directory.

- `VirtualHost`—If you want requests that come in on a different IP, server name, or port to be served from a different document root, a different server name, or with aliases pointing to different directories, then this is the directive for you. `DocumentRoot`, `Directory`, `ScriptAlias`, `Alias`, `User`, `Group`, `UserDir`, or `ServerName` can be used as arguments inside it. A couple of examples should help to demonstrate the power of the `VirtualHost` directive.

A server for `http://www.dognails.com` on port 80 with its own `cgi-bin` and document root is:

```
<VirtualHost www.dognails.com>
ServerName www.dognails.com
DocumentRoot /web/dognails/www
ScriptAlias /cgi-bin/ /web/dognails/cgi-bin/
</VirtualHost>
```

To serve all requests on port 1200, as from a separate `DocumentRoot` looks like:

```
Listen 1200
<VirtualHost *:1200>
DocumentRoot /usr/local/www1200
</VirtualHost>
```

Extensions for Apache

One of the more complicated extensions with a difficult setup process, suEXEC is a wrapper that allows CGI programs to be executed under a different UID than that under which the server is running. This is often used by ISPs that let their users maintain their own CGIs; this forces the scripts to execute as those users. This obviously strongly encourages the user to create good, secure CGI scripts. It also allows access control similar to that allowed by the password file.

Because suEXEC can open some serious security holes, its security model imposes several additional restrictions. The target program must reside in the Apache `Web space` and thus, the path to it cannot start with a / or have back references (..). Obviously, the target user and group must be valid and their IDs must be above a minimum (typically 100 or 500), which will prohibit execution as the root user or group. The target program cannot be `set uid` or gid, and the final, non-trivial restrictions are that the directory containing the program to be executed and the program itself can only be writable by the target user and they must belong to the target user and target group.

suEXEC comes in a separate C source file and accompanying header file. Before compiling suEXEC, the header file needs to be edited to reflect the particulars of your system. The following may need to be changed: HTTPD_USER, typically nobody, or maybe a "Web" or "WWW" user; LOG_EXEC, the log file for suEXEC transactions; DOC_ROOT, the root of the Apache Web space; and SAFE_PATH, the PATH environment variable for suEXEC. Then you need to compile suEXEC (gcc -o suexec suexec.c), chown it to root, set the set userID bit (chmod 4711 suexec), and copy it to its final destination.

Apache must now be recompiled to use the suEXEC wrapper. In the src/httpd.h file, you will need to add or edit a line like this:

```
#define SUEXEC_BIN "/usr/sbin/suexec"
```

to reflect where you installed the suid root suexec binary. When you start your new httpd, you should see this message:

```
Configuring Apache for use with the suexec wrapper.
```

To disable suEXEC, you can remove the binary, change its ownership from root, or unset the set uid bit.

User and Group directives in VirtualHost directives can be used to tell suEXEC the target user and group for executing CGI. Another way is for the target user to do so in HTTP requests to user directories. For example, http://thppt.org/~dweezle/somescript.cgi—somescript.cgi would be executed as the user dweezle. If neither of these conditions exists, the script will be executed as the main user and group.

PHP

One of the most useful extensions for Apache is the PHP program. PHP is actually usable as CGI, FastCGI, or compiled into Apache (linked either statically or dynamically). Which option to employ is a matter of taste and use. If you plan on using it lightly, employing it as CGI or FastCGI is fine, though for more extensive use, you will likely want to compile it into Apache, but this will raise your memory usage noticeably.

PHP is a scripting language with syntax similar to Perl and C. It is embedded within HTML, set off by a variation on the comment tag: <?>. The code within the tag is parsed (either by the server itself or the CGI script, depending on your setup), and the output, if any, replaces the tag. This is very similar to how the server side includes a function. Typically, a special extension (`.php`) is used for PHP files to tell Apache to parse the file before sending it to the client. If you plan to use PHP in most or all of your files, you may want to tell Apache to parse all HTML files.

PHP boasts many functions for connecting to and extracting information from various databases, including mSQL, PostgreSQL, MySQL, Solid, Sybase, and Oracle. See the database chapter for more information on the above database systems. Additionally, it has very powerful support for Netscape cookies, file upload, and the GD library. GD is a C library for PNG creation. PHP also has additional functionality for setting arbitrary HTTP headers (besides that which sets cookies).

SSL (Secure Sockets Layer)

As mentioned above, SSL is a protocol for sending encrypted data via a network socket. This allows for some peace of mind when transmitting sensitive data over the Web. There are two implementations of Apache with SSL: Stronghold and Apache-SSL. The legality of Apache-SSL is somewhat in question for commercial use in the U.S., as RSA claims the SSL libraries it uses are covered by patents owned by RSA. So, for commercial use within the U.S., you will likely want Stronghold. In either case, full source code is available.

Since Stronghold is well-documented and comes with commercial support, we'll go through the setup of Apache-SSL.

To use SSL with Apache, you must retrieve two things: the SSLeay and the SSL patch for Apache. These will have names like `SSLeay-0.8.0.tar.gz` and `apache_1.2.0+ssl_1.8.tar.gz`, respectively. Make sure the patch you get matches the major and minor versions of Apache that you are using. You will also need at least version 2.1 of the patch.

SSLeay can be obtained at `ftp://ftp.psy.uq.oz.au/pub/Crypto/SSL/` and Apache-SSL can found at `ftp://ftp.ox.ac.uk/pub/crypto/SSL`.

Unpack SSLeay, `cd` into the source directory, run `./Configure linux-elf` (or `linux-aout` if you don't have an older `a.out` system), `make`, `make test`, and finally `make install`. It should compile with some warnings, but pass the make test.

Unpack Apache-SSL in the root of the Apache distribution (not in the `src` subdirectory). Apply the patch: `patch < SSLpatch`. If this step produces an error, it is probably because you have an older version of the patch. Get a new version from your Linux distribution's Web site or any GNU mirror. Edit `src/Configuration` as you would normally, and change the SSL-related directives to reflect any peculiarities on your system. If you are using a fresh copy of Apache, remember to add any extras you need for other Apache modules you might be using, such as PHP.

```
./Configure
make
```

You should now have a shiny new `httpsd`!

If you get symbol errors, you may need to fiddle with the order of libraries in the link stage of the make, as well as verify you are using the correct library paths.

The httpd.conf

This will likely seem a little bizarre to anyone used to Apache's normal runtime `.config` file setup, but `httpd.conf` is the only `.config` file used. `srm.conf` and `access.conf` are both empty. For example, `httpd.conf` is included with the SSLpatch distribution. There are a few notes on setting up your `httpd.conf` that we want to give you. These guidelines should work for Stronghold as well, since it is so similar to Apache-SSL.

Edit `httpd.conf` to reflect your setup and execute `httpsd`. Try connecting to the SSL server: `https://your.host.com/` (note the "s" after the "http"). If you can't connect, check the `error_log`, the `ssl_log`, and your `.conf` file. Fix any problems and restart the server with a `kill -1 /pid/`, assuming it started on the first try, or just try to start it again.

Unless you want to maintain two sets of `.config` files, you will want to run both the unsecure and secure servers on the same binary and `.config` file. The easiest way to do this is to set up `httpd.conf` just as you would normally, except that you will need to add the contents of your `srm.conf` and `access.conf` files as well, and then use the `Listen` and `VirtualHost` directives to run the secure server on a separate port. The default port for HTTPS is 443, so you will probably want to use that. Then, simply move the `SSLflag` on directive into the `VirtualHost` directive.

Start Apache-SSL and make sure you can connect to both the non-secure server (`http://your.host.com/`) and the secure one (`https://your.host.com/`).

By default, Stronghold and Apache-SSL use version 3 of the SSL protocol. If you require SSL v2, add this line to the base level (it can't be in `Virtual-Host` or any other directive) of the `httpd.conf`:

```
SSLProtocol SSLv2
```

14.4 Logging

As you might expect, Apache supports the Common Log Format (CLF). It can also write its logs in the format used by NCSA's server; this is nice if you have homegrown log analysis tools developed for NCSA httpd.

The number of tools for analyzing httpd access logs is bewildering. Many are free, but there are commercial tools out there as well, though few run on Linux. On the other hand, more of the free ones run on Linux than on Mac or Windows machines.

Which one you choose to use is a matter of taste. We will describe a couple below, but will likely just have to try some and see if you like them.

The log analysis tool we have found most useful is http-analyze. It is free and information on it can be found at http://www.netstore.de/Supply/ http-analyze/index.html.

One particular tool deserves special note: 3Dstats. It formats its output in VRML, which you can view with a VRML scene viewer like vrweb. 3Dstats's home page is http://www.netstore.de/Supply/3Dstats/ and vrweb's is http://www.iicm.edu/vrweb.

To investigate other analysis tools for your httpd logs, a Web search on http log analysis will produce more choices than you will have time to try out.

14.5 Databases and Web Servers

With the desire for dynamic content in the presentation of large amounts of information, it is natural that databases would enter the Web equation. They are the best and fastest way (not the most space-efficient, though!) to organize and retrieve data. There is support for many free and commercial databases in the popular languages used for CGI, including Python, Perl, and C.

The choice of which database to use is dependent on many factors. Among the most important is easy access via CGI or PHP if you choose to employ one of them. For a list of database servers available for Linux, see the chapter on applications.

14.6 Setting Up a Killer Web Server

This section will walk you through setting up a "complete" Web server: Apache with PHP compiled in and integrated support for MySQL, a freeware (for most purposes) database server. While this is not a typical setup, it is an extremely powerful one that is becoming more common.

In this setup, Apache depends on PHP, which in turn depends on MySQL. Consequently, you will need to install MySQL first. It should be noted that PHP does not require any database support at all, but the idea behind this exercise is to build a Web server with very fast CGI-like features tied in with a very fast database server.

MySQL

If possible, when you are anticipating large amounts of database activity, MySQL should be installed on a separate physical disk from the document root of your Web server. The MySQL source is available from the MySQL home page at `http://www.tcx.se/`, as well as from mirror sites in the U.S. If you prefer, you can retrieve a precompiled binary distribution. There is also an active mailing list for MySQL. Information on joining it can be found on the MySQL home page. Documentation is available there as well.

The most recent versions of MySQL require recent versions of `libc`. If you don't have a new enough `libc` and are skittish about upgrading it, just install a binary version.

If you install a binary distribution, it will create a directory named `mysql-<version>` with various subdirectories for libraries, header files, and data files. If you compile and install from the source, `mysql` subdirectores will be created in `/usr/local/lib` and `/usr/local/include`. The data folders and files will be created in `/usr/local/var`.

Note the prefix path (`/usr/local` by default); it will be needed when you compile PHP and, later, Apache.

MySQL uses GNU `autoconf`. There are a few configuration options to be especially aware of:

`--prefix`	Installation directory prefix (/usr/local by default)
`--enable-thread-safe-client`	Make thread safe client library
`--without-debug`	Compile without extra debugging code
`--without-server`	Only compile client library and programs
`--without-perl`	Don't build and install the Perl interface
`--enable-shared`	Build a shared client library

After the configuration finishes, you can run `make` and then `make install`. If this is your first time installing MySQL, you will also need to install the grants database. Chapter 12 has more details on installing and setting up

MySQL. If you are just upgrading MySQL, you need only to start and restart the server.

Okay, this is the paragraph where we tell you that you need to know SQL to start using your new Web server and that this isn't a book on SQL and that you will need to either search out tutorials on the Web or buy a book on SQL. The MySQL home page has some examples in its online documentation and a separately maintained manual, more importantly, tells what additional features MySQL has beyond the standard ones. A good SQL tutorial can be found at `http://w3.one.net/~jhoffman/sql-tut.htm` and there are others to be had, as well as numerous books.

PHP

PHP is the next item to compile. You will, however, need to have Apache unpacked since at the end of the compile, the PHP module and `libphp` will be copied into the Apache source directory. The PHP home page is at `http://www.php.net/`; very complete documentation, information on the PHP mailing list, the source code, and other related items can be found there.

Since you are building only the library and not the CGI version of PHP, compilation should be easy; there is no linking step, so there are no linking errors. All the potentially sticky linking will come when you compile and link Apache. You will need to know the MySQL install root and the location of the Apache source code. PHP, as you will notice when you run the install script (something of a misnomer since it does not install anything), supports a large number of databases and enhanced file uploading, logging, and access control. Depending on your system's resources and your Web site's style, you may want to enable some or all of these.

Obviously you will want to answer `Yes` to MySQL support. If you have any of the other supported databases, you may want to enable them as well. PHP also supports the `GD` graphics library. If you wish to enable this, make sure `libgd` and its associated header file are in `/usr/lib` and `/usr/include`, or `/usr/local/lib` and `/usr/local/include`, or provide the directories in the list of additional directories to search for libraries and header files. It is fine to let PHP use the Linux system `regex` library, and it should find the `gdbm` library and header that come with Linux as well. Change directories to the `src` directory and run `make`.

At the end of the `make`, directions for editing the Apache configuration file will be printed. You may want to copy them into a file or editor to keep them for the Apache compilation.

Apache

The Apache configuration and compilation are straightforward. Move into the source directory, edit the file `Configuration`, and make the changes indicated at the end of the PHP `make`. The configuration file is loaded with various modules you can disable or enable by commenting or uncommenting the appropriate lines in the file. In general, the slimmer you can make the server, the better. Comment out what you obviously don't need. If you're not sure, leave the module in. If you anticipate having large numbers of users to authenticate, you will probably want to enable a database-based authentication scheme using `(g)dbm`, MySQL, or mSQL. A complete list of modules and their descriptions can be found at `http://www.apache.org/`.

After you have finished editing, run the `Configure` script and then `make`. If you have linking errors, 90 percent of the time they can be solved by rearranging the list of libraries in `LFLAGS` in the `Configuration` file. Most of the rest of the time it is simply a forgotten library or library path. Persevering though a little trial and error should result in an `httpd` binary. After testing the server a little, you will likely want to strip it to save on memory requirements.

If you still can't get your server to link, the best forums for help will likely be the PHP and/or MySQL mailing lists, unless you believe the problem to be unrelated to the addition of these packages.

Now check `httpd.conf` and `srm.conf`.

Under Linux, Apache is commonly set up as follows:

- The `httpd` binary lives in `/usr/sbin`.
- The logs are kept in `/var/log/http`.
- The configuration files are in `/etc/http/conf`.
- The document root is `/home/httpd/htdocs`.

All of these are alterable. Obviously, you can keep the server binary wherever you choose. The configuration files' location is settable on the command line, and the log location and document root are settable in the configuration files.

To tell Apache to parse `.php3` files with the embedded PHP parser, add a line like this to your `srm.conf`:

```
AddType application/x-httpd-php .php3
```

If you want to parse every file and end them all in `.html`, change ".php3" to ".html" in the statement.

Now start up the server. With the above setup, you would enter `httpd -f /etc/httpd/conf/httpd.conf -d /home/httpd`. Make or edit (if it already exists) an `index.html` in the document root. Somewhere in the document, add a line like `<? phpinfo(); ?>`.

The `phpinfo` function should spit out a few screenfuls of CGI environment variables and configuration information. If it doesn't, check to make sure you added the correct line to your `srm.conf` or `httpd.conf` to tell Apache to parse `.php3` or `.html` files, and then make sure you have the right extension on your file and `mod_php` enabled in your Apache source `Configuration` file.

The PHP documentation describes how to connect to MySQL databases either locally or remotely, as well as the usage of the various functions for performing queries and database and table administration.

There are other goodies you may want to consider adding to your server. If you use lots of Python or Perl CGI, you can embed the interpreters for these into Apache. Respectively, these modules are `PyApache` and `Mod_Perl`. If you wish to enhance security, you can use digest authentication instead of basic authentication. Also you can add in SSL support as mentioned earlier in this chapter. Finally, there are modules for powerful URL rewriting using `regex` pattern-matching and replacement, correcting misspelled URIs, and tracking users through the site using cookies. New modules are being added all the time and not all are shipped with the source. Check the Apache Web site for the most up-to-date list.

14.7 Streaming Audio and Video

Streaming is an alternate way to deliver content. Rather then waiting for an entire movie file to download before starting it, the data are displayed as they are sent (more or less; there is some buffering). This, of course, means that the client can start displaying the data much sooner. Additionally, it is easy to then send and output streams from streaming input (as opposed to a static file).

With the rising demand for multimedia content on the Web, sooner or later (probably sooner!) you will need to be able to serve streaming audio and video from your Web server. Lucky for Linux, RealNetworks makes its RealServer for Linux.

The basic version is free and intended for personal and single-site use (i.e., ISPs do not get to use the free version). Installation is as simple as uncompressing the distribution file, running the setup script, and answering some configuration questions.

RealServer will deliver both live and on-demand (stored in a file) streams. The default port for the server is 7070.

The Plus version, which is not free and not yet available for Linux, can be used by a hosting service. Additionally, the Plus version has enhanced performance, a printed manual, GUI, and, as you might expect, technical and upgrade support.

The default installation directory is `/usr/local/pnserver`. After the installation script completes, change to the install directory and start the server:

```
# bin/pnserver server.cfg
```

You will be prompted to register the server. You can skip this step if you wish without any effect on the functionality or performance of the server. Point your Web browser at the machine you installed the server on, port 7070. You will be prompted to enter the username and password you provided during setup. This will bring up a page with links to some samples, the server status page, and links to some areas on RealNetworks' Web site.

Test the server by trying some of the sample files to be sure it's running. RealMedia files can be placed in `/usr/local/pnserver/content` and accessed via URLs like `http://www.foo.net/ramgen/audio.rm`. You can also set up aliases or subdirectories for human users to place their own files in.

Generating Content Files

Various encoders exist for creating real audio and video. Unfortunately, only an audio encoder exists for Linux. To encode video or audio/video, you will need an MS Win32 machine or a Macintosh.

The media encoder, `rmenc`, for Linux is free as well and can be used to convert `.wav` and `.au` files into RealMedia files. Additionally, if you have the OSS sound drivers, it can listen to your soundcard's output and record that.

If you wish to record individual tracks from your CD-ROM, you can use `cdda2wav` to make `.wav` files and convert them using `rmenc`.

14.8 Summary

This chapter scratched the surface of what has become an incredibly huge and complicated subject in just a few short years. We discussed two types of servers, secure and insecure, as well as two methods of implementing them, the common forking server and the newer and less common multiplexing server.

Because of its popularity, extensibility, and power, we went into detail about Apache and its two secure derivatives: Apache-SSL, a freeware secure server of questionable legality in the U.S.; and Stronghold, a commercially supported and legal secure server available in and outside the U.S.

We also discussed various methods for interacting with the system the server is running on: CGI and SSI, as well as PHP, a scripting language designed to be embedded into HTML and then parsed by the PHP interpreter running as CGI or FastCGI or compiled into Apache.

Setup and configuration of a server for streaming audio and video were examined. Additionally, tools for creating content files were also discussed.

Lastly, we went through the compilation and setup of a non-secure Apache server with PHP compiled into it. In turn, PHP was configured with MySQL support so it could access MySQL databases locally or remotely on other machines.

X Windowing System 15

Giving a nice graphical
front end to Linux

The X Windowing System (or just X, if you like) is a windowing system designed to give a GUI to UNIX.

The implementation of X for Linux is XFree86, and it is almost always installed as part of a normal Red Hat installation. While installing X is not required, it makes administration much easier due to the graphical applications that Red Hat provides to administer the system. The power behind X is that you can change just about any operation of the interface, like the way menus are presented and the contents of the menus. There's even an interface that closely resembles Windows 95, in case you need a familiar face.

15.1 X Concepts

The idea behind X is a client/server setup. The server is really an X protocol server on the user's console, which handles the display to the screen. The

253

server then talks to clients, such as a window manager and applications and puts them on the screen.

The configuration file for `XFree86` is called `XF86config` and it is located in `/etc/X11/XF86config`. This file contains setup information for your mouse, the video card you're using, and the type of display (monitor) that you're using.

The programming for XFree86 allows you, as the user, to set your monitor and video card to much better resolutions than you can get by default through Windows 98 or other video graphics array (VGA) modes. The default modes (640X480, 800X600, and 1024X768) are still available, and very easy to set up. To get custom modes, you'll need some information about the video card and your monitor (video bandwidth, horizontal frequency, and vertical frequency).

15.2 Setting Up X Using Xconfigurator

Red Hat's Xconfigurator program gives a simple text-based interface for setting up X. The drawback is that you have less control over the screen modes, but you do get choices for the standard video rates (640X480 through whatever your monitor and video card support).

Before running Xconfigurator, make sure that your mouse is set through Red Hat. Run the `mouseconfig` program to set this in case you need to. You can also check `/etc/sysconfig/mouse` to make sure the settings look correct.

Xconfigurator can be started by the root user as `/usr/X11R6/bin/Xconfigurator`. If your video card can be detected, it will be listed; otherwise, you will get a list of supported cards and you can select the card that most closely resembles yours. For the most part, this is a list of chipsets that X supports. It should be easy from your video card documentation (or by looking at the video card) to find out what chipset is being used in your system.

Next you'll be asked about the type of monitor you have. If yours is not on the list, select something close to what you have and see if it works—you can always re-run Xconfigurator in case your first configuration doesn't work. You can also select `custom` or `standard monitor` or `standard multisync`. The `custom` selection will ask for the horizontal and vertical settings of your monitor, which you can find in the monitor's manual.

The screen will blink a few times to test the monitor and video card settings. If the program cannot determine how much video memory you have, you will have to select the amount that you have. Then you'll be asked to select whatever video modes you want to use as a combination of resolution and color depth. Eight-bit color depth is 256 unique colors, 16-bit is 65,536 colors, and 24-bit is true color (16 million colors). X will start in the lowest resolution and color depth listed unless you tell it at startup to change to a different color mode. The best bet is to choose a few settings in the 16- and 24-bit areas, unless you need 256-color support. Also remember that more colors take up more memory, so if you have under 32MB, you may want to use 8-bit mode. Once the program completes, there will be an XF86config file in /etc/X11. You can edit this file to make changes about the mouse you have or modify other settings. Xconfigurator doesn't autodetect any wheel-based mice (like the Microsoft Intelliwheel), but you can get a program like imwheel to add support. You can find the latest version of imwheel at http:/ /www.freshmeat.net.

15.3 Setting Up X Manually

To configure your X system with default modes, make sure your X server is installed. For normal VGA modes, this is the X_VGA file. Going from there, the Mach32 server is called XF86_Mach32, the S3 server is called XF86_S3, and so on. Since these servers are included on the Red Hat CD-ROM as .rpm files, you can easily install the desired server. See the chapter on RPM for more information on installing .rpm files.

The XF86config program will allow you to set up some default video modes. Starting the program as root gives a few configuration screens and some text to read. Then you get into the configuration section. Select your mouse type (Microsoft, MouseSystems, Bus, etc.). The preference here is to select a three-button mouse, since X will allow you to use all three buttons. If you select a two-button mouse, you'll need to press both the left and right mouse buttons to simulate the middle button.[1]

The next few options depend on the type of mouse you selected. If you selected a three-button mouse, then you won't need to select Emulate3Buttons. Next you'll need to enter the location of the mouse, which may be /dev/mouse. If /dev/mouse doesn't exist, enter the /dev file that has your mouse in it. Remember that COM1: under DOS is /dev/ ttyS0 under Linux, and so on. A few other options may follow, including using the ALT key as the "meta" key to generate characters not normally available on your keyboard.

---

[1] When you see Emulate 3 Buttons later on, this is what it's talking about.

Next is the monitor configuration section. This is where you need to know the horizontal sync range. There are nine predefined monitors you can choose from, and a tenth allows you to define your own range.

WARNING: Be sure that the numbers entered here are correct, because a wrong monitor and video card pair can damage your monitor, video card, or both.

Next is the vertical sync. Here you have a choice of about four monitor types, plus one to let you define your own. Once the vertical sync is set, you can enter information about your monitor. This section isn't necessary, as it allows XFree86 to use multiple monitors at the same time. You can either press ENTER and use the default for each, or enter a unique identifier for your monitor, along with a vendor name and model name.

Once this is completed, you set up the video card. It's important to select the correct video card because two video cards from the same vendor can have very different hardware internally. Selecting the wrong card can damage your card or monitor.

Now you get to select the type of server to run. If you selected a video card that has an accelerator chip supported by XFree86, you'll be able to select that X server.

The options are as follows.

1. The `XF86_Mono` server, which has 640x480 resolution with two colors, black and white. This should work for all VGA cards. If you suspect a problem with your video card or are unsure of the type of video card you have, this may be a good starting point.

2. `XF86_VGA16` server, which is also 640x480, but with 16 colors. This should also work with all VGA-compatible cards.

3. `XF86_SVGA` server, which provides super VGA (SVGA) resolutions with 256 colors. Most SVGA cards will work with it, but may not have the best acceleration.

4. `Accelerated` server, which is for accelerated cards. This gives more than 256 colors for most servers, and higher resolutions. These servers also utilize any of the faster chipsets in most modern video cards.

5. The server for the video card you selected earlier.

If you select the fifth option, the best server for your card is set up for installation.

Now you must give information about your video card. First you'll probably be asked about the amount of video memory on your card. You'll get five selections from 256K to 4096K (4MB), and a sixth selection that allows you to enter your own amount.

Once that is completed, you'll be allowed to enter a description for your video card similar to the monitor descriptions above. You can either press ENTER through the entries, or type in the description, vendor, and model of your video card.

If you have an S3- or AGX-based video card, you may need to know the type of random access memory digital-to-analog converter (RAMDAC) the card has. The RAMDAC is used to get high color (greater than about 32K colors) from the server. Choose the appropriate option if you have those cards and know the RAMDAC type, or you can just press ENTER.

Some video cards also have a programmable clock. Most clocks are not programmable, but if yours is (some Diamond cards and some S3 cards are), enter the type of clockchip you have. It should be found in your owner's manual, or on the card itself. If you don't have a clockchip, just press ENTER.

At this point, the XF86config program will attempt to find the clocks that your card supports by using the X -probeonly command. This command doesn't start X itself, but asks the video card to return what clocks it knows about. These clocks are important to determine the correct resolutions you can use.

Starting X

Now you should be ready to start X. Doing this is simply a matter of getting to a command prompt and typing:

```
> startx
```

This will start the X server in the lowest color depth and resolution you selected. If you configured your server to use 8-bit color (256 colors) and also 16-bit color (65K colors), just typing startx will start the X server in 8-bit mode. To start it up in 16-bit mode, use the following:

```
> startx -- -bpp 16
```

For the sake of extra memory, you may want to log out of other virtual consoles (VCs) before starting X. You can start multiple shells called xterms from within X. You can switch to a VC while in X by pressing CTRL-ALT-Fn, where n is a number between 1 and 6. The first X server usually uses VC 7. You can see what VC is being used when X starts up, or by going through the VCs.

Once you enter the `startx` command, you should see some text fly off the screen. The screen will change to a graphic screen and a mouse cursor. The window manager will then start. If something doesn't work right, you can press `CTRL-ALT-BACKSPACE` and this will immediately drop you out of X.

While you cannot change color depths within X, you can change the resolution by pressing `CTRL-ALT-Minus` (–) and `CTRL-ALT-Plus` (+). These will cycle through the resolutions set up for your color depth in decreasing and increasing order, respectively.

15.4 gdm

The gdm program is a graphical login window that is used instead of the regular text-based login and password prompt most UNIX users are familiar with. It's better for use with newer users or in a lab environment, since the user doesn't have to issue any commands to start X. You can automatically have gdm start on boot by changing the default runlevel to 5 (see Chapter 3 for more information on runlevels). You can test out using gdm by switching to Runlevel 5 using the `telinit 5` command.

15.5 Using X Window Managers

The way that X looks is determined by two things: the contents of the window and the window manager. The windows merely interact with the X server and there is no real way of moving the windows around the screen, or resizing the windows. This is the job of the window manager. The window manager places a border around the window and can provide maximize (full-screen) and minimize (iconize) buttons. The window manager also allows you to resize, move, or kill windows. The window manager provides for menus and the general "look and feel" of the X display. Operating systems like Windows NT combine both the display manager and the window manager, so if you're new to Linux, this may take some getting used to.

There are a few different window managers available with Red Hat, such as fvwm-95, AfterStep, KDE, and GNOME. Each window manager has its own look. Some of these window managers (such as Enlightenment and GNOME or KDE) have their own libraries, so programs can be specifically written to tie the application into the window manager.

Even though the windows look different, they perform many of the same functions. One advantage that most of the window managers have over Windows 98 or NT is support for virtual desktops. That is, you can have more than one main window (also called the root window) available to you at one time. This lets you have a neater X desktop, or it can let you open more windows and be able to see all of them.

fvwm2-95

The fvwm2-95 program is an extension of FVWM, which has a Windows 95 look and feel. However, the interface is much more configurable. You have the advantages of the task bar and Start menu, but you get additional features such as "focus follows mouse," where the current window is wherever the mouse is. You also get the advantage of configuring all the mouse buttons however you like. This is the most popular window manager for those coming from the MS Windows environment since it's so familiar. The nice advantage, though, is that fvwm2-95 doesn't crash.

The .fvwm2rc (or .fvwm2rc95) file contains startup information for FVWM. Many of the commands are similar between fvwm2 and fvwm2-95. Since for our purposes the two window managers are rather similar, we'll use .fvwmrc to talk about both the .fvwm2rc and .fvwm2rc95 files.

Focus

There are three ways to determine which window has the "focus," that is, which window will be controlled by the keyboard. The first method is the one you're most familiar with—click in the window to make it the active window. This is called ClickToFocus and it is turned on in the .fvwmrc file with the following:

```
Style "*" ClickToFocus
```

The other two methods, MouseFocus and SloppyFocus, are very similar. MouseFocus means that wherever the mouse pointer is has the control. SloppyFocus is the same as MouseFocus, with the exception that if the mouse pointer leaves the window but does not enter another window (for example, goes to the root window), the window you were just in remains focused. You can turn on this focus method with either of these options:

```
Style "*" MouseFocus
Style "*" SloppyFocus
```

Menus

Besides the regular `start` menu that has about the same configurability as the Windows 95 `start` menu, there are also menus available if you left-click on the root window. These menus are defined in the `.fvwmrc` file. The menus are pretty much self-documenting. The `AddToMenu` line adds a menu definition called `Quit-Verify` that has a title of `Really Quit Fvwm?`

    The next lines define the items in that menu. A + at the beginning of a line means it's part of the menu, followed by the text in the menu. You can include an icon in this if you enclose the icon name in `%`. The last part of the menu line is the actual command. The `Restart` in this menu means to quit FVWM and then start the named program. This allows you to quit FVWM and start another window manager. If a menu option has no text and an action of `Nop`, then it will create a separator in the menu. Replacing `Restart` with `Exec` will start the new program without quitting FVWM—but note that it's not a good idea to start multiple window managers.

```
#
# This menu is invoked as a sub-menu—it allows you to quit,
# restart, or switch to another WM.
#
AddToMenu "Quit-Verify" "Really Quit Fvwm?" Title
+ "Restart%mini-turn.xpm%"    Restart fvwm95-2
+ "" Nop
+ "Start twm"                 Restart /usr/X11R6/bin/twm
+ "Start MWM"                 Restart /usr/X11R6/bin/mwm
+ "Start olvwm%mini-olwm.xpm%" Restart /usr/openwin/bin/olvwm
+ "Start olwm%mini-olwm.xpm%" Restart /usr/openwin/bin/olwm
+ ""                          Nop
+ "Yes, Really Quit%mini-exclam.xpm%" Quit
+ "No, Don't Quit%mini-cross.xpm%" Nop
```

Modules

One of the reasons that everyone likes FVWM2 so much (besides the configurability, cheap price, number of people who have configuration files, look and feel of Windows 95, etc.) is the fact that many functions of FVWM are in modules that don't always have to be loaded in memory. This allows one configuration to have a very bare-bones setup, while another setup may have all the bells and whistles (literally).

    Modules get started either in the `.fvwmrc` file or they can be started from the menu. Here are some of the major modules you'll see in FVWM2:

Pager—Sets up a virtual desktop, allowing you to have multiple desktops to work in. FVWM can also be configured to start specific programs in specific virtual desktops for easier use.

Task bar—This is one of the critical parts of FVWM2-95. The task bar acts very much like the task bar of Windows 95, giving a list of running programs, the current time, status of any incoming email, and the ever-popular `Start` menu.

Buttons—If you look above the task bar in the FVWM2-95 window, you'll see a series of buttons, a clock, and the desktop (the pager module). This is the button module, and it cannot only create buttons to start programs (Netscape, xterm, etc.), but it can also have the output of some programs running inside it. The clock and FVWM pager are two examples of this. Some users have CD players, system load programs, and other programs running within the buttons. As with most FVWM functions, the style, size, contents, and location of the buttons can be set from within the `.fvwmrc` file.

Audio—Yes, if you choose, you can have FVWM make noises when you do things within FVWM (opening windows, starting FVWM, stopping FVWM, etc.).

Auto—This module allows you to automatically "raise" (bring to the front) a window after a certain amount of time. The window must have the focus for the allotted time before the window gets raised.

GNOME

GNOME stands for the GNU Network Object Model Environment. GNOME's goal is similar to KDE: It aims to provide an open source, user-friendly, feature-rich desktop environment. Unlike KDE, it does not have a built-in window manager; rather, one may use any of several window managers that make use of GNOME's features. GNOME also is standards-compliant, using common, open standards for object brokering, drag-and-drop, documentation, and 3D programming.

GNOME uses GTK+ as its toolkit. One of the great features of GTK+ is its themeability. This feature allows you to change the look and feel of GTK+ applications without recompiling them.

GNOME also uses an object model named Baboon for interoperablilty between its components. Baboon complies with the CORBA specification.

Getting GNOME

GNOME 1.0 comes with Red Hat 6.0 and subsequent versions should include current or nearly current versions of GNOME. At the present time, development is proceeding rapidly enough that you will likely want to update GNOME independently of Red Hat.

Information on getting and installing GNOME can be found at `http://www.gnome.org/start/getting.shtml`. Unfortunately, the number of packages that comprise the base GNOME installation is quite large. The total is nearly 50 RPM packages. In addition, if you plan to compile or develop GNOME software, you will need the additional 17 or so GNOME development packages.

Download all the files to the same directory and run `rpm -Uvh *.rpm` to upgrade/install all the packages. You may run into version dependency problems. If you do, you will likely have to remove the conflicting packages.

Alternately, you can compile GNOME and its associated programs from source. There are still about 50 archives to download and compile, for which you will need a couple hundred megabytes of disk space and a lot of time.

GNOME Features and Applications

The family of GNOME-aware applications is growing and developing at a rapid pace. Many applications are still in beta or even alpha, but are still usable.

All GNOME software applications share these features:

- Session awareness—When you restart an application, it is restored to the state it was in when shutdown occurred.

- Drag-and-drop—GNOME supports several drag-and-drop protocols, including Xde and the X windowing system's drag-and-drop protocol.

- Internationalization—The uniforum internationalization standard and localization allow a new language to be supported without recompilation.

- 3D—GNOME uses Mesa, a free implementation of OpenGL, a popular 3D programming application.

- DocBook SGML standard—Documentation can be viewed directly with the GNOME help browser, converted to HTML for viewing over the Web, or converted to PostScript for printing.

A number of traditional Linux utilities and user programs have GNOME-aware versions. To name a few:

gtop—A graphical replacement for top, gtop shows the normal top-like display, plus graphs of memory or CPU usage.

gftp—A graphical FTP client. It supports simultaneous downloads, resuming of interrupted downloads, proxies, and more.

Electric Eyes—ee is an image viewer, similar to xv.

gEdit—A simple GNOME-aware-based text editor.

gtalk—A talk daemon and GTK-based talk client.

gmc—A GNOME-aware file manager.

Balsa—A GNOME application for reading email. It supports POP and IMAP, as well as the reading of local mail.

Scores of other GNOME-aware, or at least GTK, applications exist: IRC clients, GNOME interfaces to other languages (Python, Perl, C++, Pike), games, financial packages (a la QuickBooks), and scientific programs, just to name a few.

For a complete list of software, as well as information on its state of development, see the GNOME software map at `http://www.gnome.org/applist/list-martin.phtml`.

Configuring GNOME

The GNOME Control Center can be used to configure nearly every aspect of GNOME. Functional items such as which window manager to use, keyboard and mouse parameters, session management and MIME handlers can be configured, as well as more trivial aspects such as backgrounds, themes and sound triggers.

The following shows a screenshot of the control center.

Figure 15-1 GNOME Control Center

GNOME Window Managers

GNOME can be used with any window manager, although unless the window manager is GNOME-compliant, you will be missing out on the full power the combination can deliver. To start GNOME upon starting X, comment out the line that starts your normal window manager and add this line to the end of your X startup file: `exec gnome-session`. If you want to use GNOME but don't want the session management (which works only with GNOME-aware applications), add `exec gnome-wm` instead. The X startup file is usually `~/.Xclients`, `~/.xinitrc`, or `~/.xsession`. There should be no other `exec` statements in the startup script. A short example:

```
#
# .xsession, run from an XDM based login
#
# start the gnome terminal (an xterm replacement), Gnome midnight
  commander
```

```
# (a file manager and more), and the Gnome panel (and application
  launcher)
#

gnome-terminal &

gmc &

panel &


#

# start the window manager - commented out since gnome starts the wm
  now.

#


#fvwm2 &


#

# start gnome with session management

#

exec gnome-session
```

To set your default window manager and add or delete window managers to GNOME, run the `Control Center` from the GNOME panel. Go to `Window Managers` and add, delete, and change window managers as you want.

Two popular window managers are nearly fully GNOME-compliant: Enlightenment and IceWM. Some others are partially compliant; among these are FVWM, WindowMaker, and SCWM.

Enlightenment is the window manager preferred by most GNOME users it seems. It is highly configurable and feature-rich. This does not come without a price, however. Many Enlightenment configurations are very resource-intensive. More information on Enlightenment, or "E" as it is sometimes called, can be found at `http://www.enlightenment.org/`.

Enlightenment comes with a separate configuration tool, e-conf. With it, you can tune E's behavior with great detail. Various sound and visual effects can be added as well.

A basic E desktop can be seen in Figure 15-2.

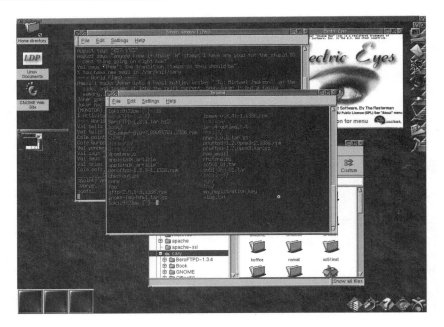

Figure 15–2   Basic E desktop

IceWM is a leaner, less feature-full window manager. It tries to be compatible with mwm (the CDE window manager), as well as faster and less resource-intensive than E. It is not designed to be highly configurable or support fancy looks. There is a utility for converting fvwm2 menus to IceWM menus, as well as a configuration tool. For more information, see `http://www.kiss.uni-lj.si/~k4fr0235/icewm/`.

FVWM is discussed more completely above. To make FVWM GNOME-aware, you need the fvwm2gnome package. Information on it is available at `http://fvwm2gnome.fluid.cx/`.

WindowMaker is a window manager that tries to emulate the look and feel of the NextStep GUI. It is relatively fast and feature-rich, as well as easy to configure. See `http://windowmaker.org/` for more information.

SCWM, which stands for the Scheme-Configurable Window Manager, aims to be highly dynamic and extensible. It includes an X11 scripting facility that supports powerful features through the Guile- (a Scheme implementation) based configuration language. Additional functionality can be introduced via compiled, dynamically loadable modules.

KDE

In case you ever wanted the functionality that Windows 98 has without all the excess baggage, there's KDE. Like Windows 98, many of the functions of the desktop are integrated with the application software. KDE comes with its own HTML browser that, while not as full-featured as Netscape, does the job quite well. The only drawback is that for applications to take full advantage of KDE, they have to be written to work with KDE, and use the `Qt` library. However, there are a number of applications already written in KDE from CD players to editors to games.

When KDE is installed on a system, you can switch to using KDE as your default window manager by using the `switchdesk` command. This will allow you to change window managers and select KDE, GNOME, or AfterStep.

Once that's done, you can just start X and KDE will start with default settings. One nice feature of KDE (and GNOME, for that matter) is that both can run each other's programs, so you could have a GNOME-based application running within the KDE window manager. GNOME and KDE also share drag-and-drop functionality, so you could drag from a GNOME application to a KDE application and the data will get transferred correctly.

The Desktop

By default, the KDE screen looks like a jumble of concepts pulled from Windows 95, MacOS, and CDE. That's intentional. The top menu bar contains a list of running programs, no matter what virtual screen you're in. The bottom menu bar contains the `Start` button (which looks like a large "K") and icons representing other menus or applications along the width of the bar. The center contains a list of the virtual screens available. By default, four virtual screens are started. To the immediate left of these tabs are two small buttons, one an `x` and the other a padlock. The `x` will quit KDE and X, returning you to character mode. The padlock will lock the screen. We'll get to configuration of this later on. The right side contains "docked" applications. These are applications that may be running in the background, but don't necessarily require a window. This is similar to the docked applications you see under Windows 98. Sample applications that use this include the PPP dialer, mail programs, Kpilot (for 3Com PDAs), and language settings. To the right of these docked applications are the current date and time.

You'll note that spaces at both the far left and far right of this menu bar contain small arrows pointing offscreen. These arrows allow you to collapse the entire bar to the left or right side, hiding it from view altogether. If you click one of the arrows, you'll see the bar collapse and be replaced with a small arrow pointing into the center of the screen. Clicking that brings the menu bar back.

The left side of the screen contains a list of icons that are drag-and-drop-capable. Dragging a file from the File Manager to the printer sends the file to the printer, or sending it to the Trash icon sends the file to the trash can. Other icons, like the CD-ROM and Floppy, mount the CD-ROM or floppy drive (assuming you're root, or you have user in /etc/fstab) and then open up a File Manager window for that directory. The Home, Templates, and Autostart icons bring up File Manager windows. Home opens the home directory (duh). Autostart allows you to copy applications to start when KDE starts. The Templates window allows you to build your own icons and settings. You can create device entries (if you have a ZIP drive), FTP and WWW URL icons, MIME settings, and applications.

To show how this works, let's add Netscape to the main window so you can kick it off at any time. Open the Templates window and select the Program icon. Drag the Program icon to the desktop and let go of the mouse button. You'll get a menu list of Copy, Move, and Link. Since we want a new icon, select Copy. Then, right-click on the new icon and select Properties. Under General, change the name of the file to Netscape.kdelink. Select the Execute tab and enter /usr/bin/netscape. You can also select a new icon (instead of the gear) by clicking the icon button and selecting a new one. Under the Application tab, enter the name of the application under Binary Patter (Netscape) and a note under Comment (we put in that Browser thing). We don't need to change anything else, so just click OK. Once that's done, you'll see that the icon changed; the name now says Netscape, and if you put the mouse cursor over the icon, you'll see a small box pop up that reads that browser thing.

Configuration

KDE has the ability to configure every aspect of its operation and interaction with the user. The KDE Control Center, available from the KDE main menu, is the primary way to configuring KDE (see Figure 15-3).

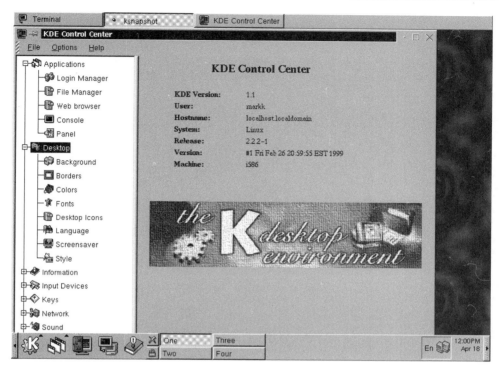

Figure 15–3 KDE Main Menu

The main screen shows information about the versions of KDE and Linux, along with login and machine information. The left side of the window contains the following list of configuration menus:

Applications This menu can set up the `Login Manager` (kdm, which is the KDE replacement for xdm), the built-in `File Manager` and `Web browser`, `Console` operations, and options for the bottom and top panels.

Desktop This section sets `Background` images, window `Borders` and `Colors`, `Fonts`, `Desktop Icons`, `Languages`, `Screensavers`, and miscellaneous `Style` settings, including MacOS and Windows 95 style settings.

Information Much of the information from `/proc` is reported here, including Samba, SCSI, processor, memory, and sound status.

Input Devices Here you can control keyboard configuration (auto repeat, style of keyboard, and keyclicks) and mouse configuration (acceleration and mouse settings).

Keys   To make the transition from MS Windows a bit easier, KDE has support for many of the keys you're familiar with, including ALT-F4 (close application), ALT by itself to focus the keyboard on the menu, and a few others. You can set the configuration of the keyboard in the KDE Control Center, under Keyboard Settings. You can make assignments for a number of different functions, or stick with the globals. There are two sets of keyboard settings: Standard Shortcuts, which are recognized by KDE-aware applications and represent commands like Insert, Paste, Close, Save, Undo, and so on; the other set of assignments is known as Global Shortcuts and represents commands like Close Window, Window Iconify, Switch to Desktop, and so on.

Network   KDE comes with its own Talk daemon and client. You can configure sounds on a talk request and talk clients. You can also set an "answering machine", in case you get a talk request when you're not at your machine. Or, you can forward talk requests to another machine or user.

Sound   There are two sets of sounds that you can configure. First is the system beep that comes out of the speaker. You can configure the volume, pitch, and length of the beep. It at least makes you sound better than the standard beep. The other set comes through the sound card and is activated by things like windows opening and closing, starting and shutting down KDE, and other events.

Windows   There are two special key combinations that KDE uses for switching windows: CTRL-TAB switches between virtual desktops, if enabled; ALT-TAB switches between windows, and there are two ways that this can work. If enabled, you can make ALT-TAB switch between windows only on the same virtual desktop. The other setting sets how ALT-TAB switches between windows. KDE uses the same method as MS Windows, where pressing ALT-TAB, releasing ALT, and pressing ALT-TAB again will switch back to the first window. This allows you to quickly jump back and forth between two windows. The CDE mode will advance through the windows in one direction only, making you cycle through all the windows.

The Applications

Many developers have started making their applications KDE-aware, so they will interface with the window manager. In some cases, the applications have been re-written to do this. There are also unique applications specifically written for use in KDE. Here's a list of some of the applications available:

- kvt—`xterm`.

- kpackage—Install RPM or DEB (Debian package) files.

- `kedit`—Text editor.

- kfm—File manager and HTML browser.

- aKtion!—Based on the xanim movie viewer and can play `.AVI`, `.MOV`, and `.MPG` files.

- kview—Graphics viewer.

- kvoicecontrol—Adds simple voice control to KDE.

- klyx—KDE-aware version of the LyX word processor.

- kmp3—MP3 audio player.

- kPilot—Synchronizes, installs files, and backs up software for 3Com Pilot PDAs.

- korganizer—Calendar application that can also tie into kPilot.

- ksendfax—Sends faxes using `mgetty+sendfax`, `hylafax`, or `efax`.

Many of these applications can be started from KFM by using MIME types. Clicking on a `.JPG` file starts kview, clicking on a text file starts a text editor, and so on. When KDE goes to open a file, it first looks up an application based on the extension, so KFM knows that `foo.gif` is to be opened by kview. If that fails, KFM checks the "magic" header of the file. Most file types have a few bytes in the front that identify the file. Once this is complete, KDE looks up the MIME type under `/usr/share/mimelnk/{mime-type}.kdelnk`. For example, the configuration file for `image/gif` is located at `/usr/share/mimelnk/image/gif.kdelnk`. KDE knows that kview handles `image/gif` MIME types because the definition for kview includes handling the `image/gif` MIME type. The `kview.kdelnk` file is located in `/usr/share/applnk/Graphics`.

To make configuration changes on a per-user basis, you can go to `/home/user/.kde/` as a directory prefix instead of `/usr`. If you install KDE from `ftp.kde.org`, the prefix for `kde` is `/opt/kde`. Keep this in mind if you upgrade.

More applications and their current status (stable, unstable, etc.) can be found on the KDE application page, located at `http://www.kde.org/current.html`.

15.6 User Programs

The default X setup has a bunch of user programs, including shells, utilities, and a couple of games. These programs all have a few default options that you can set when you first start them. We'll show this by introducing `xterm`, which is the X terminal emulator. It is almost the same as logging into the shell. The big difference is that the `.login` file is not read, but the `.cshrc` is instead.

Here are a few of the common options you can use with almost all X programs:

```
-display <host>:<display>
```

sends the display (not just the output) to the named `host` and `display` number. In most cases, the display can be 0.0, which means the first X server and the first display on the X server. The program still gets executed on the remote CPU, but the window gets displayed elsewhere. This setting will override the `DISPLAY` environment variable if it's set. If the `DISPLAY` variable is set and the `-display` option is not used, the window will automatically be displayed on the host and the display set in `DISPLAY`.

```
-bg <color>
```

sets the background color of the window. The `color` setting can either be a name of a color (`grey` or `blue`) or a collection of RGB (red, green, blue) values in hex. The syntax for this is `rgb:h/h/h`, where h is a hex number relating to the amount of red (in the first slot), green (in the second slot), and blue (in the third slot) needed to make a particular color. The hex number can be one to four characters long, depending on the number of colors your X server supports. For example, `rgb:0/0/0` is black, while `rgb:ffff/0/0` is red. A list of colors that have names is available in the `/usrX11/lib/X11/rgb.txt` file. Each entry has the RGB values in decimal (0 to 255) and a name, which can be used instead of the `rgb:h/h/h` entry.

```
-fg <color>
```

sets the color of the foreground.

```
-fn <font>
```

specifies the default font to use in the window. You can get lists of available fonts using the `xfontsel` or `xlsfonts` programs.

```
-geometry <WIDTH>x<HEIGHT>+<XOFF>+<YOFF>
```

sets the size and position of the window. For `xterm`, this is in terms of characters, so a geometry of:

```
> xterm -geometry 80x25
```

would create a window that is 80 characters wide and 25 lines long. XOFF and YOFF set where the upper left-hand corner of the window should be placed. In the case of a positive XOFF or YOFF, the offset is from the left or top side, respectively. For a negative XOFF or YOFF, the offset is from the right or bottom side, respectively. Here are some example screen placements:

+0+0 Upper left-hand corner.

-0+0 Upper right-hand corner.

-0-0 Lower right-hand corner.

+0-0 Lower left-hand corner.

Note that you can enter either a geometry or an offset, but you can't enter only XOFF or a width by itself. Both the geometry and the offset must be entered as a pair. That is, you can't enter:

```
> xterm -geometry 80
```

or

```
> xterm -geometry +0
```

but the following will work:

```
> xterm -geometry 80x25
```

or

```
> xterm -geometry +0+0
```

There's one other way to specify default settings for X programs, and this is through the `.Xdefaults` file. Anything you can set through the command line can be stored in the `.Xdefaults` file, so when you start the program, you don't need to give all the options. These options are known as resources.

15.7 X Resources

An X resource can consist of four item types:

```
program.widget[.widget..].resource: value
```

where:

- `program`—Program name.
- `widget`—One or more levels of widgets, which are sub-portions of the window. A `widget` can be a button, menu, scrollbar, option list, and so on.
- `resource`—The "least common denominator" of the widgets. The `resource` may be used by more than one program. For example, `geometry` is used by all X programs and is a `resource`.
- `value`—What the `resource` gets set to. Can be a number, Boolean (true or false), color, or some other value. It depends on the `resource`.

Any text from an exclamation point (!) to the end of the line is commented out.

To get from the most-specific widget (`program`) to the least specific widget (`resource`), the widgets must be combined. These combinations can be specified by either a period (`.`) or a star (`*`). A period indicates a tight binding, and a star (or asterisk) represents a loose binding.

In a loose binding, the link between two widgets does not have to be direct, and it acts almost like a regular expression in `grep`. That is, you can have an entry such as:

```
*geometry: 80x25
```

This says that all `geometry` settings will be `80x25`. While this is good for text-based programs, a graphical application with a setting of 80x25 pixels would be rather small indeed.

If you have a particular program, you can then become more specific. That is, if you want all programs that use the vt100 widget to have a geometry of 80x25, you can make the setting like this:

```
*vt100.geometry: 80x25
```

And you can get even more specific. Say that you want your terminal emulators to have a size of 80x25, and you want your Seyon[2] emulator to have a size of 80x40. Then you would have two settings of:

```
xterm.vt100.geometry: 80x25
Seyon.vt100.geometry: 80x40
```

Here you have tight bindings. The `Seyon` program uses the `vt100` widget, which sets the `geometry`. Using a loose binding for Seyon as follows:

```
Seyon*geometry: 80x40
```

would cause all of the windows that `Seyon` creates to be `80x40`. Since Seyon creates a few graphical-based windows, this would bring us back to having graphical windows that are 80 pixels by 40 pixels.

Note that you can replace tight bindings with loose bindings. The following two entries have identical effects:

```
Seyon.vt100.geometry: 80x40
Seyon*vt100*geometry: 80x40
```

Here are a few sample entries that apply to `xterm`:

```
xterm*scrollBar: true !    Turn on the scroll bar on the left side
xterm*geometry: 80x25 !    Set the size to 80x25
xterm*background: gray68 ! Gray background
xterm*foreground: black !  Black characters
```

15.8 X Applications

Along with `xterm` and Seyon, there are a number of other client programs that you can run. Almost all X programs use the `-display`, `-geometry`, and `-background` commands, plus some extra options. Note that while these options override the settings in the `.Xdefaults` file, it is really up to the window manager to make the settings. These options (and the settings in `.Xdefaults`) are really suggestions to the window manager. The window manager often allows the requests, but there may be a case where the window manager does its own thing.

- `-fg <color>` or `-foreground <color>`—Foreground color.

---

[2] `Seyon` is a terminal emulator.

- `-fn <font>` or `-font <font>`—Default font.
- `-iconic`—Starts the program as an icon.
- `-title <text>`—Gives a window a title.

Available X applications:

- xmh—E-mail handler.
- bitmap—Bitmap editor.
- xman—X interface to the man program.
- xclock—Digital or analog clock.
- xcalc—Calculator.
- xkill—Kills a window.
- xwd—Dumps a window image to a file.

There are also other X applications not part of the X project that are sometimes installed with Linux:

- Seyon—Communication program.
- Xsysinfo—System information (CPU idle, memory free, and so on).
- Xpaint—Paint program.
- Ghostview—Views PostScript files.

As Linux's popularity has grown, so has the number of "non-server" applications. These range from the frivolous to the so-called personal productivity applications usually associated with Windows or Macintosh desktops.

Most of the applications we have discussed so far have been server-oriented or programming languages. The few exceptions have been office suites, word processors, and spreadsheets.

Here we want to talk about some of the "fun" software for Linux. These packages range from pure eye candy to the semi-useful to various games. Some of these were developed under Linux; others have been developed elsewhere; and some even pre-date Linux.

Useful

Wine

Wine (`http://www.winehq.com/`) not an emulator, or so the authors say. Wine is really two components in one. First, it is a way of running many Win16 and Win32 applications under Linux. Second, it is a way of compiling Windows applications for use under Linux. Companies like Corel are assisting with Wine development since it will reduce the amount of time needed to port their applications to Linux. A full list of applications that are supported under Wine can be found at the Wine Web site. Additionally, Wine will run only on Linux for x86 chips.

VNC

VNC stands for Virtual Network Console. Using a browser that runs Java, like Netscape, or a Java client that runs on any OS that runs Java, you can view a UNIX or Windows 95/98/NT screen on a remote display. In a UNIX machine, you get a new X display started, and under MS Windows, you get control of the actual screen. This makes it similar to PCAnywhere. Using this, you can get an X display on Windows, or access a Windows machine from a Linux box. Very cool stuff.

Eye Candy

Xsnow

This is a silly little program that creates snow on your X desktop, which accumulates on your window tops. Periodically, a sleigh pulled by reindeer flies across the screen and it blizzards. Run it around Christmas to get in the holiday mood. Figure 15–4 shows Xsnow.

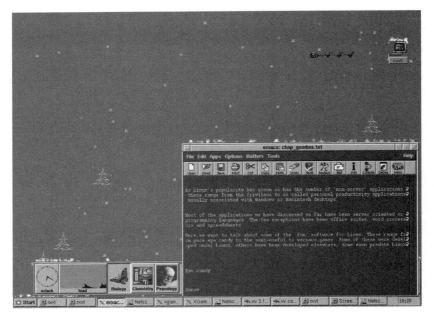

Figure 15–4   Xsnow

Xcthugha

Xcthugha is another CD player. Compared to the interfaces of Workman and Xmcd, it is pretty thin. However, Xcthugha's forte is not its interface; it's what else it does with the music. It creates a visual representation of the sound stream.

Depending on the music and the individual, it induces anything from mesmerization to motion sickness. It can be run in an X or full-screen VGA mode. Under X, it can run in a window, in the root window, or as a screensaver. Finally, it can be used in client/server mode.

Figures 15–5, 15–6, and 15–7 show Xcthugha, its control panel, and the CD controls (reached by typing `F1, c`).

Figure 15–5 Xcthugha in Action

Figure 15–6 Xcthugha Control Panel

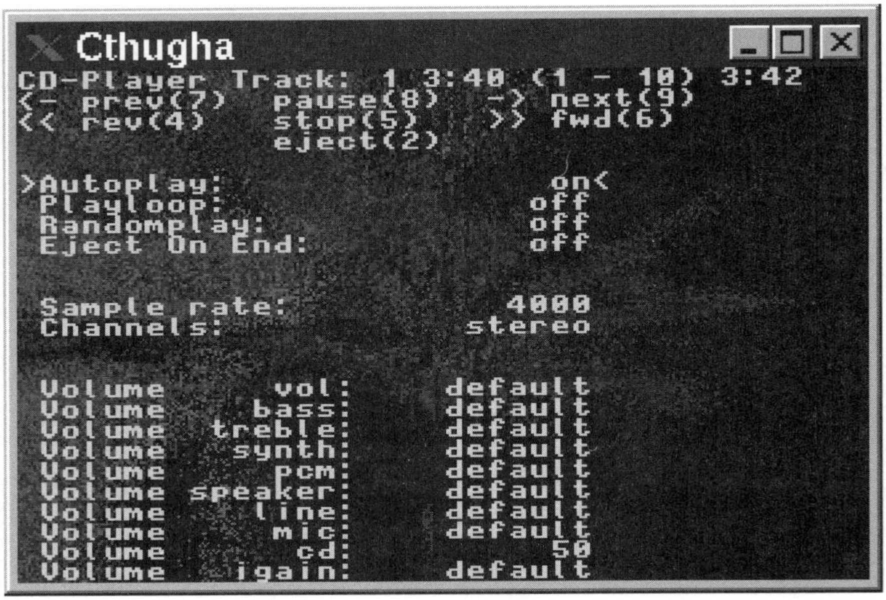

Figure 15–7   Xcthugha Status Information

Semi-Useful

WorkMan

Sure, a basic CD audio player comes with almost every OS these days, but why be satisfied with just play, pause, stop, and skip? WorkMan is a very full-featured CD player. It sports play lists, a CD database, balance control, play modes, and just about everything else you would expect. Many WorkMan users make their CD databases available for download. Figure 15–8 shows the main WorkMan interface that you use to control the CD player. Figure 15–9 shows the track and CD information screen used to input tracks, play lists, and so on.

Figure 15–8 WorkMan Control Panel

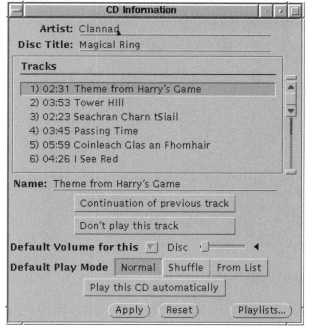

Figure 15–9 Track and CD Information

As a result of its SunOS heritage, WorkMan requires the Xview libraries to run. To compile it yourself, you will need the header files as well. Luckily these are freely available.

xanim

If you ever wanted to watch `.AVI` and `.MOV` files on your Linux machine, then xanim is for you. It brings up a window that shows the movies along with a control panel to fast-forward, rewind, and so on. Due to licensing restrictions, the version of xanim distributed by Red Hat cannot include the functionality to play some `.AVI` or `.MOV` files. However, you can download the necessary files from the xanim home page to add in the functionality yourself.

SoundStudio

As its name implies, this is a full-featured application for recording, mixing, and editing sound. It is commercial software, but the Linux pricing is very low. Also, it uses Motif, so be sure to get the statically linked version if you don't have Motif. The main window of SoundStudio is shown in Figure 15–10.

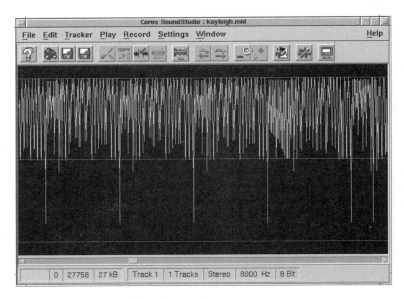

Figure 15–10   SoundStudio window

RealPlayer

RealNetworks makes a free version of their integrated RealAudio and RealVideo players for Linux. With RealPlayer, you can listen to and/or view streaming audio/video served from RealNetworks' streaming audio and visual server.

RealPlayer can run as a standalone application or as a plug-in for Netscape. The plug-in version will not play video in an 8-bit color display, although the standalone version will.

Real has recently released a beta version of their G2 player for Linux, and they do offer streaming servers and encoders so you can create your own content for your Web site.

Amusements and Games

The number of games for Linux is increasing every day. Hey, you need something to do while waiting for the kernel to recompile. There are a number of Web sites that are dedicated to gaming on Linux; for example, `http://www.happypenquin.org` and `http://www.linuxgames.com`.

In addition to the games listed here, Wine will allow you to run many Windows 98 games under Linux, including Starcraft and Unreal.

xpat

For those of you who want just a simple game, xpat may be for you. It's a collection of Solitaire games (including classic Solitaire and the "freecell" games that are so popular on other operating systems).

Quake/Quake II

It's not hard to ignore these rather popular games (and their predecessors—Doom and Doom II). Quake and Quake II are available for Linux and provide all the same features that are in the Windows versions. Linux provides three display types for playing: X11, SVGAlib, and 3Dfx. The X11 interface brings Quake up in a window and allows you to play with other applications up at the same time. The SVGAlib allows for full-screen play, but requires root access and exclusive use of the screen and keyboard. The 3Dfx version (GLquake) uses the `Mesa GL` library and a 3Dfx-based 3D card to provide superior texture mapping and graphics. The `Mesa` library and 3Dfx can also be used with VRML applications to make very high-quality graphics. Check the Id software home page (`www.idsoftware.com`) for more information about Linux Quake.

Civilization: Call to Power

If this isn't proof that Linux has come into its own arena for gaming, we don't know what is. The latest version of the Civilization series has been ported to

Linux as a commercial, off-the-shelf program. Be sure that you pick up the
Linux version instead of the Windows version.

15.9 Using Remote Displays

The biggest advantage of X over Macintosh, Windows 95, and even standard
Windows NT is that X can send the output of a program to another X server.
That is, you could be running a program in New York, with the display in an
office in Massachusetts. Or, programs can run across an office, allowing you
to control a Linux machine from anywhere.

Three things are required for remote displays to work. First, there has to
be a TCP/IP connection between the two machines. This can be Ethernet,
PPP, ATM, and the like. Next, the X server (where you'll be watching the
program) has to know that a client wants to send a display. This can be done
with the xhost program. Running xhost + will allow connections to your X
server from anywhere. Running xhost +host adds host to the list of
machines that can access your display. You can deny access using xhost -
host. Note that by default, only the local machine has access to your display.
Every other machine that wants to send a window to your display must be
given access. The third item is that the client program needs to know where
to send the display. This can be done using -display or by setting the DIS-
PLAY environment variable. We prefer setting the DISPLAY variable.

Displays are set with two items: the host to display on and the X server
running on that host to display to. The server itself is broken into two parts:
the server number and display number. Since X can handle multiple monitors at the same time, you will need to specify the host, X server, and monitor
to send the client program to.

Fortunately for most Linux installations, this is easy. The X server and monitor always begin counting at 0, making the first X server 0.0. Tie this in with the
hostname (let's call it wayga), and you get the setup shown in Figure 15–11.

```
setenv DISPLAY wayga:0.0
```

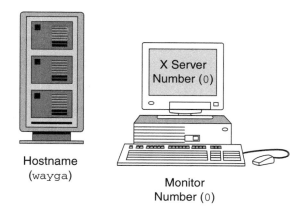

Figure 15–11   Xview of your computer

15.10 Major X Libraries

There are a number of libraries available for X that should be mentioned here. Many are available already on Red Hat, but some may need updating, depending on the application you are trying to run or compile.

Qt

The Qt library from TrollTech is the library basis for the KDE Window Manager. It's written entirely in C++, though there are hooks to interfaces with Python and Perl. One of the limiting factors of KDE and Qt is the licensing of the library. Qt has recently greatly relaxed its licensing requirements, and many have confirmed that the Qt library can now be considered open source.

GTK/GLIB

These libraries were originally developed to provide a graphical widget library for GIMP, which stands for the GNU Image Manipulation Program. They are now part of the basis of the GNOME environment and Enlightenment Window Manager.

LessTif

`LessTif` is designed to be a Motif clone and implement much of the API from Motif 1.2. There are a number of applications written for Motif that now work with LessTif, including the free Mozilla browser.

Mesa

The `Mesa` library is an open source version of OpenGL, the standard for 3D graphics under UNIX (see below). In addition to doing software-based 3D transformations, it also allows you to use 3D cards such as the 3Dfx-based voodoo series cards to display 3D applications. There are a number of applications using `Mesa`, including realistic flight simulators and VRML viewers.

15.11 Commercial X Resources

A number of commercial products related to X11 are available. Here we try to give you a fairly complete list and short description of each. Few of these packages are available for architectures other than the x86, though Alpha and Sparc versions are beginning to crop up.

Xservers

AcceleratedX

AcceleratedX is a high-performance replacement for the Xservers that come with XFree86. It is produced by XiGraphics (`http://www.xinside.com/`).

AcceleratedX supports hundreds of video cards, considerably more than XFree86 alone does. Additionally, it supports more monitors and often supports higher-resolution monitors than XFree86. Typically, it will also squeeze better performance out of your video card and monitor. However, this increase in performance comes at a cost; AcceleratedX will also consume more system resources than XFree86.

XiGraphics also makes a multiheaded Xserver, allowing you to run X on up to three monitors simultaneously.

Metro-X

Metro-X is another commercial Xserver. It also boasts support for more cards and monitors than XFree86, though not as many as AcceleratedX. Its performance is not as good as AcceleratedX's either. It does, however, cost less and consumes fewer resources. Metro-X has support for up to four displays built in.

X Libraries

In addition to the many additional freeware or shareware X libraries and toolkits, there are a couple of commercial toolkits for X.

Motif

Motif was developed by the Open Software Foundation. Its specification is freely available, which has allowed the LessTif project to work on a free clone of Motif.

Motif is popular because it provides a number of widgets that allow for the building of complex and powerful, but aesthetically pleasing, GUIs. It is somewhat resource-intensive, but most developers find it a fair trade.

Red Hat (`http://www.redhat.com/`) ships Motif 2.0.1 for the x86, Alpha, and Sparc platforms.

OpenGL

OpenGL is a three-dimensional graphics library developed by SGI. It has quickly became a standard part of nearly every 3D developer's toolkit. Most Linux users can use the `Mesa` library and a supported 3D card on Linux.

CDE

The Common Desktop Environment (CDE) is an effort by several commercial UNIX vendors to make a common X/Motif-based environment for use on all X desktops, thus providing a common look and feel, regardless of which platform you are using.

15.12 Summary

X is the most popular standard for graphics display on Linux and UNIX. It can be configured however you want, providing the control and interface that suits you best, instead of having to change the way you work to suit the operating system. The applications that are available for X rival those of Windows 98, and more are being written every day.

Securing Linux 16

*It may not seem easy, but
it has to be done*

With most of the machines in the world connected via the Internet, security is a big concern, whether you have hundreds of machines or one dial-up machine.

No system can be completely secure from outside attacks. Anyone determined enough has a good chance of cracking[1] into your system. The best thing you can do is to prepare yourself and your machine, make it as hard as possible, and be able to detect when you're being cracked.

---

[1]Contrary to popular belief, people who break into systems are called "crackers" and not "hackers."

16.1 Physical Security

The first part of keeping a system secure is making sure the hardware cannot be tampered with. Part of the C2 security specification for computer systems says that the computer must not be physically accessible to anyone without access. That is, it can't be on the network and must be in a locked room to begin with. Chapter 2 has a good list of instructions to keep a typical PC reasonably secure from outside attacks. To quickly sum up:

- Lock the BIOS and set the BIOS to boot only from the C drive.
- Don't use LILO or at least make it boot directly into Linux.
- Don't have DOS or any other OS on the machine.
- Lock the PC case.

You should also have people on hand to assist with problems and prevent anyone from having the chance to take a computer apart.

16.2 Software Security

This section is just a bit larger than the hardware security section, and for good reason. With TCP/IP having over 65,000 ports available for connecting to a single machine, this gives anywhere up to 65,000 and beyond possible ways for a cracker to enter your system.

Monitoring Software

Programs like COPS and TripWire allow you to routinely monitor your system to detect possible holes or to detect some forms of break-ins. You should probably get both programs and use them routinely. A program like SATAN will monitor an entire network and report on possible holes. Since many crackers probably have a copy of this, it is probably best to beat them to the punch and run it on your own network before they do.

Preventing Root Logins

The first way that crackers cause real trouble on your system is by getting root privileges. There are a few ways to do that, and we'll list some of them here, along with suggestions on preventing such things from happening.

First, change the root password often! This way, even if a cracker does get the password, it won't be valid for too long. Also, keep an eye on your /etc/ securetty file. This file lists the locations from which root can log in directly. To get root power from any other location, you must first have a valid user account; then you must use the su command to become root. Root can only log in at the console by default (tty1 through tty8).

Another action that should be taken is to modify the su program so that only members of the wheel group can su to root. This is a big problem with the Linux su program, in our opinion. The wheel group was designed to be the only group of users that can su into the root account. This limits the number of accounts that could be cracked to get into root. However, the GNU people think this is a bit authoritarian and have designed their su program to allow anyone to su to root, assuming they have the password. Other operating systems, such as SunOS and Solaris, require a user to be in the wheel group before being allowed to su to root.

Secure Shell (SSH)

You should also start using programs that encrypt passwords as they go over the network. The SSH (secure shell) program is excellent for this, as it not only encrypts passwords, but also the entire connection. As TCP/IP works now, all data are sent over the network in clear text (i.e., not encrypted). Anyone who has a network sniffer on any machine on the network, or on any network between you and your destination, can read the password you type in. Bad stuff. The SSH program encrypts all this, plus does some host checking to verify the host you're connecting from and the host you're connecting to. You should be using this program both within your LAN and when connecting to other sites. Commercial versions of SSH for Windows and other platforms are available, allowing all the clients on the network to have secure connections.

The SSH program is designed to be a replacement for the "r" commands (rlogin, rsh, rcp), and can install itself so it replaces those commands. If your users have .rhosts files set up, SSH will still use those files. Users will not have to change their configuration much, but their connections will be more secure.

Setting up ssh requires that you run it on the machines you will be talking between. Let's call the client (your personal machine) foo, and the server (where you want to connect, do some administrative work, etc.) Bar.

Bar will run SSHd (the SSH daemon), which gets started from either the inetd or on bootup in daemon mode. If you have a lot of users with SSHd, it might be better to run in daemon mode as SSHd is always ready to make a connection.

The `configure` command sets the stage for compiling and then `make` compiles it. There are few other things you need to do for a typical installation.

The `SSHd` program runs on the server (`Bar`) and should be started by root on startup. The client machine (`foo`) then issues an `ssh` command similar to `rlogin`. The command to connect would then look something like this:

```
ssh -l markk Bar
```

If the `Bar` host is not known to `foo`, you'll get asked if you want to add it to your list of known hosts. Add the host, and you'll be able to give your password to login.

The global configuration files are located in `/etc`. These files are `/etc/sshd_config` for server configuration and `/etc/ssh_config` for SSH configuration. The options for these files are listed in the man pages for SSH and SSHd.

New hosts can be added to SSH in a global method using `make-SSH-known-hosts`, which finds all hosts in a domain that run SSH and gets their public keys. Users can add their own hosts by copying the contents of the `/etc/ssh_host_key.pub` into `$HOME/.ssh/known_hosts`. The public keys can be sent to any host—it doesn't matter if they're transferred in an insecure manner.

Users can create their own RSA keys using the `ssh-keygen` command, which creates a public/private key pair. If regular password authentication is not used, the RSA key generated by `ssh-keygen` is used. The public key (located in `$HOME/.ssh/identity.pub`) should be added to the `$HOME/.ssh/authorized_keys` of all the machines you want to log into.

tcpd

The `tcpd` program cannot only cut off your site from a bad site, but it can also specify what sites can come in. This is a kind of "poor man's packet filter," but it works pretty well for a small installation. The `tcpd` program matches up an incoming IP address with a table. If the IP address is listed in the `hosts.allow` file, the connection is allowed. If it is listed in the `hosts.deny` file, the connection is refused. If the IP address does not match an entry in either file, then access is granted. You can set up the `hosts.deny` file to deny access to everyone and then put fully trusted hosts into the `hosts.allow` file. The `tcpd` program works only with programs that are typically started with the `inetd` program. This includes `telnet`, `finger`, FTP, `talk`, and a few other programs. You can customize so no one can `telnet` in, but anyone can `finger` the machine (for example). It also allows for RFC 931 lookups, which can report on what user is on the remote machine using the identd program.

When setting up `tcpd` for allowing or disallowing connections, the access control is the same. In fact, the man page for `hosts.allow` and `hosts.deny` is the same page. The way to set up an access control is by following this pattern:

```
daemon_list : client_list [ : shell_command ]
```

The `daemon_list` is the name of the program that is running (`telnetd`, `ftpd`, and so on). The `client_list` can be any of the following:

- Strings beginning with a period (.) are assumed to be part of a domain (`.wayga.net` would be any host in the `wayga.net` domain).
- Strings ending with a period (.) are assumed to be an IP address net or subnet (128.55.213. would be all the machines that start with that IP address).
- A string starting with @ is assumed to be an NIS netgroup (`@hosts` would be all the hosts defined in the NIS netgroup).
- `n.n.n.n/m.m.m.m` is a net and mask pair. This gives finer control over the above for matching IP addresses.

There are also a few special keywords:

- `ALL`—This matches everything.
- `LOCAL`—All hosts that do not have a dot (.) in the hostname, since local hosts do not typically use the FQDN.
- `UNKNOWN`—A user whose name is not known (RFC 931 checking) or a host whose name or IP is unknown.
- `KNOWN`—Reverse of `UNKNOWN`—a user whose name is known, and both the name and address are known.
- `PARANOID`—Any host whose reverse DNS does not match the host name it's using. Sites with multiple domains may run into this if the reverse DNS and hosts are not synchronized.

The access control also accepts the word `EXCEPT` to give something like the following:

```
192.55.242. EXCEPT PARANOID
```

which would match all IP addresses from the `192.55.242.net` except ones whose reverse DNS does not match what the host says it is.

The shell command is optional and is sent to `/bin/sh` for processing. This should be a secure script that sets its `PATH` and other environment variables.

To have a completely closed off system (from the perspective of `tcpd`), start with this in your `/etc/hosts.deny`:

```
ALL:ALL
```

This will deny access for all `tcpd` services to all hosts. Next, you can start opening the system up by adding to the `/etc/hosts.allow` file:

```
ALL: LOCAL
```

which now allows all local machines to have access to all `tcpd` services.

As you add more services (POP, IMAP, `tftp`), you can add `tcpd` support as you install the service. In the `/etc/inetd.conf` file, make your line look like the following:

```
telnet  stream  tcp     nowait  root    /usr/sbin/tcpd  in.telnetd
```

The location where the command is typically run gives `tcpd` instead, with an argument of the program you want to run in the end (`telnetd` in this case).

Other programs not started by `inetd` (such as sendmail and `httpd`) have their own host-based access mechanisms built into the program. Just be sure that as you compile your list of bad hosts (or good hosts), you include them in all your programs that interact with TCP/IP.

16.3 Denial of Service Attacks

Denial of service deals with the fact that a user may be doing valid things (such as pinging your host or sending email), but doing them in a way that prevents you from getting things done. For example, a `ping` takes up at least 64 bytes and sends one at least once a second. If a malicious cracker were to send `ping`s that were 2K in size, it would flood a 28.8K modem link, making it unusable for downloading data, receiving email, browsing the Web, or anything else. The entire link would be taken up responding to `ping`s. Linux has some protection against this, but any system is susceptible to it. Another similar attack involves sending `SYN` packets to a host. The machine then opens a connection, waiting for more data. As more `SYN` packets come in, more connections open up, until eventually the machine crashes or is rendered unusable. Linux also has some protection against this type of attack, but since SYN and ping are both standard (and heavily used) functions, there is not a whole lot that can be done.

Another type of attack involves sending so much email that it floods the mail partition. Linux usually stores its email in /var/spool, which is usually part of the root partition (/). The /tmp directory is also part of the root partition. Should you get so much email that root fills up, then /tmp can't store any temporary data. This then causes crashes of various programs, such as vi, that depend on having access to /tmp. This can potentially also cause a kernel crash. The moral here is twofold: Make /tmp a mounted directory, and make /var a mounted directory as well. Also, have frequent monitoring of the mail files to make sure that the partition isn't filling up quickly. Some users may need to be told to clean out their email every few weeks. (email can typically swell to about 4MB or more per month. 4MB per month times 30 users is a 120MB /var partition, plus other files such as log files that go in /var.

You can find out more about the current state of cracks at sites like www.cert.org and www.rootshell.com. Both sites track network and software-related security issues.

16.4 Network Security

For a small office setting, it's probably best to have a single host to interact with the outside world (Web, FTP, sendmail, etc.). Protect the rest of the network using built- in packet filtering (ipchains) and other security tools.

Monitor the anonymous FTP and WWW logs for break-ins. These logs are found in /var/log. The security files you'll want to look at are located in /var/log/security. Telnet access, tcpd denial (and access), and other information are stored there.

You can disable FTP users by creating a file called /etc/ftpusers. Any user that is listed there has no ability to FTP in. List all your users in this file, including root. For users who travel a lot (salespeople or engineers working from home), either establish a dial-up connection or use very trusted hosts for connections. There is also Virtual Private Network software available to create an encrypted link between a remote machine and your servers.

For users that require only email, you can have that email forwarded[2] to an external account. This way, your external users won't have to try getting

---

[2]Check Chapter 7 for the use of email forwarding.

into your system. Also be aware of who is on vacation or other types of leave, and make sure they're not logged in.

This gives a bit of balance to the security and convenience issues. Internal employees can go out to the rest of the Internet without using proxies. Proxies can get on everyone's nerves (including yours) as they have the ability to log HTTP, FTP, and `telnet` traffic. This lacks the security of the next method, but it is one of the downsides to this kind of setup.

For a larger office setting with a lot of employees who travel, invest the time in getting programs like S/KEY and SSH set up. Also, have a full firewall set up, where you have two to three trusted hosts doing the work for the Web, FTP, and email (see Figure 16–1).

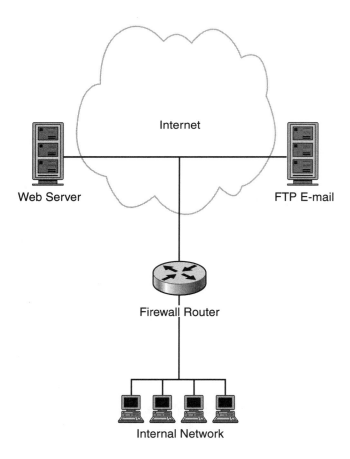

Figure 16–1   Secure environment using a firewall

All the traffic that goes in or out of the router first passes through the firewall. Anyone wanting to use the Web, download data using FTP, or `telnet` to a remote host must use a proxy, or first connect to the firewall and then perform a connection. The Web and FTP servers are almost entirely cut off from the internal network by the firewall. The firewall forwards only email from the email host—other email is not accepted (or you can have the firewall accept email). Programs like TripWire run on all hosts that have direct access to the Internet. One of the benefits of a program like TripWire is that it can monitor certain files (`/etc/password`, for example) and know when these files change. If a file is changed, it sends an alert that a potential crack is in progress.

Any remote users trying to get into the system have to log into the trusted host (the firewall) first. The firewall is the only machine that has access to both the outside world and the internal network. Once a user is verified by the firewall, they can then get access to the internal network, receive email, make connections to hosts, and so on.

Larger sites are left as an exercise to the reader, but you may want to get some books on computer and network security to assist you.

PGP

One of the earliest implementations of freeware cryptography was in PGP (Pretty Good Privacy). There are legal ways to download this software in the U.S. and many other countries. Be sure you're not breaking any domestic, international, patent, or local laws by using this software. Some countries have severe restrictions on encryption.

The main idea behind PGP is to allow personal security in sending email. The email can either be authenticated as originating from you (to prevent spoof email) or completely encrypted for opening by only another person, or both. The PGP program creates two keys: one private that must be guarded by you at all times, and a public key, which the recipient of your email must be able to read to authenticate your email.

Building PGP on Linux is not an easy thing, given that Linux has changed since the last release of PGP.[3] Patches that allow PGP to compile cleanly under Linux are available. You can find PGP by searching the major Web search engines.

To compile PGP for Linux, grab the `pgp-patcher.tar.gz` file. Put the `pgp262s.tar.gz` and `pgp-patcher.tar.gz` files in the same directory

---

[3]Version 2.6.2 of PGP was released in 1994.

(make a `/usr/src/pgp` or `$HOME/pgp` for this). Now, run the following commands:

```
tar -zxvf pgp-patcher.tar.gz
cd pgp-patcher
installer
```

This will unpack the PGP sources, patch them to work with Linux, compile them, and install the binaries in `$HOME/pgp`. If you choose to have the binaries installed somewhere else, replace `installer` with `patch-only`. This will unpack the archives and patch the files to install. You can then edit the `makefile` and have the sources installed somewhere else if you choose.

Once PGP is installed, you must generate a public/private key pair. The `pgp -kg` command will allow you to generate this. Note that you'll probably want to have multiple email addresses verify the same key (for example, if you have a home email address, one for work, one for the Linux User Group, and maybe an alumni account from your school). PGP can handle this, and you need to generate only one key, one time. The `pgp -ke` command will allow you to edit (and add, delete, etc.) the names associated with your secret key once you have it generated. When asked for your ID, put in your full name, followed by your email address. For example, my primary PGP ID looks something like this:

```
Mark F. Komarinski <markk@cgipc.com>
```

Next you're asked for your pass phrase. This phrase can be as long as you like, but be sure that you don't forget it, and that no one else gets hold of it. You'll next be prompted to type in gibberish on the keyboard to generate random numbers to use with your key. A few minutes later, your PGP key will be stored in `$HOME/pgp`. Next you'll have to generate your public key for others to read and authenticate what you send. `pgp -kx` will extract your public key in binary format. If you want the key to be in ASCII format, suitable for displaying on a Web page or using in `finger` information, add the `a` option to the mix, which stands for ASCII.

Many mailers today have access to using PGP. Readers like mutt have much of it built in, and readers like pine have patches to allow you to use PGP. Others have the email piped to PGP for verification. To sign a message yourself, use the `pgp -sta <textfile>` command. Anyone with your public key will then be able to verify that you wrote the contents. You can verify an incoming message by just piping the file to pgp, or by using `pgp <textfile>`. If you have the public key of the sender, you'll get a message saying that the message is valid, or it is not valid. If you don't have the public key, then no verification can take place. Find the public key and add it to your "keyring" by using the `pgp -ka <file>` command. The `<file>` contains the ASCII or binary version of a person's public keyring.

PGP does even more than this, including encrypting a message with multiple recipients and revoking keys listed in its documentation. Be sure to read `pgpdoc1.txt` and `pgpdoc2.txt`. `pgp -h` will give a listing of available commands as well.

16.5 Packet Filtering with Linux

Both the Red Hat 5.x series and the newer 6.x series of Red Hat have packet filtering and monitoring built in. For systems running the Linux 2.0 or 2.1 kernels, this uses the `ipfwadm` command[4]. Systems running 2.2 or 2.3 kernels will be using the `ipchains` command. We'll first go through the settings for `ipfwadm`, then show how to do the same thing using `ipchains`. Also note that Linuxconf (covered in Chapter 4) allows you to set up packet filtering.

ipfwadm

The IP firewall administration program (`ipfwadm`) allows some of the functionality of `tcpd`, but in the kernel space, before any user programs even see a packet. Unlike `tcpd`, `ipfwadm` can also filter packets that are being forwarded to another network.

Configuration of `ipfwadm` is based on a set of rules that you input using the `ipfwadm` program. One other advantage of `ipfwadm` is that it handles both incoming and outgoing packets. From your machine, you could use `ipfwadm` to not allow any data to go to `restrictedsite.com`. The request for a connection to `restrictedsite.com` gets blocked before it ever goes out on the PPP link or Ethernet line or however you connect to the Internet.

There are a total of five rules that `ipfwadm` administers:

- IP accounting.
- Input rules (packets coming into the machine).
- Output rules (packets leaving the machine).
- Forwarding rules (for when the machine in question is a router).

---

[4] Some of the later 2.1 kernels use `ipchains` as well.

- Masquerade configuration (allowing an entire network to hide behind a single IP address).

These rules are explained below.

IP Accounting Rules

The accounting rules for `ipfwadm` track numbers and types of packets that go out the TCP/IP interface. This can track incoming packets, outgoing packets, or both (which is the default). The rules for packet accounting are the same as building rules for just about everything else, so let's go through some of what it takes to build an `ipfwadm` command.

```
/sbin/ipfwadm -A -a -P tcp -S 0.0.0.0/0 http -D 0.0.0.0/0
```

The first `-A` indicates that we're building an accounting rule, and is about the only thing that differentiates this from a packet filtering rule. The `-a` indicates that we're going to append a rule at the end of the current set of rules. For accounting purposes, this doesn't matter as much; however, when you start building complex filtering rules, this will matter more. For our example, this could just as easily be replaced with `-i` for insert at the beginning of the list of rules. Next is `-P tcp`, which tells `ipfwadm` to pay attention to the TCP protocol instead of UDP, ICMP, or all protocols. Specifying the protocol is required when you're filtering specific ports, and we'll get to that in a minute. Next is the `-S 0.0.0.0/0 http` statement. This says to match a source address of anything, but coming from the HTTP port. So, an incoming packet from port 80 would be caught by this rule, but not HTTP data on port 8080, or FTP or SMTP data. The destination is specified with the `-D 0.0.0.0/0` statement, and as you can guess, this says to match with any destination. Since this is on a machine acting as a router, any machine on the internal network that gets information from port 80 from any outside source will be caught by this rule.

To take a look at the rulesets already finished, use the `/sbin/ipfwadm -A -l` command as follows:

```
[root@server markk]# /sbin/ipfwadm -A -l
IP accounting rules
 pkts bytes dir prot source                destination           ports
   14 12756 i/o tcp  anywhere              anywhere              http -> any
[root@server markk]#
```

This accounting shows that 14 packets of data came in for a total of about 12KB of data. If you wanted to fine-tune your accounting so that you could track how much incoming SMTP data you got in a day, you could just change the `http` to `smtp`, or include both in a rule. The only thing you have to remember is that the names you use to specify a port (`http` and `smtp`, in our case) have to be listed in `/etc/services`. If they're not listed, you can use the number for the port, such as `80` or `25`.

Input/Output and Forwarding Rules

Use `-I` for input, `-O` for output, and `-F` for forwarding rules. You are allowed to mix and match rules like this, but be sure that they don't conflict or the results will not be as you expected. Aside from the initial option to `ipfwadm`, the setup of the rules is the same. Unlike the accounting rules, you can set defaults for how packets that don't meet any rules should be handled. Thinking about this indicates that you would want to reject all packets, then specifically list what packets you want to accept. This is easier than letting everything in and trying to remember what to block.

Here's a sample set of `ipfwadm` commands:

```
#Set up default rules:
# By default, reject any packets wanting to get forwarded
ipfwadm -F -p reject
#Accept all incoming and outgoing packets
ipfwadm -I -p accept
ipfwadm -O -p accept
# Flush (-f) any old rules.  This is always good to run.
ipfwadm -F -f
ipfwadm -O -f
ipfwadm -I -f

# ICMP:
#Here we use -P icmp since we want to work specifically with ICMP pack-
    ets
# The two rules below help prevent our network for being used
# for a smurf attack on an outside network.  Only individual
# machines can be pinged.
#Deny packets to the IP broadcast address.
ipfwadm -F -a deny -P icmp -S 0.0.0.0/0        -D 199.105.157.255
#Some machines think that .0 is a broadcast address too. Filter that.
ipfwadm -F -a deny -P icmp -S 0.0.0.0/0        -D 199.105.157.0
#Accept all other ICMP packets
ipfwadm -F -a accept -P icmp

# bi-directional (all):
#Accept any packets from the 192.168.1.0 network
ipfwadm -F -a accept -b -P all -S 192.168.1.0/16   -D 199.105.157.0/24
# bi-directional (UDP):
```

```
# Allow outgoing DNS requests, and responses to those requests.
ipfwadm -F -a accept -b -P udp -S 0.0.0.0/0  -D 199.105.157.0/24 domain
ipfwadm -F -a accept -b -P udp -S 0.0.0.0/0 domain 1024:65535  \
  -D 199.105.157.0/24 1024:65535

# bi-directional (TCP):
#Allow responses to identd, ftp, telnet, whois, and time.
ipfwadm -F -a accept -b -P tcp -S 0.0.0.0/0 auth ftp-data ftp telnet \
   whois time -D 199.105.157.0/24 1024:65535
#Also allow gopher, 7070 (alternate gopher), anything above 1024,
# finger, e-mail, and web to go out.
ipfwadm -F -a accept -b -P tcp -S 0.0.0.0/0 gopher 7070 1024:65535 \
   finger smtp http -D 199.105.157.0/24 1024:65535
#Accept NetNews, POP and IMAP e-mail, and DNS lookups
ipfwadm -F -a accept -b -P tcp -S 0.0.0.0/0 nntp pop-2 pop-3 imap \
   domain   -D 199.105.157.0/24 1024:65535
ipfwadm -F -a accept -b -P tcp -S 0.0.0.0/0 -D 199.105.157.0/24 \
   domain

# incoming (TCP):
# Allow only one host to accept outside requests for ftp, e-mail, web,
# and POP/IMAP e-mail.
ipfwadm -F -a accept -P tcp -S 0.0.0.0/0 1024:65535 -D 199.105.157.129
   \
   ftp-data ftp smtp http pop-2 pop-3 imap
# Allow only one host to accept WWW requests.
ipfwadm -F -a accept -P tcp -S 0.0.0.0/0 1024:65535 -D 199.105.157.92 \
   http
# One other host is allowed to accept WWW requests.
ipfwadm -F -a accept -P tcp -S 0.0.0.0/0 1024:65535 -D 199.105.157.172
   \ http
# The above is examples of using allowing only a single host to receive
# requests for a service.  Based on these rules, no other hosts will be
# able to receive requests for these services.

# outgoing (TCP):
# Allow any internal address to make requests to external services.
# This is needed so the above (incoming rules) work.
ipfwadm -F -a accept -P tcp -S 199.105.157.0/24 ftp-data ftp smtp http
   \ finger -D 0.0.0.0/0 1024:65535
ipfwadm -F -a accept -P tcp -S 199.105.157.0/24 auth nntp pop-2 pop-3 \
   imap domain time  -D 0.0.0.0/0 1024:65535
```

Since the above ruleset was configured for a router, there aren't any -I or -O packet rules. However, since they're accepted by default, and we allow conventional programs like tcpd and sshd to provide security on the local machine, we could include a rule like this to prevent telnets from the outside world:

```
ipfwadm -I -a accept -P tcp -D 192.168.1.0/24 telnet -D 0.0.0.0/0
ipfwadm -I -a reject -P tcp -D 0.0.0.0/0 telnet -D 0.0.0.0/0
```

The rules must be entered in the order shown, since we want the rule allowing access to be hit first. Any connection from a host in the `192.168.1.0` network matches the first rule, and the session is connected. Any connection from another host (say `192.168.2.10`) will not match the first rule, but will match the second rule. Since the second rule says to reject the packets, the connection is denied.

Masquerade Rules

Masquerading under Linux allows a single router to act as a many-to-one connection. In locations where only a single IP address is available to connect to the Internet[5], masquerading allows a Linux machine to share that one IP address with a network. The hosts inside the network do not need any additional software (aside from a TCP/IP stack) and can all share the single connection to the Internet.

This is very easy to configure under Linux. To get this working, you need to have a machine with two interfaces on it – one going to the Internet and the other going to a local Ethernet containing the hosts you want to masquerade. You'll also need to have the machine set up as a router. Make sure this is all set in `netcfg` or `linuxconf`.

Then you'll want two commands:

```
/sbin/ipfwadm -F -p deny
/sbin/ipfwadm -F -a m -S 192.168.1.0/24 -D 0.0.0.0/0
```

These tell `ipfwadm` to masquerade any packets from `192.168.1.0` going to anywhere. Packets that go out get the return IP address of the Linux machine that is running the masquerade. Packets get tracked using some UDP and TCP information, and as a result, you may have to load in some kernel modules to get support for programs like FTP, Quake, IRC, and Real-Audio. These modules are already compiled on Red Hat and are located in `/lib/modules/preferred/ipv4`. These modules will be known because they're prefaced with "ip_masq", as in `ip_masq_ftp.o`.

Once you have the Linux machine configured, set a client to use the Linux machine as its default gateway, and start generating some traffic on the Internet.

---

[5] Such as modem dial-ups or some cable modems.

ipchains

The `ipchains` method of network administration is superior to the older `ipf-wadm` for the following reasons:

- Works with fragmented packets.
- Handles protocols other than TCP, UDP, and ICMP[6].
- Provides for easier management.
- Inserts or deletes chains anywhere in the list.

As an example of how it's easier to manage `ipchains`, here's the list of commands needed to set up masquerading, assuming that you already have routing enabled:

```
ipchains -P forward -j DENY
ipchains -A forward -i eth0 -j MASQ
```

As you can see, the commands are pretty much the same, but you don't need to specify IP addresses. All you need to know is which interface is the external one.

Much like `ipfwadm`, `ipchains` is based on a list of rules, each rule having to be passed before the packet is allowed into (or out of) the interface. You also get the three standard directions: input, output, and forward; they work the same way as in `ipfwadm`.

After this, things start to get different—or at least the options are different. Here's a sample `ipchains` firewall that is similar to the above firewall. You'll notice that many of the commands look similar. One important difference is that port listings with `-s` and `-d` (known in `ipfwadm` as `-S` and `-D`) can have only one port or range per command. This increases the number of commands needed.

```
#Set up default rules:
# By default, reject any packets wanting to get forwarded
ipchains -P forward -j reject
#Accept all incoming and outgoing packets
ipchains -P input -j accept
ipchains -P output -j accept
# Flush (-F) any old rules.  This is always good to run.
ipchains -F forward
```

---

[6] At this time, `ipchains` only handles TCP, UDP, and ICMP. However, hooks are in to handle other protocols (like IPX) as needed in the future.

```
ipchains -F output
ipchains -F input

# ICMP:
#Here we use -P icmp since we want to work specifically with ICMP pack-
   ets
# The two rules below help prevent our network for being used
# for a smurf attack on an outside network.  Only individual
# machines can be pinged.
#Deny packets to the IP broadcast address.
ipchains -I forward -j deny -p icmp -s 0.0.0.0/0        -d
   199.105.157.255
#Some machines think that .0 is a broadcast address too. Filter that.
ipchains -A forward -j deny -p icmp -s 0.0.0.0/0        -d 199.105.157.0
#Accept all other ICMP packets
ipchains -A forward -j accept -p icmp


# bi-directional (all):
#Accept any packets from the 192.168.1.0 network
ipchains -A forward -j accept -b -p all -s 192.168.1.0/16   -d
   199.105.157.0/24
# bi-directional (UDP):
# Allow outgoing DNS requests, and responses to those requests.
ipchains -A forward -j accept -b -p udp -s 0.0.0.0/0  -d 199.105.157.0/
   24 domain
ipchains -A forward -j accept -b -p udp -s 0.0.0.0/0 domain -d
   199.105.157.0/24 \
 1024:65535
ipchains -A forward -j accept -b -p udp -s 0.0.0.0/0 1024:65535 \
   -d 199.105.157.0/24 1024:65535


# bi-directional (TCP):
#Allow responses to identd, ftp, telnet, whois, and time.
ipchains -A forward -j accept -b -p tcp -s 0.0.0.0/0 auth -d
   199.105.157.0/24 \
 1024:65535
ipchains -A forward -j accept -b -p tcp -s 0.0.0.0/0 ftp-data:ftp \
 -d 199.105.157.0/24 1024:65535
ipchains -A forward -j accept -b -p tcp -s 0.0.0.0/0 telnet \
 -d 199.105.157.0/24 1024:65535
ipchains -A forward -j accept -b -p tcp -s 0.0.0.0/0 whois \
 -d 199.105.157.0/24 1024:65535
ipchains -A forward -j accept -b -p tcp -s 0.0.0.0/0 time \
 -d 199.105.157.0/24 1024:65535
#Accept POP and IMAP e-mail, and DNS lookups
ipchains -A forward -j accept -b -p tcp -s 0.0.0.0/0 pop-3 \
-d 199.105.157.0/24 1024:65535
ipchains -A forward -j accept -b -p tcp -s 0.0.0.0/0 imap \
-d 199.105.157.0/24 1024:65535
ipchains -A forward -j accept -b -p tcp -s 0.0.0.0/0 domain \
```

```
-d 199.105.157.0/24 1024:65535
ipchains -A forward -j accept -b -p tcp -s 0.0.0.0/0 \
-d 199.105.157.0/24 domain
[...and so on.  We think you get the idea..]
```

In addition to all this, there are also save and restore scripts called `ipchains-save` and `ipchains-restore` that save and restore firewall scripts. If you have a pre-built firewall script for `ipfwadm`, you can use the `ipfwadm-wrapper` script to import scripts into `ipchains` format. Once in `ipchains` format, you can use `ipchains-save` to store the new commands. Examine them to make sure there are no security issues, and you will be set with the rules in the newer `ipchains` format.

On additional feature of both `ipchains` and `ipfwadm` is that you can block incoming and outgoing connections without having to forward a packet. One use for this would be blocking ads from known advertisement sites. Another would be to prevent attacks from a specific host or network without modifying your packet filter or firewall software. Instead of using `-A forward`, use `-A input` or `-A output`. In the case of blocking ads, you'd block the output, preventing the request from going to the ad site in the first place. You would use `reject` to make the request fail immediately. In the case of a cracking attempt, you'd block the input, preventing any packets from reaching your IP stack in the first place.

16.6 Summary

Even the best of sites can get cracked with a small security hole. With your Linux servers physically secure and secured on your network, you will make it harder to get cracked.

Kernel Administration 17

Managing the
state-of-the-art Linux kernel

The kernel is the heart and soul of your operating system. It manages the memory, CPU, and disks; every piece of hardware in your system needs it to function. The Linux kernel is one of the most flexible and customizable in existence, and managing it is fairly straightforward, but can be tricky at times.

17.1 Customizing Your Kernel

In virtually every flavor of UNIX, it is possible to configure the kernel to some extent. Usually this is done by specifying a set of external, loadable modules to insert into the kernel at boot-time. With Linux, you can do this and much more. In addition to being able to insert code modules manually at bootup, Linux can also load modules on-demand and later unload them.

On top of all that, you can, since the code for the Linux kernels is freely available, compile your own custom kernel. This includes specifying which drivers and features you wish to compile directly into the kernel and which you wish to leave as loadable modules.

The Linux developers have worked hard to make this as painless as possible, so this flexibility has not cost as much in ease of use as you might have expected. The kernel has two menu-driven configuration options: one X-based and the other screen-based. Additionally, there is the simple line-based, linear configuration.

17.2 Which Kernel?

If you are familiar with Linux, you probably already know that at any given time, there are two current kernel versions: a production version and a developmental version. The developmental (sometimes called experimental) kernels typically have experimental and sometimes buggy or unstable features, though it should be noted that a truly buggy release of either a production or developmental kernel will be fixed very quickly with a new release.

Production kernels always have an even minor release number, while development kernels have odd minor releases. The minor release number is the second of the three numbers that make up the kernel version number. For example, 2.1.121 is a development kernel, and 2.2.3 is a production kernel. The next minor revision up from a production kernel is developed in parallel with the production kernel.

In general, unless you need a feature available only in a developmental kernel, it is usually best to stick with a recent production kernel.

Since Red Hat includes most kernel options as modules, it is very easy to include support for one device or another by loading in the module, or by letting `kmod` do it for you. There are, however, a few features that cannot be included as modules such as APM support. In these cases, you'll need to recompile the kernel.

17.3 Getting Ready

There are a few things you will need or want to have handy while you are rolling out a new kernel. The manuals for your peripherals and your motherboard are good starting points. You will at least need to know the model number of your various peripherals and, in some cases, some hardware settings like interrupt request lines (IRQs) and memory addresses.

You will also want to make a copy of your existing kernel and set up LILO, so you are able to boot in case your new kernel has something wrong with it or simply won't boot.

Also, you will want to have a bootable floppy (which you should have already) in case things really go awry. If you need to make a boot floppy, see the chapter on bootup and shutdown. Also, if you are a little paranoid, you might want to back up your root partition.

17.4 Adding Kernels to LILO

As mentioned above, it is good practice to keep an old, reliable kernel around that you can boot up in a pinch. LILO is the utility that allows you to choose which kernel to boot at startup. With LILO, you can also boot 386BSD, DOS, Windows 98, UNIXware, and most other operating systems.

LILO uses a configuration file, `lilo.conf`, located in `/etc`. Here is an example of one:

```
#
# LILO config file: /etc/lilo.conf
#
boot=/dev/hda1
map=/boot/map
install=/boot/boot.b
verbose=2
prompt
timeout=100
message=/boot/message
image=/vmlinuz
        label=apm
        root=/dev/hda1
        read-only
image=/boot/vmlinuz
        label=linux
        root=/dev/hda1
        read-only
```

The first line simply tells LILO what partition contains the boot sector, or if a device is specified (i.e., `/dev/hda` instead of `/dev/hda1`), which device contains the MBR (Master Boot Record). Next, the map file is specified (`/boot/map` is the default); it tells LILO where all the files are that it needs to boot an OS. Third is the boot loader. It is loaded into the BIOS and subsequently loads the selected kernel. Next is the verbosity level—higher is more verbose. The `prompt` entry tells LILO to present a prompt to allow you to choose which kernel to boot. The `timeout` is how long LILO will wait in tenths of a second before booting the default kernel. If no `timeout` line is present, LILO will wait indefinitely. In either case, simply pressing ENTER at the prompt boots the default kernel. The next line specifies the message file that contains text to be displayed before the LILO prompt.

The next three sections tell LILO about the specific kernels you want to boot. As expected, the first entry is the default one. In this case (as is typical), it points to where the kernel is installed by default: `/vmlinuz`. The `label` sub-entry is the text that is given at the `LILO:` prompt to boot this kernel, `apm` in this case. This represents a kernel recompiled to take advantage of APM sup-port. The `root` line specifies the partition containing the root directory for the OS or kernel. The `read-only` line tells Linux to mount the root partition read only, so that `fsck` can be run at boot-time. The `fsck` program cannot run on a partition that is mounted read-write.

Subsequent entries specify additional Linux kernels, each with their own, unique label, but otherwise the same as the first. A good portion of the time, this is all you will need to know about LILO, especially if you bought your Linux system already configured. However, you may also still want to use DOS and MS Windows or Windows 98 (for games, etc.). Adding entries into your `/etc/lilo.conf` for other OSes is fairly straightforward. Here is an example of an entry to boot MS DOS from a different partition:

```
other=/dev/hda5
        label = dos
        table = /dev/hda
        loader = /boot/chain.b
```

There are two new parameters here: `table` and `loader`. The first specifies the location of the partition table for the foreign OS and the second what chain loader to use to boot up the OS's kernel.

The most important thing to remember with regard to LILO is to run `/sbin/lilo` after changing anything to do with LILO (editing any of the files associated with it, updating a kernel with an existing `lilo.conf` entry, and so forth). Failure to do so could potentially prevent your machine from booting.

17.5 Modules or Compiled In?

One thing to note here is that not all drivers behave the same as a module does when compiled into the kernel. This can range from slight differences in functionality to their simply not working at all.

The choice of when to make a particular feature available as a module or to compile it is usually fairly straightforward. In general, if it is infrequently used and performs as needed as a module, you should compile it as a module. This often includes things like floppy disk drivers (in this day of networking, how often do you really use the thing anyhow?), drivers for other filesystem types, CD-ROM drivers, drivers for sound cards, and networking drivers on a machine that uses dial-in PPP for its access.

If a feature is used frequently or continually, then there really isn't much point in compiling it as a module since it will be loaded all the time anyhow. This includes items such as your hard disk controller or SCSI controller, network drivers on a machine permanently networked, AppleTalk drivers on a fileserver for your Mac network, and so forth.

In cases where functionality between the compiled version and module version differs, it is usually noted in the help pop-up for that option and in any related HOWTOs.

It should be noted that these are, for the most part, just guidelines. Ultimately, you need to compile in your kernel only what you need to boot your machine.

17.6 Dive On In!

Let's go through and outline how you might roll a kernel for a networked Linux machine you are using as your desktop machine and a file server for a network of Windows and Mac machines. You also have a sound card (they're cheap and you have a hundred CDs at home you could also listen to at work). The machine has a SCSI controller with a CD-ROM and hard drives attached to it.

First, make sure you have the kernel sources installed. Even if you do, you may decide you want to get more recent versions. The default location is in /usr/src/linux (linux may be a link to linux-x.y.z, where x.y.z is a kernel revision). Once you make your way into /usr/src/linux, type make xconfig (assuming you are in X, which is highly recommended). This will do some preliminary work and then bring up a window with buttons that take you to various sections of the kernel configuration.

As you may have guessed, the first time through it is best to start at the top and go through all the menus.

To the right of each button is a help button that gives a small amount of information on the driver and some hints to help you decide if you want to enable it or not.

Configuring the Kernel

If you are in X, run `make xconfig` from `/usr/src/linux`. If you are using a character terminal, run `make menuconfig`. And, if you are using a character terminal with poor emulation, you are stuck running `make config`.

When you run `make` with the `xconfig` option, a nice GUI pops up as seen in Figure 17-1.

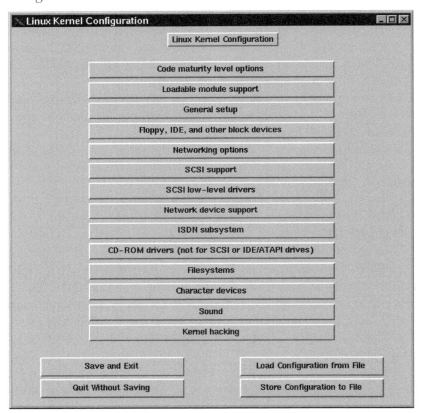

Figure 17–1   Main Xconfig screen

Once you go into a submenu, you can get help on the various options there. See Figures 17-2 and 17-3 for examples.

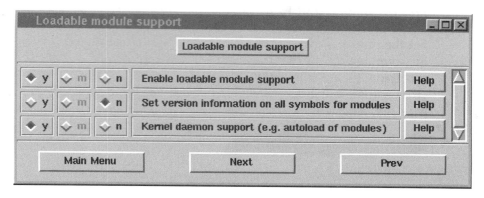

Figure 17–2   Module support screen

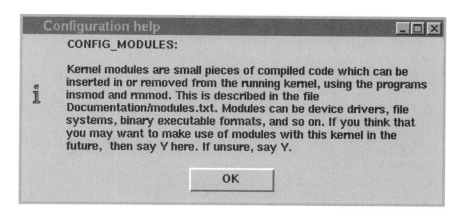

Figure 17–3   Sample help screen

Now you are ready to start configuring your new kernel.

Code Maturity Level Options

Answering Yes to the one option here will not change the kernel. It will simply give you options later on for various experimental or incomplete drivers. Say Yes; it doesn't hurt anything. You can always say No to any experimental drivers you are offered.

Some experimental modules available in the current 2.2 kernels include enhanced support for some IDE controller chipsets, IPv6, Ethernet bridging, write support for UFS and NTFS filesystem types, CODA (a next-generation network filesystem), and support for numerous pieces of less common hardware.

Processor Type and Features

cessor type appropriately, unless you have an old version of GCC
eason. In that case, you will have to say 386 or 486. If you have
PUs, enable SMP as well. If you have a Pentium Pro or Pentium
are using the machine as a workstation, i.e., you will be running X
nable MTRR as it should improve video performance.

Loadable Module Support

As you might guess, we highly recommend that you enable the use of loadable modules and kernel daemon support. Under the 2.0 series of kernels,
the kernel daemon, `kerneld`, is the program that manages the loading and
unloading of modules. It is available separately from the kernel distribution,
but ships with Red Hat. Under Linux 2.2 (Red Hat 6.0 and later), kernel
modules are loaded and unloaded by the kernel itself, using the `kmod` facility.
If you are using a 2.2 kernel, you should therefore enable the kernel module
loader option as well.

While `kmod` is not as flexible as `kerneld`, it removes a step in the locating
and loading of a module. Since the kernel never used any of the other features of `kerneld`, the replacement was made.

Both `kerneld` and `kmod` call `modprobe` to load a module, as well as modules
it may depend on. Often it is desirable to tune `modprobe`'s behavior. This is
done in its configuration file, `/etc/conf.modules`. Those that find this name
backwards can move it to `/etc/modules.conf`, which `modprobe` also knows to
check.

This file has several types of entries, but two are the most common: `alias`
and `options`.

An `alias` line does pretty much what one would expect. It assigns an alias
name to a real module name. This can also be used to turn a module off.
`Options` lines set up options for use with specified modules. Examples are
things like i/o memory addresses of peripherals and IRQ settings.

One module that almost always requires an `options` entry in `/etc/`
`conf.modules` is the sound module. For example, the entries for a Crystal
CS423x on-board sound chipset would look something like this:

```
alias sound cs4232
alias midi opl3
options opl3 io=0x388
options cs4232 io=0x534 irq=5 dma=1 dma2=0
```

Options lines can use a real module name or an alias. The main benefit of alias entries is to make it easier to use modules in general. It is easier to remember that your sound card support can be referenced by sound instead of the module named after the chipset.

To turn a module off, use an entry like this:

```
alias net-pf-4 off
```

This turns off the IPX module and also prevents the display of warning messages about it being missing should an attempt to load it be made if it isn't present.

For more details about kmod and modules in general, read the man page on modprobe and the kernel documentation on modules, typically found at /usr/src/linux/Documentation/modules.txt.

We don't recommend that you enable version information on loadable modules, but rather that you reinstall modules each time you install a new kernel.

When compiling the kernel, it is generally better to enable more options as modules than not compile them or build them into the kernel. Since modules do not take up any memory or CPU space when not in use, they allow you to have more options available for when you need them. Also, modules allow you to change options when you change cards. Installing a new sound card no longer requires recompiling the kernel; you just change the options in /etc/conf.modules.

General Setup

You will definitely want to enable networking support and System V IPC. Unless you have a very old system without a PCI bus, enable PCI support as well. You should also enable a.out, probably as a module, since nearly every executable binary is in ELF format. Choose either support for ELF or MISC. Select MISC if you want to be able to run other binary formats via a wrapper. This includes things like Python, Java, LISP, or even DOS programs via DOSEMU. You should also read binfmt_mic.txt and java.txt in the Documentation/ directory for more detailed instructions on using this feature. Most people, however, will be fine with just ELF support and running their Python scripts the old-fashioned way.

Block Devices

Enable floppy disk support, probably as a module, unless you use the floppy drive a lot. Leave out (E)IDE support if you are sure you do not need it, i.e., you have a SCSI-only system.

The various chipset support options and bug fixes can be left off unless you have an older motherboard, particularly one that uses Intel's Neptune chipset.

For the rest of the options, it should be obvious if you need them or not. Enable as you see fit.

Networking Options

There are several options you will definitely want here—namely, TCP/IP networking, UNIX domain sockets, and packet sockets.

Most of the rest of the IP and network-related options you will not need unless your machine is acting as a TCP/IP router/gateway or firewall. You might need to enable multicasting if you are going to be accessing the MBONE (the multicast backbone, which sits on top of the Internet). If you enable routing, you will be presented with options for routing strategies in the QoS and/or Fair Queuing menu.

Further down you will find support for other networking protocols: IPX, AppleTalk, and AX.25. Enable these if you need them. If your machine is going to be a server using one of these protocols, you might as well compile it into the kernel. It will likely end up being loaded nearly all of the time anyhow.

You can also enable support for IPv6. IPv6 is the next generation IP protocol. Its most compelling features are a vastly expanded address space (128 bits instead of 32), authentication, and privacy. Most Internet providers do not support IPv6 yet, but Linux will be ready when they do.

SCSI Support

Assuming we have beaten the dead horse enough, you will need at least SCSI support and SCSI disk support for your SCSI-based machine. You might also need SCSI tape and CD-ROM support as well. If you have other SCSI devices, like a scanner, you will also need to enable generic SCSI support. Unless you have a device with multiple logical unit numbers, you should say No to the option for probing all logical unit numbers (LUNs). An example of such a device is a CD jukebox.

If you are having problems with your SCSI bus, you may want to enable verbose error reporting to help track the errors.

SCSI Low-level Drivers

Enable the driver(s) for your SCSI adapters. If you are using a built-in ZIP or JAZ drive on your controller, you will need to enable its driver. See the chapter on peripherals for more information.

If you are using a ZIP drive on the parallel port, you will need to enable support for it here, too. This type of drive contains a parallel-to-SCSI converter that essentially turns the port into a SCSI host.

Network Device Support

Enable network device support (duh). After that, enable other options as you need them. In most cases, your choice should be clear. Further down in this pop-up is a list of Ethernet cards. Once again, the correct choice should be obvious, assuming you know what kind of card is in your system. Enable more than one if you have multiple cards.

Amateur Radio Support and IrDA Subsystem Support

These two menus control support for amateur (HAM or AX25) radio and infrared ports. Infrared ports are commonly found on laptops and PDAs.

Amatuer radio users should consult the HAM HOWTO or the AX25 HOWTO and `http://www.tapr.org/tapr/html/pkthome.html`.

More documentation on IR support can be found in the IR HOWTO.

ISDN Subsystem

Enable this if you need it. You will likely have to contact your service provider to find out if they support synchronous PPP and compression. Enable the driver for your ISDN adapter as well. Enable the remaining options as needed.

Old CD-ROM Drivers

Hopefully you will not need this. But if your CD-ROM interface is not ATAPI-(IDE) or SCSI-based, you will require this. In many cases, older sound cards or proprietary CD-ROM interfaces will require this setup. This should only be the case on older systems, however.

Character Devices

You will almost definitely want to have virtual terminal support, unless you plan to only use the machine from the network and/or serial port. It is also likely that you will want standard serial port support, though you can leave it out if you have a bus mouse and no modem.

Intelligent multiport serial card support is also set here. If you have a dumb serial port card (based on the 16550 or similar), it is enabled as part of the standard serial port support.

Further down are options for Unix98 `pty` support, which you should always have enabled; parallel printer support, which you should enable also if you have a parallel port ZIP drive; non-serial, i.e., bus, mice; non-SCSI tape drives; speech cards; and various devices related to timing.

If you said `Yes` to bus mice, you will be given a list of drivers to choose from in the `Mice` menu. Similarly, if you enabled watchdog timer support, a list of drivers for watchdog cards will appear.

Video for Linux

This supports video and audio capture devices and FM tuners. User programs for accessing the devices can be found at `ftp://ftp.uk.linux.org/pub/linux/video4linux`.

Joystick Support and Ftape, the Floppy Tape Device Driver

Here is another pair of fairly self-explanatory devices, at least if you've been using PCs for awhile. Enable and select the appropriate driver if you have this hardware. The joystick driver is recommended if you're going to play games, and Ftape is needed for some of the older 250MB tape systems. We don't recommend using these tapes for most systems due to the low capacity and slow speed. Most newer tape backup systems use either SCSI or ATAPI and have higher capacities and higher backup and restore rates.

Filesystems and Network File Systems

If your machine is used for shell access, you may want to enable quota support. Quota support will also work with AppleTalk users since they are "real" users and have `/etc/passwd` entries. Depending on how Samba or IPX is set up, it may be useful to enable quota for their users as well.

Leave mandatory lock support off unless you know you'll need it or you have newer AppleTalk, NFS, and/or Samba daemons.

Enable the second extended filesystem support. This is Linux's native file-system type. It will likely be safe to leave Minix, the first extended filesystem, and xiafs off as they are older and not needed in newer Linux systems.

It may be useful to enable the DOS- and Windows-related filesystem types since these machines are so ubiquitous. Enable them as modules unless you use them frequently.

Enable /proc. It's needed by several programs. You really should not even be given the option to turn it off.

You will know whether or not you need the rest of the options; enable them as necessary. In particular, you will want to include CD-ROM (ISO9660) filesystem support.

If you have a very heterogeneous LAN, you may want to enable virtually all of these for use with removable media (floppy, ZIP or JAZ drives).

Partition Types

If you want to mount and use foreign partition types, enable them here.

Native Language Support

If you enabled support for Microsoft filesystems, you can also enable support for internationalization and foreign language character sets here.

Sound and Low-level Sound Drivers

If you use the console of the machine and have a sound card, you will want to enable support for it here. You will definitely need the manual for your sound card, as there are a number of hardware parameters you need to compile into the kernel.

There are a large number of combinations of hardware and parameters—too many to try to cover here. If you are careful and keep your card's manual handy, you should not have any serious trouble getting your card fully supported (at least as far as the current drivers will allow) under Linux. Some manuals can be a little sparse, and you may have to fiddle with the settings to get your card working.

Depending on the driver you enable on the Sound menu, you will be given options for additional drivers in the Low Level Sound Drivers menu.

Kernel Hacking

Unless you are hacking and debugging the kernel, say No to Magic SysRq Key.

Compile the Kernel and Modules

To properly build the kernel the first time, issue the following commands:

```
# make dep
<lots of output here>
# make
<several bucketloads of output here>
```

Now, to install the compressed kernel in the root partition, type:

```
# make zlilo
<output ending in...>
tools/build bootsect setup compressed/vmlinux.out CURRENT > zImage
Root device is (8, 1)
Boot sector 512 bytes.
Setup is 4348 bytes.
System is 368 kB
sync
if [ -f /vmlinuz ]; then mv /vmlinuz /vmlinuz.old; fi
if [ -f /System.map ]; then mv /System.map /System.old; fi
cat zImage > /vmlinuz
cp /usr/src/linux/System.map /
if [ -x /sbin/lilo ]; then /sbin/lilo; else /etc/lilo/install; fi
Added 1 *
Added 12
Added 13
make[1]: Leaving directory `/usr/src/linux-2.0.36/arch/i386/boot'
```

If you enable any drivers as modules, you must build and install them as follows:

```
# make modueles
<a few bucketloads of output>
# make modules_install
Installing modules under /lib/modules/2.0.36/block
Installing modules under /lib/modules/2.0.36/net
Installing modules under /lib/modules/2.0.36/ipv4
Installing modules under /lib/modules/2.0.36/fs
<or something similar>
```

This last command installs the kernel and reruns LILO to update the boot map. To install it on a floppy instead, run `make zImage` (instead of `zlilo`) and then copy the image to a high-density floppy.

```
# cp /usr/src/linux/arch/i386/boot/zImage /dev/fd0
```

Reboot your machine with your new kernel like this:

```
# /sbin/reboot
```

If the new kernel doesn't boot, you can reboot again (using the familiar CONTROL-ALT-DELETE) and at the LILO: prompt, enter another kernel to boot. As you can see from the output above, there are three kernels installed in /etc/lilo.conf. If you type 12 at the prompt, the kernel corresponding to the 12 label will be booted. Recheck your hardware and the drivers you have enabled and recompile if you need to. It is also possible that the particular kernel revision simply doesn't work on your system.

17.7 Summary

Hopefully, we have managed to take some of the intimidation out of the process of compiling your own kernel. On the other hand, we also want to be sure that you take a few simple precautions in case you make a kernel that won't boot up on your system.

If you are interested in the inner workings of the kernel, you can consult various HOWTOs, in particular the Kernel Hacking HOWTO for Linux-specific information, or any of a number of books on general OS theory and design.

For more detailed information on booting and LILO, see the chapter on booting and shutdown.

System and Network Monitoring

18

Keep an eye on your system and the rest of the network

Monitor your Linux machine from the console or remotely using the syslog program and other utilities.

18.1 Syslog

The syslog program monitors kernel and user events and routes messages based on what you want to do. These events can be minor things, such as the root logging in, or they can be serious, such as a hard drive failure, kernel panic, or reboot.

The `syslogd` program gets started up at boot-time and uses the `/etc/syslogd.conf` file to know what to do. Here's a sample configuration file:

```
# Log all kernel messages to the console.
# Logging much else clutters up the screen.
#kern.*                                        /dev/console

# Log anything (except mail) of level info or higher.
```

```
# Don't log private authentication messages!
*.info;mail.none;authpriv.none                    /var/log/messages

# The authpriv file has restricted access.
authpriv.*                                        /var/log/secure

# Log all the mail messages in one place.
mail.*                                            /var/log/maillog

# Everybody gets emergency messages, plus log them on another
# machine.
*.emerg                                               *

# Save mail and news errors of level err and higher in a
# special file.
uucp,news.crit                                    /var/log/spooler
```

Any line with a # in front of it is ignored because it is a comment. Other lines are entries and consist of two fields. The first field lists the events to monitor. The second field lists what to do once an event has occurred.

Each event is in two parts, separated by a period. The first part is the facility, or type of program generating the event. The second part is the priority or severity of the event, ranging from debug to emerg.

There are twenty facilities available:

- auth
- auth-priv
- cron
- daemon
- kern
- lpr
- mail
- mark
- news
- syslog
- user
- uucp
- local0 through local7

There are eight priorities available:

- debug

- info
- notice
- warning
- err
- crit
- alert
- emerg

Facilities and Priorities

The facility/priority combination you list will report all the messages that get sent to syslog for that priority and higher. A priority of debug will report all messages, and a priority of none will not report messages.

Replacing either the facility or priority with an asterisk (*) will report for all facilities or all priorities, depending on where you put the asterisk (before or after the period). You can combine multiple facilities with one priority by separating them with a comma.

The syslog that Linux uses has a few extensions to it that are not in the original BSD version of syslog. Putting an equal sign (=) in front of a priority says to report only this priority in a list. Putting an exclamation point (!) in front of a priority says to ignore that priority and all higher priorities. Combining the two (!=) would ignore only that priority.

The man pages for the particular programs you want to monitor will usually list what facilities the program uses. Note that there are eight user-defined facilities you can use in your programs or other scripts.

Actions

The second field lists where a message should be sent. This can be a file (if the destination starts with a /), a remote host (if the destination starts with an @), all logged-in users (if the destination is an *), or a specific user (if it starts with none of the above three characters). The file destination can also be a tty file, such as /dev/console, which will send the message to the Linux console. You can also use the | character to pipe the message to an external command or FIFO.

Using remote host logging can centralize a group of computers to log all their messages to one machine. However, if the system experiences a severe problem (the Ethernet card goes bad, the kernel panics, etc.), the message for this may not get sent to the remote host. Of course, the same thing could be said for logging to the hard drive should the drive or its controller go bad.

Logging Procedures

How you log depends on what you want to log. For an initial setup, you should probably start by logging just about everything. For programs like `pppd`, this will greatly increase the amount of debugging information you have. As the system becomes stable and is working correctly, continue debugging, but change the priority to something like `warn` or `err` to keep out regular debugging information. You may also choose to have different facilities for different files. For example, you may want to send all email logs to `/var/log/maillog`, and bad logins to `/var/log/authlog`. This can make it easier to separate problems if they arrive. Bad login problems? Check the authentication log. The downside to this is that some logs may be intertwined. For example, a bad login may be the result of someone cracking into sendmail. If you don't examine the mail log, you may not realize what's going on.

18.2 Network Monitoring

There are a number of ways to keep an eye on the network to see what's going on and track potential problems. As an example, two machines that share the same IP address could easily cause trouble of which it is hard to locate the source. Other issues such as bad network cards or bad routers and hubs can also cause very sporadic and annoying problems. Having the right tools on hand can help you locate the source of trouble and fix it.

tcpdump

The tcpdump program puts the Ethernet card into promiscuous mode to see what's happening on the network. All packets seen by the card are displayed on the screen. Filters exist to see only the data that you want to see

Here are a few packets related to ARP:

```
21:49:12.480000 arp who-has mymachine.insidehost.com tell gateway.insi-
  dehost.com
21:49:12.480000 arp reply mymachine.insidehost.com is-at
  0:0:c1:b4:4f:dc
:
```

The first line is a request from gateway asking for the Ethernet address for my machine. The next line is a reply with the MAC address for that particular machine. This is fairly common, since ARP caches do not last all that long. On a good-sized network, you may see many ARP requests and (maybe) replies per minute. Since an ARP request is an Ethernet broadcast, all machines hooked by switches or hubs will see the packet. Only those machines on the same Ethernet run as the replying machine and the requesting machine will see the response, so don't worry if you don't see a lot of replies sometimes.

Here are some ICMP-related packets:

```
21:50:05.510000 mymachine.insidehost.com > ping.outsidehost.com: icmp:
  echo request
21:50:05.650000 ping.outsidehost.com > mymachine/insidehost.com: icmp:
  echo reply
```

Here we see a ping (one ping only) going from mymachine out to a remote site (ping.outsidehost.com). About 140ms later, the ping is answered with a reply. Since a ping is really sending, asking the remote side to echo data, this is how tcpdump reports it.

In this example, we're going to run tcpdump on the second Ethernet port (also known as eth1):

```
[root@server markk]# /usr/sbin/tcpdump -i eth1
tcpdump: listening on eth1
23:12:59.510000 192.168.1.15.listen > server.telnet: . ack 760059009
  win 7842 (D
F)
23:12:59.510000 server.telnet > 192.168.1.15.listen: P 1:29(28) ack 0
  win 32736
(DF)
23:12:59.710000 192.168.1.15.listen > server.telnet: . ack 29 win 7814
  (DF)
23:12:59.710000 server.telnet > 192.168.1.15.listen: P 29:199(170) ack
  0 win 327
36 (DF)

4 packets received by filter
0 packets dropped by kernel
[root@server markk]#
```

This example is pretty poor, since we're logged into the machine via the second Ethernet port. So, what we're really seeing is the data from tcpdump being sent over the Ethernet line through the telnet window. It gets messy, but it tells us a lot.

Let's take a look at two of these packets:

```
23:12:59.510000 server.telnet > 192.168.1.15.listen: P 1:29(28) ack 0
   win 32736 (DF)
23:12:59.710000 192.168.1.15.listen > server.telnet: . ack 29 win 7814
   (DF)
```

The first line is a packet leaving the `telnet` TCP port on `server` (the machine connected via telnet) and going to `192.168.1.15` on the `listen` TCP port. Because we're on a Windows 98 machine, it doesn't matter what port the data comes in on. The timestamp indicates that the time is almost 11:13 PM. You'll note that the timing goes past seconds, since Ethernet can handle 10Mbps, and that's a lot of data to put in a second.

After the destination is listed, any special TCP/IP flags are mentioned. In this case, the `P` represents "Push". This could also be `S` (Syn), `F` (Fin), `R` (Rst) or a period (`.`), meaning no flags. Next comes the data sequence number (`1:29(28)`). This allows the IP layer to reassemble packets as they come in. Next is the `ack 0`, meaning that it's expecting an acknowledgment, which is in the next line. The `win` refers to the size of the remaining receive buffer. As this buffer fills, less data will come in until the IP layer can handle all the packets remaining in the buffer.

The second line is the acknowledgment packet from the target machine to the server. If you're communicating via TCP, you need to acknowledge all packets that come in. In UDP, this is not necessary.

Among other things, tcpdump shows you ARP requests, NFS traffic, DNS lookups, and other information that you may not be aware of. Since tcpdump attempts to use names instead of IP addresses whenever possible, you may see a lot of traffic from your own machine trying to find out who everyone else is. If you want to turn this off, use the `-n` option.

Another option available to tcpdump is filtering. For example, you could filter out all telnet information and get information about who is browsing the Web with something like this:

```
/usr/sbin/tcpdump -i eth1 port http
```

This matches both local machines going out to the Web and outside machines getting information from your Web servers.

Since tcpdump only sees traffic on the local Ethernet, you'll only be able to see Ethernet traffic on your segment. You won't be able to see traffic on the other side of a router, firewall, or even a switch, unless it's an Ethernet broadcast (such as ARP or DHCP requests).

Queso

If you have a number of Ethernet segments and find an offending IP address, it may be hard to find out what that machine actually is. Is it running Windows NT? Linux? Is it a Sparc workstation? Queso (http://www.apostols.org/projectz/queso/) knows. There are a few functions of TCP/IP that are technically undefined, and it's up to the vendor how to respond. Queso is a program that checks this functionality, matches it against a database, and tells you what OS a particular machine is running. Seven packets are sent to the IP address (all valid) and the response is checked. If the response matches the list of known OSes, the name of the operating system is found. A tool like this can quickly map out what is running on a network.

Statnet

If you want to keep an eye on a network, you can use the statnet (http://www.skypoint.com/~sewilco/statnet.htm) program. It gives a single screen with an overall view of network traffic on your segment. If you start seeing strange spikes in usage, you can prevent serious problems before they start.

SNMP

SNMP stands for Simple Network Management Protocol. It defines a hierarchy of settings for an individual computer to use to tell others about its health, statistics about its use, and configuration and location information. SNMP is implemented in three parts: the SNMP daemon, MIB (Management Information Base) file, and an SNMP manager.

The SNMP daemon is provided in Red Hat 6.0 as the ucd-snmp package. It also includes a series of MIB files. MIB files are a way of describing what capabilities your machine has. Some of this can be found out from the SNMP daemon itself, but other things have to be entered. The SNMP manager is a client, or reader. These applications can query an SNMP daemon, or they can be set to receive SNMP "traps" or alerts. An alert would be something like low resources, such as a hard drive running out of space. An alert would be sent to the SNMP manager, which would then process the alert in whatever way it wants (send an email, page, fax, blink the screen a few times, and so on).

Part of the security of SNMP includes two ways of getting information. The "public" group (also called a community) is typically allowed to read but not write information. The "private" community is more for system managers who want to possibly write information or get access to more private information about a machine. More information about security settings can be found in the snmp.conf man page. You can also find examples in the /etc/snmp/ snmpd.conf file.

You can test the SNMP on your machine by using the following:

```
[user@system /tmp]$ snmpwalk -v 1 localhost public system
system.sysDescr.0 = "Linux markk.wayga.net 2.2.5-15 #1 Mon Apr 19
   22:21:09 EDT 1
999 i586"
system.sysObjectID.0 = OID: enterprises.ucdavis.ucdSnmpAgent.linux
system.sysUpTime.0 = Timeticks: (3856) 0:00:38.56
system.sysContact.0 = "Root <root@localhost> (configure /etc/snmp/
   snmp.local.con
f)"
system.sysName.0 = "markk.wayga.net"
system.sysLocation.0 = "Unknown (configure /etc/snmp/snmp.local.conf)"
system.sysServices.0 = 72
[user@system /tmp]$
```

If SNMP is not running, make sure the ucd-snmp package is installed and that snmpd is running. You can check this with /etc/rc.d/init.d/ snmpd status. If it's not running, just send a start command to the snmpd script. You can edit the /etc/snmp/snmpd.conf file or the /etc/snmp/ snmpd.local.conf file to replace system.sysContact.0 or system.sys-Location.0 and set contact or location information.

There are a number of applications for Linux that use SNMP, and here are two of them:

Scotty

Scotty (http://wwwhome.cs.utwente.nl/~schoenw/scotty/) is an implementation of SNMP using Tcl/Tk. As a sample application, Scotty comes with a program called tkined, which gives a graphical view of a network and easy menu access to many functions of an SNMP manager, including traps and Ethernet load. It can also help create a network map.

MRTG

MRTG, the Multi Router Traffic Grapher (http://www.mrtg.org), takes SNMP data from a router and displays daily, weekly, monthly, and yearly information about data going in and out of the router. The data is pulled from the router interfaces and GIF images (graphs) are created from the resulting information. These graphs give you a sense of how much data is going through your routers. Some larger ISPs are using MRTG to provide usage graphs to their customers (see Figure 18-1 for an example).

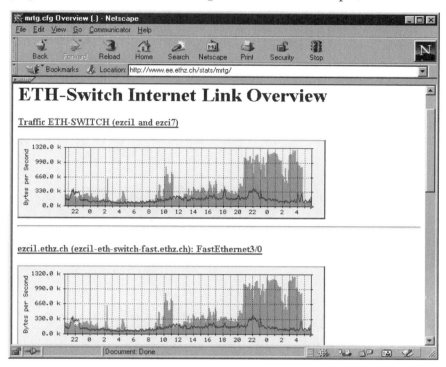

Figure 18–1   MRTG sample screen from MRTG main site

18.3 Network Monitoring Distributions

One thing you may want to think about is getting a laptop and configuring it with a mini Linux distribution. One such distribution specifically made for this purpose is Trinux (`http://www.trinux.org`). It was designed to boot off two or three floppies and exist completely in memory. Since it has a number of tools built into it, you can easily bring a laptop to a section of an Ethernet that's giving you trouble and fire up tcpdump to see what's going on.

18.4 Summary

One of the keys of having a high up-time is to know everything that is going on in the system. By monitoring your machine carefully, you can catch potential problems or break-ins before or as they occur, and fix a problem before it gets out of hand.

Backing Up   **19**
Your Data

When all else fails . . .
restore from backup!

Keeping good backups is frequently the only way to recover
from some accidents, disasters, or break-ins. Linux has a
number of methods for archiving your data, ranging from
tools like `tar` or `cpio` that come with Linux to feature-rich,
sophisticated, commercial packages.

There are a number of ways to keep backups, ranging from simply `taring`
your entire filesystem to a tape to using `dump` and a well-designed backup
schedule to running high-end commercial backup and restore programs.

Of course, you also have a variety of backup media to choose from: floppies (if you are truly desperate), tape drives (from old nine tracks up to
DAT), write once, read many (WORM) drives, magneto-optical floppies
(written magnetically, read optically), and ZIP and JAZ drives. Of these, only
the newer tape options and JAZ drives have gigabyte capacity, and only
exabyte and DAT can handle more than a couple of gigabytes. Unfortunately,
tapes are in many ways the most cumbersome to work with because of their
sequential access nature.

With the new proposed standards for CD-ROM- (and thus WORM-) based filesystems, this media will soon sport multiple gigabyte capacity. Though they will still be write once, the easier access (random instead of sequential) will likely make them popular once their price drops into the affordable range. In actuality, the technology for this has existed for some time, but the popularity of the current standard has kept it from being replaced. However, the need to store large amounts of data reliably has grown tremendously in recent years, and CD-ROMs are a big win over tape in both ease of access and longevity (decades versus years).

The rest of this chapter assumes you have some form of large capacity media on which to back up your data, though many of the guidelines are useful regardless of the media being used or its capacity.

In general, you will want to run your backup during times of low activity for two reasons. One, it is not a good idea to have lots of files open or changing while the backup is running. Some programs will lock a file and the backup will, at best, be able to skip it, or, at worst, the backup will exit or crash. Second, backing up your system will tend to consume a lot of system resources, and if your server is fairly loaded already, it will likely be bogged down considerably if you try to run the backup during "normal" business hours (whatever those might be).

19.1 tar and mt

The name "tar" stands for tape archive. Before the more recent versions of GNU, tar was not really suitable for use as a backup tool. It had no easy way of performing incremental backups and properly handling files with holes (so-called sparse files).

At the base level, you can create a cron job that will compress and archive all of your filesystems and network volumes to a tape drive every night or every few nights. There are a couple of drawbacks to this method, however.

Typically, only a small fraction of the filesystem changes over the course of even a week. Making a copy of the whole filesystem every other night is overkill. It would be better if incremental backups could be made.

It's very possible that you could have more stuff to back up than you have capacity on your particular combination of tape and drive. In this case, you would have to break up the backup and change tapes at some point to complete the backup. Once again, incremental backups would alleviate this.

If your backup, or sections thereof, is small enough, you may want to put more than one on a single tape, and then you may need some way to access a particular archive at some later point. You could use `tar`'s append feature, but then the ability to maintain different versions is lost. When the archive is unpacked, the appended files will overwrite ones with the same names that were extracted earlier.

Using tar

The `tar` command has three major functions: create a `tar` file, list the contents of a `tar` file, and extract files from an existing `tar` file. In terms of switches to `tar`, there are c, t, and x, respectively. These switches get combined with others to create an efficient means of accomplishing backup and recovery.

Other commonly used switches include f for filename, v for verbose, and z to enable gzip (de)compression. The f option requires the entry of a filename or a hyphen to indicate standard input. If multiple switches that require arguments are used, you can line up both the switches followed by the arguments, or list a switch followed by its argument. So, it is perfectly legal to run either of these commands:

```
tar -cvf foo.tar file1 file2 file3
tar -c file1 file2 file3 -vf foo.tar
```

In fact, these two commands do the exact same thing.

If the -z switch were added, the `tar` would also compress with gzip. Typically, compressed `tar` files are named `foo.tgz` or `foo.tar.gz`.

You can also compress archives with the command:

```
# tar zxvf foo.tar.gz
```

or read a compressed archive from a SCSI tape device with:

```
# tar zxvf /dev/nst0
```

When using `tar`, you must know the block size when backing up and restoring files. Get the block size wrong, and you won't be able to read the files you backed up. You may also want to change this block size if the tape drive is slow, or is higher-speed, since the default block size on some machines is rather small (the Linux version of `tar` has a block size of 20*512 bytes, or 10KB). Increasing the block size decreases the amount of overhead when writing to the tape and can increase the performance and decrease the write time to the tape. The block size is added with a -B <blocksize>

option to `tar`, where `<blocksize>` is multiplied by 512 to get the block size in bytes.

Now that we have beaten up on `tar` quite a bit, let's point out a few things that `tar` is good at doing. `tar` can archive files that are not currently needed or take a snapshot of a project. If one of your users has some data they still need but will not be using for awhile, take advantage of this to `tar` the data to a tape and remove it from the server. Also, you may need to keep snapshots of projects, but not necessarily online.

As mentioned earlier, `tar` is commonly used to create packages or distributions of documentation, source code, or precompiled software.

Finally, `tar` can be used to transfer directory trees around in your filesystem. Its many command line options let you control preservation of permissions, modification dates, and the following of symbolic links. This allows you to re-create a directory tree on another partition with more control than `cp -a`. An example illustrates this nicely:

```
# cd /newhome
# (cd /home ; tar cf —cary)| tar xf -
```

This will re-create the directory `/home/caryc` as a subdirectory of `/newhome`. It will preserve the permissions and ownership of the files and re-create (but not follow) symbolic links (assuming the links are not stale).

In general, it is not a good idea to follow symbolic links unless you know where all the links in the tree are pointing. If a link points back down to a directory that is within the archive, you will start recursively re-creating the directory tree within the subdirectory and very quickly eat up a large amount of disk space.

Using mt

To create different sections of tape, you need to use both `tar` and `mt` (for magnetic tape). The `mt` program is used to control tape devices. Since the `tar` program starts at the beginning of a block and adds an EOF (end of file) at the end of each block, you use the `mt -f <device>, fsf <count>` command to advance sections of tape. See below for a note on figuring out the `<device>` and `<count>` is the number of times to perform that operation.

For example, if you had five `tar` files on a tape and wanted to add a sixth, you would first advance the tape with `mt -f /dev/nst0 fsf 5` to get to the next block after the fifth end-of-file marker. Once you had arrived at the last EOF mark on the tape, you would then use `tar -cvf` to write new information. If you needed to recover data from a particular section, you could use

the mt command to advance the tape to the section you needed, then use tar
-xvf to restore the data from tape. You would want to use this if you were
backing up multiple filesystems to a tape. You could then have each filesystem use a different section of tape and restore only the section you needed.

Tape Operations

Another feature of tar is its use of different device names. Based on the
device name that tar uses, it can make the tape rewind to the beginning or
remain in place after completing. This is important, since if tar backs up a
directory, rewinds, and backs up another directory, the first backup is overwritten. Using mt to advance the tape is time-consuming and increases the
amount of coding you need to do to calculate how far to advance the tape.

Using the /dev/nst0 device name will tell the tape device to not rewind
after completing. Note that you'll need to use this when advancing the tape
with mt, or else the tape will rewind after being advanced! The regular /dev/
st0 will rewind after the command is completed, and can be used after a
restore to automatically rewind the tape. The mt command also supports an
explicit rewind, and if the tape device supports it, can also eject the tape.
These commands are mt -f /dev/st0 rewind and mt -f /dev/st0
offline, respectively. Other commands to mt include re-tension (forward to
the end of the tape, then rewind), status (to give a status of the tape drive),
erase (to erase the tape), and a number of SCSI-only options relating to hardware compression, buffering, density, and others. Check the man page for mt
for a complete list of the available options.

19.2 cpio

In many ways, cpio is similar to tar. It supports more formats (including the
format used by tar) and can also deal with archives from machines with different byte orders. Like tar, cpio can write or read to network devices as
well as local ones. Finally, cpio can be used in pass-through mode to copy
directory trees.

The choice between using cpio or tar to perform backups is largely a
matter of preference. If you come across a system that does not have Red
Hat installed on it, other Red Hat systems (or the RPM install file) contain a
program called rpm2cpio. The purpose of this program is to convert an RPM
file to cpio so that it can be extracted and installed on other systems.

The `cpio` program has (at last count) a billion available switches to it. Much like `tar`, these can be shortened (by us anyway) down to a few major ones you need to know about. These include: `-F <file>` to output to a file instead of `STDOUT`, `-i` for extract, and `-o` for create. These seem to make less sense than the `tar` commands, except for the fact that `cpio` thinks of the extract command as "copy in" and the create command as "copy out".

A few examples should help clarify things. One of the simplest things you can do with `cpio` is archive the files in a directory (ignoring subdirectories):

```
# ls  cpio -o > /tmp/stuff.cpio
```

To include directories, you do this:

```
# find . -print -depth | cpio -o > ~/morestuff.cpio
```

To create the file on another machine (assuming you have permission to, usually via an entry in `~/.rhosts`):

```
# find . -print -depth | cpio -o -F cary@loki:/archive/stuff.cpio
```

To extract the files from the archive:

```
# cpio -i < stuff.cpio
```

Note that `cpio` will not preserve directory structure unless explicitly told to as follows:

```
# cpio -id < ~/morestuff.cpio
```

19.3 dump and restore

`dump` is probably the best free alternative for performing backups. It makes a fairly low-level copy of the filesystem. Because of this, any type of file (including sockets and block and character devices) can be archived and files that have empty blocks in them are properly saved. Additionally, it can perform incremental backups and archives can span multiple tapes. One final nicety is that `dump` has no limit on the length of file- and pathnames.

Incremental backups are controlled by assigning a dump level to a particular backup. Dump levels range from 0 to 9, and when a dump of a certain level N is performed, all files that have changed since the last dump of level $N-1$ or lower are sent to the tape. As you might guess, a level 0 dump will dump the entire filesystem.

The *dump* program requires you to know the length and density of the media being used for the backup. In the case of devices using data compression, there is a virtual length associated with the device, which is simply the compression ratio times the actual tape length. It's usually best to be conservative here; the compression ratio is really an average—not all files compress equally. If you over-estimate the amount of compression, dump will try to write after the tape has run out and the dump will be ruined.

dump is one of the lowest-level methods for backing up your system, but it is also one of the least fault-tolerant. Unless you understand it and your backup device very well, you may want to choose another method of backing up your system.

19.4 Commercial Backup Products

BRU

The Backup and Restore Utility (BRU) is strongly based on tar but adds many more features. It runs a daemon that manages the backup schedule. It comes in two versions, the more expensive of which supports backing up NFS disks; the less expensive version works only on local disks.

BRU also comes with a menu-driven interface in both X and ASCII. The concept of backup levels is supported, and backup targets can be any character device.

Other features include the following:

- Keeps track of the number of uses of a tape to help you decide when to throw out older tapes.

- Contains powerful features for recovering data from corrupt archives.

- Has support for NIS (Network Information Services, a networked system for passwd, group, and host files, and much more).

- Has support for SMB (Samba) and Netware volumes.

- Supports archives that span more than one backup device.

BRU is available for Linux on the x86, Alpha, and PowerPC, and a lite version is included with the commercial version of Red Hat. See http://www.estinc.com/ for more information.

PerfectBACKUP+

PerfectBACKUP+ is widely acclaimed as the fastest backup and restore program. Previously sold as FASTBACK PLUS for UNIX, it began life as the UNIX version of DOS FASTBACK PLUS. It comes with menu-driven ASCII and Motif interfaces, networking support, compression, verification and recovery, and scheduling, and it is compatible with both `tar` and `cpio`. It will also back up a variety of network drives, including NFS, Windows, Netware, and Windows NT.

Other features include:

- Compression.
- Network backup devices.
- Multiple backup devices—when one is full, it will move to the next device in the list.
- Locking files during backup to allow safer backups in multiuser mode.
- Support for all file types, including sockets, pipes, and so forth.

More information on PerfectBACKUP+ is available from `http://home.xl.ca/perfectBackup/`.

BACKUP/9000

Though this is available only in beta for Linux as of this writing, it has one feature that prompted us to include it. It is designed to work with Oracle to allow live, safe backups of Oracle's tablespaces. If you are running Oracle (for SCO using the IBSC emulation; there is no native Linux version), you will undoubtedly find this feature of great use. Beyond this, Backup/9000 supports what you would expect of a commercial backup and restore program:

- Nice user interface.
- Scheduling tool.
- Support for local and network backups.
- Uses `tar` and `cpio` formats.
- Encryption.
- Parallel backups to multiple local and/or network tape drives.
- Backup of raw partitions and FIFO streams, in addition to normal files.
- Multiple backups on one tape.

19.5 Backup Strategies

How often you make what kind of backup depends on several factors, including:

- The capacity and speed of your backup device, which are particularly important characteristics for unattended backup.

- How active your filesystems are. The number of files that change per day or week. Most likely, this will vary from partition to partition.

- Whether or not you can make live backups.

- If you can't make live backups, how much downtime is acceptable and when is it least inconvenient.

In general, if more than twenty percent of a particular filesystem is changing daily, you should perform incremental backups every day or two, a lower-level backup weekly, and a full backup monthly. Lower activity levels mean you can space this out more, though there's really no excuse for not performing a full backup once a month.

Another method (if you have enough tape drives) is to perform a full backup every night. Keep 28 tapes so that you have a total of four weeks worth of data at any one time. In the event of a bug that corrupts data going back a few days (or a particular backup getting corrupted), you can restore a tape from a few days before. Then, cycle tapes every six months or so. Since heavy use of tapes can cause them to deteriorate, you'll want to replace the tapes with new ones well before this point. This allows you to store information for an indefinite amount of time. This is at a higher cost, however, since you have to buy a lot of tapes and you may not have enough storage on the tapes; but, it's one of the best and easiest ways to backup and restore your data.

Buy lots of whatever your backup media is; it's cheaper than having to pay the office for a day of doing work a second time.

For very active systems which more or less cannot be taken off-line except at 3 AM on a Sunday, it would be wise to invest in a backup utility that can perform safe live backups during periods of low traffic. You should then be able to perform unattended, incremental backups, and depending on your capacity and amount of data, unattended full backups.

More complicated databases are typically problematic when it comes to live backups. Usually, your backup utility cannot make a proper snapshot from the database's point of view. Fortunately, most databases can create a snapshot of themselves, and that can be placed in your archive. Failing this, the database will have to be taken off-line before being backed up.

You will probably want to keep some backups off-site in case of a big disaster (flood, UFO crashing into your office, dinosaur rampage, etc.). You may have to buy a new system, but at least you'll have what is likely hundreds, if not thousands, of hours of work saved.

19.6 RAID and Disk Mirroring

These are other techniques for protecting the integrity of your data. RAID stands for Redundant Array of Inexpensive Disks. It is a fairly new concept, having been introduced in 1987 at the University of California, Berkeley.

The basic idea behind RAID is that by using multiple small disks (as opposed to a few large disks) and possibly some additional "parity" data, you will be able to reconstruct data lost when one of the disks fails instead of losing a few gigabytes (albeit temporarily, assuming that you have a backup).

There are several different levels of RAID, cleverly numbered from 0 to 5. Their features are given below. Only levels 1, 4, and 5 are available for Linux, and only in software (as opposed to a hardware-level implementation).

0 Data striping—This doesn't actually provide any protection against data loss, but does enhance performance. Requires a controller that supports synchronized disks; none is available for Linux.

1 Disk mirroring—A second set of disks is used to provide a complete copy of your data. An expensive option, since you need twice as many disks.

2 Level 0 with a check disk for storing error correction information. Poor performance has made this option unpopular.

3 Level 0 with a separate disk for byte-level parity information to help reconstruct lost data. If the parity disk is lost, you lose all data integrity. Synchronized disks help boost performance despite the bottleneck of the single-parity disk.

4 Level 3 with block-level parity information stored on a separate disk. Better read performance, but worse write performance than level 3. Since synchronized disks aren't used, it can be implemented in software.

5 Level 4 with the parity information spread over the disks as well. Higher performance, since a separate parity disk is no longer a potential bottleneck. Write performance is still not as good as for level 3.

To implement RAID on your Linux box, you need a kernel patch from `http://www.linuxhq.com/patch/20-p0632.html` and a 2.0.30 kernel. The patch is still in beta and supports RAID levels 1, 4, and 5.

Separately available, raidtools-0.3 can be used to create or repair a set of RAID disks.

19.7 Summary

A variety of backup and restore tools were discussed in this chapter, ranging from simple ones that ship with every Linux distribution to commercial ones with enhanced functionality and interfaces.

In general, for sites where short amounts of down-time are acceptable, the built-in tools are fine. For "hot" backups, you will probably have to resort to commercial means.

Talking to Your Peripherals

20

It's not all disk drives and video cards!

As anyone knows, there are many more resources to be shared, served, and managed than applications and disk volumes (though we will cover adding disks, too). Scanners, modems, printers, tape drives, and ZIP and JAZ drives can all be made available to your Linux OS.

The large number of available hardware for the x86 architecture is quickly being made workable under Linux. And with products such as 3D add-on cards and CD-R writers becoming less expensive, people are starting to use them (and their computers) in ways we could barely dream of just a few years ago.

20.1 Scanners

Most scanners can be purchased with a USB, parallel, or SCSI interface. At this time, only SCSI scanners are supported under Linux, with USB support improving. There are two programs you can use to capture data from a scanner: the commercially available xvscan (`http://www.tummy.com`) and the freeware SANE (Scanner Access Now Easy, `http://www.mostang.com/sane`). As an added bonus, SANE interfaces with the GIMP program to allow you to scan an image and immediately edit it.

Many SCSI scanners will come with their own low-grade SCSI card. Unless you're sure that Linux supports the card, don't bother trying to use it.

Your kernel will need to have the generic SCSI driver compiled in it or as a module. On Red Hat, the library is `/lib/modules/<kernel>/scsi/sg.o`. Next you will need to check and possibly set the SCSI ID of the scanner if it conflicts with existing devices on your controller. The device corresponding to the scanner will then be `/dev/sg[a-f]`. Here, a would be a SCSI ID of 0, b would be 2, and so on up to f, which would have an ID of 6.

xvscan

xvscan communicates with a scanner via `/dev/scanjet`, so you will have to either create a link to the device or a copy of it. Also, if you want human users to be able to access the scanner, you will need to modify the permissions of the device file.

Assuming your scanner's SCSI ID is 3, its device entry is:

```
crw-rw-rw-   1 root    sys           21,   3 Aug 28 00:12 /dev/sgd
```

To set up a copy of the device to be accessible to users in the `scanner` group, issue the following commands as root:

```
# mknod /dev/scanjet c 21 3
# chgrp scanner /dev/scanjet
# chmod 660 /dev/scanjet
# ls -l /dev/scanjet
crw-rw----   1 root    scanner   21,   3 Aug 28 00:15  /dev/scanjet
```

SANE

SANE is designed to handle scanners, digital cameras, and cameras of the quickcam variety. It uses a number of different back-end programs to interface with the hardware and scanner, so you may want to check the SANE Web page to make sure that your scanner is supported. There may also be issues with the SCSI card, since a scan can take a few seconds—enough for Linux to think the SCSI bus has timed out. Again, check the documentation to see if this applies to you. Even if it does, it only requires a recompile of the Linux kernel.

20.2 Modems

There are a number of reasons why you might want to attach a modem to your machine:

- Faxing—incoming and outgoing.
- Backup (or primary!) network connection.
- Dial-up for remote access.

If you have an external modem, the only issue you have to worry about is having the serial port driver available. If you have an internal modem, which adds its own serial port to your machine, you may run into IRQ problems. Additionally, if the modem has a non-standard chipset, Linux may not recognize it. Any modem that is advertised as a "Winmodem" will not work with Linux. These modems, though inexpensive, rely on the CPU to do much of the processing work and should be avoided when purchasing a new machine.

In all likelihood, you will have to do nothing to get Linux to talk to your modem. The one thing needed (serial port support) is almost always present in the kernel, usually for the mouse.

If you have an external modem attached, it will attach to one of the on-board serial ports and should have no problems with IRQ conflicts. If you are installing it internally and have an IRQ conflict, there are a couple of ways of resolving it.

1. If you aren't using both of your built-in serial ports, disable one of them in the BIOS. The serial port on the modem card in some cases will simply become the lowest number serial port it can and then use the IRQs for that port. Otherwise, you may have to set the serial port with jumpers on the card. Consult the documentation that came with your modem.

2. You can use `setserial` to assign the serial port on the card to a different IRQ. If your built-in serial ports are both in use and you add an internal modem, it will present itself to the system as the third serial port. To change the IRQ, use:

```
% setserial /dev/cua2 irq 5
```

This will assign the third serial port. A number of other options can be set with `setserial`. Consult the man page for more information.

20.3 Tape Drives

There is a rather large and bewildering selection of tape drives. If you need to back up large amounts of data in a reasonable amount of time, however, you can eliminate ones using the parallel port as they have lower throughputs. ATAPI (IDE) tape drives also exist.

Assuming you decide to use a SCSI tape drive, you will need to enable SCSI tape support in your kernel, or have the `st.o` module loaded. As in installing any SCSI device, check to make sure you have chosen a unique ID for your tape drive before installing it.

Device files for tape drives contain the letters "`st`." If your tape is SCSI ID 6, it will have two device files: `st6` and `nst6`. The first is used if the device is rewinding and the second if it is not. Most tape drives are non-rewinding so you will need to refer to them as `/dev/nstn`, where `n` is the device number.

To test a new tape drive, you can use one of the backup programs included with Red Hat, or you can use the `tar` command to put files on the tape, then `tar` the files off again.

20.4 UPS

Until recently, few people thought of uninterruptible power supplies (UPSs) as peripherals for the reason that the computer and UPS didn't exchange information or take action based on the state of one or the other. Now though, this is not the case. A few years ago, UPSs with serial ports started appearing, along with snazzy GUI front-ends, to allow the battery and power level to be monitored and for actions to be set up based on conditions reported. However, only commercial OSes are supported. Some manufacturers have even published the language used to communicate with their UPS, allowing others to write their own programs for interacting with it.

There are two ways UPSs can be categorized: by how they perform their function of providing uninterrupted power, and by the level of interaction they have with the computer to which they are attached. The first has three types: stand-by, in-line, and line-interactive.

The first type simply sits and waits for the power to drop below a certain level and then, usually in a matter of milliseconds, switches to providing power via its batteries. The second actually filters all power through itself. It thus can condition the power that it puts out and kick in during brownouts. This method also provides about half the wear and tear on the batteries, obviously shortening their lifetime.

There are several programs, most of them with some sort of GUI, for talking to your UPS. Most of them are somewhat feature-poor when compared to their Microsoft Windows-based counterparts. To date, Best is the only vendor that supplies UPS control software that can be compiled for use under Linux. Most of the other tools are fairly generic and can talk to UPSs only in dumb mode.

checkups.tar—Straight from Best's Web site, this package will control their UPSs in dumb and a more advanced mode (not really a full "smart" mode). It includes the source code, which you will need to compile. In the less dumb mode, the following alarms can be detected: High Ambient Temperature, Near Low Battery, Low AC Out, or User Test Alarm. You can also tell checkups to start a shutdown when it detects that it has a particular amount of power left.

powerd-2.0—This is not the same powerd shipped with the System V `init` package. It differs in that it can be run in a master or slave mode, allowing you to manage the shutdown of other machines on the same UPS or LAN from a single, master machine. Also, powerd-2 uses a configuration file, whereas the stock powerd requires you to edit the code and recompile it when changing the configuration.

Enhanced_APC_UPSD-v1.4—Support for America Power Conversion (APC) UPSs in both smart and dumb modes.

apcd-0.5—Another APC controller. Includes support for master and slave machines. The machine designated as the "master" will signal the other machines to shut down during a power outage or low battery condition.

smupsd—A third program for APC UPSs. Supports APC UPSs in "very smart" mode. Uses a Java-awt-based tool for monitoring the UPS.

genpower-1.0.1 —A more generic UPS package. It comes with sample configurations for UPSs from Tripp and APC. Probably the best documented package mentioned thus far.

20.5 3D Cards

With dedicated 3D cards costing less than $200 and providing great 3D graphics, you can now play many of the same games on Linux as you can on Windows 98, and then some. Physical installation is performed according to the instructions. Once Linux is up and running, you'll want to download, compile, and install the Mesa 3D library. Most 3D programs require Mesa, and Mesa comes with a few demo programs to test out the functionality. Some cards (such as the 3Dfx voodoo series) require that you download some drivers from 3Dfx to complete the installation. Check the Mesa home page for more information on what 3D cards are supported. Once installed, issue the following command to tell Mesa to use fullscreen mode:

```
setenv MESA_GLX_FX=f
```

Without this command, Mesa would start up its applications in a window, which would slow down the graphics (a lot!), but you could still do 3D in a window if you required it. Once you complete some of the demo programs, grab a copy of GlQuake and blow some friends away.

20.6 USB Support

USB (Universal Serial Bus) is a method of trying to connect low-speed devices through a single connection on a motherboard. USB allows you to connect keyboards, mice, scanners, video cameras, digital speakers, and even Ethernet interfaces directly into a machine. USB provides for low-speed (1.5MB) and higher-speed (12MB) devices, allowing for up to 127 devices per machine. USB is plug-and-play, meaning that you can hot swap devices at will.

Unfortunately, few operating systems have full support for USB. At this writing, Linux has little support, but can handle a USB keyboard and mouse, since the iMac has only USB connections on it. In the coming months, USB support will be integrated into the main kernel, and many of the devices will become supported.

20.7 Adding a New Hard Drive

It is likely that at some point you will want to add additional disk space to your machine. Installing a new hard drive is a fairly painless procedure. In this section, we're assuming you are using a SCSI host adapter. Also, you presumably have SCSI, SCSI disk, and support for your SCSI controller already available, possibly set up by the vendor who sold you the machine.

This being the case, adding another hard drive is as simple as checking the new drive to ensure that it has a unique SCSI ID, installing it in the CPU case or an external case, and rebooting. Typically, the SCSI ID is set by jumpers. Where on the disk they are and how to set them should be explained in the manual that came with the disk.

Once you have the hard drive installed, you will need to create some Linux partitions on it. Start by running `fdisk`:

```
# fdisk /dev/sda
```

The number of cylinders for this disk is set to 1030. This is larger than 1024, and may cause problems with:

1. Software that runs at boot-time (e.g., LILO).

2. Booting and partitioning software from other OSes (e.g., DOS FDISK, OS/2 FDISK).

```
Command (m for help): p
Disk /dev/sdb: 64 heads, 32 sectors, 1030 cylinders
Units = cylinders of 2048 * 512 bytes

Device Boot    Begin    Start      End   Blocks   Id  System
/dev/sda1          1        1      100   102384    6  DOS 16-bit >=32
```

When you first get the drive, there can be any number of strange, possibly nonsensical, partitions on it. Just delete them with the d command in `fdisk` so you can start with a clean slate.

To add a new partition, use the n command:

```
Command (m for help): n
Command action
   e   extended
   p   primary partition (1-4)
p
Partition number (1-4): 1
First cylinder (1-100): 1
Last cylinder or +size or +sizeM or +sizeK ([1]-100): +50M

Command (m for help): p

Disk /dev/sdb: 64 heads, 32 sectors, 100 cylinders
Units = cylinders of 2048 * 512 bytes
```

```
Device Boot    Begin    Start     End   Blocks   Id  System
/dev/sdb1         1        1        51   52208    83  Linux native

Command (m for help): n
Command action
   e    extended
   p    primary partition (1-4)
p
Partition number (1-4): 2
First cylinder (1-100): 52
Last cylinder or +size or +sizeM or +sizeK ([52]-100): 100

Command (m for help):
```

By default, partitions are created as Linux native (extended 2) filesystems. If you need to change the filesystem type, for example to add a swap partition instead, use the t command:

```
Command (m for help): t
Partition number (1-4): 1
Hex code (type L to list codes): 82
Changed system type of partition 1 to 82 (Linux swap)
```

Contrary to conventional wisdom, performance-wise it is better to have a few large partitions as opposed to many small partitions, though your system's needs should probably play the largest role in determining how to partition your disk.

After you've set up your partition(s), run mke2fs on them to actually create the filesystems:

```
# mke2fs /dev/sdb2
```

Now you can mount it:

```
# mount /dev/sdb2 /tmp2
```

You will likely want to add an entry to /etc/fstab to automatically mount your new partitions at boot:

```
# device    mountpoint  filesystemtype  options  dump  fsckorder
/dev/sdb2    /tmp2         ext2          defaults  1       2
```

See the man page for fstab for details on all the options available.

If you have difficulties getting your system to recognize your new disk, booting the system with the drive in, or if you are experiencing other SCSI problems, here are a few things to check:

- Does it have power? (Hey, check the easy things first!)

- Are all the cables attached firmly?

- SCSI buses must be linear; if you have external devices, make sure you are using only one of the internal connections on your card. Wide SCSI cards in particular will often have a narrow and a wide connection for internal use.

- Does the device have a unique ID on the bus? Remember that the controller has an ID as well; it is typically 7, but 6 is not unheard of.

- Make sure your new disk isn't terminating the bus. If your bus was fine before, its termination should work with the new drive in place.

- If you are using a cable that came with the disk and have another cable you know is good, try the drive with the good cable. If it works, the new cable is very likely bad.

20.8 PCMCIA Devices and Laptop Machines

If you have a laptop, then you probably have PCMCIA available on your system. It's the way of getting SCSI, Ethernet, modems, and other types of devices onto it. PCMCIA allows for cards that are low-power, easy to configure, physically small, and standard across different architectures.

The first important thing you should do, if you have not bought a laptop, is check the Linux on Laptops page located at `http:// www.cs.utexas.edu/users/kharker/linux-laptops`. Users that have gotten Linux to work on their laptops have included their notes on how to install Linux on various models. Also of note (specifically for PCMCIA support) is the PCMCIA HOWTO located at `http://hyper.stanford.edu/ HyperNews/get/pcmcia/home.html`. This page lists PCMCIA cards that are known to exist, along with PCMCIA controllers that also work.

In short, CardBus support is still experimental under Linux, but just about all PCMCIA cards are. A full list of cards that are supported can be found under `/usr/doc/pcmcia-*/SUPPORTED.CARDS`. CardBus is a faster form of PCMCIA and is used in some high-speed devices, such as Ethernet and SCSI cards.

PCMCIA support is included with Red Hat, is installed as the pcmcia-cs package, and is activated on bootup. If cards are found at boot-time, they're activated. If after bootup a new card is inserted, it'll automatically get started. Cards can be removed without deactivation, and the PCMCIA card manager (cardmgr) will attempt to unload the drivers. If you have network cards, cardmgr will attempt to shut down the network interface and then unload the drivers. If there is network activity going on, the network modules may not unload properly.

You can also manually work with the cards in your system through the `cardctl` command. Among other commands, `cardctl insert` indicates that a card has been inserted, and `cardctl remove` stops a card. Sending a HUP signal to the cardmgr program will force cardmgr to shut down and restart all card services.

You should note that since PCMCIA drivers are kernel modules, they may need to be recompiled when you install a new kernel.

20.9 ZIP and JAZ Drives

Hard drives that support removable media became almost popular about a decade ago, but then faded. Iomega has resurrected them in the form of its JAZ and ZIP drives. Other companies have begun making comparable products, but none is currently supported under Linux.

ZIP drives have a capacity of 100MB and JAZ drives can hold 1GB. Because of their relatively large sizes, they are much better suited for use as backup media than floppy drives. Additionally, both have considerably better performance than floppy drives. In the case of JAZ drives, the performance is comparable to a SCSI-I hard drive. A ZIP drive has a seek time that is a few times longer and a transfer rate about one-fourth that of a JAZ drive.

Installing a ZIP Drive

An external SCSI ZIP drive is shipped with its own controller based on Adaptec's AHA1520, which Linux supports. Optionally, you can connect it to your existing controller. The parallel port version actually comes with a parallel-to-SCSI adapter, which will make the ZIP drive appear as if it were a SCSI device.

If you have the parallel port version of a ZIP drive, you will need to enable support for it in the kernel either compiled or as a module. If you have only one parallel port and have other devices you want to attach to it, it is possible to daisy-chain them. However, Linux will not allow more than one driver to be active on the port. The solution is to compile all the various drivers (ZIP, lp, PLIP, etc.) as modules and then load and unload them as needed.

If you have the SCSI version, you need only to support SCSI, SCSI disks, and your controller. Thus, if you plan to use the drive on an existing controller, you don't need to do anything beside attach the drive to your system. If you have the internal version and have other internal SCSI devices on the same controller, make sure bus termination is disabled or you will likely be unable to talk to some SCSI devices after you reboot.

One final note: The ZIP drive's SCSI ID can be set only to 5 or 6. This could potentially conflict with other devices on the SCSI bus, so you may need to do a little rearranging.

Installing a JAZ Drive

Since the recently available parallel port version of the JAZ drive is not yet supported in Linux, you will obviously have to use the SCSI version. As with the SCSI ZIP drive, you will need only support for SCSI disks (and SCSI obviously) and the controller itself.

The drive is shipped with its own controller. There are two versions in use. One is based on the Adaptec AHA78xx series. This series of controllers is supported by the AHA2940 driver. The other is based on the Advanced Systems family of controllers, which is also supported under Linux. As before, you may instead choose to place the drive on an existing controller. JAZ drives may be assigned any SCSI ID between 0 and 6.

Caveats

It is generally difficult or impossible to have two identical SCSI controllers in the same system because various settings frequently conflict. If you already have a controller of the type that your ZIP or JAZ drive uses, you should probably consider just putting the device on the existing controller. This will also help conserve system resources like IRQs, which frequently are in short supply.

Using the Drive

After you reboot, you may need to check the boot information to get the device that corresponds to the drive. You can retrieve boot output with the `dmesg` command. Find the section where your ZIP or JAZ drive is detected and scan down a few lines to locate the device reported for your drive.

Once you know the device, you can mount a disk in the drive. Typically, the disk shipped with the drive has a filesystem on its fourth partition. Unless you need compatibility with the OS that supports the filesystem type, you will likely want to format the drive with the Linux native ext2fs. (See the section on installing a new hard drive for instructions on formatting a disk.)

Now edit `/etc/fstab` and insert a line like this:

```
/dev/sde1/jazext2  noauto 0 0
```

The `noauto` option tells Linux not to mount the device automatically. This is typical for an entry of a device with removable media.

Using serial ports may seem a bit strange in the UNIX world, but there is a somewhat logical way of looking at it.

20.10 Quick Guide to Serial Ports

You're probably familiar with how serial ports need speed (BPS), bit size, parity, and stop bit settings. Those settings are on the software side. On the hardware side, things are a bit more complicated. The typical serial port has nine pins associated with it, as described in Table 20-1.

Table 20-1   *Serial Port Pin Settings*

Pin	Signal	Meaning
1	DCD	Carrier Detect
2	Rx	Receive Data (Date comes in this line)
3	Tx	Transmit Data (Date goes out this line)
4	DTR	Data Terminal Ready
5	GND	Signal Ground
6	DSR	Data Set Ready
7	RTS	Ready to Send (1/2 of out-of-band flow control)
8	CTS	Clear to Send (1/2 of out-of-band flow control)
9	RI	Ring Indicator (Not used)

Table 20-1 describes the pinout for a standard 9-pin PC serial connection. When a device like a terminal is connected to the serial port, you need a special pin connection called a null-modem cable. In short, pins 2 and 3 are crossed (leading Tx to Rx, and vice versa) and the RTS/CTS lines are crossed. When connecting to a modem, a "straight through" connection is sufficient.

Lock Files

To prevent confusion about who is actually using a port, there are lock files. Lock files tell other programs that try to open a port that the port is already in use. This prevents someone from opening a connection to a modem when someone else is already dialed into that same modem. The problem with this, of course, is that each program that wants to use a lock file has to use the same location. For most, this is in `/var/lock`, but it could be in `/var/spool/lock` or other locations. You can usually configure where the lock files go. The other problem with lock files is when they don't clean up correctly, which happens when a program crashes before it finishes running. Then you have lock files for programs that are no longer running, preventing other programs from using a device.

Flow Control

For the DTE and DCE to know when to stop transmitting, there are two main methods of stopping communication temporarily. First is software (or in-band) flow control, which sends a ^Q in the stream of data. Once the remote side sees this character, it stops sending data until it sees a ^S. The problem with this is that it breaks down at high speed. At anything above 9600 bps, too much data may come down the line between the time that the receiving side sends the ^Q, and the sending side processes that character and stops transmitting data. This can cause data loss. The advantage of in-band flow control is that only three wires are needed: Tx, Rx, and GND.

The other method is using hardware (or out-of-band) flow control. In this setup, two pins (RTS and CTS) are used outside the data stream to start and stop the flow of data. Since that is all these signals are used for, processing a "stop" in out-of-band flow control is much quicker than for in-band, and is recommended for all speeds greater than 9600 bps.

UARTs

A UART is the chip inside your PC that actually handles RS-232 communication. Most chips in newer PCs are either 16550s or 16550-based (meaning they will emulate the 16550 chip). Earlier PCs had 8250s and 16450s. These earlier chips could not handle speeds greater than about 38400 bps, which is inadequate for today's high-speed modems with compression. These earlier chips had only a 1-byte buffer, meaning that each time a character came in the serial port, a CPU interrupt was generated. For 9600-bps rates, this meant 9600 interrupts per second. Each of these CPU interrupts prevented the CPU from doing something else. The 16550A chips have a 16-byte buffer, which means that at 9600 bps, there are fewer than 1000 interrupts per second.[1] This gives the CPU a net gain of 8600 interrupts per second to devote to other things, such as running programs. When speeds reach 38400 bps, the difference is even greater. Most of the "dumb" serial boards use 16450 or 16550 chips to do their processing, while "smart" serial cards use anything from an Intel 80186 to a Cirrus Logic CD-2401 chip to provide greater speeds and extra functionality, like multiple serial ports per IRQ.

Modem Types

One question that is frequently asked is: "What kind of modem should I get?" There's a choice between getting an external or internal modem for your PC. Internal modems are a bit cheaper and have their own UARTs built in, which prevents data loss at high speeds. External modems don't take up a precious ISA slot in your machine (assuming your machine even has an ISA slot) and give you pretty lights to look at when downloading Web pages and FTP files. The best kind of modem you can get for Linux is an external modem, especially if you have a good 16550-based serial port,[2] for the following reasons:

1. You get the pretty lights to show that everything is working. With internal modems, you have to rely on other software to get modem states and so on.

2. You won't accidentally buy a "WinModem." These modems actually require a lot of CPU time and are not supported by Linux.

3. If you need to move modems, it's pretty easy to do so.

4. It will work with all versions of Linux, be it Linux on Sun, Linux on Alpha, Linux on PPC, or Linux on i386. RS-232 is a cross-platform standard.

---

[1]When you have a fairly large buffer, you have a point (high-water mark) where the buffer is close to being full and should be emptied. Thus, you may not always have 16 bytes in the buffer when an interrupt occurs.

[2]Linux will report what kind of UART is in your machine. You can also look at the motherboard, and you may find the chip.

Baud and BPS

To start this section, there is no such thing as a 56,000-baud modem that works with plain old telephone lines. If there were, we'd have some really fast modems out there. Up until the age of 2400-bps modems, baud and bps were synonymous. A baud is defined as the number of changes in a signal per second. To get to higher-speed modems, more bits were encoded in each baud. Thus, a 9600-bps modem has 4 bits per baud, and a 14400-bps modem has 6 bits per baud. On top of this, compression of the actual data is used to increase the throughput, making some 28.8-Kbps modems send data at up to 115.2 Kbps.

20.11 CD-ROMs and CD-R Writers

CD-ROMs are fairly self-explanatory, as support for all ATAPI (IDE) and SCSI CD-ROMS is included with Linux. ATAPI CD-ROMS get their `/dev` entry based on where they are in the chains. The master device on the primary IDE chain is `/dev/hda`, and the slave on the primary chain is `/dev/hdb`. The master on the secondary is `/dev/hdc`, and the slave on the secondary is `/dev/hdc`. Note that these entries represent the entire disk, and should only be used for specifying CD-ROMs, as they're one large partition. You can find out where your ATAPI CD-ROM is by examining bootup messages or by looking through the output of the `dmesg` command.

SCSI CD-ROMs are handled a bit differently in that the first CD-ROM gets an entry of `/dev/sr0` instead of being with the hard drives under `/dev/sd`. The second CD-ROM gets an entry of `/dev/sr1`, and so on. Again, the results of the `dmesg_command` can assist in telling you what devices are recognized. Another way of finding out is to check the `/proc/scsi` directory. This won't tell you what got assigned to which `dev` entry, but it will list what SCSI devices were found.

CD-R writers (also called CD-R burners and so on) are now getting affordable enough for people to actually purchase them. Linux has the ability to use many different kinds of CD-R and CD-RW (rewritable) devices. Two packages are first required to use them. First is the mkisofs package, which is included with the Red Hat CD-ROM. This program creates an ISO9660 image suitable for writing to a CD-R or CD-RW. The second program is cdrecord, which does the actual burning of the CD-R/CD-RW. The authors have only had access to a SCSI CD-R, so your experience may be different, but probably not by much.

We'll take the safe path first and show you the actual process of burning a CD-ROM. First, you must create an ISO9660 image. This requires enough space on a local drive to store a new image file. If you're going to build a CD-ROM that takes up 600MB of space, you'll need at least that much free space on a partition. The basic syntax for the `mkisofs` command is:

```
mkisofs -R -o file.raw /some/directory
```

The `-R` does a recursive copy, so everything under `/some/directory` gets included in the raw file. The `-o file.raw` indicates that the output of the `mkisofs` command will go into `file.raw`. This is where you'll need the space. There are two other options you may want to use. The `-V text` option includes `text` as a CD-ROM label that shows up under Windows or MacOS. The ISO9660 specification indicates that files have to be in the old DOS format of eight characters, a dot, and a three-character file extension. Fortunately, there is an extension to ISO9660 that allows for extended filenames called Joliet. Joliet allows for 64 characters in the name of each file. If you choose to use Joliet and an extended filename, add `-J`.

Now that the ISO image has been created, you can test it out by mounting it and taking a look at it. The command to do this is:

```
mount -t isofs -o loop file.raw /mnt/cdrom
```

Replace `file.raw` with the raw image you just created. You can also replace `/mnt/cdrom` with some other directory to mount on. The `-o loop` indicates that a file instead of an actual device is going to be used. This will work, and you can traverse the directories as if they were a CD-ROM. Once you're sure the image is correct, you can unmount the directory and prepare for writing.

With the raw image created, you can now burn the CD-R with `cdrecord`. First you'll need to know the SCSI ID of the CD-R. This can be found either by looking under `/proc/scsi`, or by using `cdrecord -scanbus` and looking at the results. You'll also need to know what speed your CD-R can handle. Most drives now are either double-speed (2x) or quad-speed (4x) for writing. Check your documentation for the capabilities of the CD-R.

Now down to the actual burning. The basic syntax for `cdrecord` is:

```
cdrecord -v speed=4 dev=5,0 file.raw
```

You'll need to change the speed based on the capability of your CD-R. The lowest speed is 1, so if you run into compatibility issues, try knocking the speed down. The `-v` gives a verbose listing of what's going on. The `dev=5,0` lists the SCSI ID for the CD-R device. In this case, it's a SCSI ID of 5 and a LUN of 0. For single CD-R writers, the LUN will be 0. You can replace file.raw with the raw image file you created and tested earlier. During the write process, it's best not to use the machine until the writing is complete. The CD-R is dependent on a FIFO buffer to be full to keep writing to the CD at a constant rate. If that rate drops for any reason, the writing will fail and you'll be left with a coaster.

The time to write the CD-R depends both on the size of the image you're making and the speed of the CD-R. A quad-speed CD-ROM can write a 74-minute CD-R in about 18 minutes, and winds up being about 650MB in size.

Once the CD-R is complete, you can put it in your CD-ROM drive and test it out.

The above instructions describe the hard way, but also the safest. Once you're comfortable with the process, you can turn everything into one step. The following command will create a Joliet CD-ROM on a quad-speed writer at SCSI ID 5:

```
(nice --18 mkisofs -V text -J -R /some/directory) | cdrecord -v
    speed=4 dev=5,0 -
```

The nice command provides a high priority to mkisofs, allowing it to dedicate more CPU time to building the ISO image, which is passed via a pipe to the cdrecord program.

20.12 Summary

In this chapter, we've tried to discuss a reasonably large list of hardware, but there is no way for us to cover all of the hardware available for Linux. Similarly, there are dozens of ways each piece of hardware can be problematic. We discussed how to troubleshoot the most common stumbling blocks, but less common, more esoteric ones certainly exist.

The best places for information on how to deal with problematic hardware are the HOWTOs, the manuals for the hardware, and the manufacturers. Also, some hardware types have their own newsgroups or mailing lists. These are likely to be the best places to ask for help on particularly difficult problems.

Connecting to the Internet

21

A case study in connecting a small business to the Internet

This chapter covers three items many small companies face—how to connect to the Internet with minimal cost, how to allow everyone in the company to use it, and how to protect it from crackers.

21.1 Overview

Firewalls are mainly designed to prevent unwanted activity on a network, so their basic function is to block connections from one network to another. In most applications, this would be from the Internet to your local network, and vice versa.

There are thousands of different firewall methodologies, but we will narrow our discussion in this chapter to `ipfwadm`. Let's assume that the local network is Ethernet with less than 254 machines, and connections to the Internet are made via modem. The end result will be a network with a nonpermanent connection to the Internet, but the users on the network will not have to dial a modem or remember to disconnect when finished. What they will see is a momentary pause (between 15–60 seconds, depending on your modem and ISP) upon initial connection to an outside machine. Over a 33.6-Kbps modem, three or four people actively using a Web browser at once would work quite adequately (assuming non-graphics-intensive pages, with the users randomly clicking on links. The idea is that most of the time, two people will not concurrently need the full bandwidth). Using an ISDN line will obviously make things faster, but most Linux users will have a 28.8 or 33.6 modem.

21.2 Software Versions

The configurations in this chapter use Linux kernel 2.0.30, PPP 2.2.0f, diald 0.16, and `ipfwadm` 2.3.0. If you are not planning to do IP masquerading, but still use diald, then kernel 1.2.X (X > 0) and PPP version 2.2.0x should work fine. Diald is constantly undergoing changes, and from the version released over a year ago (0.14) to the current version, many improvements and enhancements have been made.

Web pages:
```
Diald:    http://www.dna.lth.se/~erics/diald.html
Ipfwadm:  http://www.xos.nl/
```

21.3 Networking

The local network should be a private network and should not advertise its IP addresses beyond the firewall. RFC 1597 (Address Allocation for Private Internets) specifies the address blocks which are reserved for internal use only. While not necessary, using these blocks of addresses is suggested. You can alternatively use a class of addresses assigned to you by the InterNIC, but if any mistakes happen and one of your local network's IPs ends up outside the firewall, it will be ignored by the rest of the world as an invalid IP if it belongs to one of the following address blocks:

```
ADDRESS RANGE                        TYPE             # of machines
10.0.0.0 -> 10.255.255.255           single class A   1 x 16777214
172.16.0.0 -> 172.31.25.25516        class B          16 x 65534
192.168.0.0 -> 192.168.255.255       class C          255 x 254
```

For a small site, a good choice of an address block(s) to use would be one of the available class C networks, allowing 254 machines on your network. For this chapter, we will use the class C network of 192.168.1.0. There are two reserved IPs in the 192.168.1.0 block: 192.168.1.0, which represents the network itself, and 192.168.1.255, which is the broadcast address for the network. Another address to set aside would be 192.168.1.1. This is commonly the gateway machine, and in our case, the firewall. This is not necessary; it is just a good rule of thumb.

In `/etc/sysconfig/network/`, you will find a file named `ifcfg-eth0` that should look like the following:

```
#!/bin/sh
#>>>Device type: ethernet

#>>>Variable declarations:
DEVICE=eth0
IPADDR=192.168.1.1
NETMASK=255.255.255.0
NETWORK=192.168.1.0
BROADCAST=192.168.1.255
GATEWAY=none
ONBOOT=yes
#>>>End variable declarations
```

After the network is configured, reboot the machine and perform the following test:

The output from `netstat -nr` should read:

```
Kernel routing table
Destination Gateway Genmask      Flags Metric Ref Use Iface
192.168.1.0 0.0.0.0 255.255.255.0  U     0      0    28 eth0
127.0.0.0 0.0.0.0 255.0.0.0        U     0      0    14 lo
```

The output from `ifconfig` should read:

```
lo      Link encap:Local Loopback
        inet addr:127.0.0.1  Bcast:127.255.255.255  Mask:255.0.0.0
        UP BROADCAST LOOPBACK RUNNING  MTU:2000  Metric:1
        RX packets:0 errors:0 dropped:0 overruns:0
        TX packets:42 errors:0 dropped:0 overruns:0

eth0    Link encap:10Mbps Ethernet  HWaddr 02:60:8C:49:05:57
        inet addr:192.168.1.1  Bcast:192.168.1.255  Mask:255.255.255.0
        UP BROADCAST RUNNING MULTICAST  MTU:1500  Metric:1
        RX packets:0 errors:0 dropped:0 overruns:0
        TX packets:26 errors:0 dropped:0 overruns:0
        Interrupt:5 Base address:0x300
```

```
Try to ping:
localhost:      ping 127.0.0.1
local IP:       ping 192.168.1.1
other IP addresses on the network
```

If you cannot ping 127.0.0.1 or 192.168.1.1, recheck your configuration
files. If none of the machines on your local network responds, check the
cabling from your machine to the rest of the network. If you cannot ping
some of the machines on the local network, chances are there is a problem
with them, and not with the firewall machine.

Nameservers

Before continuing to the PPP section, two other files should be checked:

```
/etc/resolv.conf
order   hosts,bind
search localdns_server, ispname.net
nameserver <IPForNameserver1>
nameserver <IPForNameserver2>

/etc/hosts
127.0.0.1          localhost
192.168.1.1        gateway.localether.net
192.168.1.2        bob.localether.net
192.168.1.5        ralph.localether.net
```

We suggest keeping the local `hosts` table simple—only the names of the
machines on your local Ethernet. While it is true that adding the names of
some commonly used machines to the local `hosts` file will save a little time
when looking up names, it can lead to problems if you have a machine in the
`hosts` file that has changed its IP address.

21.4 PPP

PPP connectivity is fairly easy, since there are few configuration files to deal
with. There are only two main programs to use for PPP: `pppd`, the daemon
itself, and the connection script. Distributed with it and commonly used is a
program known as `chat`. It is a program solely designed to do a "wait for this
string, and then send this string" application. Another well-known program is
`expect`, but its flexibility and features are overkill for our application. The
default configuration files distributed with PPP will work fine, but are not

suggested to be used because they are security holes. We suggest doing the following.

There are three main script/configuration files for use with PPP. They are /usr/local/bin/ppp-on, /usr/local/bin/ppp-off, and /etc/ppp/ppp-chatfile. For security reasons, ppp-chatfile should be owned by root and file permissions should be set to 0600. This file will contain passwords and UIDs. Also, pppd and chat should be SUID (chmod +s) to allow them to read ppp-chatfile.

There are also security problems involved with this method. A fully secure method would be to use a C wrapper program that calls ppp-on and ppp-off. Both of these scripts should then be set with permissions of 0700, and pppd and chat should have the permissions set to 0100. The ppp-on script should check the ownership and file type of ppp-chatfile and make sure the lock directory is owned and only writable by root. This will ensure that a PPP session can only be started with the flags set in the ppp-chatfile and that no non-root user can create his/her own configuration file to dial out.

/usr/local/bin/ppp-on should read

```
#!/bin/sh
#       ppp-on
#
#       Set up a PPP link

LOCKDIR=/var/lock
DEVICE=modem
OUR_IP_ADDR=111.222.333.444
REMOTE_IP=555.666.777.888
NETMASK=255.255.255.0
CONNECT_SCRIPT="/usr/sbin/chat -v -f /etc/ppp/ppp-chatfile"

if [ -f $LOCKDIR/LCK..$DEVICE ]
then
    echo "PPP device is locked"
    exit 1
fi

/usr/sbin/fix-cua $DEVICE

/bin/stty 19200 -tostop

/usr/sbin/pppd asyncmap 0 lock netmask $NETMASK defaultroute modem
   crtscts      \      $OUR_IP_ADDR:$REMOTE_IP      /dev/$DEVICE      connect
   "$CONNECT_SCRIPT"
```

For most applications, only OUR_IP_ADDR will have to change. If you have a static IP, place it here; otherwise, change it to 0.0.0.0 to obtain a dynamic IP. Note that some ISPs will provide you with a static IP number, even if you leave this as 0.0.0.0. Also, the -v option, included in CONNECT_SCRIPT for debugging purposes, may be removed. The -v flag will log the conversations that it had with your ISP to /var/log/messages.

You may also have to set REMOTE_IP, sometimes referred to as the gateway. Some ISPs will automatically supply it during PPP negotiation.

```
/usr/local/bin/ppp-off
#!/bin/sh

DEVICE=ppp0

#
# If the ppp0 pid file is present then the program is running. Stop it.
if [ -r /var/run/$DEVICE.pid ]; then
    kill -INT `cat /var/run/$DEVICE.pid`
#
# If unsuccessful, ensure that the pid file is removed.
#
    if [ ! "$?" = "0" ]; then
        echo "removing stale $DEVICE pid file."
        rm -f /var/run/$DEVICE.pid
        exit 1
    fi
#
# Success. Terminate with proper status.
#
    echo "$DEVICE link terminated"
    exit 0
fi
#
# The link is not active
#
echo "$DEVICE link is not active"
exit 1

/etc/ppp/ppp-chatfile
ABORT'    \nBUSY\r'
ABORT'    \nNO ANSWER\r'
' '       ATZ
OK        ATDT5551212
CONNECT        ' '
login:         <your account>
password: <your password>
```

This is the bare minimum for your `chat` script, and obviously you will need to change the phone number, UID, and password. You may also want to add another line after the `ATZ` that changes specific modem registers to suit your application. We normally like to have the S11 register set at its lowest setting. This can be done by adding the following line, just before the telephone number in the `chatfile`:

```
OK      ATS11=55
```

After PPP is configured, start the daemon with `ppp-on` and perform the following test:

The output from `netstat -nr` should read:

```
Kernel routing table
Destination Gateway           Genmask          Flags Metric Ref Use Iface
555.666.777.8880.0.0.0        255.255.255.255  UH    0      0   0   ppp0
192.168.1.0 0.0.0.0           255.255.255.0    U     0      0   28  eth0
127.0.0.0   0.0.0.            255.0.0.0        U     0      0   14  lo
0.0.0.0         555.666.777.888 0.0.0.0        UG    0      0
   ppp0
```

The output from `ifconfig` should read:

```
lo Link encap:Local Loopback
   inet addr:127.0.0.1  Bcast:127.255.255.255  Mask:255.0.0.0
   UP BROADCAST LOOPBACK RUNNING  MTU:2000  Metric:1
   RX packets:0 errors:0 dropped:0 overruns:0
   TX packets:42 errors:0 dropped:0 overruns:0

ppp0 Link encap:Point-Point Protocol
   inet addr:111.222.333.444  P-t-P:555.666.777.888 Mask:255.255.255.0
   UP POINTOPOINT RUNNING  MTU:552  Metric:1
   RX packets:0 errors:0 dropped:0 overruns:0
   TX packets:0 errors:0 dropped:0 overruns:0

eth0 Link encap:10Mbps Ethernet  HWaddr 02:60:8C:49:05:57
   inet addr:192.168.1.1  Bcast:192.168.1.255  Mask:255.255.255.0
   UP BROADCAST RUNNING MULTICAST  MTU:1500  Metric:1
   RX packets:0 errors:0 dropped:0 overruns:0
   TX packets:26 errors:0 dropped:0 overruns:0
   Interrupt:5 Base address:0x300
```

```
Try to ping:
localhost:  ping 127.0.0.1
your ISP:   ping ispname.net
other IPs on the network
```

Another good test is to use a Web browser to try to pull up your favorite Web page, or telnet to a shell account provided by your ISP.

After testing the link, execute `ppp-off`. After this, attempting to telnet to a remote host should come back with an error stating `host not found`.

Diald

Diald, written by Eric Schenk, is available from `http://www.dna.lth.se/~erics/diald.html`. Diald is a utility used to automatically connect your machine via a modem or ISDN to your ISP when external data is requested. It will also automatically disconnect you when the connection has been idle for a specified period of time. If your PPP connection dies for some reason, diald will automatically try to reconnect. If you have a static IP and are in the middle of downloading the latest Linux kernel, this feature can be a real stress reliever. Have you ever downloaded 10MB over a 28.8 and had the modem die on the last 5 percent?

Diald's only system requirements are that you compile the kernel with SLIP enabled, and that you configure your connect protocol correctly (PPP in these examples). Diald uses SLIP to monitor network traffic, and if a non-local IP is requested, diald tells the modem to dial out and connect to your ISP.

Installation is as simple as obtaining the source code, unpacking it, performing a `make depend`, followed by a `make`, and then a `make install` as root. In the three versions we have installed on two different machines, we have never had an error message.

After installing the latest version (at the time of writing, it was version 0.16), there are three files that you will need to check. The first is `/usr/lib/diald/diald.defs`. This file is a list of internal filter rules for diald and does not usually need to be touched. If you need to make any changes, refer to the diald man pages on the format of this file.

The second file to examine is `/usr/lib/standard.filters`. You may wish to copy this file to a different location and name, for example, `/etc/diald.conf`. While leaving it in `/usr/lib` should work, we have had some problems that were solved by moving it to `/etc/diald.conf`, the location of the configuration file of previous versions of diald. This file is a list of services from `/etc/services`, and how many seconds each service will get of up-time. This doesn't mean that if you are telnetting somewhere diald will automatically kick you off while you're typing. What it does mean is after so many seconds of idle time, diald will shut the modem link down. The default file is very well-documented and easy to understand.

The third and last file is a script to start diald. We suggest starting it from `rc.local` by adding the line `/etc/rc.d/rd.diald` to the end of your `/etc/rc.d/rc.local` file. You may even just add the lines to your `rc.local` file, but it is more convenient to keep things separate so it can be run as a standalone program. Notice that we are using the same `chat` file used in the PPP section, but we are not using the `ppp-on` program:

```
/etc/rc.d/rc.diald
#!/bin/sh
echo -n "Starting auto-dialer: "
/usr/sbin/diald /dev/modem accounting-log "/var/log/diald" -m ppp
    defaultroute modem \ crtscts local 111.222.333.444 remote 0.0.0.0
    connect "/usr/sbin/chat -f /etc/ppp/ppp-chatfile"\ fifo "/etc/
    diald.fifo"
echo "diald"
```

At least the `local` option, and maybe the `remote` option, will have to be changed. If you have a dynamic IP (thus setting `local` to 0.0.0.0), this may cause some difficulties when telnetting to a machine on your local network. A static IP is highly recommended when using diald or the IP masquerading described in the following section. Also, if you know the remote IP, we suggest setting it.

The `fifo` argument is optional. The `fifo` allows diald to communicate with a few programs that come with the diald distribution for monitoring the diald activity. If you notice that your connect is slow, or if `ifconfig` reports that there are lots of errors on the PPP link, you may wish to remove the `fifo` option.

The `accounting-log` argument is also optional. This writes information about call duration to a file. It is useful if you wish to find out exactly how long your modem has been active.

After customizing this file, you may either reboot or just execute the file by hand. Depending on how recent your `/etc/services` file is, diald may complain about unknown services. A common one we've seen is `tcp.www`. If you receive one of these errors, there are two solutions. One solution is to comment out the offending line in `/etc/diald.conf` and let the catchall line at the bottom of `/etc/diald.conf` give that service up-time. The other solution is to update your `/etc/services` file to contain the appropriate information. Ideally, you should update `/etc/services`; this will give you greater control over diald, as it will allow you to narrow down modem usage.

If you check the output from `netstat` and `ifconfig` without diald making the connection to your ISP, you should see the following:

The output from `netstat -nr` should read:

```
Kernel routing table
```

```
Destination Gateway Genmask Flags Metric Ref Use  Iface
0.0.0.0 0.0.0.0 255.255.255.255 UH 1 0 0sl0
192.168.1.0 0.0.0.0 255.255.255.0  U 0 0 0eth0
127.0.0.0 0.0.0.0 255.0.0.0  U 0 0 1lo
0.0.0.0 0.0.0.0 0.0.0.0  U 1 0 0    sl0
```

The output from `ifconfig` should read:

```
lo    Link encap:Local Loopback
      inet addr:127.0.0.1  Bcast:127.255.255.255  Mask:255.0.0.0
      UP BROADCAST LOOPBACK RUNNING  MTU:3584  Metric:1
      RX packets:12 errors:0 dropped:0 overruns:0
      TX packets:12 errors:0 dropped:0 overruns:0

eth0  Link encap:10Mbps Ethernet  HWaddr 02:60:8C:49:05:57
      inet addr:192.168.1.1  Bcast:192.168.1.255  Mask:255.255.255.0
      UP BROADCAST RUNNING MULTICAST  MTU:1500  Metric:1
      RX packets:0 errors:0 dropped:0 overruns:0
      TX packets:0 errors:0 dropped:0 overruns:0
      Interrupt:5 Base address:0x300

sl0   Link encap:Serial Line IP
      inet addr:111.222.333.444 P-t-P:555.666.777.888 Mask:255.255.255.0
      UP POINTOPOINT RUNNING  MTU:1500  Metric:1
      RX packets:0 errors:0 dropped:0 overruns:0
      TX packets:2 errors:0 dropped:0 overruns:0
```

If you check the output from `netstat` and `ifconfig` with diald making the connection to your ISP, (which can be done as simply as `telnet <ispname>`) you should see the following:

The output from `netstat -nr` should read:

```
Kernel routing table
Destination Gateway Genmask        Flags Metric Ref Use Iface
0.0.0.0 0.0.0.0  255.255.255.255 UH   0      0   0 ppp0
0.0.0.0 0.0.0.0  255.255.255.255 UH   1      0   0 sl0
555.666.777.8880.0.0.0 255.255.255.255 UH   0      0   0 ppp0
192.168.1.0 0.0.0.0 255.255.255.0   U    0      0   0 eth0
127.0.0.0 0.0.0.0 255.0.0.0       U    0      0   1 lo
0.0.0.0 0.0.0.0  0.0.0.0          U    0      0   0 ppp0
0.0.0.0 0.0.0.0  0.0.0.0          U    1      0   2 sl0
```

The output from `ifconfig` should read:

```
lo    Link encap:Local Loopback
      inet addr:127.0.0.1  Bcast:127.255.255.255  Mask:255.0.0.0
      UP BROADCAST LOOPBACK RUNNING  MTU:3584  Metric:1
      RX packets:12 errors:0 dropped:0 overruns:0
      TX packets:12 errors:0 dropped:0 overruns:0
```

```
eth0 Link encap:10Mbps Ethernet  HWaddr 02:60:8C:49:05:57
         inet addr:192.168.1.1  Bcast:192.168.1.255  Mask:255.255.255.0
         UP BROADCAST RUNNING MULTICAST  MTU:1500  Metric:1
         RX packets:0 errors:0 dropped:0 overruns:0
         TX packets:0 errors:0 dropped:0 overruns:0
         Interrupt:5 Base address:0x300

sl0  Link encap:Serial Line IP
         inet addr:111.222.333.444 P-t-P:555.666.777.888
         Mask:255.255.255.0
         UP POINTOPOINT RUNNING  MTU:1500  Metric:1
         RX packets:0 errors:0 dropped:0 overruns:0
         TX packets:2 errors:0 dropped:0 overruns:0

ppp0 Link encap:Point-Point Protocol
         inet addr:111.222.333.444 P-t-P:555.666.777.888
         Mask:255.255.255.0
         UP POINTOPOINT RUNNING  MTU:1500  Metric:1
         RX packets:5 errors:0 dropped:0 overruns:0
         TX packets:5 errors:0 dropped:0 overruns:0
```

21.5 IP Masquerading

The Linux kernel is able to masquerade IP addresses behind a single IP address. Also, note that currently, all forms of network traffic are not supported. Common forms of traffic, such as mail (POP and SMTP), telnet, FTP, Web (HTTP), news (NNTP), ping, and many more are supported. Some other protocols (mostly UDP-related) are either not supported or require kernel modules to be loaded. Red Hat has modules for IRC, RealAudio, Quake, FTP, cuseeme, and others.

The simplest form of an IP masquerading firewall is two lines:

```
ipchains -P forward -j DENY
ipchains -A forward -i ppp0 -j MASQ
```

These are known as forward rules. The first line sets up a default policy (-j) to "deny" all connections unless specifically stated. You can also do a default policy of "accept," but this would defeat the purpose of the firewall. The second line appends (-A) a masquerade (-j) policy from the (-i) interface of ppp0.

You can find out more information about masquerading and rules for ipchains in Chapter 16.

The following pages include descriptions of a simple masquerading fire-wall, with some minor protection from intruders. If more in-depth informa-tion is required, read the `ipfwadm` man pages and perhaps one of the many books dedicated to firewalls. Most books will not discuss `ipfwadm` specifically, but will give theories that can be applied to your Linux box.

Below is a sample `/etc/rc.d/rc.firewall`. As with diald, you should call it from `rc.local` upon boot-time.

```sh
#!/bin/sh

PATH=/sbin:/bin:/usr/sbin:/usr/bin

#
# /etc/rc.d/rc.firewall, define the firewall configuration,
# invoked from rc.local.
#

PATH=/sbin:/bin:/usr/sbin:/usr/bin
MY_ETH0=192.168.1.1
MY_NET=192.168.1.0
MY_STATIC=111.222.333.444


# Forwarding rules
# first flush any old rules from memory
ipchains -F forward
# then set a default policy to deny everything
ipchains -P forward -j reject
# lastly, we want to masquerade the IPs from MY_NET (eth0) to
# the ppp0 interface (but we may need to stop at the sl0
# interface if diald needs to start the ppp connection first!)
ipchains -A forward -i ppp0 -j MASQ
ipchains -A forward -j sl0 -j MASQ
# Set rules
# first, flush all old rules from memory
ipfwadm -F input
ipfwadm -F output
#then set a default policy to deny everything
ipchains -P input  -j reject
ipchains -P output -j reject
# packets coming in from my local network (can only be eth0) to any-
#   where else are allowed
ipchains -P input  -j accept -s $MY_NET/24 -d 0.0.0.0/0
ipchains -P input -j accept -s 0.0.0.0/0 -s $MY_NET/24


echo "done"
```

21.6 Summary

When connecting a LAN to the Internet in a secure way, there are three items to consider:

1. Selecting a private (i.e., non-routable) network.

2. Connecting your firewall machine to the LAN and the Internet; in this example, via an on-demand dial-up line using PPP.

3. Allowing certain machines on your LAN access to the Internet and possibly disallowing access from various external machines or networks.

Appendix

URLs To Keep Track Of

http://shashdot.org/—Slashdot, News for Nerds—This site is pretty much a clearinghouse of information and discussion on Linux, free software, and technology in general.

http://freshmeat.net/—Freshmeat—As the number of open source software packages and other applications for Linux increase, Freshmeat will allow you to track new or updated packages. This list is updated every day, so you can see new packages over a period of time.

http://www.linuxworld.com/ —LinuxWorld is a Web-based magazine that has news and other technical articles. The authors are columnists for system administration issues; their column is called Uptime.

URLs Referenced in This Book

Chapter 2:
http://www.redhat.com/corp/support/manuals/RHL-6.0-Manual/alpha-inst/booklet/

Chapter 5:
http://www.kde.org/

Chapter 6:
http://www.isc.org/
http://linux.uhw.com/software/lanlord/
http://www.internic.net
http://www.isi.edu
http://www.isi.edu/div7/iana/domain-names.html
http://www.cert.org/
ftp://ftp.isc.org/isc/bind/
ftp://contrib.redhat.com/
ftp://ftp.u.washington.edu/public/asun/
ftp://ftp.kernel.org/
ftp://ftp.gnu.org/gnu/glibc.
ftp://ftp.kernel.org/pub/linux/utils/net/NIS+

Chapter 8:
http://www.samba.org/

Chapter 9:
http://www.qmail.org/
http://www.imap.org/

Chapter 10:
http://www.proftpd.org
ftp://contrib.redhat.com/
ftp://bero.x5.net/pub/

Chapter 11:
http://www.applix.com/
http://linux.corel.com
http://www.tex.ac.uk/
http://www.gimp.org/

http://www.boutell.com/mapedit
http://www.wolfram.com/
http://www.ardi.com/
http://www.caldera.com/doc/wabi/wabi.html
http://www.adobe.com/
http://www.lesstif.org/

Chapter 12:

http://www.tcx.se/ - MySQL
http://bragg.phys.uwm.edu/xforms - xforms
http://www.postgresql.org/
http://www.solidtech.com/
http://www.empress.com/
http://www.kesoftware.com/
http://www.inter-soft.com/ - Essentia

Chapter 13:

http://www.fsf.org/software/gcc/gcc.html
http://www.accu.org/
http://www.perl.com/
http://www.mrtg.com/
http://www.mozilla.com/
http://www.python.org
http://www.cs.cmu.edu/Groups/AI/html/cltl/cltl2.html (Common Lisp)
http://www-swiss.ai.mit.edu/scheme-home.html (Scheme)
http://www.red-bean.com/guile
http://www.blackdown.org
http://sourceware.cygnus.com/java/gcj.html
http://www.kaffe.org/
http://www.japhar.org/
http://www.biss-net.com/biss-awt.html
http://www.scriptics.com/
http://www.php.org/
http://www.fortran.com/fortran/
http://www.fys.ruu.nl/~bergmann/basic.html
http://www.pascal-central.com/
http://www.cobol.org/
http://st-www.cs.uiuc.edu/
http://www.cs.arizona.edu/icon/www/index.html
http://www.rexxla.org/

http://www.eiffel-forum.org/
http://smalleiffel.loria.fr/
http://www.icsi.berkeley.edu/~sather/

Chapter 14:
http://www.apache.org)\emdash
http://www.boa.org/
http://www.w3.org/pub/WWW/Daemon/
http://hoohoo.ncsa.uiuc.edu/
http://hopf.math.nwu.edu/
http://hopf.math.nwu.edu:70/
http://www.c2.net/
http://www.algroup.co.uk/Apache-SSL/
http://www.roxen.com/
http://www.zeus.co.uk
http://www.netstore.de/Supply/http-analyze/index.html
http://www.netstore.de/Supply/3Dstats/
http://www.iicm.edu/vrweb
http://www.tcx.se/
http://www.php.net/
http://www.apache.org/
ftp://ftp.psy.uq.oz.au/pub/Crypto/SSL
ftp://ftp.ox.ac.uk/pub/crypto/SSL

Chapter 15:
http://www.freshmeat.net/
http://www.gnome.org/start/getting.shtml
http://www.gnome.org/applist/list-martin.phtml
http://www.enlightenment.org/
http://www.kiss.uni-lj.si/~k4fr0235/icewm/
http://fvwm2gnome.fluid.cx/
http://windowmaker.org/
http://www.kde.org/current.html
http:://www.xinside.com/
http://www.redhat.com/

Chapter 16:
http://www.cert.org
http://www.rootshell.com

Chapter 17:
http://www.tapr.org/tapr/html/pkthome.html
http://www.tapr.org/tapr/html/pkthome.html
ftp://ftp.uk.linux.org/pub/linux/video4linux

Chapter 18:
http://www.apostols.org/projectz/queso/
http://www.skypoint.com/~sewilco/statnet.htm
http://wwwhome.cs.utwente.nl/~schoenw/scotty/
http://www.mrtg.org/
http://www.trinux.org/

Chapter 19:
http://www.estinc.com/
http://home.xl.ca/perfectBackup/

Chapter 20:
http://www.tummy.com
http://www.mostang.com/sane
http://www.cs.utexas.edu/users/kharker/
http://hyper.stanford.edu/HyperNews/get/pcmcia/home.html

Chapter 21:
http://www.dna.lth.se/~erics/diald
http://www.xos.nl/

Appendix B

Problems Using Very Large Hard Disks

Using very large hard disks in PCs can lead to problems because of the limitations of the BIOS and IDE standards on which most PCs are based. Problems arise because the BIOS can manage only hard disks with a maximum of 256 heads, 63 sectors, and 1024 cylinders because the IDE standard is based on a model that specifies the Cylinders, Heads, and Sectors of the hard disks (CHS model), but only allows a maximum of 16 heads, 255 sectors, and 65536 cylinders. The lowest limits of both of these standards combine to give a maximum size for standard hard disks of 504MB (16 heads, 63 sectors, and 1024 cylinders).

The newer Enhanced-IDE (EIDE) standard avoids this limitation by not using the CHS model. Instead, a Logical Block Addressing model is used (LBA). This model numbers all sectors on the disk sequentially.

Newer BIOS versions overcome the 504MB limitation by using an Extended CHS model that extends the maximum number of heads to 256.

The new upper size limit, from the Enhanced-IDE and Extended CHS models, is almost 7.9GB.

Linux does not use the BIOS to access your hard disk, so IDE and EIDE hard disks should not cause problems on Linux systems. If problems occur, however, Linux might be obtaining incorrect hard disk size parameters from the BIOS. To correct this problem, use boot parameters to pass the correct information to Linux. The parameter to pass is `hdx=cyl,heads,sect`, where `hdx` is the hard disk device (`hda`, `hdb`, `hdc`, or `hdd`). More information is provided below on using these parameters to create cylinder counts of less than 1024.

SCSI Hard Disks

In general, all SCSI hard disks use the LBA model mentioned above. SCSI hard disks do have a separate problem that EIDE hard disks do not have, however. SCSI hard disks larger than 1GB must have special treatment with the `fdisk` utility and while configuring the LILO boot manager. If your SCSI hard disk is affected by this problem, `fdisk` will display messages regarding the problem when you prepare your hard disk. The expert mode of `fdisk` can be used to correct SCSI problems. The LILO problems are fixed by adjusting the `/etc/disktab` file. Both of these fixes are described below with an example.

Why the Problem Arises

The problem with these larger hard disks is that the partition table must be read before any operating system becomes active. The partition table is accessed via the BIOS, which is limited to 256 heads, 63 sectors, and 1024 cylinders. Because of this, the hard disk controller attempts to convert (or translate) the true parameters of hard disks with more than 1024 cylinders into values that can be accepted by the BIOS.

The partition table itself can always be found at the first cylinder, first sector, and first header (which is the same in any translation); but because of this translation from the controller, if all data for the boot process (such as the boot loader and operating system kernel) are not found in the first 1024 cylinders, the BIOS cannot successfully boot the system.

Partitions can be created above 1024 cylinders, but you cannot boot these partitions because boot data in those higher partitions cannot be accessed until after the system is booted. This only causes trouble when a system has multiple operating systems and the user attempts to choose which to boot.

A work-around solution is to create a small Linux partition below 1024 cylinders that can be used to boot the Linux system. This partition can be as little as 15MB because it only needs to contain the kernel and root filesystem. The /usr directory and other information can be stored in a second Linux partition located above 1024 cylinders. Use the fdisk utility of another operating system such as OS/2 to create these partitions. Then use the Linux fdisk during installation to mark the partitions as Type 0x83, Linux.

A better solution is to enter the correct combination of cylinders, sectors, and heads that the hard disk controller is passing to the BIOS. Use the fdisk expert mode, as described below.

SCSI hard disks are usually reported as 64 heads and 32 sectors, giving a size of 64*32*512 bytes = 1MB per cylinder. EIDE usually reports 255 heads. The last translation is done by the operating system itself. Here Linux uses LBA to refer to the blocks sequentially from the first block to the last block on the hard disk.

Many controllers use two different models to provide cylinder numbers under 1024. In most cases, the controller first tries to double the number of heads. If this does not result in a cylinder count of less than 1024, the controller increases the actual values for heads and sectors to the maximum possible number to minimize the number of cylinders. This process is used by the extended translation of the Adaptec controllers, AH 274x/284x/294x. For example, the translation by an Adaptec controller of a 4GB disk gives a count of 255 heads, 63 sectors, and 522 cylinders. The NCR controller uses a variant by which the number of heads and sectors is chosen to provide the correct size while being within the 1024 cylinder limit. Overlap between partitions is thereby minimized because each partition begins and ends on a cylinder boundary.

Your task is to find out the translation that the controller is doing and enter the values that it passes for the hard disk into the expert mode of fdisk. As you do this, remember that the total size of the hard disk must remain constant.

For example, assume that we have a computer with a 4GB SCSI hard disk. This is more than 1024 cylinders, so fdisk gives a warning during installation:

```
The number of cylinders for this disk is set to 4095.
This is larger than 1024, and may cause problems with:

1. software that runs at boot time (e.g., LILO)
2. booting and partitioning software form other OSs
   (e.g., DOS FDISK, OS/2 FDISK)
```

When you use the `p` command to display the partition table, you see a sequence of error messages:

```
Device Boot    Begin   Start   End    Blocks    Id   System
/dev/sda1         1       1     754    771088+   6    DOS 16-bit>32M
Partition 1 does not end on cylinder boundary:
   phys=(95, 254, 63) should be (95, 63, 32)
/dev/sda2    *    97     754    1954   1228972+  82   Linux swap
Partition 2 does not end on cylinder boundary:
   phys=(248, 254, 63) should be (248, 63, 32)
/dev/sda3       1274     1954   2456   514080    a5   BSD/386
Partition 3 does not end on cylinder boundary:
   phys=(312, 254, 63) should be (312, 63, 32)
/dev/sda4       2362     2456   4095   1678792+  5    Extended
Partition 4 does not end on cylinder boundary:
   phys=(521, 254, 63) should be (521, 63, 32)
/dev/sda5       2362     2456   2707   257008+   83   Linux
/dev/sda6       2394     2707   2770   64228+    83   Linux native
/dev/sda7       2402     2770   3436   682731    6    DOS 16-bit>32M
/dev/sda8       2487     3436   4095   674698+   6    DOS 16-bit>32M
```

To correct these errors, new values must be provided for `fdisk` so that the partition boundaries match the values reported by the hard disk and controller. In this example, the 4GB hard disk shown above has 64 heads, 32 sectors, and 4095 cylinders, for a total capacity of 64*32*4095 bytes = 4095MB.

If you set the number of heads to 255 and the number of sectors to 63 (a hint that this value is correct appears in the error messages shown above), the partition still must have 4095MB. So, if 255*63*cylinders = 4095MB, then the number of cylinders would be 522.

These new values must be entered in `fdisk`. First, you must change to the expert mode with the `x` command, and then you enter the new parameters for the heads, sectors, and cylinders. In expert mode, the commands `c` (cylinders), `h` (heads), and `s` (sectors) can be used. According to the calculation above, these values should be 255 heads and 63 sectors.

Note that if you are using DOS on your system, never enter a head count of 256. This value will cause DOS to crash without comment.

Below is how the screen might look as you enter these new values in `fdisk`.

```
Expert command (m for help): h Number of heads (1-256): 255
Expert command (m for help): s Number of sectors (1-63): 63
   Warning: Setting sector offset for DOS compatibility
Expert command (m for help): c Number of cylinders (1-65535): 522
```

After these values are entered in the `fdisk` expert mode, return to the normal main menu of `fdisk` with `r`. Now, using the `p` command should show all partitions without the warnings shown in the first listing above.

```
Command (m for help): p Disk /dev/sda: 255 heads, 63 sectors, 522
cylinders Units = cylinders of 16065 * 512 bytes

Device Boot    Begin    Start    End    Blocks    Id    System
/dev/sda1         1        1      96    771088+    6     DOS 16-bit>32M
/dev/sda2 *      97       97     249   1228972+   82     Linux swap
/dev/sda3       250      250     313    514080    a5     BSD/386
/dev/sda4       314      314     522   1678792+    5     Extended
/dev/sda5       314      314     345    257008+   83     Linux native
/dev/sda6       346      346     353     64228+   83     Linux native
/dev/sda7       354      354     438    682731     6     DOS 16-bit>32M
/dev/sda8       439      439     522    674698+    6     DOS 16-bit>32M
```

If the error messages have not disappeared, you have not yet found the right values. Try again with new values until the error messages do not appear.

When you find the correct values, make note of them in your system documentation. You must enter these values each time you run `fdisk`. They are not saved.

After the correct values are entered in expert mode, you can continue working normally with `fdisk` to create the partitions that you need to install Linux on.

If you want to use LILO to boot Linux directly from the hard disk, you must list the correct partitions in the file `/etc/fstab/`. These partitions are shown from the main menu of `fdisk` once you have corrected the information in expert mode. Change the partition display of `fdisk` from units to sectors with the `u` command. The sector values shown correspond to the block values of the LBA mode.

```
Command (m for help): u Changing display/entry units to sectors

Display the revised partition table:

Command (m for help): p

Disk /dev/sda: 255 heads, 63 sectors, 522 cylinders
Units = sectors of 1 * 512 bytes

Device Boot     Begin     Start     End    Blocks    Id    System
/dev/sda1          63        63  1542239   771088+    6    DOS 16-bit>32M
/dev/sda2 *   1542240   1542240  4000184  1228972+   82    Linux swap
/dev/sda3     4000185   4000185  5028344   514080    a5    BSD/386
```

/dev/sda4	5028345	5028345	8385929	1678792+	5	Extended
/dev/sda5	5028408	5028408	5542424	257008+	83	Linux native
/dev/sda6	5542488	5542488	5670944	64228+	83	Linux native
/dev/sda7	5671008	5671008	7036469	682731	6	DOS 16-bit>32M
/dev/sda8	7036533	7036533	8385929	674698+	6	DOS 16-bit>32M

Now the start, size, and end of the partition are no longer displayed in cylinders, but in sectors (which Linux uses to access the hard disk). Enter these sector values in the file /etc/disktab. The entries in this file would look like this for our example:

```
# Dev.   BIOS   Secs/   Heads/   Cylin   Part.
# num.   code   track   cylin.   ders    offset

0x801    0x80   63      255      522     63        # /dev/sda1
0x802    0x80   63      255      522     1542240   # /dev/sda2
0x803    0x80   63      255      522     4000185   # /dev/sda3
0x805    0x80   63      255      522     5028408   # /dev/sda5
0x806    0x80   63      255      522     5542488   # /dev/sda6
0x807    0x80   63      255      522     5671008   # /dev/sda7
0x808    0x80   63      255      522     7036533   # /dev/sda8
```

The process described here is a difficult one, and we cannot guarantee your success for any particular hardware configuration. We hope that the principal steps and concepts are clear, however. If you have trouble, please contact Caldera for additional information or suggestions.

Linux-allocated Devices

Maintained by H. Peter Anvin <Peter.Anvin@linux.org>
Last revised: May 29, 1995

This list is the successor to Rick Miller's Linux Device List, which he stopped maintaining when he lost network access in 1993. It is a registry of allocated major device numbers, as well as the recommended /dev directory nodes for these devices.

This list is available via FTP from ftp.yggdrasil.com in the directory /pub/device-list; filename is devices.<format> where <format> is txt (ASCII), tex (LaTeX), dvi (DVI) or ps (PostScript). In cases of discrepancy, the LaTeX version has priority.

This document is included by reference into the Linux Filesystem Standard (FSSTND). The FSSTND is available via FTP from tsx-11.mit.edu in the directory /pub/linux/docs/linux-standards/fsstnd.

To have a major number allocated, or a minor number in situations where that applies (e.g., busmice), please contact me. Also, if you have additional information regarding any of the devices listed below, I would like to know. Allocations marked (68k) apply to Linux/68k only.

```
0       Unnamed devices (NFS mounts, loopback devices)
        0 = reserved as null device number

1 char Memory devices
        1 = /dev/mem   Physical memory access
        2 = /dev/kmem  Kernel virtual memory access
        3 = /dev/null  Null device
        4 = /dev/port  I/O port access
        5 = /dev/zero  Null byte source
         6 = /dev/core OBSOLETE - replaced by /proc/kcore
        7 = /dev/full  Returns ENOSPC on write
  block RAM disk
        1 = /dev/ramdiskRAM disk

2 char Reserved for PTY's <tytso@athena.mit.edu>

  block Floppy disks
        0 = /dev/fd0 First floppy disk autodetect
        1 = /dev/fd1 Second floppy disk autodetect
        2 = /dev/fd2 Third floppy disk autodetect
        3 = /dev/fd3 Fourth floppy disk autodetect

  To specify format, add to the autodetect device number:
        0 = /dev/fd?          Autodetect format
        4 = /dev/fd?d360      5.25"   360K in a 360K  drive
       20 = /dev/fd?h360      5.25"   360K in a 1200K drive
       48 = /dev/fd?h410      5.25"   410K in a 1200K drive
       64 = /dev/fd?h420      5.25"   420K in a 1200K drive
       24 = /dev/fd?h720      5.25"   720K in a 1200K drive
       80 = /dev/fd?h880      5.25"   880K in a 1200K drive
        8 = /dev/fd?h1200     5.25" 1200K in a 1200K drive
       40 = /dev/fd?h1440     5.25" 1440K in a 1200K drive
       56 = /dev/fd?h1476     5.25" 1476K in a 1200K drive
       72 = /dev/fd?h1494     5.25" 1494K in a 1200K drive
       92 = /dev/fd?h1600     5.25" 1600K in a 1200K drive

       12 = /dev/fd?u360      3.5"    360K Double Density
      120 = /dev/fd?u800      3.5"    800K Double Density
       52 = /dev/fd?u820      3.5"    820K Double Density
       68 = /dev/fd?u830      3.5"    830K Double Density
       84 = /dev/fd?u1040     3.5"   1040K Double Density
       88 = /dev/fd?u1120     3.5"   1120K Double Density
       28 = /dev/fd?u1440     3.5"   1440K High Density
      124 = /dev/fd?u1600     3.5"   1600K High Density
```

```
 44 = /dev/fd?u1680    3.5"  1680K High Density
 60 = /dev/fd?u1722    3.5"  1722K High Density
 76 = /dev/fd?u1743    3.5"  1743K High Density
 96 = /dev/fd?u1760    3.5"  1760K High Density
116 = /dev/fd?u1840    3.5"  1840K High Density
100 = /dev/fd?u1920    3.5"  1920K High Density
 32 = /dev/fd?u2880    3.5"  2880K Extra Density
104 = /dev/fd?u3200    3.5"  3200K Extra Density
108 = /dev/fd?u3520    3.5"  3520K Extra Density
112 = /dev/fd?u3840    3.5"  3840K Extra Density

 36 = /dev/fd?CompaQ  Compaq 2880K drive; obsolete?
```

NOTE: The letter in the device name (d, q, h or u) signifies the type of drive: 5.25" Double Density (d), 5.25" Quad Density (q), 5.25" High Density (h) or 3.5" (any model, u). The use of the capital letters D, H and E for the 3.5" models have been deprecated, since the drive type is insignificant for these devices.

```
3 char  Reserved for pty's <tytso@athena.mit.edu>
   block  First MFM, RLL and IDE hard disk/CD-ROM interface
          0 = /dev/hda      Master: whole disk (or CD-ROM)
         64 = /dev/hdb      Slave: whole disk (or CD-ROM)
```

For partitions, add to the whole disk device number:

```
          0 = /dev/hd?      Whole disk
          1 = /dev/hd?1     First primary partition
          2 = /dev/hd?2     Second primary partition
          3 = /dev/hd?3     Third primary partition
          4 = /dev/hd?4     Fourth primary partition
          5 = /dev/hd?5     First logical partition
          6 = /dev/hd?6     Second logical partition
          7 = /dev/hd?7     Third logical partition
          ...
         63 = /dev/hd?63    59th logical partition

4 char  TTY devices
          0 = /dev/console  Console device

          1 = /dev/tty1     First virtual console
          ...
         63 = /dev/tty63    63rd virtual console
         64 = /dev/ttyS0    First serial port
          ...
        127 = /dev/ttyS63   64th serial port
        128 = /dev/ptyp0    First pseudo-tty master
          ...
        191 = /dev/ptysf    64th pseudo-tty master
        192 = /dev/ttyp0    First pseudo-tty slave
          ...
```

```
       255 = /dev/ttysf        64th pseudo-tty slave

   Pseudo-tty's are named as follows:
   * Masters are "pty", slaves are "tty";
   * the fourth letter is one of p, q, r, s indicating
     the 1st, 2nd, 3rd, 4th series of 16 pseudo-ttys each, and
   * the fifth letter is one of 0123456789abcdef indicating
     the position within the series.

5 char  Alternate TTY devices
         0 = /dev/tty           Current TTY device
        64 = /dev/cua0          Callout device corresponding to ttyS0
       ...
       127 = /dev/cua63         Callout device corresponding to ttyS63

6 char  Parallel printer devices
         0 = /dev/lp0           First parallel printer (0x3bc)
         1 = /dev/lp1           Second parallel printer (0x378)
         2 = /dev/lp2           Third parallel printer (0x278)

   Not all computers have the 0x3bc parallel port; hence
   the "first" printer may be either /dev/lp0 or
   /dev/lp1.

7 char  Virtual console capture devices
         0 = /dev/vcs           Current vc text contents
         1 = /dev/vcs1          tty1 text contents
       ...
        63 = /dev/vcs63         tty63 text contents
       128 = /dev/vcsa          Current vc text/attribute contents
       129 = /dev/vcsa1         tty1 text/attribute contents
       ...
       191 = /dev/vcsa63        tty63 text/attribute contents

NOTE: These devices permit both read and write access.

8 block  SCSI disk devices
         0 = /dev/sda           First SCSI disk whole disk
        16 = /dev/sdb           Second SCSI disk whole disk
        32 = /dev/sdc           Third SCSI disk whole disk
       ...
       240 = /dev/sdp           Sixteenth SCSI disk whole disk

Partitions are handled in the same way as for IDE
disks (see major number 3) except that the limit on
logical partitions is 11.

9 char  SCSI tape devices
         0 = /dev/st0           First SCSI tape
         1 = /dev/st1           Second SCSI tape
```

```
        ...
       128 = /dev/nst0        First SCSI tape, no rewind-on-close
       129 = /dev/nst1        Second SCSI tape, no rewind-on-close
        ...
  block Multiple disk devices
         0 = /dev/md0         First device group
         1 = /dev/md1         Second device group
    ...
```

The multiple devices driver is used to span a
filesystem across multiple physical disks.

```
10 char Non-serial mice, misc features
         0 = /dev/logibm      Logitech bus mouse
         1 = /dev/psaux       PS/2-style mouse port
         2 = /dev/inportbm    Microsoft Inport bus mouse
         3 = /dev/atibm       ATI XL bus mouse
         4 = /dev/jbm         J-mouse
         4 = /dev/amigamouse  Amiga Mouse (68k)
         5 = /dev/atarimouse  Atari Mouse (68k)
       128 = /dev/beep        Fancy beep device
       129 = /dev/modreq      Kernel module load request
```

The use of the suffix -mouse instead of -bm or -aux
has also been used.

```
11 block SCSI CD-ROM devices
         0 = /dev/sr0         First SCSI CD-ROM
         1 = /dev/sr1         Second SCSI CD-ROM
         ...
```

The prefix /dev/scd instead of /dev/sr has been used
as well, and might make more sense.

```
12 char QIC-02 tape
         2 = /dev/ntpqic11    QIC-11, no rewind-on-close
         3 = /dev/tpqic11     QIC-11, rewind-on-close
         4 = /dev/ntpqic24    QIC-24, no rewind-on-close
         5 = /dev/tpqic24     QIC-24, rewind-on-close
         6 = /dev/ntpqic120   QIC-120, no rewind-on-close
         7 = /dev/tpqic120    QIC-120, rewind-on-close
         8 = /dev/ntpqic150   QIC-150, no rewind-on-close
         9 = /dev/tpqic150    QIC-150, rewind-on-close
```

The device names specified are proposed -- if there
are "standard" names for these devices, please let me know.

```
  block MSCDEX CD-ROM callback support
         0 = /dev/dos_cd0     First MSCDEX CD-ROM
         1 = /dev/dos_cd1     Second MSCDEX CD-ROM
```

```
        ...

13 char PC speaker
        0 = /dev/pcmixer     Emulates /dev/mixer
        1 = /dev/pcsp        Emulates /dev/dsp (8-bit)
        4 = /dev/pcaudio     Emulates /dev/audio
        5 = /dev/pcsp16      Emulates /dev/dsp (16-bit)
   block 8-bit MFM/RLL/IDE controller
        0 = /dev/xda         First XT disk whole disk
       64 = /dev/xdb         Second XT disk whole disk

        Partitions are handled in the same way as IDE disks
        (see major number 3).

14 char Sound card
        0 = /dev/mixer       Mixer control
        1 = /dev/sequencer   Audio sequencer
        2 = /dev/midi00      First MIDI port
        3 = /dev/dsp         Digital audio
        4 = /dev/audio       Sun-compatible digital audio
        6 = /dev/sndstat     Sound card status information
        8 = /dev/sequencer2  Sequencer -- alternate device
       16 = /dev/mixer1      Second soundcard mixer control
       17 = /dev/patmgr0     Sequencer patch manager
       18 = /dev/midi01      Second MIDI port
       19 = /dev/dsp1        Second soundcard digital audio
       20 = /dev/audio1      Second soundcard Sun digital audio
       33 = /dev/patmgr1     Sequencer patch manager
       34 = /dev/midi02      Third MIDI port
       50 = /dev/midi03      Fourth MIDI port
   block BIOS harddrive callback support
        0 = /dev/dos_hda     First BIOS harddrive whole disk
       64 = /dev/dos_hdb     Second BIOS harddrive whole disk
      128 = /dev/dos_hdc     Third BIOS harddrive whole disk
      192 = /dev/dos_hdd     Fourth BIOS harddrive whole disk

        Partitions are handled in the same way as IDE disks
        (see major number 3).

15 char Joystick
        0 = /dev/js0         First joystick
        1 = /dev/js1         Second joystick
   block Sony CDU-31A/CDU-33A CD-ROM
        0 = /dev/sonycd      Sony CDU-31a CD-ROM

16 char Reserved for scanners
   block GoldStar CD-ROM
        0 = /dev/gscd        GoldStar CD-ROM

17 char Chase serial card
```

```
        0 = /dev/ttyH0       First Chase port
        1 = /dev/ttyH1       Second Chase port
        ...
  block Optics Storage CD-ROM (under development)
        0 = /dev/optcd       Optics Storage CD-ROM

18 char Chase serial card - alternate devices
        0 = /dev/cuh0        Callout device corresponding to ttyH0
        1 = /dev/cuh1        Callout device corresponding to ttyH1
        ...
  block Sanyo CD-ROM (under development)
        0 = ?                Sanyo CD-ROM

19 char Cyclades serial card
       32 = /dev/ttyC0       First Cyclades port
        ...
       63 = /dev/ttyC31      32nd Cyclades port

    It would make more sense for these to start at 0...

  block Double" compressed disk
        0 = /dev/double0     First compressed disk
        ...
        7 = /dev/double7     Eighth compressed disk
      128 = /dev/cdouble0    Mirror of first compressed disk
        ...
      135 = /dev/cdouble7    Mirror of eighth compressed disk

    See the Double documentation for the meaning of the
    mirror devices.

20 char Cyclades serial card - alternate devices
       32 = /dev/cub0        Callout device corresponding to ttyC0
        ...
       63 = /dev/cub31       Callout device corresponding to ttyC31
  block Hitachi CD-ROM (under development)
        0 = /dev/hitcd       Hitachi CD-ROM

21 char Generic SCSI access
        0 = /dev/sg0         First generic SCSI device
        1 = /dev/sg1         Second generic SCSI device
        ...

22 char Digiboard serial card
        0 = /dev/ttyD0       First Digiboard port
        1 = /dev/ttyD1       Second Digiboard port
        ...
  block Second MFM, RLL and IDE hard disk/CD-ROM interface
        0 = /dev/hdc         Master: whole disk (or CD-ROM)
       64 = /dev/hdd         Slave: whole disk (or CD-ROM)
```

```
                Partitions are handled the same way as for the first
                interface (see major number 3).

 23 char Digiboard serial card - alternate devices
              0 = /dev/cud0      Callout device corresponding to ttyD0
              1 = /dev/cud1      Callout device corresponding to ttyD1
              ...
      block Mitsumi proprietary CD-ROM
              0 = /dev/mcd       Mitsumi CD-ROM

 24 char Stallion serial card
              0 = /dev/ttyE0     Stallion port 0 card 0
              1 = /dev/ttyE1     Stallion port 1 card 0
              ...
             64 = /dev/ttyE64    Stallion port 0 card 1
             65 = /dev/ttyE65    Stallion port 1 card 1
              ...
            128 = /dev/ttyE128   Stallion port 0 card 2
            129 = /dev/ttyE129   Stallion port 1 card 2
              ...
            192 = /dev/ttyE192   Stallion port 0 card 3
            193 = /dev/ttyE193   Stallion port 1 card 3
              ...
      block Sony CDU-535 CD-ROM
              0 = /dev/cdu535    Sony CDU-535 CD-ROM

 25 char Stallion serial card - alternate devices
              0 = /dev/cue0      Callout device corresponding to ttyE0
              1 = /dev/cue1      Callout device corresponding to ttyE1
              ...
             64 = /dev/cue64     Callout device corresponding to ttyE64
             65 = /dev/cue65     Callout device corresponding to ttyE65
              ...
            128 = /dev/cue128    Callout device corresponding to ttyE128
            129 = /dev/cue129    Callout device corresponding to ttyE129
              ...
            192 = /dev/cue192    Callout device corresponding to ttyE192
            193 = /dev/cue193    Callout device corresponding to ttyE193
              ...
      block First Matsushita (Panasonic/SoundBlaster) CD-ROM
              0 = /dev/sbpcd0    Panasonic CD-ROM controller 0 unit 0
              1 = /dev/sbpcd1    Panasonic CD-ROM controller 0 unit 1
              2 = /dev/sbpcd2    Panasonic CD-ROM controller 0 unit 2
              3 = /dev/sbpcd3    Panasonic CD-ROM controller 0 unit 3

 26 char Frame grabbers
              0 = /dev/wvisfgrab Quanta WinVision frame grabber
      block Second Matsushita (Panasonic/SoundBlaster) CD-ROM
              0 = /dev/sbpcd4    Panasonic CD-ROM controller 1 unit 0
```

```
         1 = /dev/sbpcd5      Panasonic CD-ROM controller 1 unit 1
         2 = /dev/sbpcd6      Panasonic CD-ROM controller 1 unit 2
         3 = /dev/sbpcd7      Panasonic CD-ROM controller 1 unit 3

 27 char QIC-117 tape
         0 = /dev/ftape       QIC-117 tape
    block Third Matsushita (Panasonic/SoundBlaster) CD-ROM
         0 = /dev/sbpcd8      Panasonic CD-ROM controller 2 unit 0
         1 = /dev/sbpcd9      Panasonic CD-ROM controller 2 unit 1
         2 = /dev/sbpcd10     Panasonic CD-ROM controller 2 unit 2
         3 = /dev/sbpcd11     Panasonic CD-ROM controller 2 unit 3

 28 char Stallion serial card - card programming
         0 = /dev/staliomem0 First Stallion card I/O memory
         1 = /dev/staliomem1 Second Stallion card I/O memory
         2 = /dev/staliomem2 Third Stallion card I/O memory
         3 = /dev/staliomem3 Fourth Stallion card I/O memory
    block Fourth Matsushita (Panasonic/SoundBlaster) CD-ROM
         0 = /dev/sbpcd12     Panasonic CD-ROM controller 3 unit 0
         1 = /dev/sbpcd13     Panasonic CD-ROM controller 3 unit 1
         2 = /dev/sbpcd14     Panasonic CD-ROM controller 3 unit 2
         3 = /dev/sbpcd15     Panasonic CD-ROM controller 3 unit 3
    block ACSI disk (68k)
         0 = /dev/ada         First ACSI disk whole disk
        16 = /dev/adb         Second ACSI disk whole disk
        32 = /dev/adc         Third ACSI disk whole disk
         ...
       240 = /dev/adp         16th ACSI disk whole disk
```

Partitions are handled in the same way as for IDE
disks (see major number 3) except that the limit on
logical partitions is 11.

```
 29 char Universal frame buffer
         0 = /dev/fb0current First frame buffer
         1 = /dev/fb0autodetect
         ...
        16 = /dev/fb1current Second frame buffer
        17 = /dev/fb1autodetect
         ...
    block Aztech/Orchid/Okano/Wearnes CD-ROM
         0 = /dev/aztcd       Aztech CD-ROM
```

The universal frame buffer device is currenly only
supported on Linux/68k. The "current" device accesses
the fame buffer at current resolution; the
"autodetect" one at bootup (default) resolution.
Minor numbers 2-15 within each frame buffer assignment
are used for specific device-dependent resolutions.
There appears to be no standard naming for these devices.

```
30 char iBCS-2 compatibility devices
        0 = /dev/socksys     Socket access
        1 = /dev/spx         SVR3 local X interface
        2 = /dev/inet/arp    Network access
        2 = /dev/inet/icmp   Network access
        2 = /dev/inet/ip     Network access
        2 = /dev/inet/udp    Network access
        2 = /dev/inet/tcp    Network access

     iBCS-2 requires /dev/nfsd to be a link to
     /dev/socksys, and /dev/X0R to be a link to /dev/null.

   block Philips LMS CM-205 CD-ROM
        0 = /dev/cm205cd     Philips LMS CM-205 CD-ROM

     /dev/lmscd is an older name for this device.  This
     driver does not work with the CM-205MS CD-ROM.

31 char MPU-401 MIDI
        0 = /dev/mpu401data MPU-401 data port
        1 = /dev/mpu401stat MPU-401 status port
   block ROM/flash memory card
        0 = /dev/rom0        First ROM card (rw)
        ...
        7 = /dev/rom7        Eighth ROM card (rw)
        8 = /dev/rrom0       First ROM card (ro)
        ...
       15 = /dev/rrom7       Eighth ROM card (ro)
       16 = /dev/flash0      First flash memory card (rw)
        ...
       23 = /dev/flash7      Eighth flash memory card (rw)
       24 = /dev/rflash0     First flash memory card (ro)
        ...
       31 = /dev/rflash7     Eighth flash memory card (ro)

     The read-write (rw) devices support back-caching
     written data in RAM, as well as writing to flash RAM
     devices.  The read-only devices (ro) support reading
   only.

32 block Philips LMS CM-206 CD-ROM
        0 = /dev/cm206cd     Philips LMS CM-206 CD-ROM

33 block Modular RAM disk device
        0 = /dev/ram0        First modular RAM disk
        1 = /dev/ram1        Second modular RAM disk
        ...
      255 = /dev/ram255      256th modular RAM disk
```

```
34-223 UNALLOCATED

224-254 LOCAL USE
        Allocated for local/experimental use

        Please note that MAX_CHRDEV and MAX_BLKDEV in
        linux/include/linux/major.h must be set to a value
        greater than the highest used major number.  For a
        kernel using local/experimental devices, it is
        probably easiest to set both of these equal to 256.  The
        memory cost above using the default value of 64 is 3K.

255 RESERVED
```

Additional /dev Directory Entries

This section details additional entries that should or may exist in the /dev directory. It is preferred that symbolic links use the same form (absolute or relative) as is indicated here. Links are classified as "hard" or "symbolic" depending on the preferred type of link; if possible, the indicated type of link should be used.

Compulsory Links

These links should exist on all systems:

```
/dev/fd       /proc/self/fd   symbolic    File descriptors
/dev/stdin    fd/0 symbolic   stdin file descriptor
/dev/stdout   fd/1 symbolic   stdout file descriptor
/dev/stderr   fd/2 symbolic   stderr file descriptor
```

Recommended Links

It is recommended that these links exist on all systems:

```
/dev/X0R      null        symbolic  Used by iBCS-2
/dev/nfsd     socksys     symbolic  Used by iBCS-2
/dev/core     /proc/kcore symbolic  Backward compatibility
/dev/scd?     /dev/cd? hard Alternate SCSI CD-ROM name
```

Locally-defined Links

The following links may be established locally to conform to the system configuration. This is merely a tabulation of existing practice, and does not constitute a recommendation. However, if they exist, they should have the following uses.

```
/dev/mouse    mouse port      symbolic  Current mouse device
/dev/tape     tape device     symbolic  Current tape device
/dev/cdrom    CD-ROM device   symbolic  Current CD-ROM device
/dev/modem    modem port      symbolic  Current dialout device
/dev/root     root device     symbolic  Current root filesystem
/dev/swap     swap device     symbolic  Current swap device
```

`/dev/modem` should not be used for a modem that supports dial-in as well as dial-out, as it tends to cause lock file problems. If it exists, `/dev/modem` should point to the appropriate dial-out (alternate) device.

Sockets and Pipes

Non-transient sockets and named pipes may exist in `/dev`. Common entries are:

```
/dev/printer   socket lpd local socket
/dev/log       socket syslog local socket
```

Index

Symbols
/etc/hosts.equiv 137
/etc/hosts.lpd 137
/etc/inittab 43
/etc/printcap 136
/etc/rc.d/init.d 45
/etc/rc.d/rc.sysinit 44
` 45, 46, 48

Numerics
10Base2 142

A
Alpha 231
AppleTalk 111, 133, 311, 316, 318
Applix 189, 190
ARP 88, 95, 96
ASCII 134, 164, 298, 299

B
backup 46, 57, 130, 161, 354
bash 56
BIOS 50, 290, 309, 347
BOOTP 88, 90
browser 86, 87, 193, 233

BSD 135, 137, 325

C
C 101, 193, 196, 237, 242, 243, 245, 290
C++ 193
Caldera 199
CERN 233
CERT 131, 132
CGI (Common Gateway Interface) 234, 236, 237, 238, 239, 240, 241, 242, 245, 247, 249, 251
chat 94, 366, 367, 369, 371
chgrp 55, 346
chmod 55, 242, 346, 367
console 40, 43, 96, 199, 291, 319, 323, 325
Corel 189, 191

D
database 129, 130, 131, 234, 238, 245, 246, 248, 249
dbm 248
DEC 231
diald 364, 370, 371, 372, 374

DISPLAY 272, 284

dmesg 133

DNS (Domain Name Service) 86, 94, 98, 99, 100, 101, 102, 103, 108, 129, 130, 161, 293, 294

DOS 35, 49, 50, 94, 199, 255, 290, 309, 310, 319, 351

drivers 46, 47, 95, 142, 156, 199, 308, 310, 311, 319, 354

dump 352

E

EIDE 235, 348

elm 163

emacs 193

encryption 232, 234, 297

Ethernet 46, 79, 85, 87, 88, 89, 134, 284, 363, 366

expire 102, 108

export 109, 232

F

facility 324, 325

fdisk 46, 351

filesystem 44, 109, 110, 311, 319, 355

find 46, 129, 131, 138, 159, 165, 193, 196, 236, 247, 257, 297, 316, 317, 365, 371

firewall 90, 110, 296, 297, 363, 364, 365, 366, 373, 374

FORTRAN 196

fsck 43, 46, 310

FTP 86, 233, 235, 295, 296, 297

ftpd 97, 98, 293

fvwm 258, 259, 260, 261

G

gateway 88, 90

gcc 167, 242

getty 43, 96

GID (Group ID) 54, 55

GIF 196

GNU (GNU's Not UNIX) 193, 195, 243, 291

grep 236

groups 53, 54, 130, 159, 167, 361

GUI 312, 348, 349

H

halt 35, 48

home directory 54, 56, 57, 95, 109, 146, 162, 167, 168, 240

HP 135, 156

HTTP 87, 232, 235, 237, 240, 242, 243, 296, 373

httpd 98, 232, 233, 235, 236, 239, 242, 244, 245, 248, 249, 294

I

IDE 235, 316

identd 293

ifconfig 89, 94, 371, 372

IMAP 159, 165, 174, 175, 294

init 35, 43, 44, 45, 46, 48, 49, 139, 160, 349

inittab 43, 46, 49, 50

Internet 86, 93, 99, 100, 129, 130, 131, 159, 160, 161, 164, 165, 167, 174, 235, 289, 296, 363

InterNIC 100, 129, 130, 131, 364

Iomega 354

IP (Internet Protocol) 85, 86, 87, 88, 89, 90, 93, 94, 95, 96, 97, 98, 99, 100, 102, 103, 108, 110, 130, 133, 137, 141, 143, 159, 237, 240, 241, 290, 291, 292, 293, 294, 316

ipfwadm 363, 364, 374

IRQ (Interrupt Request Queue) 347
    IRQ conflict 347

ISDN 317

ISP (Internet Service Provider) 56, 99, 235, 238, 241, 364, 368, 370, 371, 372

J

Java 237, 349
Jaz 317, 319, 345, 354, 355
JPEG 164, 194, 196

K

kernel 35, 40, 45, 46, 47, 50, 85, 89, 94,
        95, 133, 160, 198, 295, 307, 308,
        309, 310, 311, 313, 314, 316, 319,
        320, 321, 323, 325, 346, 347, 348,
        354, 364, 370
kerneld 314
kill 44, 45, 47, 48, 244, 258, 276

L

LAN 160, 235, 238, 291, 319, 345, 349
LaserWriter 156
LaTeX 192, 193
LessTif 191, 199
LILO 36
LILO (LInux LOader) 36, 50, 290, 309,
        310, 321, 351
localhost 97, 101, 102, 161
lpc 135, 138, 139, 140
lpd 135, 136, 137, 138, 139, 140
lpq 138
lpr 135; 140, 324
lprm 135, 138, 140

M

MAC 87, 88, 94
Macintosh 174, 198, 245, 311
mailq 161
majordomo 161, 167, 168, 169
make 50, 53, 55, 57, 76, 86, 88, 96, 100,
        109, 111, 129, 130, 133, 142, 156,
        160, 165, 166, 167, 168, 193, 232,
        233, 234, 238, 239, 243, 244, 247,
        248, 249, 289, 290, 292, 294, 295,
        296, 297, 298, 308, 309, 311, 312,
        320, 321, 326, 348, 353, 354, 355

man 136, 138, 139, 165, 235, 292, 293,
        325, 348, 352
mapedit 196
MBR (Master Boot Record) 49, 50
MDA (Mail Delivery Agent) 161, 165
Microsoft 189, 255
MIME 164
Minix 319
mke2fs 352
modem 85, 94, 95, 96, 294, 347, 363,
        369, 370, 371
modules 43, 94, 231, 236, 237, 244, 248,
        307, 308, 313, 319, 354
Motif 191, 199
mount 44, 45, 49, 110, 111, 146, 310,
        352, 355, 356
MS Windows 142, 199, 310, 349
        Windows 3.1 199
        Windows 95 43, 137, 142, 143, 309
        Windows NT 142, 143
mSQL 243, 245, 246, 247, 248, 251
MTA (Mail Transport Agent) 160
MTU (Max Transmission Unit) 94
MUA (Mail User Agent) 55, 163, 164
mutt 163, 298
mwm 258, 260
MySQL 243, 248

N

Netscape 174, 199, 233, 243
netstat 371, 372
NFS (Network File System) 44, 45, 87,
        98, 109, 110, 111
NNTP (NetNews Transfer Protocol) 373

O

Oracle 243
OS/2 351

P

parallel 43, 133, 134, 135, 140, 199, 308,
        317, 348, 354, 355

partition 35, 44, 45, 46, 47, 110, 295, 309, 310, 351, 352, 355

passwd 49, 53, 54, 56, 57, 94, 95, 236, 237, 318

PCL 136, 156

Perl 193, 237, 242, 245

PGP (Pretty Good Privacy) 297, 298, 299

PHP 237, 242, 243, 244, 245, 246, 247, 248, 251

    PHP/FI 242, 243, 245, 247

pine 163, 298

POP (Post Office Protocol) 159, 174, 175, 190, 294, 373

postmaster 162, 163

PostScript 136, 156, 164, 276

PPP (Point-to-Point Protocol) 43, 85, 93, 94, 95, 96, 284, 311, 317, 364, 366, 367, 368, 369, 370, 371

printer 133, 134, 135, 136, 137, 138, 139, 140, 156, 164

printtool 138

priority 324, 325, 326

procmail 161, 162, 165, 166

Python 193, 237, 245

R

RARP (Reverse ARP) 88

rc.local 371, 374

Red Hat 44, 54, 90, 95, 110, 135, 138, 160, 162, 165, 235

regex 247

resource 87, 96, 274

restore 46

RFC (Request For Comment) 159, 174, 175, 293, 364

root 35, 44, 45, 46, 47, 48, 49, 50, 54, 55, 56, 57, 86, 87, 97, 98, 100, 109, 110, 138, 145, 161, 162, 163, 168, 235, 236, 238, 239, 240, 241, 242, 243, 246, 247, 248, 249, 290, 291, 292, 294, 295, 309, 310, 323, 346

runlevel 43, 44, 45, 46, 48

S

Samba 137, 140, 141, 143, 144, 145, 146, 155, 156, 318

samba 137

scanner 316, 346

SCSI 40, 46, 234, 235, 310, 311, 316, 317, 346, 348, 350, 351, 352, 353, 354, 355

securetty 291

See Web Servers 231, 232, 233, 234, 235, 236, 237, 238, 239, 240, 241, 242, 243, 244, 245, 246, 247, 248, 249, 251

sendmail 76, 97, 98, 159, 160, 161, 162, 165, 168, 294, 326

serial 46, 95, 96, 102, 108, 134, 135, 136, 199, 347, 348

shutdown 35, 48, 50, 349

SMB (Server Message Block) 133, 137, 138, 141, 156

SMTP (Simple Mail Transfer Protocol) 87, 159, 161, 164, 373

Solaris 35, 291

Solid 243

SQL (Structure Query Language) 247

ssh 291

SSH (Secure Shell) 291, 292

sshd 291, 292

SSI (Server Side Includes) 234, 237, 238, 239, 251

SSL (Secure Sockets Layer) 232, 233, 234, 243, 244

su 56, 291

subnet 143, 293

suEXEC 241, 242

SunOS 291

Sybase 243

sync 48, 256, 320

syslog 43, 323, 324, 325

syslogd 323

T

tape drive 345, 348

tar 46, 168, 243, 297, 298, 349

TCP 85, 86, 87, 88, 89, 90, 93, 96, 97, 99, 110, 133, 137, 141, 143, 159, 161, 237, 240, 284, 290, 291, 294

TCP/IP 85, 86, 87, 88, 89, 90, 93, 96, 97, 99, 110, 133, 137, 141, 143, 159, 237, 240, 284, 290, 291, 294

tcpd 97, 292, 293, 294

tcsh 54

telinit 45

telnet 86, 96, 97, 161, 292, 294, 296, 297, 370, 372, 373

telnetd 97, 98, 293, 294

TeX 192, 193

tftp 97, 294

thinnet 142

twm 259, 260

U

UDP 87, 97

UID (User ID) 54, 55, 56, 109, 241, 369

UPS 348, 349

    APC 349

    Best 349

    Tripp 349

USENET 167

uudecode 164

uuencode 164

W

web servers

    Apache 231, 232, 233, 234, 235, 236, 237, 238, 239, 240, 241, 242, 243, 244, 245, 246, 247, 248, 249, 251

    Boa 232, 233

    NCSA 233, 245

    Roxen 233, 234

    Stronghold 234, 235, 243, 244, 251

    W3C 233

    WN 233

    Zeus 233, 234

wheelgroup 291

whois 97, 131

Windows 95 43, 137, 142, 143, 259, 260, 261, 284

WordPerfect 191

Workgroupname 142

X

X 54, 56, 90, 108, 193, 195, 199, 253, 255, 256, 257, 258, 259, 272, 273, 274, 275, 276, 284, 308, 311, 364

X86 49

XF86config 254

xfig 196

XFree86 254, 256

xterm 261, 272, 273, 275

xv 164

xvscan 346

Z

Zip 317, 345, 354, 355